Do I still have a life?

Do I still have a life?

Voices from the Aftermath of War in Rwanda and Burundi

John M. Janzen & Reinhild Kauenhoven Janzen

Publications in Anthropology, 20
University of Kansas
Lawrence, Kansas

Department of Anthropology, University of Kansas, Lawrence, KS 66045

ISBN 0-938332-20-1

To the memory

of the people of Rwanda and Burundi

who have given their lives

and to those who continue the struggle

for a more just and humane society

Contents

Preface

As this book moves to press in early 2000, twenty to thirty thousand soldiers of the Force Armée de Rwanda (FAR, the former national army under President Habyarimana) and some of the Interahamwe militia of the 1994 Rwandan genocide, continue their fight, this time in the Congo, allied with President Kabila's coalition, against the armies of Rwanda and Uganda and the Congo rebels. Burundi's low-grade civil war continues with many people displaced on both sides of the conflict. Rwanda and its allies in the governments of Uganda and Burundi insist that the FAR and the Interahamwe must be dealt with before they will withdraw their forces from Congo. The Congo War (also called the "Africa World War I") thus represents a continuation of the Rwanda conflict of 1994. Peacemaking efforts by neighboring African countries have produced the Lusaka Accords of 1999 which set the terms of disarmament and withdrawal of hostile forces. At the United Nations, a proposal for a peace keeping force has been put forward and approved. In both the Lusaka and the United Nations deliberations the central problem is the presence in Congo of foreign military forces from the Great Lakes region. The parties to the Burundian conflict continue to meet in Arusha, Tanzania.

As this opening paragraph suggests, the subject of this book—"voices in the aftermath of war"—is sadly as current as it was five years ago when we left Central Africa, indeed, perhaps even more so, since ever more "voices of war" continue to be created.

Five years, many lectures, conversations, and continued correspondence with some of our interlocutors in Rwanda, Zaire (now Congo), and Burundi have however given us advantages of hindsight regarding our experience in Central Africa in 1994, and the kind of book we have produced here. To that effect, we suggest three broad leitmotifs that readers, in particular those interested in anthropological methods and approaches, may find helpful as they peruse these pages.

The first of these leitmotifs might be called "finding ourselves doing anthropology within a relief agency." As we explain later, we did not set out to "do anthropology" in the relief work situation. Yet, that is what we were asked to do. The salient question that we can now ask, but which is still only partially answered in these pages, is what were the particular advantages and constraints of such an approach to doing anthropology? Having conducted mostly academic research in Africa previously—which is not without its biases and constraints—and having always laid out our own networks of contact, the contrast with being part of an NGO team was striking. We enjoyed amazingly quick contacts ready for instant interviews or conversations. Since ours was a church-related organization, our contacts with church agencies are relatively prominent in these pages. Because we were with such an agency, we were no doubt perceived differently by many. Now we wonder, would it have been even possible to conduct anthropological research in the refugee zone and the post-war setting without being part of such a relief work related group?

A second leitmotif might be called "the anthropology of war" or "the anthropology of genocide." Again here the advantages of hindsight suggest that war—and even more so genocide—introduces rather unique dilemmas into anthropological inquiry, particularly concerning the use of individual identities and agencies. The most acute of these dilemmas has to do with the terrain where the doctrine of "informed consent" meets with the obligation to identify "flagrant human rights abuses." Of less consequence for the discipline of anthropology, but as critical for the fate of the individual, is the delicacy of reporting heroic stories of lives risked and saved when the narrator's life might be endangered by reporting the very story he or she wants the world to know.

A third leitmotif might be that "disparate detail and vivid story gradually give way to analysis." This is perhaps true of all anthropological research but it is especially true of a work in which the focus of research was at first as inchoate as the postwar scene and peoples' lives in it. Regional settings, local communities, the repetitive plots of stories, and the evident anthropological themes of ethnicity, healing, and justice have been used to give the individual "voices" some larger sense of coherence and meaning. At an early stage of our writing, friendly critic and editor Murray Last wondered, "Is this a book?" He thought so; "a particular kind of book." He might have kindly called it a "Scrapbook" in which the individual voices are situated in a social or historic context but not so as to lose their uniqueness.

This work would not have been possible without the cooperation of the many individuals who stopped what they were doing to sit down and talk to us. But our sentiments go well beyond gratitude and recognition. the voices we heard and the stories we recorded were more like a sacred trust of the private agonies and the almost unspeakable memories individuals shared with us. We hope that we have lived up to that trust in this book.

Many people encouraged and assisted us in this research. Among them are the members of the Zion Mennonite Church of Elbing, Kansas and our family—our home constituency—who paid our way, through the Mennonite Central Committee's (MCC's) policy of grass roots support of its efforts. Our fellow MCC unit members helped us make contacts and shared their joys and frustrations, and we held many substantive discussions with them: Harold Otto, Joyce Martens, Ndjoko Mampombolo, Mukambu Ya'Namwisi, Luamba-Mbombo Clement, Cathy Mputu, and Daniel Féver, and in Burundi David Niyonzima, Felicité Ntikuranko, and Susan Seitz, who also extended their hospitality and guidance at Kibimba.

Eric Olfert and Jim Shenk, of the MCC Africa department, Cathy Hodder and Terry Sawatzky, then current Zaire/Congo country representatives, and then MCC Director John Lapp provided expert logistic support throughout our term of service and, on our return, encouraged us with thoughtful critique and financial means to devote part of the summer of 1995 to writing it all down.

We thank our colleagues in the Department of Anthropology and the deans of the college of Liberal Arts and Sciences at the University of Kansas who agreed that we should respond to this call to help in the postwar experience in Central Africa. Washburn University supported manuscript preparation with a Small Research Grant.

We thank all those who were prayerfully concerned for our safety and those who were our guides, pilots, or drivers between Bujumbura and Kigali, between Bujumbura and Kibimba, and between Bukavu and the camps; and we acknowledge the Zairian colleagues who helped us through arrival and departure gauntlets at Bukavu's Kavumu airport.

We also extend our thanks to the readers of successive manuscripts who did not hesitate to express their approval as well as their criticism, including our Food and Thought study group, David Newbury, Susan Janzen, Sara Regier, Murray Last, Harold Otto, John Lapp, Cathy Hodder and Terry Sawatzky, Danielle de Lame, Steven Feierman, Sandra Barnes, and Pierre Ndilikilikesha.

And, finally, we thank Judith Rempel Smucker and Kerry Jean Handel for their sensitive design work. Any errors in detail or judgment are ours. This research has been a challenging project that we hope will contribute to a better understanding of the events of 1994 and 1995 in the Great Lakes region of Africa.

Introduction

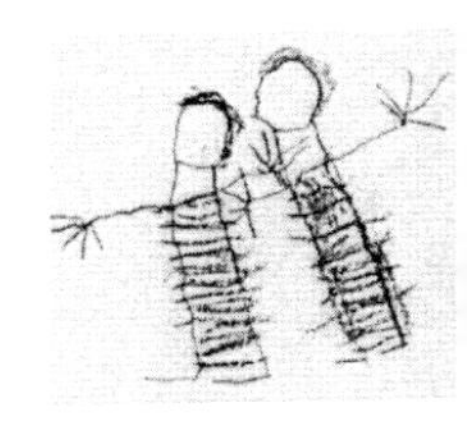

I would like to know of your impressions and understandings that you have gained after your visit, first with us refugees, then in Rwanda and Burundi. There the situation resembles for the moment a ripe abscess that threatens to burst open and to turn Burundi's situation into the same that Rwanda has lived through. If possible, could you give me a profound analysis of the situation in the two countries, an analysis of information you received and your personal understanding. That could help me in particular and others to better prepare for our future.—Habimana Emmanuel, Rwandan coordinator of the Mushweshwe, Muku, Bideka, and Izirangabo refugee camps southwest of Bukavu, Zaire, in a letter, early 1995

We need one thing—the truth: spiritual and scientific. The outside perspective could help.—Jean Pierre Rukara, Rwandan refugee in Zaire and former functionary in a government ministry

At 5:00 a.m. [on October 22, 1993] the chef de colline *called people to put up barricades. And they began to bind up Tutsi, and ran around to find others, beginning with the men, then the women. They were hunted even in the toilets, where they were killed. Their houses were destroyed and the contents stolen. Then they killed the women and children, even the pregnant women. Some collines now have no Tutsi left at all. . . . Their goal is to eliminate the Tutsi. . . . We have no hope for a better life.*—Ntacomaze Emmanuelle, Burundian widow, whose husband was killed in the first round of attacks after the death of President Ndadaye; she fled with her eight children to the military camp at Kibimba mission

The first quotation is that of a disillusioned Rwandan Hutu civil servant who left a government position a year before the war broke out in 1994 to work in a private social service agency. He fled Rwanda during the war in 1994, during which time his wife died, and found himself in a refugee camp in Zaire, where he became the Rwandan representative and coordinator of a committee charged with administering four small refugee camps southwest of Bukavu. Disillusioned anew and fearful of returning to Rwanda, he earnestly sought our advice as he was contemplating seeking permanent exile.

The second quotation is from a career civil servant in a government ministry who also found himself in a refugee camp in Zaire. He called for truth, both spiritual and scientific. However, his call for truth was not for an open examination of evidence but rather a request for serious consideration of the injustices against the Hutu revolution. In other words, his call for truth assumed that the side of the perpetrators of the genocide of 1994 was in the right and that outside investigation would vindicate that perspective. This was a voice of denial that harbored the willingness to perhaps carry out further acts of vengeance or vindication against those who would thwart his cause.

The third quotation is a voice of despair, fear, and pain, covering barely hidden emotions of anger. Although the woman's voice is a Tutsi voice, she later revealed that she is in fact Hutu and was married to a Tutsi man and therefore is the mother of Tutsi children, thereby illustrating the paradox and the pathos of the identities Hutu, Tutsi, and Twa that have so torn up the Great Lakes region of Central Africa, Rwanda, Burundi, and eastern Congo (formerly Zaire).

Many voices such as these were heard in the aftermath of the Rwandan genocide and war of 1994 and the related yet independent Burundi conflict that broke out in 1993 and simmered in subsequent years.[1] In both cases neighbor was pitted against neighbor, family member against family member, one national party against another national party, rich and powerful against poor and weak. Everything and everyone was affected. Some families survived in name alone; others were regrouping around the only adult remaining. Others wondered whether they would return home in their lifetimes. Emotions of guilt and grief, anger, and the urge for vengeance were borne simultaneously by many people.

The awesome expectations of those Rwandans, Zairians, and Burundians who hoped that two North American academics would be able to answer their perplexing questions and salve their horrendous wounds will surely remain unrealized in these pages. The Rwandan War and the continuing dilemmas of that country and of the Great Lakes region are as complex as those of any other holocaust of the 20th century—the Armenian massacres, the Stalinist purges and the Gulag, the genocide of Jews and other groups by Nazi Germany, China's Cultural Revolution, the Cambodian horrors under Pol Pot, the Balkan ethnic cleansings, and more. Decades later, each of these human disasters continues to generate soul searching, debate, and writing as survivors, next of kin of the victims, and citizens of those nations probe for answers to why and how these annihilation movements could have occurred, how they should be remembered, and what their occurrence means in the course of human events. The book is not closed on any of them. In like manner, attempts to present, analyze, and reflect on the Rwandan and Central African tragic experiences are in order.

Thus the simple act of listening to and recording stories is important because the burdens of each person's experiences are great, and the questions facing many individuals are perplexing. Giving voice to these burdens and questions is a first step for their tellers to regain their humanity and understanding and to contemplate solutions. In this light, the first and main objective of this book is to present the individual narratives that were entrusted to us during two months in Rwanda, Burundi, and eastern Zaire (now Congo) in late 1994 and early 1995.

A second and closely related objective is to put these narratives into a descriptive ethnographic account that creates a larger context within which they occurred and within which they may begin to make sense. Listening is never a neutral act. Our questions, our concerns, the circumstances of our encounters with our interlocutors, the kinds of people that we approached, and the types of subjects we explored in our questions shaped the content of these narratives.[2] A third objective of this book is to analyze selected issues, such as the fate of institutions, ethnic polarization and the uses made of ethnicity, and the nature of post-war healing.

Such an ethnographic work centered around individual stories complements and adds to the rapidly growing body of writing, commentary, and analysis that has begun to emerge around the Rwandan genocide and war and the late 20th century crisis in the Great Lakes region. First were the journalistic accounts often motivated by the urge to identify human rights abuses. A prime example of this is *Rwanda: Death, Despair, Defiance* (African Rights 1995), which along with other publications and exposés by Amnesty International offers an early portrayal of the scale and particulars of the genocide. One of the most noteworthy American publications in this vein has been Philip Gourevitch's gripping book, *We Wish To Inform You That Tomorrow We Will Be Killed with Our Families: Stories from Rwanda* (1997), which retells the drama of the 1994 Rwandan genocide and war around a handful of individuals and families so that the issues of genocide can be understood from these people's personal perspectives. After the journalistic accounts came the volumes by scholars who know the region and who were in a unique position to lay out the general picture of events quickly. A prime example of this type of writing is Gerard Prunier's *The Rwanda Crisis: History of a Genocide* (1995), an authoritative political history of the buildup to the war around the decisions of key actors. A third type of writing is the slower to appear but more carefully documented academic journals with special issues edited by the leading experts devoted to the Great Lakes region and its conflicts, such as "The Ongoing Crisis in Central Africa" (Faulkingham and Goheen 1998b), "Central Africa: Political Dynamics of Identities and Representation" (Jewsiewicki 1999), and "Ethnic Conflict: Global Challenges and Psychological Perspectives" (Mays et al. 1998), which sets forth a comparative picture of ethnic conflicts in Latin America (Guatemala, Peru, Puerto Rico), South Asia (Sri Lanka), the Near East (the Israeli-Palestinian case), Northern Ireland, and Rwanda.

A major recent work on the genocide in Rwanda that combined general analysis with documentation from war-time government archives on the actions of individuals in the administration was published by Human Rights Watch as *Leave None to Tell the Story: Genocide in Rwanda* (1999).

Despite the important place of writings such as these that suggest that the events surrounding a genocide and a war can be understood by careful historical reconstruction and disciplinary analysis that is rationally understood,[3] our point of departure is that many of the individuals whose stories we heard reflect the fundamentally irrational and incomprehensible nature of war, on the part of both those who were involved in it and those who observed it from the outside. French historian Raymond Aron, in his 1956 book *Dimensions de la conscience historique,* emphasized that few can see war clearly, that is, few are historically conscious of all dimensions of what is happening to them. Aron drew his inspiration from Greek historian Thucydides' investigation of the Peloponnesian War between Athens and Sparta, the two largest and most influential of the city-states of ancient Greece. Thucydides examined the subtle line that divides purposive individual "rational" behavior from the larger patterns of collective action. Aron, like Thucydides, was especially interested in the manner in which apparently purposefully taken actions in war become engulfed in tragic consequences unintended by the perpetrators. Neither Athens nor Sparta supposedly wanted the war, yet each was drawn irresistibly into it to preserve a self-image.

The Rwandan War and the Burundi massacres, like the Peloponnesian War, took on realities of their own far beyond the intended or even foreseen consequences of individuals. Thus the individuals with whom we spoke—to whom we listened—were often in a state of incomprehension over what had happened to them, their families, or their country. In Rwanda the perpetrators of the genocide, the Hutu elite, ended up in exile in the refugee camps along with many of their innocent compatriots. The targeted victims, the Tutsi, or their brothers and sisters who had been in exile, won the war and are now in power at the inhumane cost of a million slaughtered. The aftermath has left many individuals in a state of deep shock, anger, and denial and has left others with a false sense of security and infallibility. Coupled with these conditions is the basic realization, coming from hindsight, that the conflict is being continually renewed in slightly different ways. The conflict of Rwanda and Burundi has been extended and transposed to the neighboring countries of Zaire (Congo), Angola, Uganda, and perhaps Sudan. Therefore there is a need to listen to the voices to examine the many complex ways that rationalities and irrationalities interact in the lives of individuals, their communities, and their families. Such listening permits us also to share deep appreciation with those who may have had extraordinary clarity of judgment—recalling Aron's historical consciousness—in a moment of collective madness.

Approaching the voices of Rwanda and Burundi in the aftermath of war in this way, without fixed interpretations, leads us hopefully to a new understanding beyond the facile stereotypes. This is nowhere more important than in the way we look at the terms Hutu, Tutsi, and Twa and relate them to the realities that they may symbolize or even mask. As suggested by the three individuals quoted at the outset of this introduction, these identity terms have no simple single meaning. Hutu identity includes the disillusioned social service worker, the obdurate nationalist in denial in the face of the attempted final solution, and the Burundian widow in an internal Tutsi refugee camp. All three individuals are Hutu yet they are so different from one another.

The terms Hutu, Tutsi, and Twa have evolved in concert over the years and cannot be given single essentialist meanings. It is well to ponder the words of Burundian Quaker leader David Niyonzima, who when asked by an American student in 1996 what the difference was between a Hutu and a Tutsi said, "There is none." Many individuals of the Central African region would prefer to avoid these terms altogether, but obviously there is something to the reality of the social or symbolic constructs that generate the rancor that these ethnic terms identify and the deep gulf that causes some to kill based on these categories. Again, listening to the voices may offer a beginning of understanding of the complex realities that words and signs convey.

This book was put together, first, to respond to the pleas voiced at the outset of this introduction. A second audience is the Western reader who wishes to get beyond generalities to particular individuals and voices of Central Africa. People of the United States especially need to take notice of the Central African conflict because of the way the US government is called on increasingly to broker conflicts around the globe. The widening wars of Central Africa in 1997, 1998, and 1999 have spread to Uganda, Burundi, the Democratic Republic of Congo, Congo-Brazzaville, Angola, Zimbabwe, and beyond. Observers speak of an "all Africa war"; they may as well speak of a world war. The murder of American eco-tourists in March 1999 in western Uganda served notice that the United States and Great Britain must not continue to support the minority. The murders were a clear attempt to entangle the superpowers in the regional conflict. The United States was involved through the Defense Department's Officer Training Program, which invited most of the top military leaders of the new Rwandan government to Leavenworth, Kansas, in the early 1990s, and through US military presence in the Great Lakes region. Through their taxes Americans support the United Nations, a major player in the refugee relief work and peace brokering. Whether we like it or not, we of the West should recognize our many connections to the Great Lakes region of Central Africa, just as we are connected to the rest of the globe.

In this book we seek to situate the individual voices we heard in 1994 and 1995 within the context of their communities, nations, and region so that they may be fully human, within the one world we all share, not as distant faceless masses whom we would rather ignore.

Listening, Providing Analysis and Philosophical Reflections

We became involved in this mission of listening to voices in the aftermath of war in Rwanda and Burundi when we responded to this emergency call for help in August 1994: "Urgently needed: French-speaking volunteers with excellent relational and organizational skills to spend three months in eastern Zaire working among Rwandan refugees . . ." (*Mennonite Weekly Review*, August 11, 1994, p. 2). We became part of the action of over 150 international agencies—semi-governmental, nongovernmental, and religious—that provided airlifts of blankets, medicines, food, and shelter to the refugees and displaced in Rwanda, Burundi, eastern Zaire, and Tanzania following the catastrophes there in 1993 and 1994. Relief work in the entire region was coordinated by the United Nations, in particular, the High Commission for Refugees (UNHCR). Some of the larger and better known agencies in this action included the International Red Cross, which dealt with the unaccompanied children, the Red Crescent, dozens of nongovernmental organizations, such as Oxford Famine Relief (OXFAM), the Cooperative for Assistance and Relief Everywhere (CARE), and many religious organizations such as Church World Service, World Vision, and the international and national denominational agencies of most of the faiths of the world.

The particular organization with which we worked was the Mennonite Central Committee (MCC), a 70-year-old umbrella organization sponsored by all Mennonite and Brethren in Christ groups of North America with about 1,000 workers around the world.[4] The MCC became involved in the Central African post–Rwandan War scene primarily because Zairian Mennonites, who live in the western region of the country, wished to assist the eastern Zaire churches and communities who were overwhelmed by the refugees of Bukavu and the surrounding countryside.

A task force of Congolese Mennonites and MCC representatives visited Bukavu early in the crisis and determined to work with several local communities through the Zairian Council of Churches, the Communautée des Eglises du Christ au Zaire (ECZ). Harold Otto, a veteran of MCC work in western Zaire and a graduate of the Kennedy School of International Affairs at Harvard University, was invited to direct the MCC effort in the Great Lakes region.

The overall response of the MCC to the crisis in Rwanda and Burundi had two parts: first, material aid in the immediate aftermath of the war, including seed distribution, and refugee relief work; and, second, peace education and reconciliation. The first work was mainly with Rwandans in Zaire and in Rwandan communities inside Rwanda. The second phase of MCC work on peace education was concentrated in Bukavu and in Burundi where, with the Burundian Quakers, material support was given in some conflict-stressed locales. The MCC also provided what was called "a peace presence" in specified settings and among groups of individuals on both sides of the conflict.

When we indicated our willingness in August 1994 to work with Rwandan refugees in eastern Zaire, we thought we might be asked to distribute food and negotiate shipments through Zairian military controls or to translate for non-French-speaking workers. Having conducted anthropological research on numerous occasions in central and southern Africa, we offered our services, hoping this would somehow work out with our teaching responsibilities. In October 1994 we were contacted and negotiated a between-semesters period extending from November 20, 1994, to January

Figure 1. John and Reinhild Janzen converse with authors and theater directors Sibazuri Marie Louise and Kalisa Tharcisse in Bujumbura over coffee.

Figure 2. Reinhild Janzen records Uwimana Josephine in Kayenzi telling of her experiences during the 1994 war in Rwanda.

17, 1995. We were surprised and not a little intimidated when our assignment was defined as "listening, providing analysis and philosophical reflections" on the conflict and recent events in the Great Lakes region of Central Africa. We are grateful to Harold Otto, who, after reading our résumés, faxed a letter back to North America suggesting that "the Janzens should be invited to come and do what they do best, to offer background understanding of the conflict, for further relief, reconciliation, and healing work of the MCC."

With introductions by Otto, we were able to get off to a quick start in our listening and observations. In all, we participated in about 75 interviews that ranged from perhaps 30 minutes to several hours in length in several visits. These listening sessions, as we would call them, were concentrated in the following locales. In Burundi we spent time in Bujumbura (Figure 1), the capital, and Kibimba, a Quaker mission and commercial center that was engulfed in violence after the attempted coup d'etat in October 1993 and the assassination of President Melchior Ndadaye. In Rwanda our base was the capital, Kigali, from where we visited Butare, the center of the university and research establishment, and two communes, Kayenzi to the west (Figure 2) and Giti to the northeast. In Zaire we were based in Bukavu. From there we traveled to the four refugee camps being served by the combined teams of ECZ, CARE, and the MCC.

Some of our conversations were chance encounters that became informative; others were planned and integral to the MCC work setting. We spoke with displaced persons and refugees; peasants and tradespersons; medical, educational, and research workers; government and military officials; church officials and clergy; writers, museum administrators, and artists; journalists and diplomats. We spoke with individuals but also on occasion with clusters or focus groups, such as the displaced widows of Kibimba or the Rwandan refugee administrators in the camps of Zaire. One of us (Reinhild Janzen) sought out opportunities to obtain children's drawings of their wartime experiences in several of these settings. We traveled with one bag, a tape recorder, a notebook, and a small camera each and used whatever local transportation was available, mostly our legs, which set us apart from the dominant Non-Governmental Organization (NGO) presence and their white vehicles. We stayed in Catholic and Protestant guesthouses, with friends who worked for World Hunger, in a private home rented by the Salvation Army, and in simple hotels. Our food and lodging and travel were paid for by the MCC and we were given a small personal allowance.

First and foremost we listened to individuals and recorded their individual stories. Although we had a tape recorder, we rarely used it. Most of the personal stories were transcribed by hand in French and later translated. Invariably, people responded to our introductions as "volunteers with MCC, relief organization, anthropologist and art historian" with eagerness to tell their story. These stories, almost like a scripted plot, included the tellers' personal traumas of the war, their encounters with death, accounts of family and lineage members killed, the naming of the killers when they were known, their flight, and their seeking and finding refuge, followed by great uncertainty and continuing fear. The stories were often prefaced or concluded with the plea to be honest, to tell the truth of what happened. As predictable as the plot of these stories was the emotional subtext. The narration of these personal stories of war would come out in a tone that impressed us as being flat and emotionless. At first we did not know what we were hearing. We wondered how people who had experienced such horrors could relate them with such calm, such a seeming absence of feeling. But we came to recognize this flat tone as an expression of deep and damaging trauma. This was true not only of Rwandans and Burundians but also of some Europeans and Americans who had experienced the war and needed to tell us their stories as well. Usually our interlocutors were able to move on from their experiences to other topics only after they had told their personal war story.

However important such personal stories may be, they alone do not capture the larger picture of genocide within a war. They must be situated within a broader social and historical context. The stories are parts of dramatic events that include other actors within fuller scenes, which, in turn, are parts of a greater play. A kind of strategy unfolded in our work whereby we sought to situate individual accounts within settings that appeared to offer microcosmic case studies of the genocidal crisis and the war. Thus we tried to obtain accounts by persons on opposite sides of issues and events: the refugees who had fled and those in the home community who did not; communities that had been engulfed with violence and at least one community that had resisted; those who believed in the racial theory of ethnic categories and those who did not. Yet, given the suddenness with which we undertook this venture and given its unpredictable and potentially dangerous character, we readily admit that many of our contacts were quite accidental. We were willing to listen to anyone whose path we crossed or who came to our door or to whom we were introduced. The centerpiece of this book therefore remains the individual voices we encountered in late 1994 and early 1995.

Brief Background of the Central African Crisis

It is misleading to offer a brief background of the Central African crisis of the 1990s without presenting some of the theories that have been put forward about its causes. A few writers can be recommended for their straightforward historical background accounts of the genocide in Rwanda (Newbury 1998) and of the comparable events and issues in Burundi (Lemarchand 1994). This section introduces them for the uninitiated reader.

Rwanda and Burundi are effectively the only societies of the Central African Great Lakes region (Figure 3) where the personal identifying terms Hutu and Tutsi have evolved into a code for abusive, obscene words for which people kill and are killed. These identity designations have become a kind of shorthand for opposing political parties that vie for control of their respective states: in Rwanda the Mouvement Révolutionnaire National pour le Développement (Revolutionary Movement for National Development) (MRND) (mostly Hutu) and the Rwandan Patriotic Front (RPF) (mostly Tutsi) and in Burundi the Front pour la Démocratie au Burundi (Democratic Front of Burundi) (FRODEBU) (mostly Hutu) and the Union du Progrès National (Provisional National Union) (UPRONA) (mostly Tutsi). Why did this polarization occur?

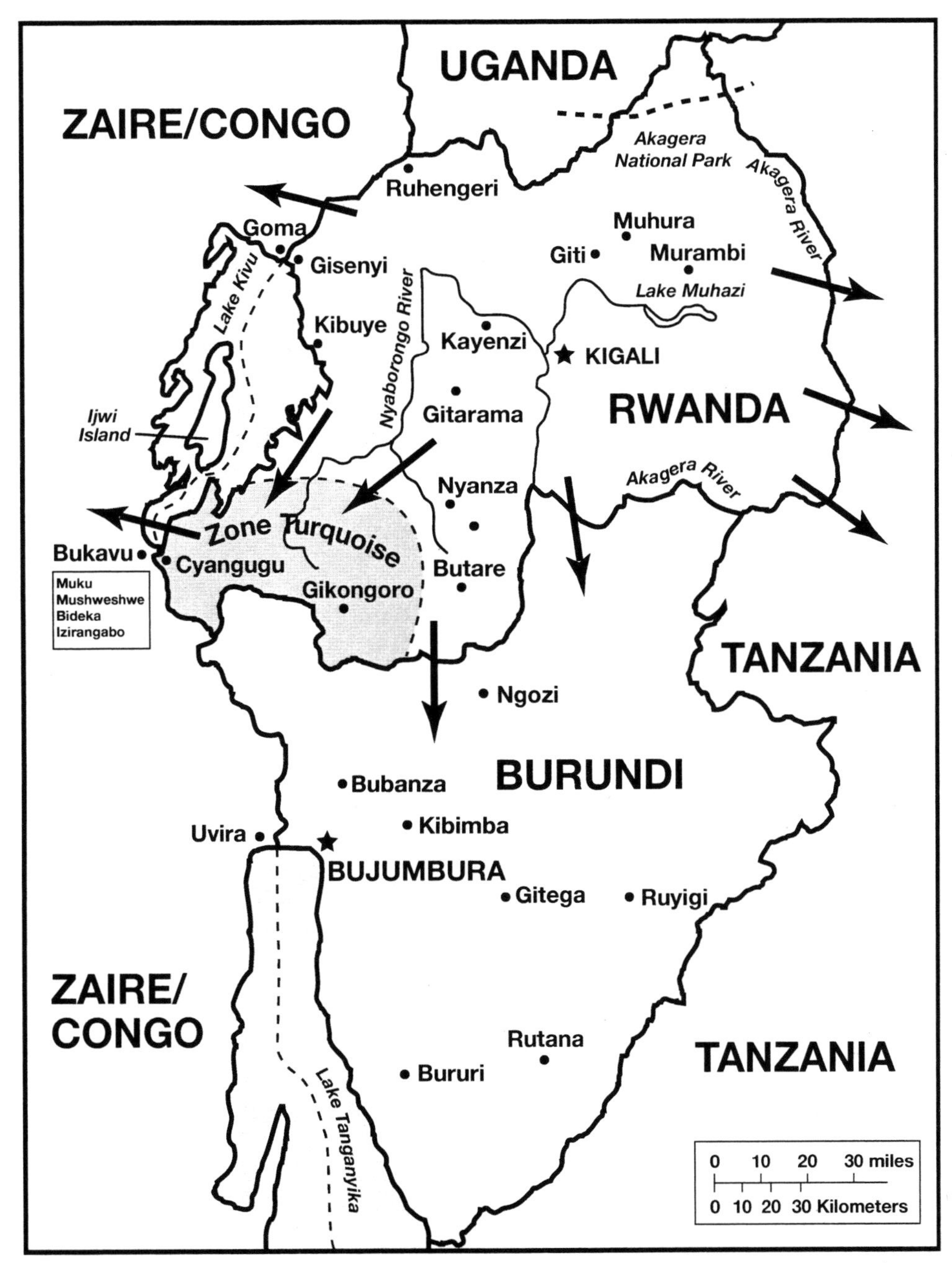

Figure 3. Rwanda, Burundi, and surrounding countries. Dashed line at top shows approximate extent of incursion of the RPF from Uganda; arrows show paths of flight of Rwandans in the 1994 war (Tutsi and moderate Hutu fleeing the genocide and, later, militant Hutu and many civilians fleeing when the RPF began its armed takeover). Enclosed area in southwestern Rwanda is the Zone Turquoise created by the French military by July 1994 for the government troops, the militia, and many civilians.

One particular historical factor that sets Rwanda and Burundi apart from the other Great Lakes region societies is their colonial history. Both were colonized by the Germans until World War I, when Belgium took control until 1960. The surrounding societies of the Great Lakes region were English colonies. The Germans ruled through the Tutsi kings, a policy that the Belgians continued, thereby adopting the British approach of indirect rule first invented in India and then applied in Africa. The formal continuation of the indigenous institutions of rulership, however, did not preserve the power of indigenous leaders. For the British in such places as northern Nigeria and Zanzibar and for the Belgians in Rwanda and Burundi centralized institutions with many hierarchies and checks and balances were transformed into a tight, repressive single chain-of-command hierarchy to facilitate labor recruitment, tax collecting, and diverse programs of "civilization." Furthermore, the Belgians worked hand in hand with the Catholic Church, which ran the schools.

Finally, the Belgians implemented a racial-ethnic policy that privileged the upper class, the Tutsi, and in the 1920s and 1930s applied to them the myth of Hamitic superiority. According to this myth the Tutsi were the race of Ham, one of the three sons of Noah, and thus of biblical descent. In effect, they were transformed in colonial eyes into inherently superior humans, born to rule, deserving of broad education. The Hutu, in contrast, were viewed as inferior, not even on the spectrum of biblical races. An identity card system begun in the 1930s imposed this ethnic and racial privilege and made it hereditary. Thus a Hutu of today is a person whose paternal grandfather received that designation. In cases of doubt regarding Hutu, Tutsi, or Twa status, the rule of 10 cattle was applied. If a man had 10 or more cattle, he was granted Tutsi identity; if fewer, Hutu identity. Cases are recalled in which brothers landed on opposite sides of this ethnic divide. A woman's identity was defined by her father's. Belgian colonial policy in the 1950s came to be determined by workers' parties, so in the colonies support swung to the Hutu, and worker-priests inspired the formation of the Hutu party.

The consequence of these colonial policies was to polarize the several sets of preexisting social distinctions and to turn them into all-pervasive, exclusive, hereditary groupings. In addition, the character of the king was transformed from that of head of the nation into stooge of the colonial government. Most pervasive, perhaps, was the erosion of belief in the religion of the region, Kubandwa, the diffuse worship and belief in Imaana. Although Imaana, the god of the peoples of the Great Lakes region, was identified by missionaries with the Christian God, the Catholic Church claimed the exclusive right to perform the public worship of Imaana and destroyed in whatever way possible the local public expressions of the Kubandwa religion.

The foregoing comments about the explanations and constructs of the Central African crisis suggest that the reality of the conflict is far more complex than a few labels or easy clichés can provide. Past efforts to put cultural terms into simple stories have yielded images and feelings that are the building blocks of terrible stereotypes that have been used with frightening effect not only by the past colonialists but also by Rwandans and Burundians themselves. The conflict in Rwanda and Burundi has been portrayed in the press as tribal or ethnic, Hutu against Tutsi. Sometimes the Twa are mentioned. In this view the term Hutu is used to mean poor peasant; the term Tutsi is used to mean cattle herder, cattle owner; and the term Twa refers to hunter-gatherers. But this characterization of the nature of the conflict is highly misleading, perhaps because the stereotypes correspond some of the time to historical and physiological reality. Some poor peasants no doubt were and are short and squat, have wide noses and thick lips, are hard-working, happy, and not so clever. No doubt there are some cattle keepers who were or are tall and thin, have narrow noses, are clever, devious, arrogant, and manipulative, and who came as conquering foreigners from the northeast.

In fact, these are just stereotypes. Hunting and gathering have been practiced in the Central African Great Lakes region for over 50,000 years. Cattle have been kept for about 3,000 years, and crops have been in cultivation for about 2,000 years. Of all the regions in Africa where cattle keeping and agriculture are practiced together, the Great Lakes region is one of the most fertile and agreeable, with its tsetse fly–free cool climate, terrain well watered by rains, and fertile volcanic soils. Prosperous Hutu peasants used to be able to become Tutsi; that is, they converted their wealth into cattle and hired other peasants to care for them.

Like other interlacustrine regions, the territories of Rwanda and Burundi have seen one form or another of centralized society for about a thousand years. The so-called Hutu kingdoms were situated along the western region of the two countries and throughout the Great Lakes region. Pastoralists from eastern highland grasslands at various times moved into and mixed with the already-present residents. Despite some outside loan words, all these peoples—hunters, farmers, pastoralists—spoke and speak a common Bantu language (Kinyarwanda and closely related Kirundi) of the Niger-Kordofanian family of languages. At the time of colonial takeover the powerful dynasties were backed by the colonizer, with the weaker dynasties suppressed. These structures of centralized kingship persisted until the 1960s, through the colonial era until independence.

Popular nationalism in both Rwanda and Burundi formed around the Hutu identity, which is associated with poor peasants. This was due in part to their poverty and the fact that they were peasants, but more so to their oppression by the colonially backed chiefs. The privilege and wealth of the Tutsi chiefs, often gained from graft in their administrative posts, came to be translated into the local idiom of cattle, although most Tutsi had no cattle and were even opposed to the rule of the chiefs. Furthermore, all Hutu chiefs (and, earlier, kings of small western kingdoms) had gradually been replaced by powerful Tutsi chiefs under the nominal control of the king of Rwanda.

When the winds of independence blew strongly in Africa, around 1960, the Belgian Governor General had a choice to either reinforce the monarchies within the repressive colonial regimes against popular demands of the Hutu or tilt to Hutu parties and identity. In a fateful decision for the future of the region, he did the latter. By 1962 the Rwandan kingdom was gone, and an independent Hutu-controlled government was in power under President Gregoire Kayibanda. Tens of thousands of Tutsi were killed or fled, including the entire aristocracy and most of the chiefs. In 1973 a coup d'etat established Juvenal Habyarimana in power; he ruled until 1994. But every time there were internal problems opposing mostly Hutu cliques, another round of Tutsi killings and flights occurred, so that by 1990 there were 500,000 Tutsi and other opponents of the regime living outside the country, waiting to return legally or, finally, by force.

The Burundian Tutsi, seeing what had happened in Rwanda, were more prudent and kept the Hutu from consolidating power. They too eliminated the kingship, replacing the monarchy with a series of military dictatorships. In 1972, following attacks by guerrilla bands allied with the rebellion in Zaire, tens of thousands of Hutu were killed. In 1993, however, President Pierre Buyoya set the stage for a popular election, in which Melchior Ndadaye, a Hutu, was elected president. But he was killed by a group of army officers after 100 days in office in an attempted military coup, setting off a bloodbath of Tutsi killings and a reprisal on Hutu by the mostly Tutsi army.

In Rwanda the governmental crisis that had simmered since October 1990, when the RPF first invaded northern Rwanda (see Figure 3), was to have been resolved by the Arusha Accords, which were to bring home all the refugees and create a government of national unity with a distribution of ministries among the several political parties. However, the government negotiated an agreement that was not supported by a clique close to President Habyarimana. As he was returning home on April 6, 1994, from another meeting with neighboring heads of state concerning implementation of the Arusha Accords, his plane was shot down over Kigali airport. Mass killings of Tutsi and opposition Hutu began within the hour as part of a master plan to eliminate the Tutsi and all Hutu who were the allies of the RPF or in any way against the monopoly of power by the governing party, the MRND. The massacres spread throughout most of Rwanda. The United Nations forces stationed in Kigali withdrew after a dozen of their number were assassinated by radical forces and because of a lack of a clear mandate from the UN leadership. The RPF, seeing the massacres of its supporters, moved to take over the country as quickly as possible. As the Forces Armées Rwandaise (Rwandan Armed Forces) (FAR) and Interahamwe militia and their families and many other people fled, the Rwandan government authorities and the clique that had seized power waged a propaganda campaign orchestrated to cause many other citizens to flee. By the time the RPF had gained control of the country, almost one million Rwandans were dead from the massacres, the fighting, or from disease connected with the flight and early weeks in exile and the camps. Close to three million were refugees in Zaire, Burundi, and Tanzania.

Along with the many relief agencies that began to work under UNHCR auspices, the MCC team that responded to the Rwandan crisis began work on a number of fronts: seed distribution in Rwanda, food and clothing distribution in the Bukavu region of Zaire, and, later, food distribution and peacemaking in Burundi. Uncomfortable with promoting refugee settlements at the expense of repatriation, the MCC decided to close its Bukavu unit in May 1995 and to support local Zairian peacemaking and community development efforts. Despite initiatives by the United Nations, the Zairian government, and other agencies to move the Rwandan refugees home, few in fact returned voluntarily. The camps continued to be supported by the United Nations, by CARE, and by many other agencies for fear of the humanitarian disaster that would result if food were simply cut off.

In late 1996 the international agencies' (unsuccessful) efforts to close the Zairian refugee camps were overtaken by another tragic military campaign of a force that would eventually call itself the Alliance of Democratic Forces for the Liberation of Congo-Zaire. The details of the emergence of this force and its subsequent conquest of all of Zaire (renamed Congo) are too complex to tell here in more than sketchy outlines and in terms of the consequences for the Rwandan refugees in the Kivu region. The Banyamulenge (the people of Mulengi) figured centrally in identifying the group that had most to gain from the dismantling of the refugee camps in southern and northern Kivu. The Banyamulenge are Tutsi who settled in the Uvira plain south of Bukavu and in a few regions northwest of Goma centuries ago for economic reasons. They formed enclaves of prosperous land and cattle owners with a penchant for client-type relationships with their neighbors. The flood of Rwandan Hutu into Zaire in 1994 and the continued life of a shadow government with anti-Tutsi militia brought great pressure to bear on the Banyamulenge. In late 1996, after tensions heightened between the Rwandan Hutu refugees and the Tutsi Banyamulenge, the South Kivu governor ordered the entire Banyamulenge community of thousands to leave Zaire within a few short weeks for Rwanda, "where they belonged." It was a fateful decision. The Banyamulenge countered that they were Zairian citizens and would not be forced into exile. With support from the new Rwandan army, they organized their own militias. After a few successful skirmishes with a corrupt and ill-equipped Zairian army, they advanced on Uvira and Bukavu, easily taking both. As they picked up local support in order to "nationalize" the movement, long-time Mobutu opponent Laurent Kabila, a name from the rebellions of the 1960s, joined their ranks and became their official head. Their goal became the ouster of President Mobutu Sese Seko.

How the rebellion moved across the country and entered Kinshasa by June 1997 is another story. The consequences of the movement of Alliance forces on the Rwandan refugees in Zaire was fateful, however. Unlike the United Nations and its array of humanitarian agencies whose mandate was to preserve the lives of innocent women and children and to foster eventual justice, at least in theory, the Alliance soldiers had no such niceties in mind. Backed by Rwanda, their short-term goal was to uproot the camps and destroy the FAR troops and the Interahamwe militias. The assault on Bukavu was so swift that in the camps of the area only those eager and poised to return to Rwanda were able to do so, during the momentary distraction of the Interahamwe and the FAR in or near the civilian camps. However, most of the civilians in the camps fled westward and northward with the Interahamwe and the FAR soldiers, away from the advancing Alliance troops. From eyewitness accounts we were able to learn that some of the individuals in the Muku and Mushweshwe camps reached Rwanda but that most of the refugees in these and other camps in the Bukavu area fled northwestward and into the dense rainforests of western Kivu, where they were at the mercy of the elements, without food and shelter. Here thousands perished.

The Alliance rebel army also confronted the large refugee camps in North Kivu where the Interahamwe and FAR troops controlled the populace. Here, however, most of the armed refugees and militia fled westward or were defeated as they were engaged by the rebel troops. Thousands of refugees who had in effect been kept hostage suddenly were free to flee eastward into Rwanda at Gisenyi. The world watched in early 1997 as 500,000 Rwandans trudged back home after nearly three years in exile. The Rwandan refugees in Tanzania were expelled some months later and similarly walked home.

The fate of the Rwandan refugees who had fled westward would become a point of contention between the United Nations and human rights groups on the one hand and Kabila's government on the other. The number of people who would later be considered missing was estimated at 230,000. Among these were most of the refugees of the Muku, Mushweshwe, Bideka, and Izirangabo refugee camps where we had worked. Many of these missing were presumed to have been killed and hastily buried in many mass graves that were identified by human rights officials along a broad trail that extended from South Kivu to Kisangani and even westward to Mbandaka on the Congo River. A few refugees reached Congo Brazzaville, having walked and hidden along a route of a thousand miles. But in 1998 units of the former Rwandan army (ex-FAR) under Augustin Bizimungu and Interahamwe militias were fighting alongside Kabila's Congo Coalition army against the rebel coalition backed by Rwanda and Uganda. The Rwandan conflict of 1994 had evolved into what some have called Africa World War I.

The Ethnographic Imperative

We did not set out to "do anthropology" or to write an ethnography in our work with the MCC, but after returning, we found we had many notes of our interview-like conversations with people. Our particular mission—to listen, to provide analysis and philosophical reflections—had been echoed by many Central Africans who told us their experiences and who asked us to tell the world. It is apparent that the contextual orientation of individual testimonies that ethnography provides may contribute to the quest for the truth in the aftermath of the human disaster in Central Africa.

We have already noted the almost compulsive eagerness with which our new acquaintances told of their war experiences. Although we continue to seek to understand the emotional logic behind these encounters, several years of study and thought have given us the advantage of hindsight, and perhaps insight, into our project. Our listening in a nonjudgmental way acknowledged the tellers' humanity and dignity. The mere offer to listen already did this. Deep trauma, even the dark experience of having killed, or as in some cases, the combined trauma of having participated in the genocide and then having had to take flight were experiences that isolated individuals from their former selves, their ordered world, and the rest of humanity.

One aspect of the ethnographic imperative, then, is to reconnect these individual narratives, the situations of their narrators, to the larger world. The creation of context is one aspect of this ethnographic reconnection. Context may be social, that is, other people within scenes and events. It is definitely temporal, in the telling of the sequence of events that shaped people's lives. Context also includes the cultural dimension of experience, that is, the ideological, moral, and sensory frameworks within which these life-defining experiences occurred. The ethnographic imperative includes attention to variation within local social events and spaces. In his review of Goldhagen's (1996) *Hitler's Willing Executioners,* Hinton (1998) identified the distinctive features of an anthropological perspective on the World War II Holocaust that Goldhagen presumes to follow. Hinton criticized Goldhagen for overgeneralizing to all Germans, rather than seeking to find distinctions between individuals in settings where atrocities were committed. He reexamined the evidence of one case used by Goldhagen in which a German police battalion was ordered to execute a community of Jews. Differential willingness, even outright resistance to kill, was evident in this case. This difference between individuals, which is also evident in the Rwandan and Burundian cases, is an important feature of the anthropological perspective, Hinton argued.

What defines the contextual dimension of ethnography is not only individual variation but also the differentiation between settings. Comparison, long a hallmark of anthropology, becomes a tool for analysis in a subject such as war and genocide. An important preparatory contact before leaving for work in Central Africa was with Murray Last of University College London, editor of the journal *Africa,* who has studied issues surrounding the aftermath of war (in Zimbabwe, Mozambique, South Africa, Angola, and Namibia). He recommended that we not dwell exclusively on the catastrophic side of war but identify those persons, settings, and situations in which the fabric of civility held or in which persons were again initiating such civility. This led us to seek situations in which there had been no massacres. Thus the comparative method common in anthropology is transparent in this work. The stories of the war in two communes in Rwanda (Kayenzi and Giti) and two communities in Burundi offer contrasting insights into the role of local authorities and councils in alternately averting or fanning the flames of conflict. These comparisons demonstrate the importance of local justice in maintaining and restoring peace.

In ethnography there is typically a tension between the individual account and the social, cultural, and historical dimension of context. Although the individual lives and particular accounts lend ethnographic poignancy and face, the context often enhances understanding of particular actions, institutions, or changes. In writing about the aftermath of war in Central Africa, we sorely needed context-sensitive analysis. But no single perspective or line of analysis can capture the whole truth of what happened or why. Therefore the individual voices in all their complexity and contradiction provide data for the long-term effort to comprehend one of the most horrifically systematic attempts to exterminate the "other" in recent times.

Ultimately, the individual stories must remain at the heart of the ethnographic imperative. If telling a story of ordeal humanizes the teller, then making sure that such a story is related in narration or in print is the obligation of the person who received the story. By publishing these stories, we are in effect affirming the humanity and dignity of the original narrator before the wider world.

Responsibility and the Ethical Dilemmas of War Ethnography

The centrality of the individual voice in ethnography, especially war ethnographies, carries with it dilemmas. North American anthropology, like medicine and a range of laboratory sciences but unlike journalism and perhaps history, has protected the individual from public gaze by the use of aggregate data or pseudonyms or other techniques of assuring the subject a measure of anonymity (or when publicity is desired, with the consent of the individual). Anthropological research protocols are often governed by procedural rules that allow participant involvement only on the basis of informed consent. Resulting anthropological writing, however, has also contributed to making informants into objects. Although these methodological structures persist in anthropology, major efforts have been made in recent years to bring voice and agency back to the individuals and communities involved in ethnographic coverage. Where anonymity is wished, pseudonyms are often used; they protect the privacy of the real person while permitting readers of the account to recognize themselves.

The responsibility to relate personal stories in the aftermath of genocidal war in Central Africa collides directly with the anthropological effort to protect the anonymity of the informant. But there are additional issues involved that make the dilemma even more poignant. In the early days after the 1994 war Rwandans and many outside journalists began identifying the names of perpetrators and victims. To identify the victims was to honor them. Thus the Rwandan Catholic journal *Dialogue,* temporarily removed to Belgium, published a special issue in July–August 1994 devoted to detailed accounts of 206 clergy and lay priests and nuns killed in the events of April and May. The compulsion to tell their story and the journalists' eagerness to get a story led to many accounts with vivid individual identification. Naming the perpetrators may also have been a way of restoring justice. Early on in reporting the war, it became clear that major human rights violations were in progress and that the world was facing massive war crimes. African Rights of London set the tone of reporting on rights violations in its *Rwanda: Death, Despair, Defiance* (1995), which identified by name and role figures deemed responsible in the killing as well as their victims. In *Bisesero: Resisting Genocide* (1997) African Rights also named perpetrators, victims, and some survivors of this remarkable story of a region where refugees and local residents came together and at a great price resisted the forces of genocide. In 1997 the government of Rwanda began to publish an alphabetized Internet list of thousands of names of participants in the genocide, their origins, and wartime roles and identities (www.rwandemb.org/prosecution/tribunal.htm).

One can understand the reasons for the publication of individual names in these writings, yet acute ethical dilemmas persist. Identifying someone in print as a genocidal killer before a court has tried that individual would of course be the worst kind of slander if the individual was innocent. We heard many accounts of individuals believed innocent who were (and still are) imprisoned. We also were told that many such accounts may involve duplicity. We heard that the easiest way to settle an old grudge or to acquire someone else's house or land was to tell the authorities that that individual had been seen with the Interahamwe or had been seen at the scene of killing. It will be years before the Rwandan Tribunal and

International Tribunal of Arusha try all those imprisoned on such charges, if that is ever accomplished. In the meantime, what practice is to be followed in writing about those known to be on such lists or in prison? We became aware that some of the individuals we had interviewed were on these lists. In the camps in Zaire we knew of the presence of perpetrators of genocide among those to whom we were providing food and shelter and with whom we were speaking. But we did not know who they were apart from a few blatant cases. Later, we were made aware of the complicity in the genocide of some of the individuals we had met in the camps and who appear in the pages of this book. They are introduced in the cases in chapter 1. Where there has been independent corroboration of their involvement in planning and executing the genocide, we identify them as such in parallel with telling their own stories, as we heard them.

The most difficult dilemma, however, concerns writing about those who stood up to their neighbors and authorities in the heat of the madness of April and May 1994 and who rescued prospective victims, often risking their own lives. These stories should be told because they too speak of a profound humanity. Yet these are precisely the people whose lives are most at risk. Just as witnesses who came forward in tribunals were killed for their stories or to silence other would-be witnesses, so these heroes of sanity in the midst of genocide are also at risk; some may accuse them of having broken ranks with the party of the genocide perpetrators, and others may believe that these heroes witnessed them killing. The awful problem for the ethnographer here is that the identification of these heroes and the full-context telling of their heroism may endanger their lives.

We have discussed these dilemmas with editors and scholars and have reached an uneasy compromise. We have decided to veil some names and situations where we believe the individuals' safety would be compromised if we identified them fully. On the other hand, we have left public figures' identities intact because their prominence makes them well known.

We have, above all, sought to convey in this writing the immediacy of our own contacts with the people whose stories and circumstances were shared with us so that the truth would be told and the world would know. Ultimately, history will be the judge of these individuals and their circumstances and of our approach to telling at least part of the story of the aftermath of war in Rwanda and Burundi.

Organization of This Book

Two broad approaches to writing are used in this book. Part I is ethnographic, that is, descriptive, and highlights the voices of individuals in the contexts of their stories during or after the war. Part II is essentially synthetic, featuring perspectives by scholars, including Rwandans, Zairians, and Burundians, on the events and issues of their societies as well as our own interpretation of the issues at hand.

We begin with "Rwanda in Zaire" (chapter 1), meaning the Rwandan diaspora in Zaire, both in Bukavu and in the refugee camps. This chapter opens with Bugingo's personal narrative. His story shows the tangled layers of experience and emotion that many Central Africans carry with them and that must be dealt with if there is ever to be closure to the conflict. "Rwanda in Zaire" is our point of departure not because that is where we went first but because the society of the refugee camps in Zaire represented Rwanda as it had existed before the war, as Habyarimana's largely Hutu Rwanda. Many of the camps, although under nominal organization of international relief organizations and the United Nations, were in fact controlled by remnants of the former Rwandan government and the militias. This control is evident in the hesitation of some individuals to speak openly or in their fear of being in the camps.

In chapter 2, "Inside Rwanda", we open with accounts of two communes inside Rwanda: Kayenzi, which experienced the massacres, and Giti, which stands out as having resisted, as did a few other communities. This comparison provides a basis for further reflection in chapter 6 on justice and healing. The fate of institutions in Rwanda is told by the voices of leaders who were trying to solve problems with much of their fellow leadership dead, missing, or in exile or who were picking up the pieces to begin anew after the war.

Chapter 3 is devoted to the "visual voices" of the war and its aftermath. Especially, the children's drawings offer a glimpse into their mind's eye and the makeup of their memories. Just as drawing these scenes of their experiences was therapeutic for the children, so the publishing of them extends the memories of the events both as document and as warning. Children's drawings also appear as documentary evidence related to events described in chapters 1 and 2.

Chapter 4, on Burundi, offers a comparison and a contrast to Rwanda within the larger setting of the Great Lakes region of Central Africa.

Part II brings together texts and thoughts that analyze the nature of the conflict in Central Africa and presents more synthetic approaches to the subject of politics and ethnicity (in chapter 5) and healing and justice (chapter 6). Rwandan, Burundian, and Zairian voices are heard here because some of the leading thinking and writing in the aftermath of war is coming from individuals engaged in the active and open-ended process of recreating their societies.

Notes

1. Use of the term war has been contested in connection with the 1994 events in Rwanda. Rwandan professor Pierre Ndilikilikesha (personal communication, June 10, 1999) argues that there was little direct combat between the two armies [the old Rwandan Armed Forces (ex-FAR) and the Rwandan Patriotic Army (RPA)]. Several authors have used the generic term *conflict* (Prunier1995; Faulkingham and Goheen 1998b); others have stressed *genocide*. We understand the term *war* in a more general sense as "a state of open hostility or competition between opposing forces or for a particular end" (*Websters Ninth New Collegiate Dictionary*, 1989), which permits us to include "low-grade warfare" in Burundi and the entire region as well as genocide as a special circumstance within war. Genocide, following the 1948 Genocide Convention (United Nations, 1951), is defined as "acts committed with intent to destroy, in whole or in part, a national, ethnical, racial or religious group."

2. Our title might have been "conversations" or "dialogues" in the aftermath of war, but we chose "voices" to highlight the centrality of the stories we heard, although clearly we conversed with those we met.

3. The case for rationality of the genocide is convincingly made by René Lemarchand in his essay "Rwanda: The Rationality of Genocide" (1995), to differentiate it from tribal war. As a strategic way of remaining in power, the radical Hutu used ethnic manipulation and killing.The irrationality to which we refer, using Raymond Aron's definition, has to do with the consequences for many in the larger conflict.

4. The MCC had its beginnings in the 1920s when central committees were in vogue. Its first project was to send food, wheat seed, and agricultural machinery to starving postrevolution and civil war Russian Mennonites and their neighbors. In post–World War II Europe the MCC distributed food, conducted refugee relocation, and organized housing construction. During the Vietnam War, the MCC tried to meet human need in a neutral way in the conflict, a stance that meant it kept its workers in Saigon after the end of the war. Today, the MCC is involved in such work as removing bombs and mines in Laos and providing teachers, health workers, and community development assistance in 50 countries. Despite its name, the MCC is a grass-roots organization. Much of the food it distributes globally comes from US and Canadian prairies. The meat that is distributed is often donated by Mennonite farmers and processed in a portable canner that is operated by volunteers. A good portion of the MCC's annual budget of $35 million is supplied by annual relief sales, such as the Kansas sale held in Hutchinson that earns $500,000 each year, and SELFHELP Crafts (now called Ten Thousand Villages), a self-sustaining marketing program of Two-Thirds World artifacts.

PART I

Ethnographies of War and Its Aftermath

1. Rwanda in Zaire

The world was awestruck in June and July 1994 when television news reports showed a third of the nation of Rwanda spilling into eastern Zaire. First came those few Tutsi and opposition Hutu who fled the massacres (although most of these were murdered in their home communities); then came the masses of mostly Hutu fleeing the advancing army of the RPF. At first the human waves simply came: on roads and overland from Gisenyi into Goma and northeastern Zaire, from Kibuye and other points by canoe across Lake Kivu, and then through Cyangugu across the Ruzizi River bridge into Bukavu. The Zairians, completely overwhelmed, nevertheless often did what they could to take the refugees in. But soon the cities and countryside were unable to deal with the masses that within a month would grow to 2.5 million. Another 800,000 refugees fled to northern Burundi, and 500,000 fled to Tanzania.

Having arrived without much food, water, or extra clothing, these masses of Rwandan citizens suddenly turned refugees were a large city without an infrastructure and a public health disaster waiting to happen. The camps stretched out as far as the eye could see on the black lava beds of Goma, under the shadow of Central Africa's live volcanoes. Digging latrines into this rock-hard soil was almost impossible. Human waste accumulated on the surface of the ground. Drinking water was unavailable, so the famished and thirsty people took to drinking out of the polluted Lake Kivu right at their feet. As cholera began to spread, workers of the UNHCR and a growing number of emergency relief agencies moved the Rwandans away from the overburdened Zairian cities into refugee camps. In the camps they distributed tents, set up emergency feeding stations, dug latrines, and tried to create safe drinking water sources.

UNHCR provisional maps drawn and circulated early in the crisis show the camps that emerged in Zaire. Figure 4 locates the large camps that took shape along the roads west and north of Goma: Mugunga, west of Goma; and Kibumba, Karengera, Katale, Rubare, and others located between Goma and Rutshuru. Camps also emerged all along the western shores of Lake Kivu down to Bukavu and beyond to Uvira, at the Burundi border. Figure 5 shows the city of Bukavu and some of the larger camps along the lake as well as camps to the southwest on the road to Lubumbashi, notably the sites of Mushweshwe, Muku, Bideka, and Izirangabo, where we worked.

In late 1994 Bukavu presented a surreal facade combining its various historical identities. Looking out over beautiful Lake Kivu, one could see the roofs of mansions that had been built on coves overlooking the lake as well as the checkerboard white and blue tent cities of refugee camps on distant hills. The largest buildings of Bukavu were the schools, churches, and hospitals that had been built in the late colonial or early postcolonial years and intended to be monuments to the best of European and African collaboration. In 1994 those buildings stood faded and rusted but were still in use, monuments to the elite that tried to maintain them. Public buildings, such as the abandoned Bukavu post office, were in even sorrier state, revealing the complete collapse of government infrastructure. The new University of Bukavu, one of Zaire's decentralized private universities, demonstrated the determination of Kivu civic leaders and businessmen to carry on, despite the collapse of the state. Shops and markets along the main streets were full of goods, evidence of productive Kivu agricultural suppliers and the merchants' access to East African ports.

The underlying tensions in Bukavu were visible to anyone who tried to find them. The Zairian military emerged from their barracks every morning to man their roadblocks—to harass and detain

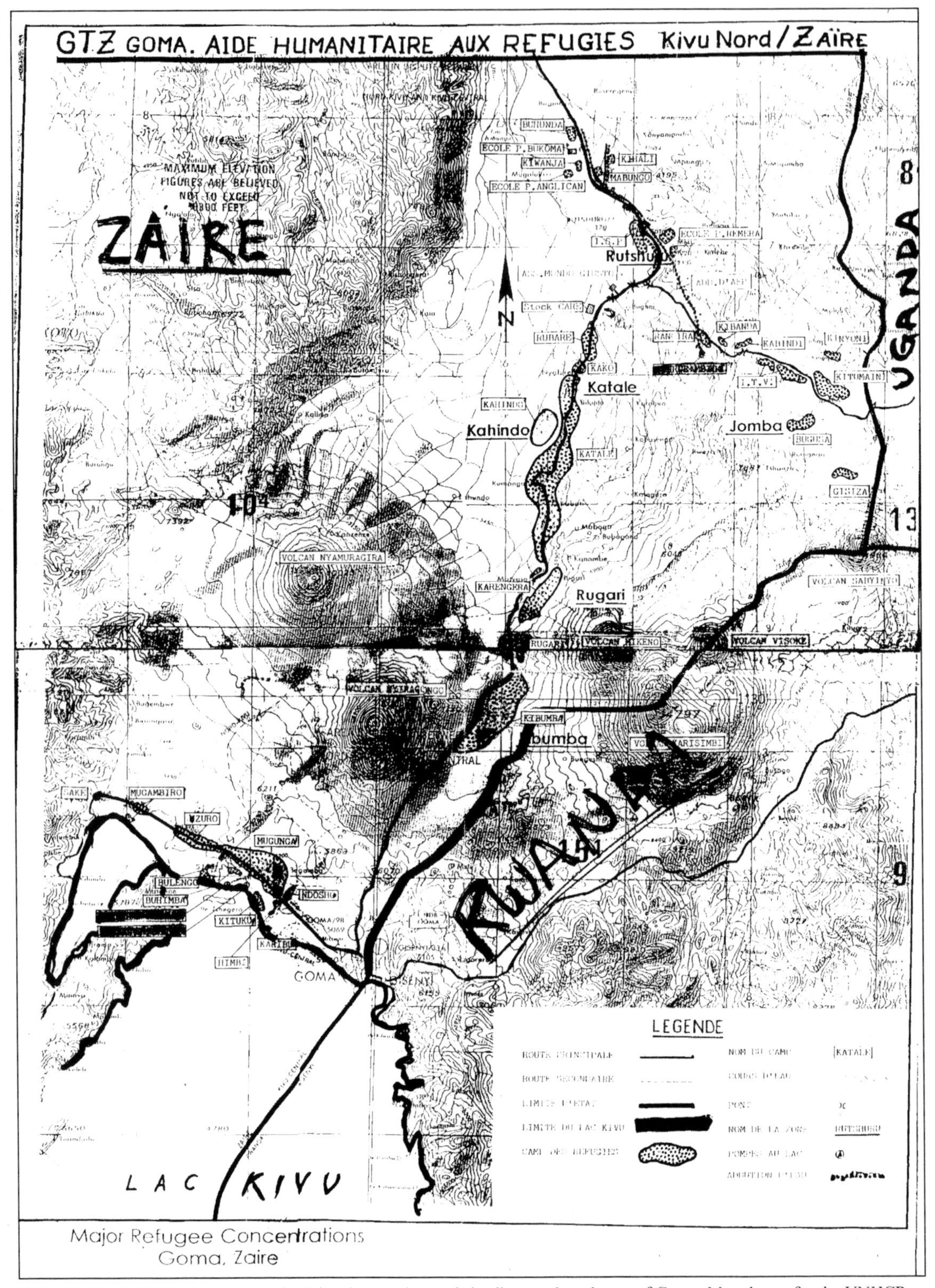

Figure 4. North Kivu refugee camps in Zaire along major roads leading north and west of Goma. Map drawn for the UNHCR (courtesy R. van der Meer).

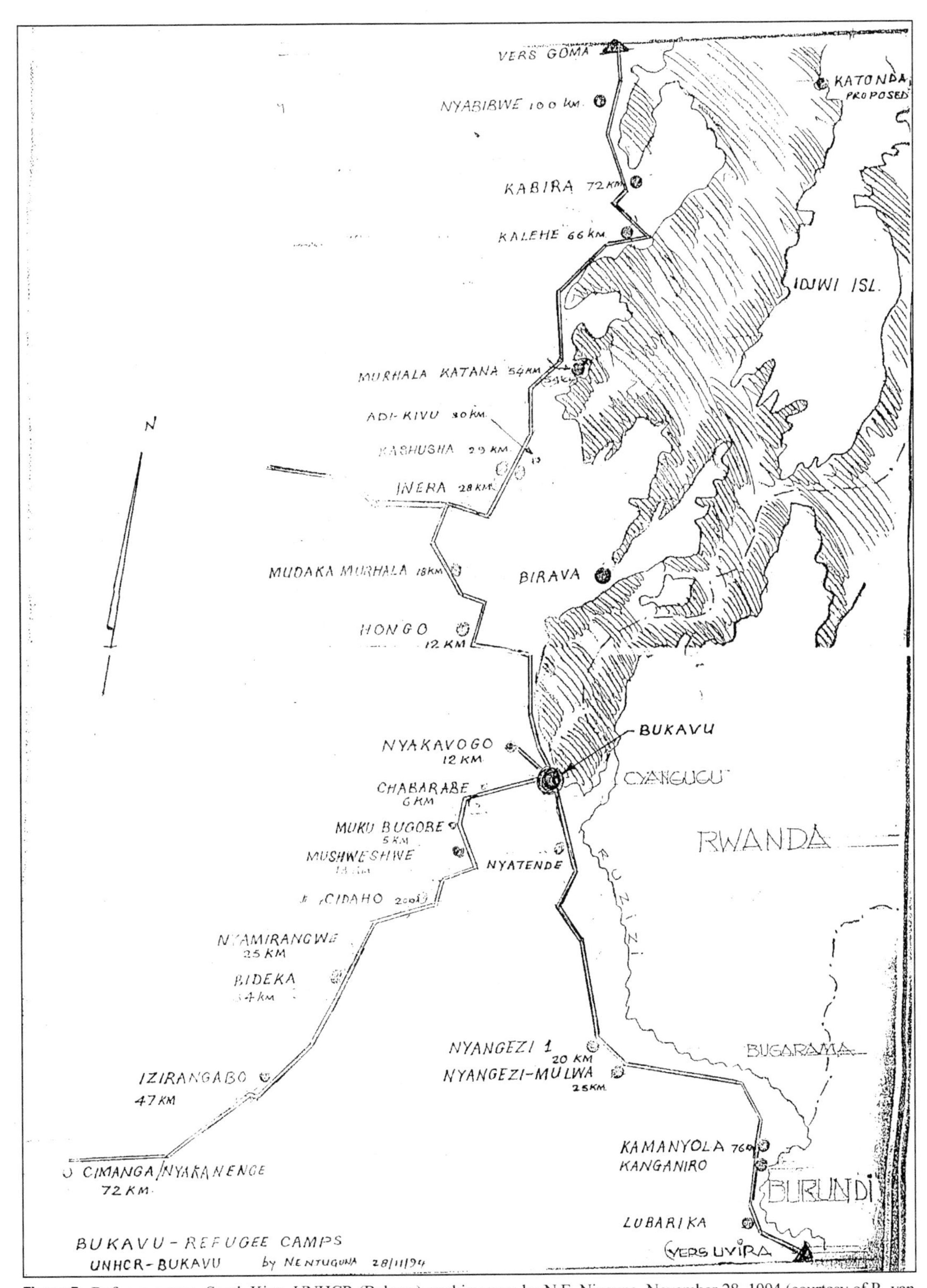

Figure 5. Refugee camps, South Kivu. UNHCR (Bukavu) working map by N.E. Njuguna, November 28, 1994 (courtesy of R. van der Meer). Note camps Mushweshwe (13 km), Muku (Bugobe) (18 km), Bideka (34 km), and Izirangabo (47 km) from Bukavu.

drivers, citizens, Rwandan refugees, and foreigners until they had earned enough bribe money for their daily needs. These soldiers also guarded the borders at the bridges over the Ruzizi River leading into Rwanda and at the Kavumu International Airport north of Bukavu. One of the camps of Rwandan soldiers—of the old FAR—was set up near the Ruzizi River just south of Bukavu, from where cannon fire was exchanged with the RPF armies across the border inside Rwanda. The UN headquarters was set up at the north end of Bukavu's main street, several blocks north of the guesthouse where we lived. A stream of white UN and related agency vehicles along with assorted private cars, taxi-minivans, and pedestrians moved by from early morning until late night. On a good day one had the impression that this cosmopolitan community, thrown together by history, could go on indefinitely as a world city; on the other hand, there was the equally fearful possibility that it could explode at any time if the several armies camped around the city became entangled with each other.

Many Zairians with whom we spoke betrayed the rising tensions between them and the Rwandans over many issues. Zairians were deeply disturbed by the fact that the refugees had cut down many trees in Bukavu and in the countryside for use as firewood and that they had helped themselves to stores of food and crops in the fields without paying their "hosts." In general, Zairians felt that the Rwandans were pushy and domineering and that they would take over if their occupation were to continue for long. Disagreements and fights did erupt over these issues. Local church and civic organizations such as the Ligue Zairoise pour la Paix emerged to mediate conflicts between civilians and between Zairians and Rwandans to keep the military out of the picture, especially the Zairian military, which was known to fuel conflict with often deadly consequences.

By 1995 it was apparent that the Rwandan presence in Kivu was putting significant pressures on Zairian public officials, the outcome of which was not yet clear. Weak government authorities tried to keep the armies apart, but the dominant Hutu forces in the camps were forcing the hand of the Zairian officials to support them. Although Kivu society had not been divided by the categories Hutu and Tutsi, such pressures came to be felt. Zairians with the stereotypical features of Tutsis said they felt endangered. In 1996 these pressures from radical Rwandan Hutu forces prompted Kivu area Zairian officials to move against the Banyamulenge, Tutsi communities on the Ruzizi plain south of Bukavu. The Banyamulenge refused to leave, instead invoking their Zairian citizenship as a reason to fight back. They received support from the new government of Rwanda and formed the core of the rebellion that ultimately ousted President Mobutu.

One of the first indications of the strength of this rebel movement was their success in defeating or routing the units of the Zairian National Army with which they engaged. By late 1996 the growing rebel army [Alliance Démocratique des Fronts de Liberation de Congo-Zaire (Alliance of Democratic Forces for the Liberation of Congo-Zaire)] had taken Bukavu and regions to the south. The implications of this for the Rwandan refugee camps in the area were far-reaching and disastrous. All the camps in eastern Zaire were dispersed, including the FAR, the Interahamwe militia, and their sympathizers in the camps. Most of the noncombatants in Goma area camps were able to return to Rwanda once the Alliance forces had engaged the soldiers and militia who had held them hostage for over two years. A few of the noncombatant refugees in the Bukavu area were able to return home, but most, including the refugees of Mushweshwe, Muku, Bideka, and Izirangabo, were among the 230,000 missing Rwandan refugees assumed to have been massacred or to have perished of exposure, hunger, or disease on their flight westward. Therefore most of the Rwandans in Zaire who appear in these pages are voices from history whose fate remains unknown.

1.1 *Do I Still Have a Life?* One Terrified Man's Search for Repatriation

I was a refugee in my own country before the war.
—Bugingo, former soldier of the Rwandan Army, Hutu

Among the Rwandans who frequented the Protestant Guest House of Bukavu where we lived was Bugingo (a pseudonym of his own choosing). He was one of the 20,000 Rwandan refugees who had remained in Bukavu after the others had been moved to camps along the lake or along one of the other roads at a distance from the city. At first it was not clear why he came to us or what he feared. A Zairian in our group suggested that he perhaps had committed some terrible offense against humanity that he wanted to confess. Later, we discovered that he was among those many unfortunate Rwandans who had been drawn into the killing while trying to flee from it, thus probably accounting for the tangled emotional state he displayed. One morning I (John) sat with him and agreed to listen to him as he poured out his anguish. The narrative here does not immediately find a direction other than fragments of his life story. The reader will need to exercise some patience to hear him out and reach beneath the surface to the depths of his troubled being, which is sadly not just the story of one Rwandan youth whose aspirations were shattered but the plight of many youths across Africa. According to David Newbury (personal communication, 1996), Bugingo's life "is a story of the struggle of a Rwandan youth to gain acceptance into the intellectual class, to no avail. Especially after 1990, amorphous power was the major ticket to success in Rwanda."

Bugingo said he was really 42 years old, although his identity card indicated he was 37. But his identity card was lost when his clothes were stolen. He told us early on that he had attended a Catholic primary school in Rwanda and was first in his graduating class of 41 students. The teacher normally would pass 7–10 students on to secondary school. He asked for applications to seminary and to public school so he would have a place to go if accepted. Bugingo's story continues in his own words and in excerpts from the correspondence we carried on with him for several years (most of Bugingo's words and writings have been translated from French; he sometimes wrote in English).

In an interview on December 16, 1994, in Bukavu, Bugingo recalled his education and the problems he faced as a Hutu. His experiences mark his first disillusionment. Much more would follow.

> You could enter the priesthood, if you felt called. I opted for both exams. [When the results were to be announced], we all went to the parish. I was third in the results. We went with our parents to the priest. But he didn't encourage anyone at this time. Then the hierarchy spoke in church. Later, the students were interviewed. My parents were not Christian, my father was polygamous. When I was asked if my parents were Christian, I explained. Then a new list was posted, and I was excluded from those who could continue their studies. On the official exam, not one had passed. I tried to find out what the priest and the teachers were doing in this. It turned out that only the students with Christian parents were passed.
>
> My big brother found me a place in a private school. Two years later, I discovered that I had no future there, for it wasn't a good school. It was a Christian school run by an ex-priest, so it wasn't really a seminary. Then I went to a youth service *[service de jeunnesse]* near a military camp, to do agricultural work. I was asked to decide if I wanted land to become a cultivator, but I was too young. Teams would work the land, but I wanted another type of work. So I returned home.
>
> Meanwhile, I prayed with my sister, and at home. We went to a bishop to find me a seminary place, although I was four years older than the others. The bishop said, continue to pray, and God will show you the way. They helped me with readings and other studies and in finding funds to attend the catechists' school *[Ecole des catechistes]*. After one year the school was closed.
>
> During the vacations, a friend advised me to write to another catechists' school. So I was admitted to a seminary for adults, to become priests or to go to other vocations of the church. At the end of this year of studies we were discouraged, but at 22 years of age, I was encouraged to become a priest. However, I had met a girl and now wanted to marry.

Bugingo continued with the story of how he entered the military.

> A friend encouraged me to become a soldier. I was tempted and got the necessary certificate from a friend; that is, we created a false ID. I was accepted and entered. They knew of this falsification. But [they let me continue anyway]. The commander simply demanded good work. So I worked at this for 10 years. I studied sport, combat, karate with Koreans, so I could apply to the Presidential Guard. After this I returned to my unit, in the Bugesera, near Gashora, the military camp of the Gako Training Center. They learned I had karate training and invited me to teach them in the evenings. I was very isolated, they had time.

Not much later, Bugingo's trouble with military officers began.

> In Gako camp there was a commander of the commando training who was mean and beat his men and oppressed them. I didn't know any of this and didn't want to meddle. He told me to stop the karate training to only a few, he wanted all the men to learn it. I understood nothing of his and their intrigues. For some reason the commander began to see me as his enemy or rival, but I continued to train the few, not understanding the commander's motives. Each time he wanted to punish me, the officers protected me. I was perplexed at all this. Maybe I was naive. In any case, the commander was replaced by another. When he arrived, it appeared that he had been banished to this camp. Again, I was singled out for punishment by him. This happened in connection with a festival of the Rwandan Army that was to be held in Kigali. Each center sent individuals for the parade, and I was included. We trained to do a good performance. We were in Kigali; it was the day of the parade and the performances. An officer had resisted training for this. Why? He plotted to take my place. I asked my platoon chief what was going on. He said, it has been decided, the other one is older and has seniority. So I ceded, and went as an observer.
>
> Then I heard they were looking for me. Now, the performances were changed, and others were put in instead of those who had practiced. The one who had taken my place was accused of not wanting to participate. I was interrogated, accused, incriminated falsely, and sentenced to 15 days of punishment. I demanded a hearing and asked for witnesses. They sent the commander of the one who hadn't wanted to participate. They assured me it would be all right, but they didn't write out an official attestation.
>
> Meanwhile, I applied to train as a military teacher and was accepted. But I first wanted my papers. The commander refused. They put my things in a jeep headed to go to Kigali. But I wanted first to clarify my status. I went to the commanders. They sent me with a letter to my old commander. But he refused, accusing me of having intrigued against him. So I left for Kigali and told my new commander about all this, calling into question the old commander.
>
> So I followed the course in military education. The new commander, he too began to harass me. I had a knee injury. I met my commander in the hospital with two officers who were not participating in the course. He promised to remove my earlier sanction in six months. But then he was transferred and replaced by another commander.
>
> When the course was completed, I went to the adjutant chief to seek to remove this punishment from my record. They agreed, but they kept punishing me, again, to humiliate me. I was transferred to a higher military school and presented myself to my new commander and told him of the unjust punishments. He told me to write to the Chef d'Etat Major. But I was again frustrated, for they refused to consider my appeal. This was in 1982. [Instead of hearing my request to clear my record], I was sent to a unit in the northeast of the country, at Mutara, where the army sent soldiers who had a reputation for lacking discipline, whom they monitored closely with a surveillance sheet *[fiche de surveillance]* and a photograph. It was intimidating and humiliating, but it only lasted several days.
>
> Eventually I was sent back to the officer's school at Bugesera, and my commander was the one with whom I had had all the problems, but he experienced so much malaria that he was sent away and replaced by a new commander. Two years later I was sent to Ruhengeri to teach physical sport. I had four units.
>
> From this appointment I was sent to the border to Uganda, where I directed a detachment. I did all the patrolling myself. One day I arrested some smugglers who were trafficking fraudulent merchandise and brought them in. I reported on my radio to headquarters and asked them what to do. The commander said, take notes, take the merchandise and the men to customs, get a copy signed by the customs agent, have it witnessed, and send a copy to the commander. I did all this and thought I had done right.
>
> Awhile later, I was at the canteen, where I met my commander. I told him I had the copy of the paper and would give it to him. He wasn't interested in it right then. He wanted to leave and asked me to go with him in his car. I went with him. I soon discovered that what he was going to do—and wanted me to do—was to engage in something illicit, which I was reluctant to do with him, namely, to visit a prostitute at a brothel *[deuxieme bureau]*. I had my fiancée, so I couldn't go along with this. We drank, and he danced with the prostitute. Then he told me, "This is how we work." More drinks, more music. He asked me why I wasn't interested. I waited. Finally, we left and passed

policemen on the road. The commander was clearly unhappy with me, and after this time we became unfriendly.

Bugingo married his fiancée, but his problems continued.

I married then but am now divorced with one child. Does this divorce too have something to do with my troubles with officers and commanders? I spoke to my parents and entered a Christian group. But my wife didn't want to go with me.

Bugingo picked up his story again after the brothel experience. His marital problems soon surface.

I was returned to my old unit in the Akagera Park, and again I thought I might be subjected to punishment. I spoke to the chaplain and to the commander and told him that my marriage was in trouble. The commander's advice was, "Beat her and make her obey," but I refused this advice. Then, we went to the court for a divorce, but for three years they refused to give it to me. Again, the court told me to beat my wife. She went to sorcerers to provoke me.

Bugingo needed a new identity card to replace the one with sanctions on it.

Normally, to leave an army unit, you need to give two years advance notice. They moved me to Kibuye in the west. [I was still interested in clearing my record.] They said, to get a new ID, give us your old ID card and you can have an attestation in lieu of an ID; it's an interim ID. I thought I was being hassled because I wanted a divorce. What to do? The procurer again told me to beat my wife [to bring her into line]. I was about to move. She lived in a house nearby now. I was in the barracks. We took the same car. Was this a trap? She got into the car, and she began to throw bananas at me. I hit her. They separated us. When we arrived at Kibuye, the commander asked me to explain myself. He accused me of lies. I wrote a response. They asked me for my ID card, and I gave them the attestation. It was 1990 now, at the moment of the war.

The war in Akagera was beginning, and Bugingo was sent to the front, still without proper identification.

I went to Gitarama for a week, demanding my ID, but [I got] more excuses. Then I was sent to the front, where there were no administrative services. We under-officers were to wear red armbands. The officer told me I'd be killed. What? Later, we were told to remove the bands. I was under-officer of a unit, with artillery support behind us. "You approach," we were told. The officer accused me of being afraid. It was night. The [RPF] enemy attacked. Our soldiers began to flee because the officers were gone. Where was the commander? Major? "Did you order them to flee?" He said, "Stay with the 12 soldiers," and he left and didn't return. In fact, they all left, some 30 km back from the front. We were alone. There was another attack the next morning. Some were killed; the rest of us fled. We found the commander and the others. They had reported that I was missing, or dead. We regrouped. The *Chef d'Etat Major* and others passed by in a jeep headed for Kigali. Our unit also went to Kigali, but they told me to stay behind and hold the front. The leaders fled. "You, the under-officers, you stay. We'll leave." I stayed, the others left. There was another attack. I fled on foot, and more retreating. I fled into a banana grove where I removed my officer's uniform and officer's shirt. I took my weapon apart, and left it there.

All of a sudden I saw another comrade, and we continued together. We heard a vehicle approach. We used a password to identify ourselves, but they didn't reply. Were they the enemy? They asked us to surrender and demanded to see our identity cards. I tried to explain [why I didn't have mine]. My colleague defended me, backing up my story. They appeared to believe me, but they wouldn't say who they were. I took them to my weapon [to back up my story]. They said not to touch the weapons; they couldn't make them work, but they took them anyway. We were then accused of being deserters and were taken to the commander. He turned out to be the one who had taken me to the prostitutes. He had also fled. He took me to Kigali in a jeep.

We were interrogated about the events, and the transcription they made was accurate. After two or three days we were taken to another camp in Kigali and put in a cell where we were given an interrogation. The interrogator transcribed this in the form of Q and A and asked us to sign. I contested his version of things, but I signed not to have further troubles. They needed a pretext to explain the events and to have scapegoats. We were kept a week in the central prison in Kigali. Then there was another interrogation. When my six month [sentence] was nearly over, I was liberated by a committee. It was now April 1991.

Bugingo returned to his wife after his release from prison, but the marriage was over.

I was again forced to take up my married life. My [now ex-] wife wrote a letter, to which I added some lines, asking to get to court. So they preferred to liberate me. The divorce was granted, and I was expelled from the army. Now I was without anything.

I returned to my home community *[colline natal]*. I went to the mayor for a paper requesting to get my things . . . I obtained a new identity card with "cultivator" on it. Our family's domestic had broken his arm in a fight. I took him to Kigali to help him, and while there I visited the parish priest, because I had decided to live away from my

> parents [in Kigali], with a brother who was a teacher there and was married. I had no papers with me. I went to find papers in another commune. I was now completely adrift *[déraciné]*. I sought work. But my brother's wife began to hassle me, inspired by outside persons. She entered my room one day and threw out all my things. Then she and my brother fought, and she left. This prompted him to go to court, and they were divorced.

Bugingo blamed some his problems on sorcery.

> There is a history of sorcery behind all this. At least, this is what my parents were told. My brother went to an *umfoumu*. When you go to a diviner, you are asked to respect their rules. They say they get their knowledge from God and the spirits. The two women—my wife and my brother's wife—used sorcery for their own ends. Intellectuals use women for their ends. People say you're a victim because of sorcery, because of a curse. But they say this to persuade and deceive the public. If you're a Christian, you can settle these things.
>
> After the divorces, the two women began to agitate against us. They went to the military, and someone told us they'd kill my brother. He didn't believe this, saying it was merely a continuation of the first affair. But who was behind all this?

While trying to pick up his life, Bugingo found himself in the midst of the massacres of 1994.

> Then the war broke out. It was April 1994. My brother was in Kigali. We lived near the airport and worked for the French. He went with the French [to the protected zone (see Zone Turquoise in Figure 3)]. I stayed. The neighbors tried to implicate me in the killing and the pillaging. I told them I was not at all interested in this since leaving the military. So, I found a ride to Butare with a vehicle. I went to the theology faculty where I had a friend. Suddenly, [the war broke out in Butare] and [my tormenters] knew I was there. I was nearly killed four times. They asked me, "Why are you here?" I told them I was a teacher.
>
> "But your card says you're a farmer. You're an old soldier!"
>
> "This man is suspect," they said to each other. "Cut off his head."
>
> So they took me to the communal pit. They wanted to take my money, so I gave it all to them and they freed me.
>
> I returned to my friend from the theology faculty, and we went to a Belgian unit of Doctors without Borders. We were arrested by the military. There were lots of questions and orders.
>
> "If he's an ex-soldier, kill him."
>
> "If he's a teacher, kill him."
>
> "If he's a cultivator, . . ." My friend vanished and I was alone. Christ saved me. I went to the president of the court *[cour première instance]* and presented them my ID card. There were more questions. A professor in Butare from my commune saved me from this situation. But there was more harassment, and I was again rescued by him. We fled together to Gikongoro and Cyngugu and then to Bukavu. I found refuge with an Anglican bishop in Bukavu behind the college.

Halfway through Bugingo's story I (John) began to suspect that he really hadn't done anything wrong in the war. By the end of his account, however, I knew that he was one terrified man who had gotten caught in the crossfire of the genocide, which left him terribly tangled emotionally. He kept referring to "them" or "they," as if someone was after him. So I asked him who was going to get him. He spoke of the military authorities and their accomplices who had tried to kill him in Butare. But he also spoke of sorcerers possibly working for others, using the women. Sorcerers, the military commanders, assassins, and evil women fused in his mind. He was staying with about 50 other refugees at the Anglican bishop's compound in Bukavu. Some of them were families; others were loners like him. There were some Tutsi. All seemed to have in common fear for their lives in the camps.

Bugingo was the first Rwandan we spoke with who could be said to have displayed severe post-traumatic stress. He was trembling and sniffling when he finished his story of how he had escaped Butare. I offered him the section on fear in a religious tract available in the guesthouse and directed him to several Bible passages. He read them, and then I asked him if he wished me to pray with him. He said yes, and I did. Then he told me of having been hassled by the Zairian soldiers, who told him his identity card wasn't adequate. We invited him to eat with us, and he ate heartily. He spoke of his parents, who he thought were in a Goma camp, and of his brother in Tanzania. We urged him to seek the services of a search agency to confirm their location.

After this lengthy interview and counsel that lasted the better part of an afternoon, I (John) realized that none of the reports I had read about the war describe the emotional terror people had gone through. Bugingo was nearly killed four times fleeing war and the unjust harassment in the military. He should be crazy. He was clearly sick with fear. By the time he left, he seemed more composed because he had been able to tell his story to someone. Before he left, he expressed the desire to find some work, not just for the money but to have something that would distract him from his fear.

Bugingo came calling again the next afternoon (December 17, 1994) with four letters for us to take to Kigali and post in the mail. He again wanted to talk, so we sat down and he prayed as he had the first visit. Again he raised the possibility that his string of troubles—his exclusion from good schools, his hassles with the military commander, his marital troubles, the war—were caused by sorcery (by the *umufumu*). He said he felt like a refugee in his own country even before the war. Emotionally he was more settled than the previous day, but his analysis was, if anything, even more calculating. It was as if he could see the pattern connecting the words of others.

> My father had said, "You are making yourself sick and confused by your pursuit of legal recourse." My mother and mother-in-law went to the *umufumu* together to get my marriage to stick: my wife's various evil words and poisoning attempts and the commander's words "You will die." . . . And then my new misfortunes. Do I still have a life? Would you help me emigrate to Canada?

I thought intently about all this and discerned through all the rhetoric a negative self-image that internalized the hostilities or allowed them to destroy his self-image. So, I suggested to Bugingo that he stop dwelling on the past, that he couldn't change it wherever he might be—Kigali, Bukavu, or Canada. I told him that he should know that God loves him fully, as all of us, despite our flaws, weaknesses, and failures. God's love is unconditional. With this, he could gain courage and self-confidence. He needed to accept himself as created in the image of God and begin anew. He should try to do things well and right one day at a time and to seek accomplishment in each day. Reinhild brought him a meal, which he ate eagerly as if he had been receiving little or no food.

Bugingo then began to wonder out loud if he might return to Rwanda. I told him it seemed to me he had done nothing wrong. Perhaps his being a soldier in the FAR would be held against him but he had been expelled before the war, after all. Daniel Fever, the French Pastor on our team, spoke with him about this too. He pointed out that there was another under-officer who was a witness to his imprisonment. Also, the commander who had harassed him had been killed, so he couldn't testify against him. Bugingo decided to write some friends and a missionary contact in Kigali for their help in getting assurances that he could return.

Later, I discussed this case with Zairian pastor Mukambu Ya'Namwisi of our unit. He said that fear of sorcery and low self-esteem are part of a profile in Central Africa common to many people who are plagued by self-doubt. Giving people hope is important. Congolese psychologist Masamba ma Mpolo (1981) suggested that witchcraft suspicions are an unconscious search for ego integrity and individuation. In the Rwandan context the interiorization of a negative other could be especially damaging, suggesting that Bugingo was trying to clarify his emotional state by getting this source of his trouble outside of himself.

Some days later we delivered Bugingo's letters to their destinations in Kigali, and we mailed another from Nairobi. I also wrote to Bugingo to tell him that I had delivered or mailed his letters in Kigali. I added that I had been told that a Baptist chaplain of the FAR had returned to Rwanda from Goma with three FAR soldiers. After a week or two of reeducation, the chaplain is again at work in Gako camp, and the soldiers have been reintegrated into the Rwandan army under its new leadership.

Bugingo's next year and a half would be spent in the security of the Anglican bishop's enclave of Bukavu. From there he could exchange letters with various friends and acquaintances, including us in the United States. Excerpts from our correspondence with him follow; Bugingo's letters reveal his continuing search for contacts in Rwanda that would assure him safe passage home and a secure existence there. Further details about his fears and his role in the war emerge little by little in the letters.

Bugingo to the Janzens: Bukavu, February 4, 1995

> . . . As for my news, it is without special change, except for the worst that happened to me Friday, 23 December 1994, when the men whom we call "thieves" entered my tent during my absence and stole all that remained of value in my bag. I use the term "worst" because of the photographs, the dearest of all that I had, the photos. I remain convinced that all these things will come back to me and that is what I pray to God.
>
> Since almost nothing remains of my own, I benefited from the generosity of my compatriots in the same community as the Anglican bishop [of Bukavu], and since I already had asked Joyce Martens to help me with clothes, she put me in contact with Clement [of the Mennonite team] but he,

after checking his stock, could find only women's clothing; he offered me a sack of these to distribute to the women and girls of our Anglican community. I had the luck of finding two men's T-shirts in this stock which happened to fit me, so I kept them for myself. Clement also promised that the next distribution would come soon and, apart from the missing photographs, I was nearly restored. Obviously, the clothing does not spare me the harassment by soldiers, who, for the moment content themselves with demanding from me my identity card and proof of Rwandan citizenship, so that I am not [suspected] and treated like a spy of the Rwandan Patriotic Front on an espionage mission!

I give thanks to God for a letter from Peter Andrews in Tanzania; it is perhaps a reply to my very first letter which I wrote him via the International Red Cross. I also received another letter from the guard of the Kigali diocese, which was a reply to the letter I gave you when you left. This is all to say that I am experiencing the increase of divine blessings through you. May God bless you.

Returning to God's will in my future and in the current state of affairs, you were right to invite me to not dwell on the past and to look at life with new eyes (which is not difficult when one has washed them with tears). God is always ready to help me for he has accepted me and loves me as I am. I must add to this that Daniel told me that Christ died for you and me and all those who believe in him, more than the whole world. These are the good memories engraved in my mind.

My letter also has the objective of conversing with you over who I should consult among those who know me the best, regarding my desire to engage in further study of literature, for the rest can wait till later. By the study of literature, I mean my desire to learn languages and to improve those which I already know somewhat, so as to understand better when I see more clearly. Do not worry about my vocation as God's minister, for I can always do that even in an occupation that doesn't seem to be closed, as long as I have the will, the means, and am predisposed to doing it.

Excuse me for all this discourse that I produced and many thanks for the effort you have made to read it. I hope to read good news from you in the near future, and pray for you that the Eternal may bless you.

P.S., Monday, February 5, 1995

May God be blessed, last night in passing by the Guest House to give them the letter you have, your letter of December 28 had been there for me almost three weeks, according to Cathy. I have already read it and am very happy for all the news. I did not know that the Andrews are at Kigali because their letter, recently received, suggests that they were at Mwanza in Tanzania. They were probably visiting when they met you.

As far as my repatriation is concerned and the work of Reverend Pastor Nsabimana Jean-Baptiste [chaplain of the Rwandan army who returned from Goma], it is all very interesting, all the more so because this chaplain is an old friend of mine; we grew up together and know each other well without thereby sharing the secrets of our lives. He is the one who gave me the counsel to leave the seminary to go into the military and who arranged for me the forged certificate of study that I presented upon entry [into the army]. We are here at the point of tackling my repatriation and my reintegration into society, after the highs and the lows I experienced, and the sinking of a household in which he played the role of middleman in the engagement, and later mediator between spouses, this all has the flavor of a tragicomic adventure novel!

So I will write him to demand information on the modalities of repatriation since after everything I experienced in military service, reintegration into the military must not be undertaken without a time of reflection and calmness. Still, may the will of God be made manifest through all these events, however insignificant and full of absurdity.

Bugingo to the Janzens: Bukavu, March 3, 1995

It is again a pleasure to be able to send you a letter. I had the chance to meet Joseph at the Protestant Guest House of Bukavu and he was with a friend who was returning to France and agreed to transmit the letter that you have before your eyes as well as those to Daniel Féver and Joyce [Martens].

The news is about the same, but there has been a general census of all the Rwandan refugees in Zaire, and that led me to think of preparations for repatriation. I saw on the papers into which we were being registered headings about "passport for vehicles" *[feuille de route pour véhicules]*, but that could have to do with other matters.

I have not yet received a letter of response from the Reverend Pastor military chaplain of Gako, and I intend to send another letter via UNHCR as the protector promised to forward it. I prepared another letter to the President of UNHCR Sagako Ogata to request help with studies to prepare for another professional career. God willing, this could become a solution to my problems. Would you please kindly continue to contact benefactors who could be sensitive to my case. God will not fail to respond favorably, for the life of a refugee in Zaire is above all increasingly full of deceptions.

The best of health, and may God bless you.

P.S. Excuse me, if I am obliged to use even the back side it is because an idea came to me just after ending the letter. I want to go back to our conversation the other day at [the Centre d'Acceuil Protestant (the Protestant guesthouse)]. Several sentences in your counsel came to mind. Concerning the judgment of others, certainly leaders, I apologize and regret having often made judgments, rightly or wrongly, in this place being mostly revolted both internally and externally. This was totally groundless, given that the work of leading is not easy, errors are always possible, such as the wrong appreciation of situations and individuals. May God forgive me in the name of our savior Jesus Christ.

Would you please communicate to me if the letter that I gave to Joyce reached you, I hope she was the one who put the address of the Mennonite Guesthouse in Nairobi, and when she told me that you had already left for the United States, I did not have the presence of mind to ask her if she knew your address in the U.S.

Bugingo's Appeal to the UNHCR: Bukavu, March 22, 1995

The UNHCR headquarters was located not far from where Bugingo lived and even closer to the Protestant guesthouse. In his plea for support and protection, Bugingo details his fear of the old FAR and militia in the camps all around Bukavu. This letter to Sagako Ogata, Japanese president of the UNHCR, yields the permission to remain legally in the city and a small payment of support, which greatly relieves Bugingo. This letter, which Bugingo sent us in July 1995, repeats some of his story as told to us, but there are significant additional details. Our translation of this letter retains some of the French idioms to convey the tone of Bugingo's deferential language.

Madam President,

I the undersigned, Bugingo O., Rwandan refugee in Zaire, sheltered at the Anglican Bishopric in Bukavu for eight months. I have the honor to address myself to your highness, in order to ask you to kindly bear witness to my grand indulgence in finding a permanent solution to my security and my future. In effect Madam, beyond the misery which has hit the land and its population in general, I have particularly known the worst political persecutions before and during the war which continues.

What exactly happened? I am an ex-soldier and I served in the army from October 1975 until 1990. But on 23 October 1990 I was imprisoned without trial for six months and then discharged without reason. I was released on 15 April 1991.

Imprisoned soldiers in that period of the war were commonly considered accomplices of the political adversary of the regime in place. But in the detention dossier, as with most of the other soldiers, I was branded a *deserter*.

Here is the truth of this affair as far as I know it. It all began in 1980 when I was a young sergeant and military instructor in the Bugesera Military Camp of Gako.

The commander of the Instruction Center was the late Colonel Munyengango Francois, who had officers under his order with whom he did not fail to have conflicts; especially in the evening while they shared a glass of beer, the colonel went a little too far, including physical attacks.

They did not tolerate this very long because certain ones knew that in the past I had done six months of training in karate with the Koreans (who called it KiEksuc); these officers asked me to teach them these techniques in the evening. I didn't realize the conflict that this would cause between them and their chief. I accepted with pleasure to teach them because that meant for me a more agreeable occupation than sitting behind a glass of alcohol. It is thus that I attracted the hostility of my boss who saw in these karate exercises a threat to his authority if ever it came to physical force. Captain M. would witness to this because he was the victim of attack [by the colonel] several times, as was Commander N. and many others.

To return to that which concerns me, the commander of the center swore he would launch an unjust punishment against me; he launched intrigues. I did all I could to have this affair investigated by the military authorities. Thanks to his knowledge and his authority, he blocked my requests for appeal and I waited several years, during which I was silenced in military academy and let it pass.

It was then that the officers of the Rwandan army ganged up against me and established what one calls a surveillance file *[fiche de surveillance]* against me, apparently destined to put the authorities on guard for a dangerous person but in reality to invite them to take oppressive vengeance on me.

We are now in 1985, six months before my marriage. An officer, Colonel R., commander of the Commando Batallion of Ruhengeri, tried to get me to lead a life of sexual and alcoholic debauchery. I resisted him not only for virtue but also out of respect for my future wife and the happiness of my home. Perhaps it was naive to have confided all this to my wife after our marriage.

Life in the home became impossible. The woman accused me of not being like others and wished me death or imprisonment. She went out every night between 8 and 11 p.m., she took money and other goods; she caused two wounds to my sexual organs; she began a tale of venereal disease and obliged me to have myself examined in a medical laboratory; she continually tried, without success, to get me involved in sorcery. She left a packet of poison on the table and later tried to deny it. I finally noticed that she was not the only one in on the act, given that all this was reinforced by Colonel N., who was the commander of the military camp, who did his best to erase the traces of this story of poison.

In 1987 when I began my request for divorce, the persecutions increased and all civil and judicial authorities, backed up by the military authorities, reinforced her with their protection—which could not hide all [her deeds].

To avoid the reality of the facts, they tried to entice me to commit acts of physical violence toward her, not to mention sexual and alcoholic debauchery, as well as sorcery. Since I did not accept their proposition, they imposed multiple and varied afflictions on me, such as unfounded punishments, fines, machination of complicated situations to accuse me of errors, rejection of promotions, degrading and unjustified moves, combined judicial and professional actions, up to and including imprisonment and being dismissed from my position without warning.

The divorce would not be granted until some months later. During my imprisonment, the director of the prison allowed me to correspond with my wife. But because I used the paper to correspond with the tribunal instead of my wife, they no longer allowed me to correspond with her and even forbade me from being in contact with the court by letter.

To come back to my imprisonment: its preparation had been launched three months earlier at the start of the war [with the RPF] of October 1990. An agent of Command Headquarters came to my unit to collect several military identity documents, including mine. The local administrative service gave out substitute forms with the justification that I should wait for a duplicate form. Later, I was assigned to a new unit where this substitute attestation was taken from me with the promise that I would be given a new identity corresponding to the new unit. Each time I requested a new attestation form, they told me that I should be patient; this continued until the day of the outbreak of the war on October 1, 1990.

I intensified my reclamations during the two weeks prior to our departure to the front. But Chief Adjutant M. and Adjutant N., who were employed at the secretariat, rejected my appeals with the word that they were busy with more urgent work. This was an exasperating intrigue provoked by the commander of the operation, Colonel Innocent R. He had been the one at the origin of the conflict between us because I had rejected his propositions to keep him company in the affair of sexual and drunken debauchery.

So I departed to the front without any identity documentation. I hoped that a secretariat service would follow us to the battle front and still furnish me with the card that I needed. But the officers organized my isolation from the rest on the battlefield. Suddenly, they sent military police to arrest me, who also demanded to see my identification, knowing full well that I didn't have any. Following this I was treated [line missing from bottom of page]. The interrogations were supposed to begin anew several times in order to establish a dossier whenever their intrigue appeared the least possible. It is then that I was imprisoned.

After being released and my divorce accepted, the mayor of my home commune took the battle again and took sides with the other authorities. He refused to issue me papers of free circulation within the country. He told me he had received verbal orders that, despite my release, I remain under surveillance.

I fled to the commune of Kanombe, where the appropriate identification was issued to me. But I became conscious of all the threats that surrounded me so I requested asylum to Canada through the Canadian Consulate in Kenya. This was at the end of 1991 or early 1992, but I never got a response.

My persecutors did not give up. They took advantage of my unemployment and tried to offer me work so that they could continue the surveillance and entrapment. But I rejected them all and took advantage of the post of Professor of Physical Education in a private college in Kigali. This would represent yet another item on the list of reasons why I should be executed, for the college in question had the reputation (wrongly) of being a fiefdom of the political and military adversaries of the regime in power.

Around the time of Christmas vacation 1993, a group of policemen plotted the assassination of my brother—we were living together—I do not think I was directly the target of this attack. I nevertheless went to open an investigation with the United Nations Military. While I was awaiting the outcome of this investigation, the Rwandan war of 1994 broke out.

In May 1994 I escaped arbitrary execution three times and was two to three steps away from ending in the communal pit. Each time it was the intervention of a member of a militia who saved my life.

The testimony of Jean Baptiste N. (who currently lives in Bideka [refugee camp]) will tell you that it all began with the suspicion of a militia member who insinuated that I was an accomplice of the Belgian group Doctors without Borders who were said to support the military and political adversaries of the regime in power.

The fact of having worked as professor at [a] college made the situation worse, because they found in my identity documents a piece of paper with several notes in English. They concluded that my collaboration with an enemy who attacked from an English-speaking country was evident and could no longer be questioned. But what excited them even more was my imprisonment and my discharge from the army during the war [of 1990].

Here in Bukavu, in December 1994, all my personal effects were stolen, probably for the purpose of going through them and the photographs as evidence for further reconnaissance of me.

Believe me, Madam, that this recital of my misfortunes is not the whole story but that my fear of going into the refugee camps is well founded and is based on the annoying experience of earlier harassment. You would do me a great service in saving me from having to go live in the camps.

Considering my 15 years of military service in the Rwandan army, a large number of soldiers of the old regime know me, either from the instruction centers or from the elite units. Even if most are apart from the other refugees, some are found in each refugee camp, however few these may be. There is even one of them among the 54 refugees here in the [Anglican] Bishop's quarters. Happily, he is a fervent Christian.

The former soldiers who may or may not have participated in the war, who were demobilized for various reasons and are today found in the camps, are continuing to collaborate with the militia who are found throughout the camps.

As a former professor in one of the important scholarly communities of Kigali, as former referee of volleyball games in Kigali as elsewhere in Rwanda, it is easily possible that a student, a player, or a spectator would recognize me, even if they speak well of me. This could have serious consequences for my security if I were forced to go into the refugee camps.

My security is even less assured in Zaire now than in 1990, given that the agents who imprisoned me on behalf of my persecutors sought several times to have me exiled in Zaire for whatever pretext. One of these agents was Adjutant R. of the Presidential Guard, who counseled me to come and seek the most powerful sorcerers. Another agent was the functionary of the Presidence of the Republic H.C. who told me he had seen my name on a list of persons to track down by persecution and imprisonment if possible. Zaire represented a favorable setting for them to track me down and entrap me.

The problem of my security and my future is far from being solved, even in Bukavu. But in waiting for the favorable moment to return home, I solicit your indulgence for urgent support in order to survive, since I do not have any further resources.

Secondly, support for the time being in the form of identification is in the works. Perhaps there may follow settling in a country where my security is less threatened.

Hoping for a favorable response from you, I ask, dear Madam, that you accept my most profound respect.

The next few letters were sent to North America with a bundle of other letters destined for Kigali. Bugingo asked us to read the letters to the president of the International Tribunal, the chaplain of the army, the head of the college where he had taught, and Margaret Court, a British missionary and old acquaintance. We were to read the letters and forward them if we thought they should be forwarded. Court was then to do the same. Her reply to us, to be forwarded to Bugingo, follows after the letters. The mailing also included Bugingo's letter to the president of the UNHCR. The convoluted trail taken by these letters is indicative of the complete absence of official mail between Rwanda and Zaire, between the Rwandan authorities and the refugees in Zaire.

Bugingo to Margaret Court: Bukavu, July 6, 1995

Greetings and welcome to Kigali. I received a letter from Felicity Angus sent to me from Uganda, and she told me of your return to Kigali. Day before yesterday, Tuesday morning, I accidentally met an old colleague professor of [my] college in Kigali who had passed there last April. As a Zairian, he had no security problems. He told me about the struggle of the remaining professors whom he met at the college, which has already taken up its activities. He also gave me much news of the college which has been open for some months. This all made me experience a growing nostalgia. I thought of all the promises made to me to facilitate repatriation. At the UNHCR they gave me all the details needed for one wishing to return and assurances of security and of welcoming—yet it seems not to be enough. Your presence encourages me because I have only three or four acquaintances in Kigali, but I do not yet know what agreements there are between the UNHCR and local authorities concerning repatriation. I tell myself sometimes that one obliges people to pass through the transit camps or also other destinations without considering the declared choice of the concerned party.
I hope you will give me details relative to this and send them to me here.

The details of my news includes praise to the Savior because, recently, He accorded me special assistance of $60—from the UNHCR. It is a good sign that repatriation will not be delayed. I do not know if my letter of 1 April reached you. I gave it to Rev. Kalonji, the diocesan secretary from here who was going to England, where he will stay for about a month. It would be a pity if it would get lost, since it is the first [letter] to you. Thank you for your prayers that you have offered for us, and the good courage in the organization of the welcome for the repatriated believers whom you mentioned in your letter.

Greetings on my part to my sponsors Andre and Marie Anne to Reverend Rulinda. To the family of Pastor Gilles Williams to the Andrews of Inkuru Nzizi if they are at Kigali.

May God bless you.

Bugingo to Margaret Court, July 16, 1995

Again great greetings! It is one week ago that I received the letter from our sister Felicity Angus from Uganda. It was she who told me of your return to Kigali. I am sending you together with this letter another that I wrote immediately after having learned the news of your presence at Kigali. I had not yet sent it when a profound thought came to me that I would ask you to facilitate my repatriation in as much as you are in Kigali.

It is now quite awhile that I continue with the support of the UNHCR of Bukavu attempts to obtain my repatriation. They are ready to facilitate the movement of all persons who wish to return to Rwanda, but the gossip circulates everywhere that each and every person who returns to Rwanda goes either to prison or to transit camps where a selection is made of the victims to be executed by implicating them in the genocide; whereas those who are acknowledged to be innocent are sent to their country homes of origin. This may be true, it may be false, but my greatest preoccupation is that they add that someone who was at the barricades during this war crisis, he cannot escape the accusation of being implicated in the genocide. This seems monstrous to me, given that even some victims of the genocide succumbed after months to this dirty work, hoping to buy their freedom through obedience [to the authorities]. Personally, I refused [to participate] in Kigali despite the pressure, but at Butare after more than a month in which I experienced all the threats of execution, I ended by helping to save my skin. Happily my conscience is free of a single drop of bloodshed. The dirty work was nearly finished. We only stood guard.

When I related my concerns to [the UNHCR], they said that it was a matter for the Rwandan authorities. Then I told myself that I could write a letter to the Ministry of Repatriation and Reinstallation of Refugees demanding a guarantee of safe return without fear if indeed the stories are nothing but intimidation.

I hope that the transmission of these letters (because I have written one to the director of [my] college as well) will not be a burden for you. Thanks a lot for agreeing to the sacrifice above all of your time that this may cost you.

May the Savior be with you. See you soon, maybe.

P.S. I must not close without telling you that one day last week, there was an exchange of gunfire between the Rwandan and Zairian military (according to the inhabitants of Bukavu), which is a bad sign for the Rwandan refugees above all. The more time passes in finding a way to send this letter, the more ideas I have. There is also a letter for the president of the tribunal of the international court with its seat in Kigali.

N.B. Would you please agree to read all the letters that I have sent you to determine if they are worthwhile to be sent, since they are all the fruit of a reflection or a decision taken without consulting anyone else. As always, I hope to receive the best of your advice in your reply. If, concerning my repatriation, it is as easy as my optimism tells me, I would like to stay at the Guest House of Biyogo as my first destination. Would you reserve the minimum for a repatriated person. The copies are not very readable, but I can make others when I am in Kigali.

Bugingo to Ruolodo Alfled, Director of the College, Kigali: July 20, 1995

It is an unequaled pleasure to be able to write you this letter, and it is also a pleasure to learn that life in the college has resumed. I know this thanks to professor Maroti Valentin, whom I met here after his visit to Rwanda and to the college.

Forgive me if I begin by telling you who I am. You will recall a former professor of physical education who, after the war of April 1994 in Rwanda, found himself in asylum at Bukavu now for nearly a year. I have continued to dream of repatriation. The news which Mr. Maroti told me in passing provides me with a foundation for my decision. To be reintegrated to my place at the college would not only reinstate my meaning in life but also would keep me from having to go back to the countryside, where I do not know exactly what would await me.

I do not want to close this letter without deploring the terrible turn of events and noting that almost all the survivors still feel the shock in the depths of their being. I think with new emotion of the disappearance of one of your daughters. May the earth be soft for her and may her sacrifice be a source of benediction for her family as to the entire community of faithful.

I hope to hear from you soon and why not to see you soon if my dream persists and becomes reality. Please, if possible, convey my greetings to all the college's leadership, employees of various offices, professors and students, workers, watchmen, and everyone.

Bugingo to the President of the International Court of Rwanda: July 20, 1995

I, the undersigned, Bugingo O., Rwandan refugee in Bukavu, Republic of Zaire, have the honor to address myself to your highness in order to request you to please accord me protection that would include my repatriation. Following which, I solicit an audience to seek counsel and to lodge a complaint against the perpetrators of the harassment I experienced before and during the armed conflicts which my country has experienced.

In addition to my situation as refugee is the aspect of entrapment that becomes ever stronger and is thus the main reason my free repatriation is compromised. For further clarity, I invite you to read the annexed copy of a letter I prepared for the President of the United Nations High Commission for Refugees. It outlines the multiple menaces of execution I experienced and witnesses to the traumas that awaited me if I would persist in refusing to participate in rounds of duty at the barricades.

Hoping for a favorable outcome from you, I ask you to agree, Monsieur le President, to this expression of my most profound respect.

John M. (and Reinhild) Janzen to Bugingo: June 25, 1995

I hope that you receive this letter, one way or another. A thousand excuses for delays in my correspondence. I received your letters of March 3 and April 2. Thank you! The first of the letters arrived only in April. Joyce Martens [of the Bukavu MCC unit] brought it to us when she visited. She told us of the departure of the Mennonite unit from Bukavu. Later, she visited Pastor Daniel Féver in France. For us, the members of this unit from US, France, Ethiopia, and Zaire and the Rwandans with whom we worked and spoke, despite the shortness of the encounters, were of an extraordinary intensity. They created for us a formidable esprit de corps. . . .

I have much appreciated your letters. Above all, in the first letter I was struck by the way in which you recall the words of our first encounter. I must confess to you that in my spring seminar on "Healing the Wounds of War in Africa" I shared this letter with the students. One of my students noted that the African concept of "the power of words" was evident in your lines.

In the second letter you speak of the theft of your possessions and your lack of clothing. It seems that you were able to keep your sense of humor when you were obliged to distribute a package of women's clothing in order to find something for yourself. I trust you were able to find a solution to this problem. If you receive this letter, it means you are still at Bukavu. We rarely hear Bukavu mentioned in the news, but the greater part of the Rwandan refugees are still in Zaire apparently.

I am subscribed to an electronic network known as "Rwandanet." Every evening I read messages of Rwandans and others from France, Quebec, and elsewhere in the world. By this medium I receive some news from your corner of the earth. But the official press no longer interests itself in Central Africa, except when there is violence there. Yet I know that most of the people of interlacustrine Africa are intelligent, sympathetic, courageous humans.

Dear Bugingo, may I ask of you the favor of using your words and your letters in our writing on the war and the conflict in Rwanda and Burundi? In our exchanges from the first day after having explained your misfortunes over the years, you asked me the question, "Do I still have a life?" *["Est-ce-que j'ai encore une vie?"]* These words, precisely, phrased the difficult question of most Rwandans. We would like to use these words as the title of our writing which we hope may appear as a book. Does this meet with your approval?

The Rwandan drama continues on all fronts. For the most part the news is bad. But today I read a newspaper article—which I enclose—to the effect that the Kigali government is ready to negotiate with "the refugees" in Zaire if they distance themselves from those who committed the genocide. It was an article published in *Le Monde* in France last week. Let us hope that this news will open the way for a future peace.

We are taking the opportunity of sending this letter with the new MCC coordinators to Burundi and Rwanda. They are Lauren and Suzanne Yoder, who will replace Harold Otto. The Mennonite work will focus now on Burundi, where they are assisting the Quaker community in the midst of the national conflict there.

Let me close in English, because I know that you enjoy challenges of language, and I am considerably more at home in English than in French. Dear Bugingo, we wish for you and all the Rwandans in Zaire that you find your way back to your home soon, and that your situation will give you joy. Have you received any news from the Rwandan army chaplain whom you wrote? That this man is the same one who encouraged you the first time to join the army is a remarkable coincidence. Did he respond to you? What is the outcome? We are curious to learn.

Bugingo to the Janzens: Bukavu, July 22, 1995

. . . Thank you very much for the joy your letter offered me, for the photo you sent me that caught first my attention. At least I'll be able to tell about the whole family in remembrance of this photo. Thank you also for the sheet of newspaper with information about my country. Yes, it is very hopeful if politicians are really willing to make it become true.

Thank you again for having paid so much attention to my letters, and no mind if you share one of them with your students, it rather sounds great. Excuse me, dear John, I don't understand well the meaning of the remark your student made about my style, the power of words, "la puissance des mots." I wish it would be something one may be proud of. I am sorry not to know the sentences that made him say so. I am sorry not to be good at arts. In the beginning I dare said "puissance des mots" meant boldness.

There is no more problem about clothing, for the whole community did its best to supply my need.

You no longer hear news about Bukavu, as you say, but some gunshots have been exchanged between Rwandese soldiers and Zairians. Rwandese attempted to pour out former Rwandese soldiers from a Zairian military barracks in Bukavu. The gunfire began at about 10 o'clock and ended about 7 p.m.

Let me go on with French in order to be sure there will be less mistakes. The idea to use my words or my speech in your writing would be all the more welcome because it comes at the very moment when I had the idea to launch a trial a propos of all that I had lived before the International Tribunal of Kigali. I believe moreover that these writings would serve if their production would take place at the same time as the trial. But I fear that the publication of these writings would take place at the moment when I would find myself still in Zaire or elsewhere where I am still alongside my persecutors. But you have my "green light"; as for the title "Do I still have a life?" and for these writings, you are free to use my words. But for my security here in Zaire and that of my family, my persecutors have often made use of them. It is necessary to think twice about this before publication.

Forgive me, I nearly forgot to tell you that I had the good blessing recently that is to say the social service of UNHCR accorded me $60—in June and perhaps there will be more in the future, God willing.

As far as the chaplain who is responsible for the repatriation of the former soldiers, he did not reply, neither to my two letters nor to a message I sent via the Red Cross. This latter was returned to me with the notice that I did not have a precise enough address. I intend to send another message soon. But, to put it briefly, I have not had a reply.

I wish you a good vacation and I wait impatiently for your news. May God bless you

Bugingo to Janzens: Bukavu, August 2, 1995

Because I continue to reread your letter and study the photograph, I write again as if it is the first reply to your letter, in any case I do not know which of the two letters [I am sending] will reach you first, to justify my attitude. I have entrusted the first to an Australian missionary who leaves for vacation tomorrow, August 3; he will mail it when he arrives, whereas this one will be entrusted to an agent of the United Nations High Commission for Refugees who will mail it. . . .

To return to the big favor which I expect to ask of you, it is almost impossible to send my mail toward Kigali. Would you do me the favor of reading all the letters which I have put in the same envelope to see if you find anything compromising. Send them to the address which I again repeat here. [Margaret Court's address is given.] She will also read everything and transmit them [to their destination] if possible and if she judges it necessary. The mail is voluminous enough, I must end my chatter. I look forward to hearing from you soon.

May God bless you.

John M. (and Reinhild) Janzen to Bugingo: October 8, 1995

I have here before me your letter of August 2, received a week or 10 days ago with the other letters. I have sent them on to Margaret Court several days later. . . .

November 11: The letter was interrupted by a three week trip.

I will not comment much on your ideas of repatriation. The circumstances there are difficult for me to discern at this distance. But I appreciate your judgments, they seem correct. Let's leave things as they are for the time being.

News from Rwanda has died down here, which is basically good news, I think, because the media are more concerned to cover war than to cover peace. I think letters are a better way to touch the actual details of daily life and reality.

We have just received a letter of a family of 14 of mixed ethnic identity whom we assisted to cross the boundary from Rwanda to Zaire last December, and whom we met in Kigali one week later. The young man explained to us that all was well and that he had returned to his studies.

By the same token we received a sign of life from Mr. Otto, who is now in the United States after his time of service in Burundi and Rwanda. The efforts of MCC continue in Burundi with the Quaker Church. I do not know if you have any news of the Zairian Mennonites.

This is the news from here. I have many exams to read. I await your next letter.

Margaret Court to the Janzens: Kigali, November 11, 1995

Thank you for your letter of 25th September and the many enclosures from Bugingo. I have read all of these and after considerable thought and consulting one or two people, I do not think that delivering his letters would be a very helpful exercise. He only draws greater attention to himself; he would be better just to come. Perhaps you are in contact with him and can pass on this opinion to him.

John M. Janzen to Bugingo: November 27, 1995

I just received a letter from Ms. Court in Kigali; you will find it on the back of this one.

The first point to note: My letter arrived at its destination together with your several letters.

The second point: you read English well enough to understand what she is saying. She did not pass your letters on for the reasons she indicates. She says it would be best for you simply to return.

We hope that you remain in good health as long as you remain in Bukavu.

Here, life is more or less normal for the moment. . . . It was almost a year ago that we were in Bukavu.

Bugingo to the Janzens (in English): Bukavu, January 1, 1996

. . . Thank you for the two letters including Miss Court's message. I am sorry my reply comes too late; it is due to unsteadiness of my decision to go back to my homeland. I still have a hard time to make my mind up because we are surrounded by information according to which repatriation gives way to assassination, arrestation, sojourn in camps or to be backed in countryside in order to make farmers out of everybody. All of this is not encouraging and you know, there is no way to get true information since post service Kigali–Zaire does not function; only people in other countries can decide easily because they can send and receive letters from their friends or to their friends in Rwanda. I'm still hanging on hope to be repatriated soon but at a time not known exactly. I don't know any news about Zairian Mennonites; once, a long time ago, I've seen Clement from Kinshasa, but he left soon after unloading some containers full of clothes for refugees.

This past week a tragedy broke out in Goma city where a senior soldier has been killed by a grenade explosion. The local way of investigation made a lot of killed other people, including refugees in Goma town. I've got Christmas gift very interesting, a set of five books that begins by a story of a discovery of holy scriptures at Qumran. They are written in English, it's not only teaching me about the Bible origin but also new words and English expressions. I wish to read you soon and thank again for the news. Please tell me something about the printing of the document "Do I still have a life?" if it's ready. I'd like to have a copy. I hope it is better to send it to Kigali until I am back there.

P.S. Would you excuse me for asking you another favor, to send the enclosed letter to the chaplain in Kigali because I have not received any response from him. Even the message via the Red Cross was returned to me citing insufficient address as the reason. Thanks yet again.

John Janzen to Chaplain Nsabimana: January 20, 1996

On behalf of my friend Bugingo, I send you this letter that he sent to me. [The letter is reprinted in the next section.] I became acquainted with Bugingo in Bukavu last year in my work among the Rwandan refugees. It seems that Bugingo has tried several times, without result, to write you. I hope that this letter reaches you without delay. I am ready to transmit a reply to Bugingo if necessary. Please accept my warm regards, Rev. Chaplain.

Bugingo to Chaplain Nsabimana: Bukavu via Nairobi, January 2, 1996

It is for me a great honor to write to you yet again. I was discouraged due to lack of a reply on your part, but I have learned that mail passes much more easily via a third country. I will limit my words to New Year's greetings for 1996 and a brief message. Would you write and give me all the details regarding repatriation and any news of my son. I do not know if he is at Musasa, but I believe that you know him, perhaps. Would you give me also other news about my family, as well as about yours. If I would not be horrified by all the stories which are being told concerning voluntary repatriation, I would already have returned. It is for the journey with a group of persons who are strange to me, which gives me fear, above all when I recall the arbitrary execution threats which I experienced at Butare. I believe I would have the courage if I could have the possibility of traveling by car from Bukavu to Kigali. Please inform me.

Please do everything possible to write me if possible. Do not hesitate to spend the money needed to send your letter to the address on the back.

John Janzen to Bugingo: January 20, 1996

How great to receive a complete letter from you in English (of January 1), and today your letter dated January 2 with the letter to chaplain Nsabimana Jean-Baptiste. I have sent his letter on to Kigali with a cover note. Let us hope and pray that he will receive your letter and offer help for your repatriation. . . .

Thank you for the New Year's wishes. We certainly extend to you our best wishes for this year and hope it will be the year in which you safely return home to Kigali. We wish for you a reunion with your family members, and a return to work. We also pray for peace in your country, Rwanda.

You ask about the Mennonites of Zaire, who almost all live in the west, in Bandundu, Kasai and South Kasai, and Kinshasa. Pastor Mukambu [Ya'-namwisi], whom you met in the [Protestant guest-house] in Bukavu, lives in Kinshasa and can be reached at the following address [the address is given].

The Mennonite Central Committee representatives in Zaire [Terry Sawatsky and Cathy Hodder], who also live in Kinshasa, can be reached at this address [the address is given]. However, the MCC work in the Rwanda-Burundi region is now concentrated in Bujumbura and Gitega, where the replacements of Harold Otto [Lauren and Suzanne Yoder] are living and working to help the Quakers with peacemaking there. [The Yoders' address is given.]

I hope that you can make contact with some of these good people.

I am glad that you received five books for Christmas, especially the report about the "Dead Sea Scrolls" from Qumran. I too have read about those discoveries, and the way they have changed biblical scholarship.

I can tell you that our writing project *Do I Still Have a Life?* is almost ready. We have been told by the highly-esteemed historian of Rwanda, David Newbury, that we must protect our sources and characters by making them anonymous, or at least giving them pseudonyms. This means more work for us. Do you have a pseudonym for yourself? You will certainly receive a copy of our writing, but I do not think I can send it through the mail to Bukavu at this time.

In looking at your letter one more time, I must say that your English is really very good. There are some mistakes, but I can understand the sense of each sentence. I will close here and repeat our wish for you in this New Year. We pray for your safe keeping as you look for a way home.

Bugingo to the Janzens (in English): via Kenya, April 17, 1996

Receive my greetings and my best wishes. I hope the Easter Day brought you all blessings. Myself I had wonderful time with the community of missionaries here in Bukavu, we attended a dawn Easter service at a Guest House of Grace Church and we share a memorable morning tea afterwards.

I are got to apologize for having not sent you this letter earlier. Therefore I confess my laziness and my emptiness of mind. I am so concerned with getting an idea that may shed a light to a possibility of my repatriation. By the way the meeting I are made not long ago with an UNHCR agent gave me more hope. Thank you again for your letter of January 20, 1996; it reached me on February 16th, 1996. . . .

Thank you for giving me the addresses of Mennonites peoples as well. I plan to write them soon, as I've got some stamps and aerogrames this afternoon. It is very good news that our writing project "Do I still have a life" is almost finished. This matter of protecting characters and sources seems to be inasmuch obvious as our Lord's answer to the question "Do I have Life" is certainly "You must have life." As for a pseudonym for myself, there is one that can fit, "Bugingo." It means LIFE, literally, but is more meaningful religiously. This past days, a gunshots exchange from both sides (Rwanda and Zaire) made people of Bukavu upset. One of Zairian military barracks Panzi was a chosen target of Rwandese bullets because there are some former Rwandese soldiers [there]. About three persons died and some others wounded. On last Monday, a Zairian plane flying from Kinshasa by a new pilot (according to local information) missed his landing to a Zairian aeroport Kavumbu Bukavu, and by mistake landed at Kamembe aeroport Rwanda. Then it was taken as hostage by Rwandese authorities who suspected it to have done so spitefully in order to fulfill another warlike mission.

Some of the camp's refugees in Zaire are now under Zairian soldiers' control; they have already surrounded them. Trouble are stirred up in Masisi, northwards Kivu region, some Kinyarwanda speaking citizens are sneaked away from Zaire and have got shelter in northwest Rwanda as forcibly repatriated. These very people and Rwandese authorities declare their citizenship to be Zairian, and that the fact of spreading Kinyarwanda is not enough to justify what they are suffering. Probably Zairian soldiers and former Rwandese militiamen are just using this way in order to loot their belongings. They say to be all born in Zaire, some of them a long time before 1959 event.

In hope to read you soon, I close mine here. God bless you.

Bugingo alludes here to the Kinyarwanda-speaking Zairians in Masisi, one of the communities of the so-called Banyamulenge, or Zairian Tutsi. By late 1996 the Banyamulenge along with their south Kivu fellow Kinyarwanda-speaking Zairians and with the help of Rwandan soldiers began their assault on the Zairian army posts and the Rwandan Hutu refugee camps. Bugingo perceived that he was faced with a choice between the frying pan of remaining in Bukavu or the fire of returning to Rwanda. He chose to return to Rwanda in July 1996, as is described in his next letter, written almost a year after the previous letter.

Bugingo to the Janzens: Kigali, April 15, 1997

I wish you a very happy new year 1997 even if this comes too late. I haven't sent you any letter for a very long time. I judged better to write one as soon as I got back home. Unfortunately trouble was on bait on my way back. I was arrested just before I made a second step on Rwandese ground. I was imprisoned, allegedly because I was a former soldier regardless of being dismissed since 1990. I was the only one among other prisoners.

I was released from jail on January 18 and sent back to my home place on 2 March 1997. So I spent eight months on my way. It is very bad news that my father died while I was in prison and I couldn't know it until I reached my home. Before I left Bukavu in July 1997, I got a letter from Mennonite representatives of Bujumbura. They told me some addresses for Mennonite representatives in Kigali; unfortunately, immigration Zairian officers obliged me to destroy those documents and I couldn't remember any on my arrival to Kigali. It would be very helpful if you could send me some together with the document whose title is *Do I Still Have a Life?* I hope you already know that the missionary Margaret [Court] left Kigali around August 1997. I expect to read you soon.

John M. Janzen to Bugingo: June 5, 1997

What a joy it was to receive a sign of life from you, in your letter from April 15th, and to read that you had reached home, despite some delays of eight months. We breathed a prayer of gratitude because we feared the worst. News from Bukavu after November was of war and flight. We knew that many of the Rwandan refugees with whom we worked had fled deeper into Zaire and are among those who ended near Kisangani. How fortunate for you that you decided to "bite the bullet," as we say, and return home, even though it meant a time in prison.

It is not too late, I think, to wish you a happy new year, and it is still later than your letter. This new year will be sad for you because of your father's death. We are sorry for that. We wish for you and your family some comfort in your time of bereavement.

[Your question regarding the document] "Do I still have a life?" can be answered with a definite "Yes, Bugingo does have a life!" I will send the manuscript when I know it is safe to send it. There are still very many original names in the document, and the safety of some of those people might be at risk if the wrong people read it. I will possibly send it [by means of] a private route. I would like to finish the work of pseudonyms. I need pseudonyms for many people . . . .

Bugingo to the Janzens: Kigali Rural, August 27, 1999

This opportunity to send you a message is welcome, it'll certainly tell you what happened with me since two years of silence. It was not long after I got your letter of June 5th, 1997, just on July 11th, [that] I was rearrested and imprisoned, instead of understanding in spite of a great and courteous display I made of my document of identification. I was driven in prison where I've spent two years and 9 days. . . .

. . . this last experience was the worst I have ever lived inasmuch as death was more active in our cell than anywhere else. The only similarity with other situation is that they never told me why I had to be detained, until we were all asked to confess our crime and to apologize. Some of us were responsible of some crime so, they conferred them and wrote apologetical letters. Then all of us, except three people only, were set free at a number of 232 people in all. Afterward we have had three weeks in a solidarity camp and were set free on August 13th 1999. There in solidarity camp we were told that all of this problems are mistakes due to confusion that gets its power from evil deeds that go along with war evil activities.

To say the truth about pseudonyms, I have prepared a lot of, but after being arrested, I had everything away out of my memory. If you still need them, hold on untill I get a letter from you.

I am sending you this letter on my way to my elder brother home . . . many people are stunned to see I am still alive and I have hard time to tell them all I have lived. The most valuable of this is that people's faith grows stronger and stronger.

All my best wishes and my kind regards to your children's families.

Bugingo to Janzens: Kigali Rural, October 15, 1999

All my greetings . . . to you and to your whole family! I do not know if any previous letter sent about one month ago has reached you, if it did you already know what happened with me within this two just years of silence. I was preparing pseudonyms for the different characters in "Do I still have a life" work when came a new arrest. I spent two years under custody and was set free on August 13, 1999 without any charge against me.

Please be helpfull in this situation and protect me from this evil abusive plans. The only wrong I have done is to decline the offer (a job) they proposed me after my first releasement, since it consisted of being involved in criminal and political activities—you know, accusing falsely someone and have him condemned injustly . . .

Put me in touch with any honest international lawyer you happen to know in Kigali . . . I'd like to have his assistance and advices about my protection, and why not a foreign citizenship in order to complain safely against the authors of my hardship . . .

Through Bugingo's continuing saga it is possible to discern the deep divide that exists in post-genocide Rwandan society. The bitter ironies of his case show how right he was to be fearful and anxious about his future. In retrospect, it is clear that his options were somewhere between the frying pan and the fire. His story demonstrates how difficult it is for a Rwandan individual of his experience, his knowledge, his acquaintances, to simply become an ordinary citizen. It also reveals the extent of fear of the Rwandan government and the lengths to which officials in the New Rwanda were willing to go to collect intelligence and maintain control, and to use individuals toward that end.

1.2 To Return Home or Not to Return Home

We live in a state of chronic fear:—Philippe, a refugee after his return to Rwanda, June 12, 1996

On the minds of many of the refugees with whom we spoke in the camps surrounding Bukavu was the burning question of when, under what circumstances, or even if, they should return home to Rwanda. Bugingo's story (see section 1.1) reveals one man's desires, fears, and hopes. For those who knew they had not been involved in the massacres the question was, Could they safely return? Then there were the Zairian soldiers who patrolled the roads between the camps and the final crossing points to Rwanda, and they were known to rob Rwandans of everything valuable to permit this crossing. No one offered protective escort service, it seemed. Even if one could reach the border safely, rumors inside the camps suggested that most Hutu would be imprisoned, even killed, if they returned. The sources of these rumors were often hearsay or single-anecdote accounts from passers-by. They were also encouraged and fanned by authorities of the old Rwandan government and militants in the camps to keep the masses of refugees where they were. Radio Rwanda invitations designed to assure the refugees of their safety were seen as a trap. So the Hutu ideology—or at least anti-RPA (Rwandan Patriotic Army) ideology—created a kind of cosmology that reinforced itself through supporting anecdotal information.

Among the refugees with whom we became best acquainted in the small camps of Mushweshwe, Muku, Bideka, and Izirangabo and in Bukavu, we were aware of those who had returned home, those who were eager to do so and awaited the right moment, and those who sought our assistance in returning. In this section we relate briefly the stories of several families from Kayenzi commune and Kigali. We focus our attention on the families from Kayenzi because we visited this commune in Rwanda in connection with seed grain distribution and would be returning there after our time in Zaire. Many of those who had fled Kayenzi were in Muku camp. In this group were the families of Mujyambere Mathias, the pre-1992 bourgmestre, and of Makarakiza André, a high school physics teacher. Another family of teachers, Mbaduko Gabriel and Sekimonyo Francoise, who had fled to Muku earlier with the others, had returned home. Their accounts will be given later (section 2.1).

Figure 6. Mujyambere Mathias, front row center, and Makarazika Andre, back left, in Muku refugee camp, December 1994, with their families.

Figure 7. Letters and clothing bundle taken to Kayenzi from Muku by the Janzens in late December 1994.

Muku Camp, South Kivu, Zaire

Makarakiza André and his wife intended to return to Kayenzi, as did Mujyambere Mathias and his family (Figure 6), both of whom were good friends of Sekimonyo Francoise and Mbaduku Gabriel. In fact, Makarakiza, the physics teacher in Kayenzi secondary school, had been back to Kayenzi with his 13-year-old son to get reestablished. He left his son behind with Sekimonyo and her family and returned to Zaire to get his family. However, while in Zaire, he and the others who intended to return got cold feet because of rumors and reports. What were these?

One of the Kayenzi refugees, in whose plastic tent I (John) received hospitality and a meal of beans and rice, expressed the most common sentiment in a letter to us in late January 1995:

> Every day one's file [dossier] is added to, grows. Vengeance, settling old scores, jealousy, the absence of judicial institutions, the seizure of property, etc. . . . It suffices that you are accused of collaboration and it is finished. "You did not stop the murderers," or "You have collaborated with the genocide." . . . Only God knows the guilty ones, and in any case they are not numerous, and they are certainly known.

Knowing that we were going to return to Kayenzi, these families and others in Muku prepared letters for their families and friends there. Makarakiza also sent a shirt to his son in Kayenzi (Figure 7).

An Ethnically Mixed Family

We became aware of an ethnically mixed family from Kigali when one of their numbers, a young man named Philippe, spokesman for his family of 13, including adults and children, came to the Bukavu guesthouse one afternoon in December 1994. His drawn face betrayed the tension he was experiencing. He wished to speak with *"la direction"* of the Mennonite team because he and his family did not feel safe in the camp where they were living. Out of earshot of the Zairian members of the team and Rwandan workers in the house, he confided to one of the American workers that his family was multiethnic—some were Hutu, others Tutsi—and that they had been threatened in the camp. Thus they had left the camp and come to Bukavu where they felt they were safer. But their accommodations were not good, and they desired help in either relocating or perhaps even returning home. They feared being robbed by the Zairian border guards and were not sure of the legal paperwork required to cross the border.

Philippe was Hutu, as were his father and his four siblings; his mother was Tutsi, as were her two brothers, who were with them. His mother's brother together with his wife and their two children and his sister's two children constituted the entire group. In the climate of even the small well-kept camps of Mushweshwe, Muku, Bideka, and Izirangabo they felt unsafe. When asked by a member of our team, they said that there had not been physical attacks but that they feared their identity, which they had kept secret, had been revealed or discerned. In any case, a verbal threat or remark had been construed by Philippe to mean that they had been discovered. One other family of mixed identity was known to the Zairian staff at one of the camps, information that was not shared with the Rwandan committee members.

The next day, Joyce Martens, unit leader of the Bukavu team, went with Philippe to the UNHCR command post down the road in Bukavu. The staff member suggested that it would be advisable to go to the Zairian governor's office to receive a pass so as to move without turmoil through the Zairian checkpoint at the Ruzizi River into Rwanda. In the general vicinity of Bukavu there were two border points where one could cross. Philippe and his family could either go down the road from the UNHCR, where a UNHCR bus would take them to Cyangugu, from where they would be repatriated to their home in Kigali, or they could take a taxi to the border directly across from Cyangugu and walk across. From there, a UNHCR bus would take them home. Martens and a Zairian staff member went to the governor's office with Philippe to request the letter. After several days and another visit, the papers attesting to the family relationship and assuring them safe passage were acquired.

The Mennonite team discussed this case of prospective repatriation at some length because it was the first of its kind during our time in Bukavu. It raised the kind of policy questions that relief agencies must often resolve quickly and with little preparation. The UNHCR initially encouraged repatriation in the early months after a relative peace had settled over Rwanda. Then, in the face of reported arrests of returnees, the UNHCR withdrew its endorsement of such a policy. Instead, they offered instructions to those who expressed an interest in returning to Rwanda but took no responsibility for protecting them or ensuring their security. Philippe and his family were subject to possible arrest the moment they crossed the bridge into Rwanda. We decided we would offer our help because Philippe obviously wanted to return home. We would monitor this case closely and, pending the outcome, leave any larger policy issues until later.

Thus, on December 22, 1994, the eve before we were scheduled to fly to Kigali, we again met with Philippe to arrange a place in Kigali where we could confirm his family's safe return. We departed on December 23 from Bukavu airport, with the usual hassles and payoffs to the Zairian military and customs officials who rummaged around in our luggage for a long while, hoping to extract another payment. The thought entered our minds that passing this border was a daunting enough prospect to discourage all but the most strong-hearted refugees. If each case required as much help as we were devoting to Philippe's family, then it seemed that few of the 2.5 million refugees would ever return.

In Kigali we daily checked the contact point to inquire whether Philippe's family had arrived. A week passed and there was still no word. Then, on December 30, one day before we were scheduled to continue southward to Butare and Bujumbura, after a long day of interviews, we went to the Kigali central market one last time to find a few mementos. What followed at the market of Kigali seemed providential serendipity. Suddenly, before us in the throngs of thousands, like apparitions, stood Philippe and his mother. They were as awestruck as we. Faces beaming, we shook hands and embraced. They wished to withdraw to a less public spot for a photograph together. We then returned to our hotel with Philippe to hear his story and to celebrate his family's return.

Philippe told of his family's crossing and return home. He had gone one more time to the UNHCR with Joyce Martens to confirm arrangements for their repatriation. Then, on December 24, the family took a taxi to the Cyangugu border crossing accompanied by French pastor Daniel Féver and several Zairians of the Mennonite team. There was no problem with the Zairian border guards. The family spent a night at Cyangugu in a UNHCR transit shelter. On the following day they traveled by UNHCR bus to Butare, where they spent three days. Finally, on December 29 they traveled on another UNHCR bus to Kigali, arriving the night before our meeting. Philippe was relaxed and happy. Their house was occupied by someone else, but they thought that they could arrange themselves with the occupants. In the meantime, they were staying with friends. We toasted their safe return and wished one another a happy new year.

A year and a half later we received a letter from Philippe that reflected the continuing tensions within Rwanda.

Philippe to the Janzens: Kigali, June 17, 1996

It is with a great nostalgia that I write this letter, embracing you affectionately and asking your forgiveness that I delayed my sincere thanks for your most recent letter.

Dear father, you would be unable to grasp the joy my mother and I experienced when we received your letter with the beautiful photographs [of you and us at the market in Kigali]; it is a reassuring sign that you really thought of us.

All the same, this joy did not last very long, for, several days later my father was arrested for reasons thus far unknown. We ran all over the place to begin inquiries on the causes of his arrest. These inquiries did lead to something in his favor. We received assurances of the Inquiry Commission that they would release him because they had not a single witness against him. We have waited and waited but without results. When I recall that my elder brother was killed by the militia of the former government and that we fled the country because they wanted to kill my Tutsi mother, and now my Hutu father is arrested arbitrarily, I am overcome by disgust with life *[je me sens dégouté par la vie]*. Not a single member of my family was mixed up in politics, not previously nor now, but we are victims here and there of political tensions whose reason I fail to understand.

We live in a state of chronic fear of eventual attacks from abroad without forgetting the consequences that could bring. Truly, dear Father, you must pray to God to extend his hand over the innocent souls here on earth. I count fully on your prayers, hoping that the Lord will give me the strength to endure the heavy burden of family responsibilities and my studies at the same time (*Psalms* 146:5–8).

I cannot close without greetings from those who are together here with us. . . .

May his blessings and peace be yours, sent to you from God our Father and Jesus Christ our Lord.

To return home or not to return home was indeed the question. Fear of arbitrary arrest or arbitrary accusation and arrest and Philippe's fear of being discovered and disgust at life after his father's arrest in Kigali, sketched the refugees'—and many other people's—limited options. The presumption of suspicions felt by and accusations hurled at innocent people merely because of who they were or where they had been was as forceful as accusations of actual wrong-doing.

1.3 *Les Sites:* Mushweshwe, Muku, Bideka, Izirangabo

They were called "sites," not refugee "camps," because the latter term could make one think of concentration camps. This was the wisdom in the thinking of the local worker teams with the Zairian Church (ECZ), which was providing the linkage between refugees and local Zairian congregations and communities, CARE, which was supplying some of the medical provisions and food (Figure 8), and the MCC, which was supporting much of the local camp coordination and supplemental food as well as other social service and humanitarian programs (Figure 9).

Each of the four Rwandan refugee communities near Bukavu that were assisted by the MCC carried the name of the local host community of ECZ-affiliated Baptists who had initially taken in the refugees, indeed, had invited them to resettle from the city of Bukavu, where they had camped in the open after fleeing across the Rwandan border at the Ruzizi River. The red earth road to these camps led up the escarpment south of Bukavu into the hills and mountains, through Ngweshe country. This area is one of a number of Bushi kingdoms, each with its own king *(Mwami)*, related in general to the Great Lakes region kingdoms. Ngweshe is the largest and currently most politically prominent of the Shi kingdoms, although it is not of the order of these kingdoms because it broke off from Kabare (David Newbury, personal communication, September 1995).

The hillsides in Ngweshe were dotted with freestanding fenced-in homesteads composed of three or four thatch- or tin-roof mud-brick houses for people and cattle surrounded by steep plots of gardens and fields. But the verdant hills and fields were not terraced as in Rwanda, and some showed signs of erosion. There were also expansive tea plantations, mission stations, and market centers such as Mugogo, where every type of imaginable good was traded, from medicines to livestock to clothes to gold. We watched how 46 grams of gold dust was weighed on a small hand-held counter balance and changed hands for the equivalent of about $800.

In the vast valleys we saw cultivated marshes and, on the rises and ridges of higher land, many refugee camps, big and small. At least two of these were just for unaccompanied children who were so troubled and sometimes violent that they were too much of a disturbance in a regular camp. From a great distance these camps all looked like tidy white resorts sprinkled by well-intentioned plan-

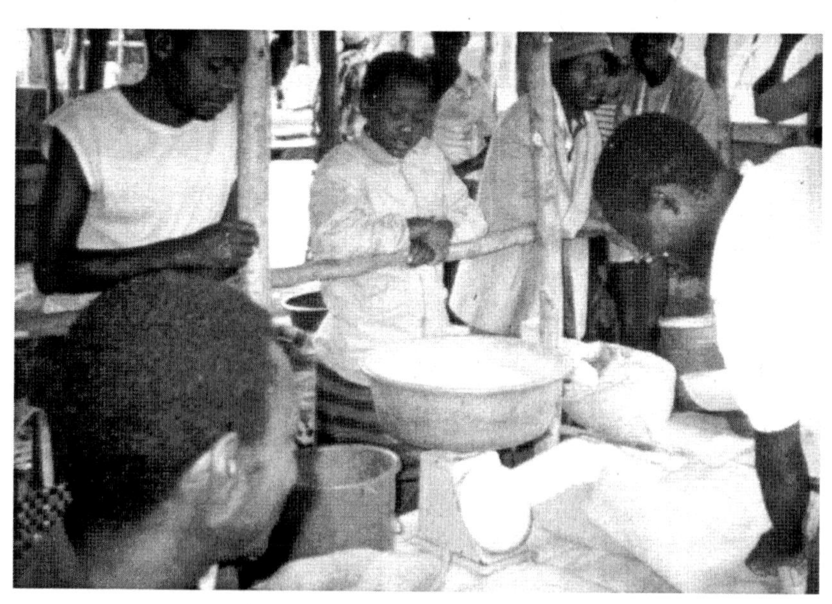

Figure 8. Emergency relief rations of flour and beans being distributed to Rwandan refugees, Muku Camp. The rations were provided by CARE, local volunteers, and the MCC. This scene was repeated throughout all the camps overseen by the UNHCR.

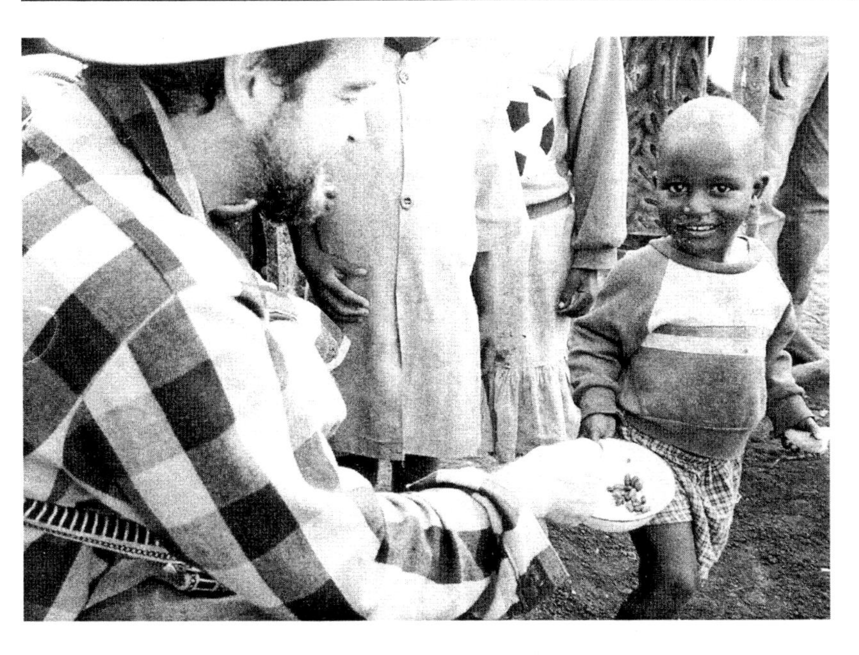

Figure 9. Rwandan child offers his bean dish to Harold Otto, MCC coordinator for Great Lakes relief work. This photograph was used in publicity and wrongly interpreted to show Mennonites distributing food to needy people. In fact, we took it because the boy showed great generosity in offering his few remaining red beans to Otto.

ners among the lush green of this beautiful and fertile piece of earth.

Other camps, spread over the slopes of the hillsides on the west bank of Lake Kivu or elsewhere near Bukavu or in the open countryside southwest of Bukavu along the main paved road, were usually much larger. Downstream from Bukavu, near the Ruzizi River, was a military camp for the exiled FAR. At Cimanga or Nyakanenge, between Mushweshwe and Bideka, beyond some large tea plantations, was another large FAR military camp of 14,000 soldiers and their families. These tent cities caught the eye, with their shining white plastic tent sheeting in straight lines on the hazy distant hillsides. The magnitude of what they signified was elusive and daunting; it was easier to imagine them as intentional installations of some peaceful and progressive human community than a national army in retreat, still organized and intent on fighting its way back to control of Rwandan soil.

The United Nations and nearly 200 NGOs in Rwanda and the refugee camps of Zaire, Burundi, and Tanzania provided a hastily erected infrastructure that gave tent cities the illusory appearance of permanence (Figure 10). Beneath this impression was the financial outlay of expenses for all relief and peacekeeping operations that was approaching $1 billion at the close of 1994.

The four MCC-CARE-ECZ supported camps were small by comparison, harboring 1,000–2,500 refugees each. They were said by some of the inhabitants to be more humane than the large camps, to have a more distinctive community ambiance. Each was nested within a local Zairian Baptist congregation-community. The pastors, deacons, and lay members and representatives of the Rwandan refugees formed local committees to run the camps. The ECZ had its own coordinating committee separate from the local Baptists; the Rwandans had their own coordinator of the four camps, Habimana Emmanuel, formerly of the Rwandan Ministry of Social Services. Although we were well aware that a hidden dimension of organization in these camps was likely carried over from Rwandan social and political structure, this was not as overt in these four camps as in the larger camps where militia and other elements of Rwandan government openly controlled food distribution and other services. The culture of refugee camps, the Rwandan refugee camps, and of these four camps in particular were reviewed in mid-1995 by a team of evaluators representing about 30 of the NGOs (Pottier 1996; de Lame 1996). The four camps with which we were affiliated seemed in any case to be well thought of by refugees, because in December of 1994 there were still daily arrivals of refugees who had heard that food distribution and safety were good here (Figure 11).

As these four sites were being constituted in August and September of 1994, each developed a distinct profile as a community. Izirangabo was composed of about 80% Rwandan Baptists from the Butare region. Bideka was largely Anglican, with inhabitants from all over Rwanda. Muku con-

Figure 10. Chabarabe, a large tent city of Rwandan refugees outside Bukavu, December 1994. The camp was uprooted in late 1996, and its Rwandan inhabitants took flight westward, deeper into Zaire.

Figure 11. Rwandan refugee camp in Mushweshwe, southwest of Bukavu. Photo by Joyce Martens.

with inhabitants from all over Rwanda. Muku contained the Rwandan Presbyterian hierarchy and a number of government administrators from Gikongoro prefecture.

Relations between the local Zairian host communities and the Rwandan refugees also varied from camp to camp. Some relations became tense over the loss of trees cut for firewood, over access and use of scarce water resources, over the use and abuse of existing buildings (especially the Zairian school buildings), and over jealous feelings regarding the attention and relief goods received by the refugees from the international NGOs operating in the area. There were also some hard feelings at the dispensary in the Izirangabo camp, where Zairians paid for their medicines and treatments while the refugee patients received them free of charge. In Izirangabo the refugee children took over the local school; the local people withdrew their children because of insecurity from the nearby military camp. In Bideka the local school offered to accept refugee children for the price of $5 each, plus other fees, which many say they could not pay. So in Bideka the refugees started an open-air primary school for their children. At Mushweshwe the local community shared their classrooms easily with the refugee community by using them in alternating shifts.

Drawings by children from the Mushweshwe refugee camp illustrate camp life. We explore this subject more fully in chapter 3 but give a brief overview here. Bigirimana Jean Pierre, age 14, drew UNHCR tents made of plastic sheeting inside of which people are sleeping on the ground (Figure 12). In the drawing we see people getting water from an outdoor faucet in the ubiquitous large plastic gasoline canisters or tending a cooking fire in the open.

The essential element for survival, water, is also captured in other drawings with motifs of water faucets and the carrying of water in large containers. Two daily chores, the fetching of firewood and the hauling of water, occupied a great deal of everyone's time in the camps and was often illustrated by the children.

Another recurring motif is the UNHCR logo on

Figure 12. Getting water and cooking food. "The refugees simply sleep on the ground, like this." Note name given to plastic tents by refugees, *burende*, "armor". Drawing by Bigirimana Jean Pierre, age 14, Mushweshwe camp, Zaire; pencil and color markers on paper, December 1994.

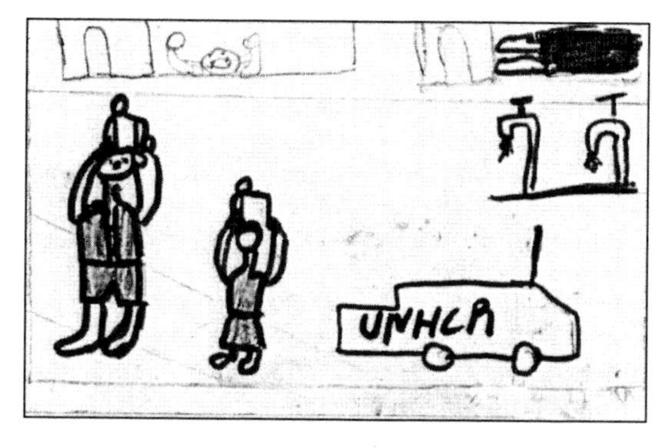

Figure 13. Details from Rwandan children's drawings of their experience in Mushweshwe refugee camp: (top) drawing by Niwenshuti Jean Claude, age 15; (middle) drawing by Nomnyijamana Sylvie, age 14; (bottom) drawing by Mukeshimana Pelopie, age 13. The UNHCR insignia was pervasive in the camps and shows up prominently in the children's drawings; "shetting" was one of many variations of the spelling for sheeting that we encountered.

tic sheeting of the refugees' crowded shelters. Sometimes in front of the UNHCR tents we see a person sitting at a table or standing, using wireless radios, probably CARITAS or CARE personnel. Other times a child drew the flag of aid organizations near the tent city. That some families were able to flee in their cars is also documented in the drawings. One child shows a Rwandan public transportation bus filled with refugees on the road to the camp in Zaire. It was the stripped skeleton of just such a bus that we passed on our serpentine road everyday to and from the camps. But it is the many crowded tents of UNHCR plastic sheeting in the refugee camp of Mushweshwe and many others like it in the Bukavu region that remain a prominent motif in the drawings.

Many of the children in the camps played with toys they had improvised themselves (Figure 14). Habimana Joel (figure 15), a teacher at the Mushweshwe camp school, helped us collect some of these toys. There were balls made of tied-up plastic bags or banana leaves, hand-carved tops made to spin artfully with whips made of sticks and vines, ingenious cars and trucks made of bits of scrap wire and tin and rubber, or vehicles constructed of matchboxes with the tin caps of beer bottles serving as wheels (Figure 16). String games were improvised from bottle caps and bits of plastic fiber from relief food bags. Whistles made of bark and leaves were popular (see Figure 14). We watched one little girl practice her knitting skills with a pair of rough sticks and scraps of yarn gleaned from the women's knitting projects.

The daily work of surviving was difficult in the camps. When the sun shone, it got very hot very

Figure 14. Refugee child with whistle made of bark and leaves, Mushweshwe camp, Zaire, December 1994.

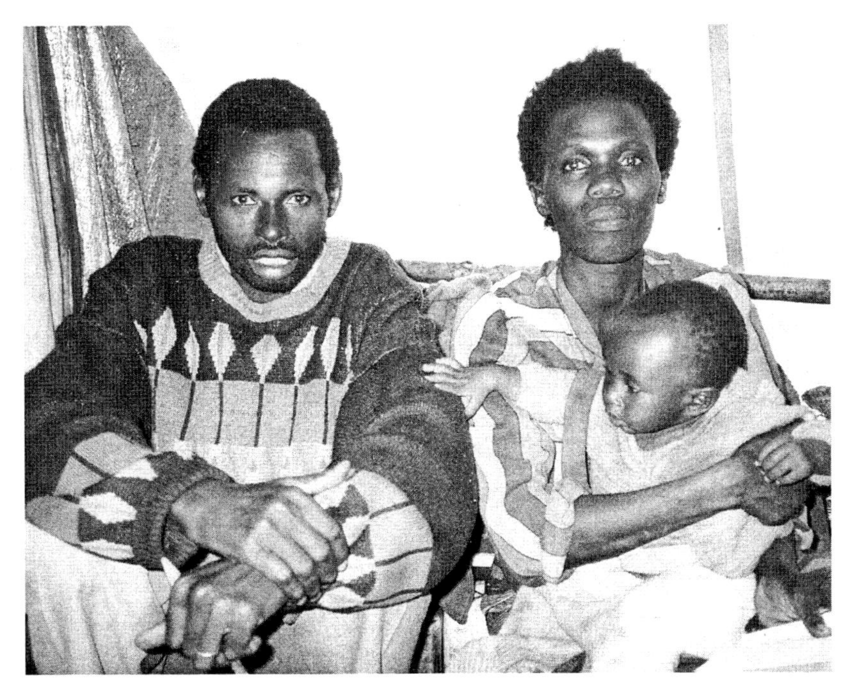

Figure 15. Habimana Joel and his wife and one child from Kayenzi commune, Rwanda, in their tent where they live with their five children, Mushweshwe camp, Zaire, December 1994. Habimana, as a teacher in Kayenzi, was in charge of the school at this camp and assisted us in obtaining children's drawings as well as a small collection of toys the children had made.

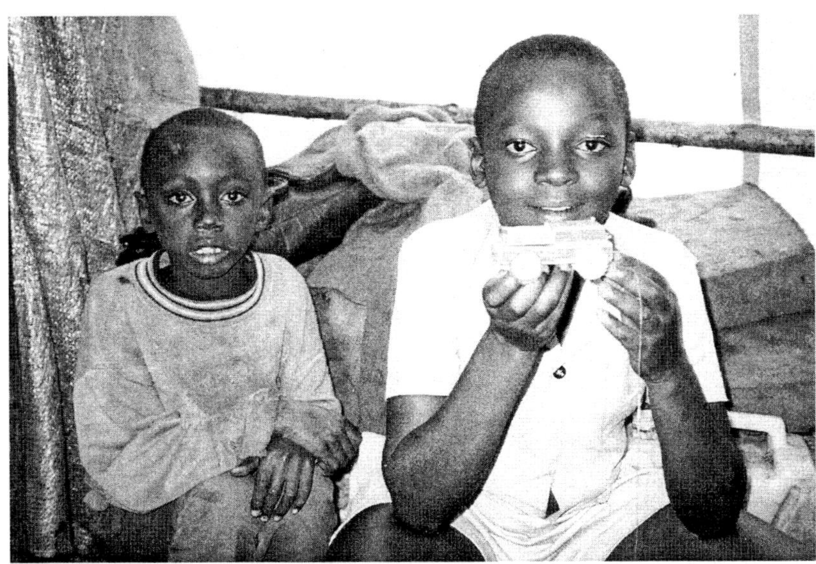

Figure 16. Two children with a toy truck made from a matchbox and bottle caps. Mushweshwe camp, December 1994.

quickly under the plastic covering, as in a greenhouse, and there was much condensation. Conversely, during cold and rainy weather, it was chilly and damp in the tents. Each tent had to accommodate as many as six adults and children. Constant chores were the fetching and carrying of water for cooking and washing from a communal faucet or spring and the procurement of firewood and kindling for cooking. Some families constructed makeshift shelters of laced-together laths, waddle and daub, or plastic around their improvised cooking hearth, which was dug into the earth next to the entry of their tents, to protect the fire and the pots of rice and beans from the rains (Figure 17).

The fronts and backs of many plastic-covered shelters had been constructed of just such waddle and daub walls, to create dividers that were at least the height of a person. Some families became quite ingenious at creating a bit more dignity by adding a tiny veranda-type seating space in front of their tent where they could receive visitors and watch the goings-on in the camp. Washing or shower shelters that remained open to the sky were improvised by tying together leafy branches behind many of the tents. At a distance there were rows of latrines, also covered with plastic sheeting. The boards surrounding the latrine trenches were slippery and flies swarmed around them. Some stalls had been privatized with hand-built half-doors and locks. At Izirangabo a special type of circular brick latrine was built, modeled after the supposedly odorless model developed by MCC worker David Klassen. It was fitted with round roof slabs of poured concrete. The odorless part of this latrine model, however, had not been achieved. They stood like a row of sentinels on the edge of the camp.

Many women engaged in activities that helped to keep up their morale and provided sorely needed income. At the Bideka camp a group of women created a simple earth oven with scrap metal sheets; they baked tasty white bread for sale (Figure 18). We visited the "studio" of a seamstress who was working at her foot-treadle machine while her co-worker cut the pattern pieces on a rough table (Figure 19). Other women at the Mushweshwe and Bideka camps wove grass mats to cover the bare dirt ground in the tents and to serve as mattresses. Women's groups were organized for the purpose of Bible study or classes in sewing, knitting, crocheting, and embroidery. We received requests for more Bibles and for more yarn, thread, and material. At the Izirangabo camp we observed a group of women engaged in English language study, squatting in a little circle between tents. Many women continued to value grooming themselves, especially with complex hair plaiting that took much time to complete.

One of the women in Izirangabo, fourth grade teacher and mother Rachel Nyirahabiyambere from the Nyakizu commune in the prefecture of Butare, told us about her flight and how it happened that she and her Baptist-pastor husband, their six children, three adopted children, and a nephew came to this particular camp. They had left their home in mid-August 1994 because they heard gunshots. It was 11 a.m. The children were at home because it was vacation time. They walked for four days. "We didn't wash, we ate raw potatoes, we slept in the forest." Once they reached Bukavu, they slept along the road there, as did thousands of other refugees, for an entire week. "We helped each other with food, whoever had something shared it." In Bukavu Nyirahabiyambere's husband and other refugee Baptist pastors made contacts with local Baptists and Mennonites, and that is how they came to the Izirangabo camp.

An elderly woman whom we visited in her tent, which she shared with six others in Izirangabo, told us of her flight from Nyamagabe in Gikongoro prefecture. She heard many gunshots, people began to get killed in her commune, and refugees passed by her hill. Two of her older sons decided to leave, and she went with them. They fled on foot, taking along some clothes, sorghum, a mattress, two goats, and two cows but no pots or pans. When the animals got too tired, they sold them. They got 15,000 Rwandan francs for the 2 cows and 4,000 Rwandan francs for the goats. The woman wanted

Figure 17. A refugee family's "kitchen" protected from rain by plastic sheeting stretched over bent twig frame, Izirangabo camp, December 1994.

Figure 18. Rwandan refugee women bake bread for sale in a makeshift oven, Bideka camp, December 1994.

to go back to Rwanda, where she left her fields. Even though she felt grateful for the food distributed by CARE in the camp, she wanted to tend her own fields rather than receive aid. One of her sons, who was the ECZ-MCC chauffeur and who translated her Kinyarwanda for us, added that she had never learned to read or write.

Idleness, listlessness, hopelessness, and depression affected the refugees in the camps. Professional men—doctors, teachers, lab technicians—seemed to have the most trouble accepting their new situation and finding a meaningful way to cope. One physician burst into tears of frustration while relating his story to us. We saw many men merely lounging about or playing the traditional 32-hole board game *Ikibuguzo* (Figure 20) when they were not splitting logs for kindling or involved in the camps' organizational work. In Kashusha, one of the huge camps near Lake Kivu that housed 48,000 refugees, the paths between tents were literally paved with beer bottle caps.

The MCC team that worked in this setting for three months and that we joined for two weeks in December 1994, consisted of Cathy Mputu, a social worker from Kinshasa; two Zairian pastors, Mukambu Ya'Namwisi and Ndjoko Jean, also from

Figure 19. Seamstress at work with sewing machine she brought on flight, Izirangabo camp, December 1994.

Figure 20. Rwandan refugee men playing board game, Bideka camp, December 1994.

Kinshasa; the merchant Clement from Kinshasa, who acted as an accountant for the MCC work and as a critical liaison to the church, mercantile, and governmental hierarchies in Bukavu; the French Mennonite pastor Daniel Féver; and Joyce Martens, an American nurse and local unit coordinator. This team was housed in the Centre d'Acceuil Protestant (CAP) in Bukavu, a base from where almost daily journeys to the camps were undertaken. We traveled in a four-wheel drive vehicle rented from the Rwandan Baptist church leadership that had fled to this region and recongregated mainly at the Izirangabo camp. This van was taken care of and driven most skillfully by a Rwandan refugee chauffeur. The guesthouse of the CAP is located among the once beautiful villas of the expatriate community of Bukavu and not far from one of President Mobutu's estates, with a view of Lake Kivu. But in 1994 this view included the white tent city of a distant refugee camp on the shore of the lake and unaccompanied Rwandan refugee children playing in the yard—constant reminders of why we were all there. The guesthouse saw a continuous stream of Rwandan refugees who needed assistance and who needed to tell their stories and of Zairians who were involved with assisting the refugees.

On most mornings the trip to the refugee camps on the treacherous dirt road leading out of town through the city began by squeezing our four-wheel drive van through the narrow passages between endless rows of market stalls and countless street vendors—many of them children—with their cardboard boxes holding anything from bubble gum to matches to tomato paste to shoe polish, past masses of people walking along with dealers and money changers who swiftly moved from one prospective customer to the next with fancy attaché cases and calculators. Frequently we would be stopped by Zairian soldiers who demanded to see the car's permit and proof that we were "missionaries." When they began their day's work, they put on a hostile and threatening demeanor, acting like bandits, until they had collected enough money for the day's needs or until it began to rain. It was said that they were not being paid. One day, halfway up the escarpment in a lonely area, a Zairian armed soldier appeared out of nowhere and held up our car. It was only because Pastor Ndjoko spoke with him in Lingala and assured him we were missionaries going to the sites that he waved us on without demanding payment.

The road leading out of Bukavu was always a scene of unimaginable red-brown muddy chaos. When the afternoon rains began, the road dissolved into quagmire and mudslides. But somehow the huge trucks, loaded to bursting with firewood or bricks or manioc as well as people, and the "buses" that carried four times as many people as any standard safety code would allow, managed to pass each other and get to their destinations.

The beautiful landscape, the breathtaking view of Bukavu along the glistening waters of Lake Kivu as we climbed or descended the steep mountainside by more than 500 meters, was in stark contrast to the miserable mud and clapboard huts covered with rusted tin cowering on naked red earth so precariously that the next torrent of rain threatened to wash them down the mountain. And yet life was throbbing along this road and a profit could be turned from the presence of the Rwandan refugees. For example, we saw people wearing raincoats fashioned from UNHCR plastic sheeting, a store displaying duffel bags made of this sheeting with the UNHCR logo prominently imprinted, and leaky roofs of local homes covered with such sheeting as well.

The French and Zairian pastors on our team conducted Bible studies and peace seminars in French on subjects of forgiveness and accountability, mostly for the men in the camps, but the sessions were also attended by a few women. Furthermore, they assisted with the periodic food distribution of rice and beans, but this work was handled for the most part by local Zairian and Rwandan refugee workers. Our team member Clement, a Mennonite merchant from Kinshasa, played a critical role in this, as he networked, in suit and tie and highly polished shoes, among the local Kivu elite to facilitate transportation and distribution of relief goods. Ironically, in the midst of all this human disaster, Clement once had a fit of exasperation when he couldn't find his shoe lasts. He and Joyce Martens were in charge of accounting responsibilities for MCC's budget in this entire operation.

Cathy Mputu organized seminars for women who could speak or at least understand French and women who were leaders in the camps' women organizations, among them one of the three Rwandan Presbyterian women pastors. Because far fewer Rwandan women than men continue in school long enough to learn French at the secondary level, the participation in Mputu's seminars was of course smaller numerically, but it also included local Zairian women. Mputu devised an intriguing blend of Bible study and women's liberation teaching titled, "Comment prendre sa responsabilité en tant que femme Chrétiènne" ("How does one take one's responsibility as a Christian woman?"). She concluded that a Christian woman can do anything and does not have to be bound by customary restrictions so long as her work honors God. It became clear during the discussion that many of the women feared their husbands, that many husbands were polygynous, and that many women who attended church had husbands who didn't. Mputu emphasized the story of the Samaritan woman, especially its application to the Hutu-Tutsi conflict, as an example of overcoming social boundaries and limitations with agape love. She further emphasized dramatically how Jesus, dying on the cross, was able to forgive his tormentors, that Christ's love was large enough to do that. "What love! This love, mes chères mamans rwandaises—this love we must practice. For the Christian to pardon is also to forget." Then she asked the question that all refugees would need to ask themselves: "What do I say to my enemy when I first meet him or her?" Mputu was assisted in her efforts by women from the ECZ churches in Bukavu.

An important part of these meetings was the food that was shared at the beginning and at the end. Mputu brought rolls and honey from Bukavu to eat with the tea at the start of the sessions, and after discussion and singing, the women of the camp that hosted the meeting served a big meal in the best dishes they had brought along on their flight—an indication of their middle-class status, because they had been able to flee Rwanda in a vehicle. We could see how those with some savings or newly found income could supplement the relief food of rice and beans with vegetables and meat from local markets. These meetings also provided the women with an occasion to get out of their tents, to dress up, to socialize, and thus to keep up their courage and their hope.

In addition to these women's seminars, Mputu organized sewing, embroidery, soap making, and other project sessions with women's organizations in the camps. Further, as a special Christmas gift, she initiated an MCC donation of large quantities of salt, a rare commodity in the relief food distribution.

Of course our team was well aware that this social outreach to refugee women in the form of Bible studies and discussion may have benefited mostly those of the middle class, meaning those well enough off to have gone to school long enough (meaning secondary school in Rwanda) to learn French, because the discussion groups were conducted in French. But this was due to the limitations of circumstances, not to policy or intent. It was reasonable to expect that the women who participated would speak about what they had said and heard in wider circles. The active outreach to women, and to men, regardless of their social standing or possible implication in the genocide, was above all aimed to help confirm their dignity and their humanity.

A few months later, between April and May of 1995, the MCC decided to end its relief involvement in the camps when the United Nations began to work actively on the repatriation of Rwandan refugees. Well aware of the disastrous effects of what has been termed "the refugee business" (Maren 1997), the MCC opted for continued support of peace work in Bukavu and Burundi through local organizations. This was especially true in light of the growing awareness that the relief work in the Zairian refugee camps was strengthening the forces of genocide for renewed attacks on Rwanda. Later, we would learn from someone who had visited these camps that relief blankets were being sold to raise money for, among other things, arms (de Lame 1996; de Lame, personal communication, 1997). The camps near Bukavu were broken up in November and December 1996, and the remaining refugees who had decided against returning to Rwanda dispersed into the interior of Zaire. By mid-1999 some Rwandans were still known to be wandering in the forests of Zaire (Pierre Ndilikilikesha, personal communication, June 10, 1999); others were fighting with the Congolese army against the Rwandans and Congolese rebel forces.

1.4 Conversations with Refugee Church Officials

Just as the refugee camps in Zaire represented a cross section of the communities of Rwanda, so they harbored segments of Rwanda's institutions. The churches tragically mirrored the deep rift that had emerged in Rwandan national society. More will be said of this situation in chapter 2. Here, we report on conversations held with some of the leaders of the Presbyterian Church of Rwanda, who had fled to the Muku camp (interviewed on December 15, 1994).

The Catholic Church in Rwanda was decimated in the events of 1994. Of the 400 ordained clergy in the church before that point, 200—mainly Tutsi—were killed in April and May by militia; later, as the RPF moved in, 40 mostly Hutu priests fled to Goma (Nzabahimana 1994; van Hoyweghen 1996, p. 395). In addition, the archbishop of Rwanda, Vincent Nsengiyumva, was killed, as were a number of bishops, by the RPF. Many of the 2.5 million refugees in Tanzania, Burundi, and Zaire were Catholic. We return to the Catholic Church in Rwanda in sections 2.3 and 2.5.

Some of the Rwandan Protestant churches, although far smaller numerically than the Catholic churches, saw their leadership and their membership torn apart by the same forces that had divided the nation. For example, in the Baptist Church, of 56 pastors in prewar Rwanda, three were killed and 50 fled to Zaire; only three remained in Rwanda (Brubaker 1994, p. 4). An estimated 40,000 members also fled and were in exile, although the leadership returned before the end of 1994 (see section 2.3).

The Presbyterian Church of Rwanda demonstrated some of the strains that resulted from the war and a divided leadership. The head (legal representative) of the national Presbyterian Church of Rwanda, Twagirayesu Michel, was in the Muku camp along with some of his pastors, whereas the executive secretary, Gakinda Gédéon, stayed in Rwanda. Although Twagirayesu continued in late 1994 to be the official head of the church, Gakinda effectively took over the leadership role because of all the decisions that needed to be made. This section continues with Twagirayesu's account of the war and its impact on the church. Gakinda's perspective is given in section 2.3.

Many pastors were lost in April and May 1994, and others have died since then, even recently. Twagirayesu seemed not to know how many had survived or where they were. (Church authorities inside Rwanda later indicated that of the church's 70 pastors and evangelists, 10 had been killed in the war and at least 13 (Brubaker 1994, p. 4) and as many as 41 fled to Zaire. Of these, 26 were in the Bukavu area and 15 were in Goma in late 1994 (including pastors and evangelists) (Gakinda Gédéon, interview, Kigali, December 28, 1998). The Bible School for the training of evangelists and a theological school and faculty in the Butare Seminary were also decimated. The deans were murdered and the faculty dispersed. They had 12 students at the time of the war, one of whom was killed (Gakinda Gédéon, interview, Kigali, December 28, 1994).

Pastor Twagirayesu, legal representative and official head of the Rwandan Presbyterian Church, a refugee in the Muku camp, Zaire, was accompanied for our interview by two of his pastors, Pastor Nzamutuma Lelathiel of Kamembe parish, Cyangugu, and Pastor Manirakiza Venant of Kibuye parish. I (John) had made the appointment to see the Presbyterian leaders through the camp coordinating committee. When we met one afternoon near the football field of Muku, the distant mountains around Bukavu were visible; the western mountains of Rwanda would have been visible, but the rainy season clouds were forming. Yet the chasm that divided these men from their home was enormous. In order not to broach the painful questions of what had happened—why they were in exile—and because I knew nothing about the particulars, I asked them first about the history of the Presbyterian Church of Rwanda.

The history of the Rwandan Presbyterian Church mirrors the colonial and the independent history of Rwanda. The church originated in 1907 in the work of the Bethel Mission during German colonial rule in Rwanda. This origin placed the church in the German Reformed tradition; the name Presbyterian came much later. Bethel abandoned its work in Rwanda in 1917 with Germany's defeat in World War I and the loss of its African colonies. Just as Belgium took over the territory Ruanda-Urundi, so the Société Belge de Mission moved in to recruit Dutch and American Protestant missionaries from a variety of denominations, including the Presbyterians, the Baptists, and the Adventists. By the mid-1950s, a group known as *Les amies du Rwanda* (friends of Rwanda) among Swiss missionaries to Belgium became interested in the Rwanda missions. The conservative wing of the Reformed Church of the Netherlands, not the state church, also became involved. Only in 1980, in collaboration with the Swiss-Belgian and Dutch churches, did the German Reformed Churches again become involved in Rwanda, this time with an independent national church.

The national Rwandan Presbyterian Church that grew out of this mission work emerged in 1969. They had debated which denomination to belong to. They chose to be Presbyterian but independent of the Scottish and American churches that used this name. Today, they are members of the World Council of Reformed Churches, the All African Council of Churches, and the World Council of Churches.

Twagirayesu explained the organization of the Rwandan Presbyterian Church. His detailed accounting of parishes, districts, and synods made clear the extent of the fracture caused by the war. The church is a national church and covers the entire country. Its National General Synod meets once a year. Delegates, including an elder and a pastor, come from all 54 parishes. Also represented are the 20 evangelization fields, and six regions, each with its own president (but these do not correspond to the governmental prefectures). Also represented are the heads of the social services—departments of education, medicine, schools, and rural development projects. The synod has three delegates from each region. The legal representative of the church—Twagirayesu—is president of the National Synod, which is separate from the church's administration, headed by Gakinda.

In response to my question of why they had fled, whereas others in the leadership had stayed, Twagirayesu had this to say:

> Those who stayed, it was by accident for some; they couldn't leave, happily they stayed. Others were on the road, bogged down, and stayed. It's good that there are some who stayed, that there are colleagues there. But they can't visit the parishes. There is very little news—short messages from the general secretary in Kigali. . . . We would like to have a meeting with those who are in the country. The German mission would finance such a meeting at Nairobi [for us to begin] to work together. The church should serve as the basis of reconciliation. If those [now in Zaire] "speak the same language" as those [who stayed], a meeting is possible. In such a meeting we could inventory the return and reconciliation and mutual pardoning of members and reintegration of the church.

"Was ethnicity a factor in the separation?" I asked.

> No, the criteria for pastoral recruitment are that one must have the vocation, the call, and be competent. For recruitment of pastors the local community and the council of elders must support it. Then there must be confirmation at the regional, synodal, and synodal council. In fact, of the six regional presidents, there are three of each ethnic identity, Hutu and Tutsi. Thus this representation was both the source of the integration and the source of the division.

Were church members involved in the massacres?

> The "movement" was popular and members were carried along with it. So yes, some were involved. It is a great setback for the church, ours and in general. The Nairobi conference will be the point of departure of national reconciliation.

What did the church do to deal with the issues?

> In 1990 the churches—Protestant and Catholic—met, created a *comité de contact* to contact all the forces for peace. They did a lot, met with the president and political parties regarding the refusal of the parties and the RPF to stop the war. The churches tried to mediate, to find a peaceful solution. When the war broke out this year [1994], the church was completely overwhelmed. Some of the heads were killed. At the moment the Arusha Accord was to take place, they met—May 13—to demand of both parties a stop to combat. [The Prime Minister] Kambamba met with us, not the RPF. Everyone was now dispersed, even the May 13 meeting was difficult. It was impossible to stop the massacres. They started the same night as the president's death and spread everywhere. Access to anyone was impossible. The youth took power. With their barriers and machetes and arms the militias took over. The church became powerless at this moment. If you tried to do anything, you were threatened.

Does the church still have credibility? Is it still a voice of hope?

> In the services here, much is as before. There's repentance being heard in the camps. The church is

> a force, but weak in the face of political events. In the camps the message of reconciliation is heard here and there; the church preserves its credibility. The church could reunite. But the two political tendencies are strained. Even the political parties expect the churches to do something. There was a recent evangelical event in Nairobi that showed the way.

The event in Nairobi to which Twagirayesu refers is a meeting of Rwandan church officials and representatives who had sought refuge in Nairobi that was held on November 4, 1994 (Dirigeants d'Eglises rwandaises 1994).[1]

About the youth and the church Twagirayesu had this to say.

> Not just those who killed, but the RPF youth, the future with these youth who learned to kill, trained to reject the value of human life, the church has a huge work ahead of it. There have been youth services, house building projects. Those who survive and were protected by Christians, they gave a testimony.

He continued to describe the historical background of the Presbyterian Church in the context of Habyarimana's Rwanda, suggesting that "the problem" of ethnic difference in national society had been largely forgotten until the RPF attacked and aroused sentiment.

> The church was accused of tilting toward the Tutsi, but we were national. We had nearly forgotten the problem, but the RPF roused it. . . . There was a time when the problem wasn't visible. The MRND tried to deal with peace and equilibrium through participation in power at each level through a quota for each group [Tutsi and Hutu]. During the period of 1973–1990, the youth even forgot the problem. With the war in 1990, the sons of Tutsi refugees invaded, the assassination of Ndadaye in Burundi, the Arusha Accord was problematic in its implementation, the sentiment that roused tension, assassinations of various visible important Hutu politicians. [In the] February 1993 attack on Ruhengeri, many Hutu people [were] killed and mutilated. All this crystallized the sentiments, which were set loose by the death of the president. A Tutsi minority said, "Do you think the Tutsi will continue to be oppressed?" Extremists on both sides roused the hatred.

This testimony by the head of the Presbyterian Church in exile echoed the perception of the old culture, and the MRND-dominated government, which prevailed in the camps. This group of Presbyterian leaders had sought refuge with the government leaders who were also there. Although Twagirayesu had been active in prewar attempts by church leaders to bring political pluralism into Habyarimana's government in the early 1990s and to initiate dialogue between the government and the RPF, he could not erase his own deep political involvement with the MRND. He had been on the provincial MRND council in Kibuye prefecture. With church members from other denominations, he had given strong public support to Habyarimana's government (Longman 1995a, p. 197).

Yet the Presbyterian Church leadership mirrored the national society. What could have accounted for the inclination of some to remain and others to flee, given their otherwise noble effort to disregard the ethnic divide in their church membership and organization? In a publication shortly after the war, American scholar Timothy Longman wrote about two Rwandan Presbyterian parishes he had studied in western Rwanda from 1992 to 1993 (Longman 1995b). In the parish where the local Presbyterian leaders were part of the elite that felt increasingly threatened by the political reforms and the return of the exiled Tutsi, the leaders had fallen in with the genocidal plot to target local scapegoats to assert their control over local institutions and resources. In the other parish, where the Presbyterian leadership was more populist—indeed, it was made up of peasant and poor individuals—the church ranks did not fragment. Although local government leaders still initiated killing, this was done from the outside rather than emerging from within the community.

A leitmotif that runs through many accounts of the Rwandan conflict of 1994 is how class division and access to institutional power appear to have led many leaders to become involved in the national movement to preserve privilege and control. By the same token, those who felt alienated from such privilege used the movement to gain opportunity or to seek revenge.

1.5 Conversations with Refugee Rwandan Administrators

We had hoped to contact individuals, families, and administrators on both sides of the border to better understand the war and its aftermath. Since visiting Kayenzi, we had been led to believe that the immediate prewar bourgmestre of Kayenzi, Mbarubukeye Jean, would be in the camps where we would be working. Instead, the Kayenzi bourgmestre we met in Muku was Mujyambere Mathias, Mouvement Democratique Republicain (MDR) (Democratic Reform Movement) bourgmestre until 1992. He had quit because of the chaos of multiparty reforms and because of MRND policy to have only its own bourgmestres in office after 1992. On hearing that there was an American professor who wished to talk with refugee Rwandan administrators in Mushweshwe and Muku, several other men presented themselves, including Laurent Bucyibaruta, préfet of Kibungo until 1992 and the préfet (governor) of Gikongoro until he fled to Zaire in 1994; Jean Pierre Rukara, functionary in a government ministry; Mutwarabili Narcisse, bourgmestre of Musebeya commune, Gikongoro prefecture; and Muragazi Gabriel, bourgmestre of Mwendo commune, Kibuye prefecture. We held three meetings (on December 14, 16, and 20, 1994) in which a variety of issues were discussed. I (John) began with an open-ended question about what had happened in Rwanda and what they thought should be done. The account of these conversations and the impression that was given by this group of men at the time follows here. Gradually we would become aware of the extent to which the reality depicted by them was like shifting quicksands of a subsurface stream.

There was a great civility among these administrators. Our talks were like academic seminars. Topics ranged freely, and opinions, when they differed, were respected. At one point, in a discussion over the geographic features of the region, we were trying to establish the exact point of the continental divide northeast of which streams flowed into the Nile River and the Mediterranean Sea, south of which they flowed into the Indian Ocean by means of the Zambezi River, and west of which they flowed into the Zaire River and the Atlantic Ocean. On a clear day from our perch in the Muku camp we could see distant mountains that were sometimes snow capped. In this December rainy season we were often shrouded in fog or finding shelter from the rain. To solve the question of which watershed we were on, Bucyibaruta went to the next room in the house in which he lived to get his *Petit Larousse,* which he had brought with him in his flight. What forethought.

Rukara opened our first session with a general statement. He expressed his thanks for Mennonite help, especially the peace perspective they promoted. There was a need for material and moral nurture and a need for dialogue between the Rwandan population inside and outside the country. The Mennonites and others could play a role in this reconciliation. Then he emphasized that "we need the truth—spiritual, scientific. The role of the exterior perspective could help." He went on to elaborate what he meant, complaining bitterly about the international media:

> The war broke out in 1990, but the truth isn't being told. There were 960,000 displaced Rwandans already in October 1990, most of them poor peasants.[2] If the truth had been known, the international community could have stopped the war. The press saw Rwanda from one perspective, usually. I implore you to seek the truth on the whole story, even with its political dimensions.

I asked him which press he had followed. Rukara answered, "BBC, French radio, Belgian radio, 'La Libre Belgique.' But the press followed the RPF version of reality." As a functionary, he said, he had written about human rights. The other side (the RPF) had used weapons and bombardments:

> The press didn't hold to the rights in their reporting. The average American won't know the difference [between the sides]. I'm not for arbitrary arrests nor massacres of villagers. Universal human rights are universal, not to be abandoned by any journalist. Rwanda has need of the truth, including [the views and experiences of] all the poor peasants in hiding.

Then he related his own experience in the war of 1994:

> I was at my house. I left Kigali because of bombs falling, morning to night, not because of politics or a search for food. A bomb fell near my house. I left with my wife and seven children, all survived.

Bucyibaruta continued the conversations with a general overview of events in Rwanda since 1990. Bucyibaruta was the image of a senior official who had facts and policies at his fingertips—tall, calm, authoritative. He had risen through the ranks of the Rwandan civil service, from the days before 1972 when he had been a researcher at the National Research Institute. A member of the MRND party, he served as préfet at Kibungo until 1992, when he was appointed governor of Gikongoro. Bucyibaruta admitted that there had been ethnic policies before 1990 with which he did not agree. But before 1990 the Hutu and Tutsi had lived together. The war introduced tensions, but people still continued to live together until President Habyarimana was killed.

With the political reforms of 1992 Mujyambere told how he had become a member of the MDR, one of the parties that organized in opposition to the MRND, along with the Parti Liberal (Liberal Party) (PL), the Parti Social Démocrate (Social Democrat Party) (PSD), and the Coalition pour la Défense de la République (Coalition for the Defense of the Republic) (CDR). The ethnic composition of these parties was as follows: MRND, mostly Hutu with some Tutsi; MDR, mostly Hutu; PSD, half Hutu and half Tutsi; PL, mostly Tutsi; RPF, mostly Tutsi. The CDR was formed after 1992 and represented militant Hutu nationalists. Mujyambere described the growing life of these parties in Kayenzi, where he had been bourgmestre.

> Most of the parties organized their own youth movements to enhance their chances in forthcoming elections. This was the source of a great deal of turmoil. Party youth movements not only waged a war of words and deeds on each other, such as burning each others' flags, especially those of the government party MRND, they also physically assaulted officials and obstructed government at local levels and disobeyed local laws. In Kayenzi they closed communal offices and forced the subprefet of Kayenzi to walk 20 km with them. In Kayenzi the population intervened, and these youth were beaten away, but the communal vehicle was commandeered for a year. An extraordinary, uncontrollable disorder emerged. These youth movements were even able to influence the military.
>
> People saw that by protesting the MRND, which was in power, they were inadvertently working for the RPF, destabilizing the country; people began to boycott public institutions; undiscipline was generalized, and the authorities could do nothing to stop this. The army was at the front, not available to combat the internal conflict. It was out of this situation, to defend itself against the militancy of the other movements, especially after the second [1992] attack by the [RPF], that the MRND organized its own youth movement, which would become the Interahamwe. The CDR, a more militant nationalist party than the MRND, also emerged at this time.

Mujyambere, as a member of the MDR, supported multiparty democracy, in general. But he had this to say:

> We forget that people in underdeveloped countries haven't learned what multipartisme [a multiparty system] requires. In Africa many coups d'état are supported by outsiders. These coups were tolerated by the powers. We should have first involved the army, then talked [to the RPF]. The customary system and the state and democracy . . . —Rwandans have not figured it all out. Even Museveni says it's too early to introduce multipartisme. You need many intellectuals [to make it work].

As the national political scene became increasingly tense following the 1992 attack from the north by the RPF, the Habyarimana government, while negotiating for power sharing following the terms of the Arusha Accords, was in fact launching a rearguard action that we now know was a desperate attempt to hang on to power. In addition to military training of the Interahamwe, local officials who were true to the MRND party were appointed. Thus Mujyambere lost his position as bourgmestre of Kayenzi and was replaced by Mbarubukeye, an MRND hard-liner. A number of attacks on enemies of the regime had already been undertaken at this time.

Bucyibaruta's comments reflect the MRND stance, although it is now clear that his words were guarded. When asked about the reasons behind the war and the genocide, Bucyibaruta stressed that it was necessary to see first what the RPF had done in 1990, that the RPF had been at fault for the war of 1994. Here is one of his early formulations on the question of who or what had precipitated the war:

> The RPF's reasons for attacking were that (1) Tutsi were being abused and needed to be defended; (2) they wanted to have a democratic regime and return to the country. Outside, it was the return of the

> 1960 refugees. Inside, it was saving their ethnic group and having democracy. [Yet] the war broke out just when democratic pluralism was begun, which would have led to elections. People were ready to have democracy. It was not necessary to "save the Tutsi" because we lived in harmony. Some said that there were posts not open to Tutsi, e.g., préfet, bourgmestre. But there had been some, even politicians and functionaries. In 1982, Tutsi were ministers and parliamentarians. They were in such positions. The democratic way would have opened up. On the refugee question, there were talks going on, and contacts. If the solution was not satisfactory, international contacts could have helped. If the invasion [of 1990] was accepted by the international community, it was because they were behind the RPF, to destroy the existing government. They did not want Habyarimana's government.

I pressed him to talk about the 1994 war and how it had been fought. Again Bucyibaruta evaded the question, except to say:

> All Rwandans of good will regret the killings. War only destroys. But the war isn't over. Now we need to try to resolve the conflict, or else it will explode again sooner or later. This [explosion] will not necessarily be [because of] the refugees returning, but from within. In a few months, those who stayed, there will be discontent over what the RPF is doing. We have information that those Tutsi who didn't support the RPF are not well regarded.
>
> No, the war wasn't justified. The RPF started recruiting Tutsi within the country from the 1960s on, from inside the country. . . . Why were they recruited to destabilize the country? This only aroused ethnic conflict. When the RPF entered Rwanda, simple Hutu peasants were killed. One of my people in Byumba went to Kigali. His parents were killed and buried in a ditch. No, the RPF wanted to eliminate all who opposed them.

Eventually, after this outburst against the RPF, he returned to the massacres in Rwanda in 1994. He suggested, in effect, that it was important to remember who was responsible for the genocide.

Bucyibaruta's position on the massacres was that there had been a regrettable ethnic and political conflict between opposing sides in the Rwandan political landscape. But the international press and the international community had supported the RPF against Habyarimana's government. On another day, he elaborated his views of how the actual war had begun and why it had taken the form it did.

> The Interahamwe were the youth of the MRND. After the war broke out, the RPF considered all who opposed to be Interahamwe of all the youth movements. In Kigali there were a lot of people below Ste. Famille parish, and the RPF bombed the region, including the Red Cross hospital. The CDR had no organized youth; the Liberal Party had a youth movement. The Social Democrats also had a youth movement. But the RPF had adherents across the land and planned the assassination of the president so there would be trouble. When the trouble would break out, it would be easy to know who would be for them, who against. All who were not there, would be against them. But not all Tutsi were for the RPF. But, many gathered anyway, because they risked [being attacked by the RPF].

This version of the war by Bucyibaruta merits careful reading because it is the narrative of someone who others have indicted as a major instigator of the genocide in his region. He is suggesting that the Tutsi gathered in churches and other places because they were part of an RPF conspiracy. Even those who were opposed to the RPF were there, for fear of reprisals. In effect, he is saying, they were killed by their own kind. He continued:

> There was a confrontation. Not just Tutsi died, even more Hutu died. Since the April troubles [of 1994], an uncontrollable movement erupted. There were Tutsis in the hills, others in the churches or in communal buildings. We found some documents; they had advance brigades in the communes. In case of war, they would have these advance brigades. They had some weapons distributed, for example, at Kabuye, Lubonde, and other armament centers. Even in the churches these documents were found.

Bucyibaruta then came to the moment of needing to explain the killing of all these Tutsi gathered, as he said, for the movement by the RPF, although he did not come right out and say that they were killed.

> When there would be a confrontation, the local administrators needed to defend themselves. The RPF attacked after the killing of the president. The administrators were obliged to defend themselves. No gendarmes or others were ready or available [they were at the front]. One ran here and there, but [there were] mutual massacres between Hutu and Tutsi. A confrontation between everyone ensued. The authorities were in great insecurity. The RPF, as we all, regret the deaths. But the RPF isn't interested in the Tutsi population but was simply interested in power.

Thus, in Bucyibaruta's explanation, the general instability introduced by multipartisme and the agitation of the youth movements followed by the conspiracy of the RPF within the population led to

BIZIMANA Francois		Rutonde, Nkunga
BIZIMANA Jean-Baptiste	Membre du comite prefectoral du MRND, Ex-Bourgmestre	Rutonde
BIZIMANA Jean	Bourgmestre	Nyarugenge
BIZIMANA Leonard	Membre du comite prefectoral du MRND, Enseignant	Musange
BIZIMANA Mathieu		
BIZIMANA Vincent	Commercant	Kabarondo
BIZIMANA	Militaire FAR	Murambi Mbogo
BIZIMUNGU Augustin	Chef d'Etat Major FAR	
BIZIMUNGU Casimir	MINISANTE	
BIZIMUNGU Come	Ex-Prefet de Kigali-Riral, MRND	
BIZIMUNGU Teleshore	Ex-Agent de MINIPLAN	
BIZIMUNGU	Paysan	Kayonza
BIZIYAREMYE Francois		
BIZIYAREMYE	Agriculteur	Murambi, Mbogo
BIZUMUREMYI (Lt)	Membre escadron de la mort	
BIZUMUTIMA Francois	Membre du CDR	Rutare
Bizumwami Uzziel	Commercant	Kigoma
BUCYANAalias NGALISI)	Cultivateur	Nyaruhengeri
BUCYANA Martin	Conseiller du secteur	Gisuma
BUCYIBARUTA Laurent	Ex-Prefet	
BUDIGIRI Innocent	President des Interhamwe, secteur Kiyanza	Murambi, Mugambazi
BUGERE	Conseiller de Secteur	Kinigi, Kabwe
BUGINGO Capaoral GD	Gendarme	Kabarondo
BUGINGO Dominique		Muhazi, Ruhunda
BUGINGO Edouard	President de MRND	Rusumo, Musaza
BUGINGO Joseph prefectoral du MRND	Ex-Bourgmestre, membre de comite	Gisovu
BUGINGO Musa	Agriculteur	Kabarondo
BIGUNGO	Directeur du CERAI	Kibeho
BUHAKE Aminadabu	Coordinateur des operations des miliciens	
BUHIRIKEJoseph	Commercant, membre de reseau Zero	
BUHOBERO	Agriculteur, MDR Power	Kigoma
BUNANI Charles	Interahamwe, Chef de service ORTPN	

Figure 21. Segment from section B of the category 1 "List of Planners and Organizers of the Genocide," which includes Laurent Bucyibaruta, former prefet of Gikongoro. In terms of the Organic Law of August 30, 1996, category 1 perpetrators include (1) persons whose criminal acts or whose acts of criminal participation place them among the planners, organizers, instigators, supervisors, and leaders of the crime of genocide or of a crime against humanity; (2) persons who acted in positions of authority at the national, perfectoral, communal, sector, or cell level or in a political party and fostered such crimes; (3) notorious murderers who by virtue of the zeal or excessive malice with which they committed atrocities, distinguished themselves in their areas of residence or where they passed; and (4) persons who committed acts of sexual torture (Rwandan Embassy Web site).

a general outbreak of mutual killing. To clinch his point, Bucyibaruta noted that the Tutsi who were not for the RPF had been suddenly put in danger. This explained the death of Vicar Gasabwoya Innocent of Kabgayi near Gitarama. It explained the case of Kajuga Robert, a Tutsi, and head of the Interahamwe, who had fled and taken refuge in Goma, Zaire.

Without detailed human rights documentation in hand at the time, it was difficult to gain a clearer picture of the massacres and the war that this general defensive account by the top official of Gikongoro and one of its bourgmestres yielded. Only later did we begin to learn what might be the truth. In Butare a retired priest told us that he was one of the few survivors of a grenade attack on a church in Gikongoro in which he had taken refuge. The vicar of the cathedral in Butare, when he heard of our conversations with Bucyibaruta, said that Bucyibaruta was one of the main perpetrators of the massacres in his area. African Rights' *Rwanda: Death, Despair and Defiance* states that in Gikongoro the killers included a sous-préfet and four bourgmestres (1995: p. 117), and that the killing "began immediately after the death of President Habyarimana. Rwandese agree that the massacre of the Tutsi in this prefecture was carried out systematically and speedily, to an extent possibly unmatched elsewhere. Survivors describe Gikongoro as a 'region of graveyards'" (1995: p. 227).

More complete understanding of what occurred in Gikongoro during the genocide in 1994 is provided in the voluminous *Leave None to Tell the Story: Genocide in Rwanda* (Human Rights Watch, 1999), where witnesses' accounts and governmental archives are used in a painstaking reconstruction of events. The first attacks in Gikongoro (the commune Muko) were led on April 7, 1994 by assailants from Mwendo commune in Kibuye prefecture where Muragazi Gabriel, MRND party leader, was bourgmestre, and sous-préfet (1999, p. 313).

The assailants moved from Muko commune to the nearby commune of Musebeya, where local bourgmestre Higiro Viateur, with the help of local police, resisted the aggression and protected Tutsi, and held meetings urging people to resist the attacks (1999, p. 318). The two contrasting trends gave the préfet opportunity to show his leadership. But Prefet Bucyibaruta, having returned from a meeting in Kigali called in mid-April by the interim government, issued lengthy statements urging his bourgmestres to maintain order, not to pillage, and to remain vigilant against "the enemy," the RPF. Thousands of Tutsi, who were at first protected in Musebeya were to have been taken to Butare, but they were not allowed "by the authorities" to continue from Gikongoro, and were instead taken to a new technical school at Murambi and massacred. Bourgmestre Higiro was replaced by an MRND loyalist bourgmestre who followed through with the killings.

A pattern of duplicity is evident in Gikongoro, as elsewhere, in which the authorities encouraged calm and order, yet seemingly turned a blind eye and a deaf ear to parallel network that led the massacres. In Gikongoro Lt. Col. Aloys Simba, who had been close to President Habyarimana, played this role. Préfet Bucyibaruta's edicts encouraging calm and efforts to enforce the peace by keeping weapons out of the hands of militia were belied by the ease with which the parallel network of assassins continued their work and the quickness with which those, like bourgmestre Higiro, who resisted, were replaced (Human Rights Watch 1999, pp. 320–329).

As we have read each new revelation of the details of the genocide in Gikongoro, our understanding grows of those conversations we held with administrators in Muku and Mushweshwe camps. Bucyibaruta, governor (préfet) of Gikongoro, Muragazi Gabriel, bourgmestre of Mwendo commune in Kibuye, and Mbarubukeye Jean, bourgmestre of Kayenzi, were cited on the List of Planners and Organizers of the 1994 Genocide (see Figure 21). The man who called himself "Mutwarabili Narcisse, bourgmestre of Musebeya commune," may have been the man who replaced bourgmestre Higiro who tried to save the Tutsi.

It is not surprising that Bucyibaruta and the other administrators said that the refugees were afraid to return to Rwanda. However, they couched this in terms of the RPF's brutality and arbitrary arrests rather than their own guilt and fear of judgment. Bucyibaruta's explanation of the killings, in effect, blamed the victims for their own deaths. It was unclear whether this was a stance that had been rationalized for our benefit, or was the honest perspective of his view of events that betrayed a massive denial of genocide and continuing shock that he and his associates were refugees in exile.

1.6 Who Speaks for the Refugees?

I (John) visited Habimana Emmanuel, spokesman and coordinator of the Rwandan refugees of the four sites (Mushweshwe, Muku, Bideka, and Izirangabo) in his office in the school in Muku where he showed me the computer he had received for his work. He then invited me to come to his tent where his sister served us rice and beans and we were able to talk in quiet.

As a well-educated Hutu, Habimana had become a functionary in the Rwandan Ministry of Social Affairs, a post he held until March 1993. He saw the administration becoming increasingly politicized in the face of growing tension in the land, in part because of the divergence of positions between the government and the RPF. He quit his position in the Ministry of Social Affairs and began to work for CARITAS, the Catholic relief organization. He had worked with them for reconciliation in Rwanda, especially in the northwest of the country, for a year leading up to the war. His disillusionment with the Hutu cause and his reading of history led him to a deep pessimism over the future of his people. In our conversation he traced the historical events that had led to this present situation, almost as if there were direct causal threads leading back through the years since independence and back into colonialism.

When I asked Habimana to explain to me the sources of the conflict, he doubted that its base was really ethnic and that the history they had learned in school was really true. But he began his account with a recital of the "three ethnies" origin account he had been taught.

> There were three ethnic groups, the Twa and the Hutu, who are Bantu, and the Tutsi, who are Nilotics. The Twa were hunters in the forests, whereas the Hutu ran the society. The Tutsi came with aggression, crowned their kings, making the Hutu their serfs to do corvée labor.

The contradictions in this mythohistoric account of Central Africa are apparent in what Habimana does not say: There was no mention of pre-Tutsi kingdoms nor an explanation of how the Nilotics adopted a Bantu language. "Bantu" seemed for Habimana to be an all-encompassing identity that included cultural and physical features alike.

Habimana continued his narration with the impact of colonialism:

> Then, the missions came and wanted to install themselves. They took the situation, as it was, to be accepted. The Belgians wrote that the Tutsi are a superior race. If we detach ourselves from them, we can't succeed, they reasoned. Rwanda experienced the politics of apartheid in the 1930s. All this was revolting to the majority. Hutu chiefs were even replaced with Tutsi chiefs by the end of colonization.

The Wine Has Been Poured, and We Must Drink It

Habimana's narration of this history of Rwandan was brief. He had not experienced much of it firsthand. Even the "Hutu revolution" that followed it seemed distant to him from the vantage point of a Zairian refugee camp. But he conveyed the sense that it had set in motion the fateful course of events that would lead to the Rwandan holocaust for which he and his kind must pay. He searched out some of the connections between government policies of the two Hutu republics and their consequences.

> The missions began to change their ideas, and political parties were founded. Pressure was put on the chiefs, but they refused, saying, "No, [the Hutu] are our serfs." The king was chased out, elections were held, and we had democracy! Some Tutsi were chased into exile. They tried to return several times.

Habimana's account of independent Rwanda explains when and how things began to go wrong with the ethnic quota system, or the "politics of equilibrium."

> The first regime [of independent Rwanda] was elected. But then the second regime imposed the northern military over the southern intellectuals. There was a massacre against the intellectuals in the center. Since 1973 [under Habyarimana], we have had a military regime. The laws were changed, officially, to have equality by ethnicity and regions, that is, quotas. Thus there was here a

> legalized difference [or quota arrangement] in regions and in ethnicity. This was bad legislation, especially as concerns *la loi scolaire* [laws pertaining to education]. It gave the minister of education the right to determine 5% of the graduates on his own discretion, so as to calibrate ethnic equality. This meant he privileged the northern region, his own, at the expense of the Tutsi and others. Usually, each year in Rwanda, 100,000 students would graduate from primary school, to compete for 4,000 positions in secondary school. The minister could determine 5% of these 4,000, thus 200, who would go on to secondary school from among all the graduates. He would usually support mediocre ones from his region. This was rotten legislation! It naturally provoked the good students, and the Tutsi, who were given 10% [or 400 positions]. But, most Tutsi, even when excluded, were still able somehow to manipulate the system, including private schools. Tutsi students were often financed by Hutu. So, many Tutsi went into business and non-governmental organizations; many are in good positions around the world. In Canada and Belgium the Tutsis are well known. Their cause is well publicized. And, in the administration they were better placed and better paid.

Habimana also criticized the exclusion policies of the government and spoke of the disastrous consequences to which they led.

> The next mistake of the Rwandan government was in 1982, when Obote took power [in Uganda] and shut out the Rwandans. The Rwandan government also chased them out; they had no place to go. This pushed them into solidarity and they began to plan for war. The government's policy on this was that there was no more room for them, for more people in the country. . . . There was also the matter of passports, that the government wouldn't issue passports to the Tutsi living outside Rwanda.
>
> Before the 1990 war there were contacts between the two sides and newspaper coverage of the two communities. But after the 1990 war it was complete suspicion between the two. The Hutu said to the Tutsi, "We'll get you and your Hutu accomplices." There was recruitment of Tutsi children by the RPF. In the 1980s there were rumors of a coup d'état. The Minister of Internal Security of the Central Government, a Hutu, fled and sought exile in Uganda, joining the [RPF]. The current president also fled. Both are northerners. Some soldiers also fled or were paid off.
>
> The [other side] then had a third of the country. There was widespread complicity within the administration. Politics was relatively open. But I doubt the sincerity of the people. Even those who got what they wanted, they weren't satisfied with the Arusha Accords. The Foreign Minister signed things that weren't even negotiated, e.g., the presence of the RPF military in the city of Kigali. Thus, the two armies were side by side in many places. With the [arms] embargo [against Rwanda], the effect was to privilege the RPF.

Habimana then turned to the effect of all this on the self-image of the people, in particular those who had identified with the Hutu revolution.

> There was an evolution of attitudes. Vis-à-vis Tutsi supremacy, the Hutu internalized their sense of inferiority. There was great jealousy of those in power, great difficulty of sharing in political, economic, and social life. The late president [Habyarimana] had a lot in common with the Tutsi, and this angered the people. Whereas the Tutsi developed the economy, the Hutu felt increasingly isolated.

Reflecting this isolation and resignation, Habimana concluded his account of the whole affair with a poetic summation.

> Now world opinion is on the side of the Tutsi. It's going to be difficult to pardon a people that has done what is done. The wine has been poured, and we must drink it.

A Sense of Foreboding

This sense of fatefulness for Habimana had strong implications for the future of his country and for him and the refugees around him.

> What are the consequences of the war? Land has been taken. All houses are occupied. We have millions outside. The RPF is consolidating its power. The news continues to speak of new massacres. People are afraid to sleep in their houses. Many inside the country want to leave but can't. How can this build peace? Anyone can be accused of being an Interahamwe. They are killing, but more subtly. They are seeking vengeance. People are arrested and disappear. There is no examination of the sources of information.

His comments turned to the refugees, whom he represented.

> Who is speaking on behalf of those who have fled? Is the international community aware of all this, the 4 million? Are they all assassins? Why must they be victims?
>
> The RPF says we can return. We know those who have returned and have been killed. [Agents of the government] come seeking particular individuals and relatives among the refugees. They infiltrate the refugee camps. They pay Zairian soldiers to help them.
>
> Among the Rwandan refugees, the United Nations has a bad reputation. Why? The UN abandoned the people when they were most needed. They are liquidating the camps now. This plays into

the hands of the RPF. The refugees feel that the UN is partial.

The Rwandans need a voice, especially the refugees. Don't incriminate all the members of the old government. I [as a functionary of the Ministry of Social Affairs] didn't know of any plan. I don't believe there was one. The Tutsi functionaries would have known of it. The ministers would have acted differently, with all the houses they had.

Habimana spoke of the possibility of reconciliation.

Can reconciliation happen among all these people who can't share? It cannot be otherwise; some will kill themselves [before reconciling]. Negotiations are a long way off. If one wants to invest in education, that would be one way to contribute to reconciliation. But those who are in the good houses in Rwanda now, they aren't interested in reconciliation.

His recipe for peace included the need to

disarm everyone, keep the border from becoming a battle zone. Negotiations will begin. People still have arms. But is there a willingness at all to negotiate? The Rwandans should live together. But these were neighbors, drinking partners, who killed each other. Peasants kill if they're told to do so. We've been victimized by extremists. The RPF was never satisfied. Look at what happened in Burundi. The model transition to democracy blew up. Now? It was all done in bad faith.

Habimana kept returning to the theme of injustice perpetrated on the Rwandan people but kept trying to understand for himself why the war had happened.

Habyarimana was for the Arusha Accords. The Tutsi say he was killed by Hutu extremists. Who had the most to gain from his absence? One fault was that he drew too much power to himself, and the day he'd be eliminated, it would all collapse.

How can confidence be reborn among the people? We used to talk of history to instruct people. We used to talk of the press. Now we need to highlight the refugees and the internally displaced, their social life, and the need to share the country's wealth, and the importance of multiple parties in government. Both sides need to forgive and repent. Neither side can hide anything. It is insupportable to let the killers go around with impunity. But it will take generations.

On February 2, 1995, Habimana wrote to us from Muku camp; the letter that follows was hand-carried to the United States and mailed to us from inside the United States.

Greetings from me and from my large social family, as well as from all the refugees in those of our camps which you have visited. We are still here; we are waiting impatiently for a better development.

With regards to the general assistance, we are still receiving aid from MCC, the first phase of which will end on the 24th of this month. Only, we do not know at all what will follow. We trust that God will not abandon us.

For us, the general situation stays the same and there is not one hour that passes that we do not think of our return. The position of Kigali seems to us to be categorical, to exclude the refugees of Rwanda. How will this end? We appeal to God for hope.

I would like to know of your impressions and understandings which you have gained after your visit, first with us refugees, then in Rwanda and Burundi. There, the situation resembles for the moment a ripe abscess which threatens to burst open and to turn Burundi's situation into the same that Rwanda has lived through. If possible, you could give me a profound analysis of the situation in the two countries, an analysis of information you received and your personal understanding. That could help me in particular and others as well to better prepare for our future, in order to discern whether we must table our return to Rwanda or whether we must henceforth and now envision contacts in order to find another country of asylum, especially since we judge that life (above all from the point of view of security) is very difficult.

I dare to hope that this will reach you.

We do not know whether Habimana survived the dispersion of the camps by the Alliance Forces for the Liberation of Congo/Zaire in late 1997 or whether he fled westward into the rain forests of Kivu and Maniema.

Notes

1. The background of initiatives by Rwandan churches—Catholic and Protestant—to broker a peace between the RPF and the government, their continuing attempts during the war, and the current situation are summarized by the Dirigeants d'Eglises rwandaises (1994).

2. Some place this figure at 70,000 internally displaced (David Newbury, personal communication, September 20, 1995).

2. Inside Rwanda

The wounds of war that heal most quickly are the destroyed or damaged buildings that are restored or the crops or pillaged food stores that are replanted and harvested. Far more long term are the emotional scars that people suffer, including the memories of physical and psychological pain, loss, and trauma. The conflicts in a civil war such as the Rwanda conflict, which led to neighbor being alienated from neighbor, leave scarred relationships and communities that are difficult to restore. These human consequences of war usually last well beyond a lifetime. If there is healing, it does not erase the scars; healing consists in a new social tissue of relationships and understandings as people begin to trust one another again. In this chapter we look at the aftermath of the 1994 war in several communities and institutions in Rwanda and at the long-term consequences of war on children. Our stay in Rwanda was concentrated in four centers: Kigali, the capital; Butare, the southern university and Catholic center; and Kayenzi and Giti, two of Rwanda's 147 rural communes.

In the absence of an official Mennonite presence in Rwanda we were introduced to people by Harold Otto, our regional unit coordinator. In broad consultation with other Rwandan and foreign agencies, Otto defined the MCC's mission within these other agencies' priorities (Figure 22). Thus the MCC distributed Ugandan seed grains in Kayenzi through the Salvation Army, and provided financial and logistical support for a meeting of in-country and exiled Protestant pastors that was organized by the Rwandan branch of African Evangelistic Enterprises (AEE). The MCC also affiliated with the Rwandan and Burundian Quakers through the office of the Evangelical Friends in Bujumbura and the presence of Willard and Ann Ferguson, Quakers who at the time were stationed in Kampala but had been in Rwanda at the outbreak of the war. The MCC's presence was thus a patchwork of short-term projects.

We arrived in Kigali on December 2, 1994, sharing a taxi from Bujumbura with Otto. We checked in at the Ste. Famille Catholic Guesthouse

Figure 22. NGO representatives attending a biweekly briefing meeting with United Nations and Rwandan government officials, Kigali, December 1994. Briefings included security reports and articulation of UN and Rwandan government policy announcements.

Figure 23. Ste. Famille parish church (right) and guesthouse (left) in Kigali.

(Figure 23). The Ste. Famille parish had been the scene of some of the most gruesome aspects of the genocide earlier that year, including the unforgettably atrocious scene of the Hutu parish priest pulling out a revolver after mass and killing known Tutsi congregants. Ste. Famille's guesthouse was open despite the intermittent flow of water and electricity, the lack of a variety of foodstuffs for meals, and a staff shortage. Many of the regular staff, we were told, had been massacred or had fled.

Postwar Kigali bore many signs of the battle that had raged in April and May. First, the militia and army massacred the regime's opponents and all Tutsi. In the second phase of the war the RPF shelled the center of the city as they moved in and drove out the Rwandan army. Buildings with shattered windows, walls, and roofs, burned vehicles, bunkers at every intersection, and occasional signs warning pedestrians not to cross empty lots because of uncleared mines were apt reminders of recent war. Youthful RPA soldiers were everywhere, stationed at intersections, at entrances to banks, and at the post office, office buildings, and hotels, or they drove around in their war machines—pickup trucks with machine guns mounted on the back that had been hastily yet creatively painted in camouflage colors over the markings from whatever company, mission, or NGO the vehicle had been commandeered. Personnel from the United Nations and hundreds of NGOs were everywhere. The restaurants of the city teemed with journalists from all over the world.

Rwandans in postwar Kigali fell into several obvious categories. There were those who had survived the war in place, but these did not include hard-line supporters of the previous regime. Most visible and prominent of course were the returned and returning "Ugandan" exiles, including the victorious RPF soldiers, officers, and civilians. Many of these spoke either Kinyarwanda or English. There were also the "Burundians," those Tutsi who had been in exile in Burundi and were opening up businesses or taking positions in government.

When sanitary conditions at Ste. Famille worsened, we moved to the house of an international NGO, Food for the Hungry, which was also involved in emergency food distribution. When we returned from Bukavu just before Christmas, we stayed at the Isimbi Hotel, across from the gutted MRND and guarded party headquarters. Later, in early January 1995 in Butare, we lived in the guesthouse of the bishop of Butare across the street from the war-torn chapel of the Catholic Secondary School. All these places of residence provided good opportunities for continuing our work of observing and listening, trying to understand and to interpret what was going on in Rwanda in the aftermath of the war. We did not have our own vehicle, so we usually walked in the cities. Some of our long-distance trips were done by taxi or by hitching rides with diplomats and NGO workers.

Our contacts with the rural communes of Kayenzi and Giti were dictated in the first case by refugee and relief work and in the second case by a coincidence of meetings. Secondarily, ethnographic rationale gives these two communes an extraordinarily interesting set of contrasts. Many of Kayenzi's families who fled to Zaire ended up in the Mushweshwe and Muku camps, where the MCC was at work. We wished to listen to personal accounts from those who had fled, those who had stayed, and those who had fled and returned home. The visit to Giti was compelling because it offered such a striking contrast to Kayenzi in terms of the war's character and impact. Both communes had prewar resident populations of about 45,000 inhabitants. In Kayenzi communal counts suggest that 8,000 were killed in the genocide massacre, 98% of them Tutsi; in Giti there were no killings organized by community officials, although massacres raged all around. Giti also hosted many refugees from the fighting to the north between the RPF and the government troops in 1990 and 1993. Communes such as Giti, which experienced no government-instigated massacres, are few. Yet, compared to communes such as Kayenzi, they offer a wealth of insights. Giti shows how and why the fabric of civil society held together and the extent to which these differing outcomes were due to the willful work of individuals and groups.

Butare is a remarkable town in southern Rwanda and is the site of the National University, the National Museum, and the national institutes for scientific research and technology. It is also a center of Catholic learning, with religious orders, a seminary, and several Catholic schools and the Reine Astride Cathedral, which dwarfs all other buildings in the city. We stopped at the cathedral on our initial drive into Rwanda. We spent four days in Butare on our way back to Bujumbura in late December 1994 and early 1995. Butare, named Astride in Belgian colonial times after the Queen Mother, was the brain center of the Great Lakes region of the Belgian colonial empire. L'Institut de Recherche Scientifique et Agricole au Congo (IRSAC) was an agricultural experiment center and research station for the exploration of the use of natural resources in this fertile region of Central Africa. It became the National Research Institute. The school for colonial civil servants' children was in Butare, where because of the favorable climate, family vacations were also often taken. The European school became the National University. Butare also became the center of Catholic education and the center of several orders and religious congregations, 25 of which survived the war. The Catholic seminary of Butare and its diocesan life continued as a center of Catholic life and thought allied with the university and the National Research Institute.

The fate of institutions sections in this chapter consider the impact of the war on churches and the research establishment; these groups represent some of the many institutions and groups that can be identified as Rwandan civil society. We were able to talk with the leaders of several churches, this time from within the country, and we heard accounts provided by other individuals and published reports. At the National Research Institute we were able to talk with the new general director and several section directors. The institutional aftermath of war ranged from partial continuity of staff and circumstances to division and total disruption or complete replacement of personnel. The accounts offer insight into the impact of civil war and the challenges of rebuilding a country.

To gain insight into the ways in which decisions and actions of individuals shaped the war and its aftermath in communities and institutions, we had to broaden the basis of documentation from particular persons' voices to the concerted voices of groups of individuals who were in ongoing relationships of friendship, neighborliness, work, and power, especially across ethnic lines. It becomes clear that many people in Rwanda did not align like robots into the stereotyped behavior of Hutu and Tutsi. Rather, the war and its aftermath unfolded as a continuing drama in which there were no clear-cut scripts. Individuals made spur-of-the-moment life-affecting choices, the most crucial of which was whether to go along with the "madness" and possibly kill to protect themselves or to risk their own lives to save the life of another.

Stories of the children of war came to our attention almost daily during our stay in Central Africa. The 1994 war in Rwanda possibly produced far more parentless children than others because of the motive and the method of the killing. Everywhere we went in the war zone, we were made painfully aware of the overwhelming phenomenon of "unaccompanied children," a term promoted by UNICEF and caring agencies in preference to "orphan" for reasons having to do with the way international conventions try to reunite these children with their parents or other next of kin and to deter the booming baby business that flourishes, we soon discovered, around every war and impoverished region of the world.

2.1 Six Families of Kayenzi

Portrait of a Rwandan Ridge

Kayenzi is characteristic of a particular picture-book Rwanda, with its terraced hillsides dotted with neat homesteads, many now built of kiln-dried bricks and tile roofs, and small plots defined by banana groves and eucalyptus trees (Figure 24). In the background on a clear day the distant mountains of the Zaire-Nile continental divide are visible. In the rainy season dramatic clouds provide generous water for the volcanic soil to yield its bountiful harvests of beans, sorghum, green vegetables, corn, and coffee. Long-horned Central African cattle, small herds tended by shepherd boys, graze in road ditches or in the few remaining small pastures (Figure 25). Bee keeping is common (Figure 26). The Rwandan landscape is the most fully cultivated of any area in Africa. There are few empty spaces outside the national parks, and cultivated land is no longer fallowed (Figure 27). In recent years agricultural techniques such as terracing and draining of marshes so that they can be cultivated have provided additional land for some people (Figure 28). Still, in many areas of the north and northwest, rural densities reached 1,000 people per km^2 with average land holdings of less than half a hectare (2.2 acres) per family.

Kayenzi commune and Kayenzi Subprefecture are bordered on the north by the Nyabarongo River, which begins in the eastern foothills of the continental divide not far from Lake Kivu but circles northward and eastward and then southeastward around Gitarama Prefecture, past Kigali, eventually joining the Akagera River, which flows into Lake Victoria, whose waters ultimately flow into the Nile and the Mediterranean Sea (see Figure 3).

The scattered homesteads of Kayenzi are typical of East African highland societies that combine cultivation with cattle keeping; the homesteads and small adjoining farms are served by occasional commercial and administrative centers distributed mostly along ridges connected by dirt roads that link to the paved highways leading to the cities of Rwanda. In addition to the communal offices and agricultural cooperative buildings, Kayenzi's center includes a state-run hospital and health center and both public and private primary and secondary schools. Kayenzi, like most of the centers along

Figure 24. Terraced fields and homesteads, Kayenzi commune, Rwanda.

Figure 25. Herd boy with cattle, Kayenzi, December 1994.

Figure 26. Beehive tended by a beekeeper in Kayenzi. Beehives and honey are important features of Rwandan life.

ridges, has a market that, in African fashion, meets on scheduled days so as to complement other markets in the area (Figure 29). Overlooking the market is a small commercial center where local merchants tend their shops and offer a few other services (e.g., tailoring, a small eatery).

Kayenzi, as in much of Rwanda, has adherents of several religions, the most numerous being the Catholics. Presbyterians, Baptists, Seventh Day Adventists, and Muslims are also represented. These religious groups have their centers and their meeting places along the ridge road.

Many of the 45,000 inhabitants of Kayenzi, as counted in early 1994, before the war, trace their history back many generations in this place, where they were part of the combined economy and way of life of cultivation and herding. This is true, for example, of the local lineage of the Gesera clan, as portrayed by its spokesman, current bourgmestre Nkurikiyinka Damien (interviewed in Kayenzi on December 4, 1994). His patrilineal Tutsi family traces its genealogy six generations in Kayenzi, a time period that saw revolutionary changes in the relationship of people to land and in the way control of this relationship was handled. At the beginning of this period the local ridges *(collines)*, were governed by chiefs appointed by the king and his subchiefs. Theoretically, the king owned all the cattle and the land, which were allocated to the people. In fact, local families and individuals controlled particular hills or parts thereof and extended rights to land and cattle. This system was

common in highly centralized societies across Central and Southern Africa (e.g., Tswana chiefdoms of Botswana, the Lozi kingdom of western Zambia, the Luba kingdom of Zaire). In Rwanda there were land chiefs, cattle chiefs, and regiment chiefs, who coordinated for the kingdom the particular resources of land, livestock, and the warriors, respectively. This system also existed in Kayenzi. Wealthy and powerful families leased out or subcontracted to those in need their cattle and land in the *ubuhake* arrangement, whereby these partners would care for the cattle and work the land of their lords. It is a gross oversimplification to suggest that all cattle keepers were defined as Tutsi and all cultivators as Hutu, as today's stereotypes would suggest. Not only did both Hutu and Tutsi control land and cattle, but there were also both wealthy and poor Hutu and Tutsi,

Figure 27. Aerial view of Rwandan settlement showing widespread *colline* or ridge pattern of single-standing homesteads surrounded by terraced fields of sorghum, bananas, coffee, and vegetables. Little free pasture survives in this area near Kayenzi, central Rwanda.

Figure 28. Kayenzi peasants in fields with Jacques of the Salvation Army, inspecting progress in emergency relief seed planting. Previously, the MCC had also distributed seed grains through the Salvation Army. Each NGO was appointed a local commune or region to cover the entire country.

Figure 29. Kayenzi market, on market day, December 1994.

then as today. For present purposes it is sufficient to emphasize that a relatively flexible, redundant, and multitiered structure of authority was, as Nkurikiyinka pointed out, streamlined by the Belgian colonial regime into a single administrative hierarchy paralleled at the upper levels by the Belgian colonial state structure.

Under rising pressure for land, Nkurikiyinka said, the big estates were divided in 1956, and each family received its own land to cultivate. He remembered that when he was 12 years old, there were still empty spaces to cultivate and many more open pastures. Since then, fields have become close, with boundaries marked by named *imiyenzi* trees, which cannot be cut down. Each community or commune has a land register and measurements. Each hill has a name. The right to these registered land plots is ten years by statute. This 1956 land tenure system, very different from that under the old chiefs and the kingdom, continues to the present. In theory, the land claims were enforced and border disputes were settled by local courts and the courts of first instance. However, access to land and to justice are two volatile background issues of the current Rwandan crisis. Land pressure has been mentioned as a source of conflict between neighbors and even brothers. Nkurikiyinka, as the recently appointed mayor of the new RPF-led government, categorically denied the charge by the late president Habyarimana that there was not enough room and land for all Rwandans. The subject of land disputes was raised by several of the people in Kayenzi with whom we spoke.

The six families in this section all lived in Kayenzi before April 6, 1994. In December 1994 two families were in the Muku refugee camp in Zaire. They were introduced in section 1.2. We can reconstruct the drama of the war and its aftermath through several family members: Uwintije Celestine, Mbaduko Gabriel and Sekimonyo Francoise, Nkurikiyinka Damien, Mujyambere Mathias, Makarakiza André, and Ndayambaje Ibrahim.

Other members of the community enter the picture as passing actors, but we were not able to interview them. We became minor actors in this story because we entered the lives of these people, especially when we carried letters between Kayenzi and the Muku refugee camp. To the extent possible, we have continued to correspond with some of these families of Kayenzi.

The First RPF Attack in 1990 and Multipartisme up to 1993

After the armed incursion of the RPF across the Uganda-Rwanda border in October 1990, Kayenzi became the scene of growing tension and polarization. Mujyambere Mathias, a Hutu, was mayor at that time and was responsible for the local administration of the introduction of multiparty reform. This resulted from both structural adjustment in Rwanda in connection with loans from the International Monetary Fund and continuing peace talks between Habyarimana's MRND party and the RPF, which was seeking to return to Rwanda.

The introduction of multiparty politics and the turmoil surrounding the elections (see section 1.5) set the stage for the radical polarization that led to the massacres in Kayenzi. Mujyambere joined the opposition party MDR. He disliked the direction politics was taking. Those mayors, like Mujyambere, who joined opposition parties were replaced by MRND loyalists in 1992 when the RPF attacked northern Rwanda for the second time. In Kayenzi Mujyambere was replaced by Mbarubukeye Jean. (Mujyambere and his family fled to Zaire, to the Muku camp, and remained there.) It was Mbarubukeye who recruited some of the restless unemployed youth into the Interahamwe, the MRND and CDR youth organization, and sent them off to receive special training in killing. It was Mbarubukeye who led the attack on opponents of the regime, including some of his own Hutu staff and all Tutsi in the populace.

War Erupts in Kayenzi

The Rwandan war of 1994 can be seen in terms of two phases: first, the massacres of the regime's enemies; and second, the advancing attack by the RPF. Both phases occurred in Kayenzi, with some overlap, creating horrible killing, fear, and chaos. The accounts that follow include some repetition, like the replaying of the same film. But they demonstrate that various people and families reacted differently to the same unfolding event because of their different social situation and their own unique location in the chaos of the war, with often fateful consequences. Obviously these accounts are by survivors and do not include killers. The first two accounts are by targeted Tutsi men who miraculously survived but whose families were decimated. The second two accounts are by Hutu women who fled with their families but returned.

Nkurikiyinka Damien is the sole surviving male of a large, old Tutsi lineage of Kayenzi. He survived with his wife and children; they took in one grand-niece, whose parents and family were killed in the genocide. He was a secondary school history teacher before the war and was appointed mayor by the new government. He said the return of Sekimonyo Francoise, another refugee, made possible the beginning of his healing. He wanted eagerly to hear from us that Mujyambere, the former mayor of Kayenzi, would return. Nkurikiyinka and his family are devout Catholics, and he sometimes leads local worship.

Nkurikiyinka related in an interview in Kayenzi on December 4, 1994:

> The massacres took place in full light of day with lots of witnesses. Some who participated in the massacres have fled; this is the case with [Mbarubukeye Jean], the former mayor who coordinated the killing and himself killed some; he personally shot the veterinarian and the agronomist and his family, both of whom were Hutu, because they were protecting Tutsi.
>
> In Kayenzi there were some but not many Interahamwe. They had bayonets, they had grenades, small hoes, with which they hacked people. Everyone was afraid of them. They were young unemployed youth who joined the Interahamwe. But there were also good boys, who were good earlier, who also joined. But they all fled. Military and people of the hills also participated in the killing, even 12–14-year-olds.

Nkurikiyinka, like other Rwandans who experienced extreme loss of family in the massacres, was seemingly emotionless about the experiences. Only once in our afternoon conversation did he choke up, but mostly he told the story of the massacres, how he and his family survived, and the history of his lineage and the commune in a matter-of-fact tone of voice that betrayed a surreal mixture of shock and self-control.

> My mother, my father, 3 brothers and 2 sisters, 6 paternal uncles and their entire families—a total of 130 individuals—were killed. Myself, my wife and children, and one grand-niece were all who survived in our lineage. The genocide was nearly accomplished.

At this point in his deliberate narrative he, like so many others who experienced a terrible ordeal, told of those remarkable exceptions of acquaintances and strangers who had resisted participation in the massacre or who were not killed in selective instances for reasons of neighborliness, friendship, and other special circumstances.

> Our life was threatened three times. The first time a friend paid off the assailants after the Interahamwe came. The second time it was soldiers who came to my door. Our little daughter told the soldiers, "Kill us all so we can be together in heaven," whereupon the soldier lost interest; he didn't want

> her blood on his hands. The third time an Interahamwe acquaintance protected me.
>
> Only the grace of God can explain why we survived; perhaps because I had tried to do well by my people as a teacher and church worker, leading services in the absence of the priest.

Nkurikiyinka continued:

> Many of my lineage were killed by a grenade. They were put in a huge pit, then burned. Now the bones are protruding from the dirt. I do not know who killed my parents. There are many stories and rumors. As a leader of the community and as a Christian, I only want to follow the truth and not repeat these stories unless the truth is known.

Most outside observers of this Rwandan massacre of Rwandans have had a hard time understanding, really grasping what would lead to an attempt to eliminate an entire segment of a society. Nkurikiyinka had an answer to our question. Although he had earlier said that there was enough land for everyone, he later admitted to us that there were rivalries over land even within families. But he insisted that this was not the real source of the hatred. That came from elsewhere, he explained.

> One source of the hatred of Tutsis had been the politics of ethnic equilibrium, requiring only one Tutsi to nine Hutu in entry positions to secondary school. This was the quota system; it was well known even in the United Nations. They didn't want [the Tutsi] to advance, but many had nevertheless. It was also used in hiring, but they had gone into business instead.
>
> Second, the authorities refused to give passports to those expatriates who wanted to return even for a visit. The government thus and in other ways prevented them from returning.
>
> Third, when they negotiated to share power and return, this had created further hostility. When they came back by force, that was too much.
>
> Then there was the rhetoric of hate by the president's family. Even before Habyarimana's murder on April 6, 1994, one of his family had ranted [on Radio Mille Collines] about *kunyuza abatutsi iya Nyabarongo* [to send the Tutsi away through the Nyabarongo River], meaning they should be eliminated. Then, on April 7 the massacres of Tutsi began.

These reasons given by Nkurikiyinka seemed to be symptomatic of even deeper causes that he would or could not articulate. Nkurikiyinka drew a statistical picture of the Kayenzi massacres. Of 45,000 persons who had previously lived in Kayenzi, 8,000–9,000 were killed, 98% of which were Tutsi; 500 had fled, mostly to eastern Zaire.

Ten Days in the Pit

Another powerful witness of the genocide was Ndayambaje Ibrahim (interviewed in Kayenzi on December 7, 1994). Ndayambaje, a 29-year-old Muslim, identifies himself as a poor Tutsi peasant farmer. He is a survivor, with his younger brother, of a massacre that killed most of his family. He was rescued by his Hutu Muslim godfather from a pit filled with corpses. He met his tormentors some months later and spoke with them about their deeds. He was working for the Salvation Army in Kayenzi when we met him.

> Above all, the war was against the Tutsi *ethnie*. The inhabitants of the other race, the Hutu, took the decision to kill all the Tutsi. The administration agreed to this action. The people began to take their neighbors to kill them. They used machetes, hammers, knives, and spears. People were thrown into holes and left there [Figure 30]. I left home to come to the commune. Then I met the enemies, who hit me, cut me, tied me with cords, and took me to the pits at the commune. Before they could cut off my head with a machete, I jumped into the pit. They threw rocks at my head. In the pit, very deep down, I encountered the dead. This was April 16 or 17.
>
> I stayed in the pit for two weeks. They threw other bodies into the pit and threw more rocks at me, telling me I needed to die with as much pain and suffering as possible. They said, "You are the enemy." I stayed there, in pain, without eating or drinking, with all my wounds. [He showed me his scars and broken tooth at this point in his narrative.]
>
> I prayed to my God. After 10 days a man came, my godfather, and he heard my cry.

Ndayambaje's godfather was the man who had taught him to drive and who had introduced him to the Islamic faith. The extraordinary courage of this man is demonstrated by the way he approached the Kayenzi mayor, who had just coordinated the genocide, to rescue his godson, a Tutsi, from the pit. Ndayambaje's account continues:

> [My godfather] was at the communal offices, where he said, "I will get my son to give him a good funeral." He let down a cord, told me to grab hold. I was too weak, so he made a sling and pulled me out. The administration, hearing [I was alive], said to take me to the hospital. But after three days in the hospital, the enemies who had thrown me into the pit heard I was in the hospital. They came to get me to put me in the pit again. Hearing this, my godfather stole me from the hospital and took me to his house where I stayed hidden for two months until the next administration took over.

Figure 30 a + b. (a) Ndayambaje Ibrahim beside the pit into which he jumped to elude his assassins. He spent 10 days among bodies of other victims, bits of whose remains can still be seen (b).

Only later, after the war, would Ndayambaje learn from his 8-year-old brother that his father and mother and all his other siblings except for an older sister living elsewhere had been killed by the Interahamwe. They had packed his family, with many others, into a building and then thrown a grenade into it. The 8-year-old boy had somehow survived.

Flight to the Zone Turquoise

Uwintije Celestine was a teacher and her husband had worked at a government ministry before the war. Both are Hutu. They rescued and hid three daughters of Tutsi friends who were massacred. Uwintije and her family fled with the girls to Cyangugu during the opening stages of the war and later returned to Kayenzi. Uwintije and her husband now run a shop in Kayenzi; her husband became a merchant, as did most Rwandans after the war. Their small store in the Kayenzi commercial center overlooks the market. In the small clapboard space they sell hard orange-red palm oil from a big barrel, dried beans from large sacks, sugar, flour, sorghum, batteries, salt, USAID cooking oil, detergent, and little cans of tomato paste. Uwintije belongs to the Seventh Day Adventist church, whereas her husband and her children are Catholic.

Uwintije related her most significant experience at the time the war broke out (from an interview in Kayenzi on December 4, 1994).

> Some Tutsis fled and hid after April 21. The three sisters arrived, daughters of a friend who was killed. We are Hutu, but because of God's love we keep them. The Interahamwe gave us much trouble. They would have killed the girls, but we paid them and they left. When the soldiers of [Prime Minister] Kambanda came, they also killed the Tutsi. We saw that soldiers and Interahamwe were fleeing past here, we saw some who knew us. Then bombs of the Rwandan Patriotic Front began to fall behind the stores. We also fled because of the Interahamwe. We left June 20, before the soldiers of the RPF arrived.
>
> We hoped to go where they wouldn't know us. We thought at Bukavu there would be more [of a chance that the girls would be discovered] so we chose to go to Cyangugu where there would be French soldiers to protect us. We wanted to save the children until peace. We saw that the RPF was beating those who had committed crimes *[malfaiteurs]* and we were afraid that we would be accused.

Uwintije described their life in the French protected Zone Turquoise.

> At Cyangugu the French soldiers were not a problem either. There were empty houses, left by those who had killed and fled. We stayed in a private school, we took food along. The French weren't able to keep some from killing and pillaging. The Interahamwe continued to kill in the camp till today. A doctor from here fled to Bukavu; some saw him, and they knew him and killed him, even though he is Hutu. Maybe because of his studies in the United States? Who knows. In Cyangugu, life wasn't bad, but we had to find food supplemental to relief goods. Schools finished there. Adults worked with the French to distribute food. We were unemployed otherwise. In the school two to three families lived together. Cooking was done outside. Not much trouble with health, because the French opened a hospital. Women giving birth were hospitalized.

After two months at Cyangugu in the French protected zone, Uwintije and her family needed to make a choice; the French were pulling out, and many of the Rwandans who had sought sanctuary in the Zone Turquoise were moving on to Zaire rather than face the RPF. She described their decision:

> My husband, however, decided to return. "God is the judge," he said, "Let's return." We returned on the 18th of August, my husband, our family, and the Tutsi girls. We had the pickup of a friend with which we had fled, so we returned. It took two days and was not a problem.

On their return they found the scars of the war in Kayenzi, not the least in family lives lost.

> We lost the wife of my husband's brother and their daughter. In my husband's family there were three persons lost, and my family lost four. The Interahamwe in my family were killed by the RPF. This was during the war. We found their bodies at their house. The head of their household was a licensed psychologist. In my husband's family a woman and her child died. They did not find their bodies. Down the hill, one was killed by the Interahamwe and we found the body.

Uwintije also detailed the looting of their household. She explained that her house had been totally pillaged during their stay at the camp at Cyangugu.

> At our house here, everything was stolen, much was broken. We found some of the goods and furniture. This table is new. Otherwise, everything you see here was given back. We knew who had taken the furniture, linen, casseroles, and tableware and simply asked for these things to be returned.

One afternoon I (Reinhild) went out on a walk with one of the teachers to the school where Uwintije had taught, where the depths of the war's wounds on the community became apparent. She spoke of many things that were on her heart. She mentioned reliable sources in the area who knew a lot about the "events." It was said that the RPF killed many people in July, dumping the corpses into destroyed outhouses, and that an investigation into this situation would shed bad light on the RPF. It was also said that many people left their churches after the war because they saw Christians do terrible things. Before the war there were about 540 children in the primary school, but in 1994 two classrooms had been closed because so many children had died; the school buildings, consisting of two rows of mud-brick structures covered with corrugated-tin sheets and packed dirt floors and wooden shutters over glassless window openings, were used by refugees fleeing Kigali right after the war started; the refugees cooked inside some of the classrooms, where one can still see walls blackened with soot.

A small group of children attached itself to us while we visited some of the classrooms. There were lessons in English, French, ecology, and arithmetic written in chalk on the blackboards. I saw no books, no papers, no visual aids, no equipment other than long rows of rough planks as benches and equally rough raised planks as tables and lots of blackboards. In the corner of one class a short grass broom and plastic water container stood ready for the constant battle against fleas. Schoolchildren carried small cardboard chalkboards on which to practice writing. Between the two rows of classroom buildings, at the end of the large bare yard stood a Presbyterian chapel where the youth choir was practicing. The teacher asked them to sing for us. There were several drums, one of which was used to accompany their singing. The only church furniture was a pulpit platform constructed of plastered mud bricks and backless low benches also made of mud bricks and covered with straw matting. Here too, wooden shutters covered the glassless window openings. From this hillside we could see the Nyabarongo River into which bodies were dumped by the hundreds and thousands.

I asked Uwintije whether she would encourage her children, including her three adopted daughters, to draw what they remembered of the events that led to their flight to the French zone at Cyangugu. I left paper, pencils, and a box of crayons

Figure 31. The genocide in Kayenzi, drawn by Umukesha Carine; pencil and crayon on paper, December 6–7, 1994. In narrow horizontal bands are the images of the Interahamwe militias armed with clubs and machetes, hacking and clubbing their victims to death and tossing the dead into great communal pits or into the river; in the bottom band people flee with all their belongings, some carrying loads on their heads, herding cattle along, while bodies lie along the road. The only colors used in Umukesha's drawing are green for grass and roadside forest and red for blood of the wounded and the dying and for cooking fires.

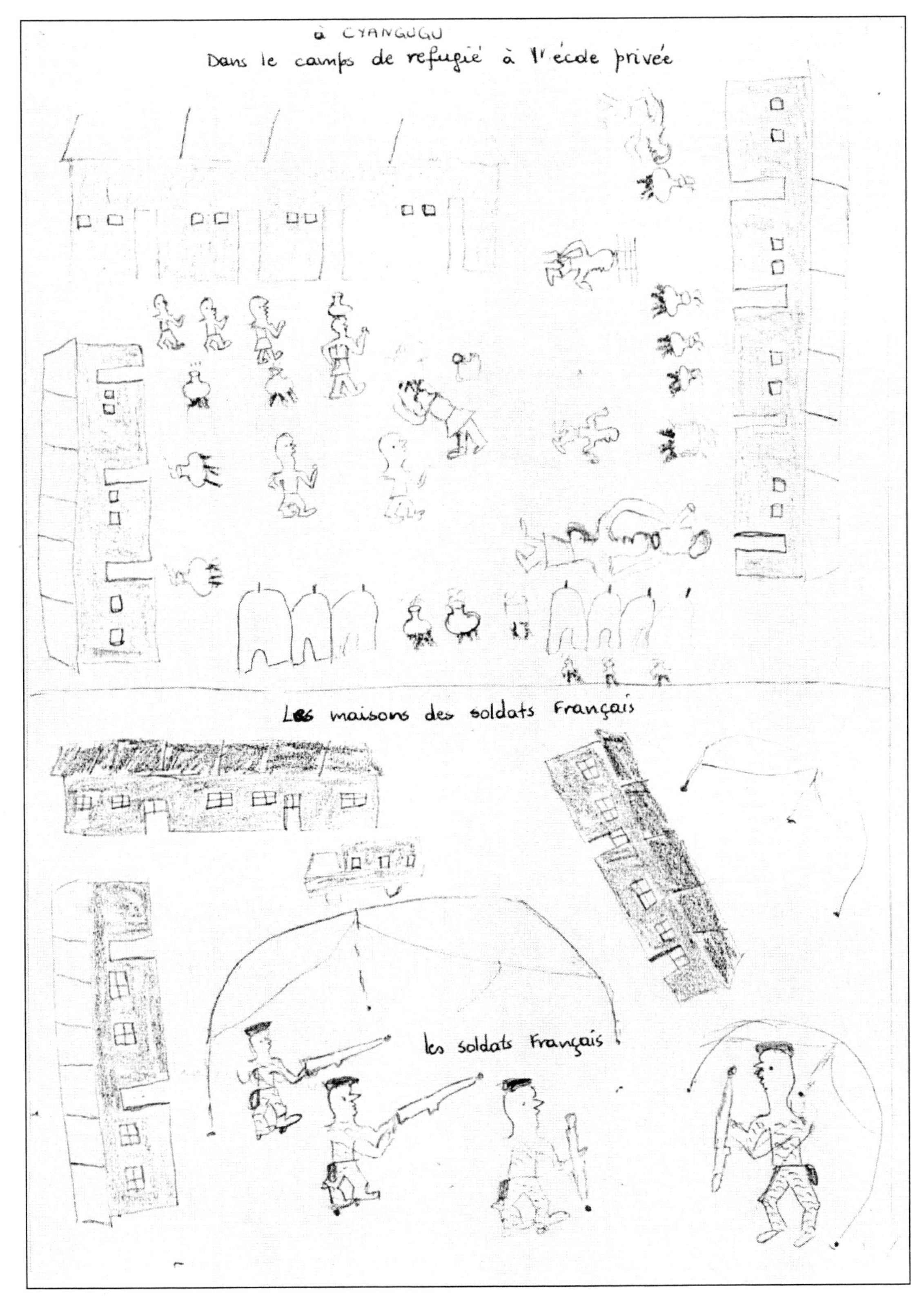

Figure 32. The flight to the French-protected Zone Turquoise, drawn by Umukesha Carine's. The drawing shows the refugee camp in a private school at Cyangugu with the many outdoor cooking fires, the French soldiers and their tents, and the makeshift grass huts of other refugees.

with her, saying I would appreciate collecting the drawings the following day. When I returned to Uwintije's house, she gave me four drawings: one by her 20-year-old children's maid; one by a 16-year-old orphaned girl (see Figures 31 and 32); one by Uwintije's 6-year-old daughter; and one by her 5-year-old girl. These drawings record the mass killings of Tutsi by Interahamwe militia, the dumping of bodies into rivers and pits, and the flight of people to the Zone Turquoise. The storyline and the compositional organization of the images in all four drawings are identical, so that one can assume that the teacher in Uwintije assembled the children around the large table in the family's living room, under the same lantern light, and suggested the sequence of events that the children then drew with much narrative detail. It may be that the younger children copied from the older children, but each contributed her own emphasis and unique motifs. In one drawing several women are carrying babies on their backs and many small children are amid the stream of refugees. Another drawing shows how during their flight the refugees cook along the roadside and how cooking fires burn brightly under the pots. The 5-year-old adds a scene of pillaging to the massacres of the Interahamwe. Two figures set a house roof on fire while its inhabitants flee, carrying possessions on their heads.

Fear and Flight

Mbaduko Gabriel and Sekimonyo Francoise, husband and wife, were teachers at a private school in Kayenzi. Both Hutu, they fled to Zaire on foot with their family in the second phase of the war, ahead of the advancing RPF army. They were refugees in the Muku camp for a time and decided to return to Kayenzi. They had just completed a new house when the war broke out. After returning from the refugee camp, Mbaduko earned his livelihood as a small merchant and by renting his house to an NGO. The couple has four children who are in their early 20s and teens.

Sekimonyo's account (from an interview in Kayenzi on December 4, 1994) gives a description of the arrival of the fighting after the downing of President Habyarimana's plane. Almost like a medieval account of the approaching plague, the massacres come nearer and nearer.

> It started in Kigali. We heard they were killing. One didn't know exactly what was going on. On the hill [Kayenzi hill] there were massacres, one after another. Everyone was angry. Then it reached here. Then we heard killing on our *colline;* it had arrived here, at the neighbors. . . .
>
> In order to save our lives, we left everything behind, including our livestock. When we decided to flee the advancing RPF troops, we took one suitcase, some food, a little cash and walked and walked, sleeping along the roadside or in schools or abandoned houses.
>
> We left before the arrival of the RPF, because we heard they killed. We—our whole family—fled to Zaire, leaving June 26, on foot, with thousands others fleeing. All the places, then Bukavu. The nights were passed on the road or in schools. Same with cooking, on the road. We brought clothes and food—what we could carry, like beans. When we got there, we needed money to live. We sold our radio to a Zairian. We arrived [at Muku] when the Mennonites began their work. The children went to get water, and so forth. We stayed in a school classroom, because school was on vacation. There were few diseases in that camp of about 1,000.
>
> We were there one month. Then we heard the battle was over from others who had stayed here. We heard the RPF was killing those who had killed, but since we were innocent, we returned. We took a taxi. There were pastors with us. Others are still there, like our neighbor [Mujyambere Mathias] next door. Because we had no support, we decided to leave. Others with more means stayed.

Sekimonyo continued her account of what they found when they returned to Kayenzi.

> The house had been robbed bare. All we had was suitcases and a cooking pot. All the rest had been taken. No furniture, no cooking utensils; even the curtains were gone. We were able to find the chairs. We knew who had taken them, and they were returned. Others gave us a few things. We had just moved into the new house, but now we rent it out to earn money.

As for the human losses in her family, Sekimonyo said:

> My mother and brother, his wife, six children, in Kayonza commune, they were not there. We asked their neighbors who said they were dead. I hope they fled, and I wait for a letter, but nothing so far. No corpses, either, have been found. They say the RPF took them away in a truck, but we don't know whether they're alive or not.

The story recounted by Sekimonyo and Mbaduko was similar to that of Makarakiza Andre, who had also been a secondary school teacher in Kayenzi. A Hutu, Makarakiza fled with his wife and family to Zaire. He too returned to Kayenzi with his son in October 1994, when Sekimonyo returned with her family. Makarakiza then left his son behind, intending to return with his wife. However, he became fearful of returning and continued to stay in the Muku camp with the other refugees from Kayenzi who did not return. Like so many other Rwandans, Makarakiza's family became split—some inside the country and others outside, a reflection of the larger constructions of reality that tore at the fabric of Rwandan society.

The Struggle between Conflicting Realities

We became aware of the gulf between conflicting versions of reality held by the several segments of Kayenzi and, more generally, Rwanda when we traveled from Rwanda, including Kayenzi, to Bukavu and Muku in early December. It was not exactly a Hutu-Tutsi division of reality but a division between those who believed they could live in the new Rwanda and those who had committed crimes and could not return. Between these two camps there were many who were afraid to return. They might not have committed crimes but they feared unfounded accusations.

When we were in Kayenzi, just before traveling to Bukavu, we agreed to take many letters along. We asked our Kayenzi friends what we should tell those in the Muku camp. The responses were indicative of where the speaker stood in the versions of reality.

Nkurikiyinka, who was working with the new government as mayor, encouraged us to tell the refugees in Zaire to come back. All Rwandans must come together and construct a new Rwanda. He noted that about 100 families who had fled had returned, such as Uwintije and Sekimonyo. They live well. He urged us to tell the refugees that it is not true that soldiers kill those who return.

Sekimonyo, Nkurikiyinka's neighbor who is on speaking terms with him, had a different response to the question of what we should tell the Muku and Mushweshwe refugees from Kayenzi:

> The Muku people, what should one tell them? I don't know. When you see what's happening among the neighbors . . . When we returned, many were dead, who were said to have killed. It takes only one to say "you participated" and you're taken. There is no inquest. The Tutsi who didn't get killed name groups that killed, and maybe you were among them. Those with us have no guarantee—thus one cannot encourage them. If there would be a tribunal, one could judge these things. We've seen how people have been put in prison. We don't know what happens to them. Where? I don't know. Numerous ones from here. When we returned, we wrote those [in the camps] to come; some there did participate, others not.

Sekimonyo identified how the massacres had polarized people who had been the best of friends before the war.

> In this commune there were few Interahamwe. They were of the president's party. Here we were of the party MDR, and one of the ministers was from here. . . .But the massacres drew out vengeance; Tutsi took revenge on those who killed their kin or [were rumored to do so], even if it wasn't true.

Uwintije told us of precisely such a case, her own sister.

> The RPF imprisoned people who have not killed. My older sister—she is 44 years old from the commune Taba—was beaten by Interahamwe because she hid Tutsi. The Interahamwe also ate her two cows. She is now in prison at Gitarama, accused by Tutsi who were neighbors. A Tutsi woman accused her of being Interahamwe. Other neighbors said she was innocent. This accuser may have had an old grudge against her.

When we returned to Kayenzi in late December 1994, we brought many letters from the camps near Bukavu. We walked over to Uwintije's house near the commercial center to say hello and to deliver some letters to her. We also had letters for Sekimonyo's husband, Mbaduko Gabriel, and mayor Nkurikiyinka Damien. The letters came from these people's friends and relatives in the Muku camp.

Uwintije in her unique open, querying, careful way invited us in, and we talked for a while. She obviously wanted to know what it was really like in Zaire, what was happening there. She again spoke of arbitrary arrests in Rwanda.

> A Kayenzi man had returned from Zaire. He was well for a while. Then he began his commerce with his truck, people and goods. Just outside of Kigali at a military checkpoint he was told that his truck had been used by the Interahamwe and that it was being confiscated as evidence by the military! He panicked, fled into the bush, and hasn't been seen or heard from since then. The truck had possibly been stolen by the Interahamwe, but was that a reason to confiscate it and arrest this man? Or were the soldiers simply using this as a pretext to steal the truck?

Uwintije was worried about her husband, who, as a merchant, meets many people; some of the contacts are danger-filled.

> You buy produce from someone as a merchant; that person is accused of being an Interahamwe, and suddenly you are charged with having been an accomplice to the massacres.

Later, Mbaduko came by, having earlier encountered us on the path from the commune, and joined us back in his house behind that of the mayor. He also wanted to know of conditions in the camps in Zaire. We gave him our impressions. Soon he opened up and told of all the arbitrary arrests and lack of security.

At the end of the afternoon, as we were preparing to return to Kigali, I had occasion to meet with Nkurikiyinka. He had been suffering from malaria and diarrhea and looked gaunt. I explained that we had come to deliver letters from the camps in Zaire, from the Kayenzi people at the Muku camp in particular. He asked about his friend Mujyambere. Did he intend to return? I told him what I had heard: that Mujyambere was well, with his family, and that the only reason he had not come home was because there was no place on the truck he had wanted to take. I spoke of the thinking among many of the refugees we met that the old government still spoke for them and that there was a lack of security in Rwanda because of the arrests of people. I emphasized that it seemed to me that isolated accounts (e.g., the theft of cars and killing of night watchmen by RPF soldiers at the Tanzanian embassy, the flight of a man across Lake Kivu because someone wanted to steal his tin roof) were gossiped about to form people's opinions but that they had little good, objective, verified news from Rwanda. I suggested to Nkurikiyinka that there should be some way of bridging the gap between the two realities and told him this is what we were hoping to do in taking letters back and forth. No other agency or postal service was doing this.

Nkurikiyinka the mayor had quite another view on the issue of two realities, repatriation, letters, and security perceptions. First of all, he judged that the people in the camps were getting a lot of false information either from the extremists in the old government or from the very letters that were being sent to them. There were other issues at play. He suggested that some of the people writing to their refugee friends and family were purposely warning of insecurity and arbitrary arrests to keep them away. Why? Because these people—some very close to him—were now occupying houses and using land that would have to be shared if their refugee relations were to return.

I (John) must confess that I had never thought of the possibility of such a manipulation, but I quickly recalled the stories as told in Rwandan folktales and in Burundian author Katihabwa Sebastian's collection of brothers feuding over cattle and land and killing each other over them. I wondered, Were we contributing to this false impression by carrying letters? Nkurikiyinka said that it was useful for agencies such as the UNHCR and the International Red Cross to report names and conditions in camps and at home, but it was not helpful to spread false rumors. Was he referring to our letter exchanges?

Before we departed, Nkurikiyinka reiterated that those who had not committed massacres had nothing to fear and should come home. The guilty would be arrested and tried, beginning in mid-1995 in collaboration with the international tribunal.

Vengeance, Fear, Justice, Forgiveness, Healing, and Hope in Kayenzi

The contradictory realities described by these six families fueled a broad gamut of actions and attitudes among the families and others in Kayenzi. Nkurikiyinka, the mayor, was in charge of the arrests of known killers, along with the RPF soldiers who occupied the commune, with their occasional roadblocks. By mid-December 1994 he had made 21 arrests of individuals who had been taken by the army or police to prison in Gitarama, the court of first instance. His statement of what would happen to them was that "they will be tried by the law." He distinguished sharply between two types of killers:

> Those who were forced to kill, they will be judged but they must come back to their families; they may ask for forgiveness. Perhaps they will be forgiven. God forgives. The second group are animals *[bêtes]*.

Uwintije held similar views of those who had killed.

> The former mayor organized the *Interahamwe*. But all who killed must be judged. Their families have lost them. One is waiting for these killers and when they are in prison, they'll be punished.

Nkurikiyinka and Sekimonyo, neighbors, represented most poignantly the combination of tension and the bonds too complex to divide into opposing sides. The ties between Nkurikiyinka, a Catholic teacher, member of a six-generation Tutsi family in Kayenzi, and newly appointed mayor, and Sekimonyo, a middle-class Hutu whose family had benefited from the decades of independence in Rwanda, were forged by a lifetime together as teachers and neighbors. Nkurikiyinka, the most grievously hurt of any of the families by the near extermination of his lineage, told us how much he cherished Sekimonyo and her husband. He said he owed Sekimonyo his sanity and that "she had healed me by coming back from the refugee camp."

In other words, with her returning, he was able to visualize a future with all Rwandans who had not committed grievous crimes. He still hoped for a united Rwanda that could be rebuilt. He had nothing but scorn for the three-ethnic-group theory of Rwandan society, which he dismissed as a pure lie *(un mensonge pur)*.

> The colonialists used the terms Hutu, Tutsi, and Twa; this classification didn't exist before then. These terms, this ethnic classification, became a poison. Although 98% of those killed were Tutsi, the ethnic question is one of the past. We live in Rwanda, and we are Rwandans.

Sekimonyo and her family had cast their lot with the new Rwanda by returning home. On the surface all seemed well. They had rented their house to the Salvation Army for use in the postwar food distribution and health support which Nkurikiyinka oversaw at the commune. Yet the threads that held this particular social pact together were thin and strained. When Sekimonyo visited us with her son, she passionately gave us her view:

> If there is more vengeance, the cycle of violence will go on. We have need of justice first; then perhaps there can be forgiveness. When someone has committed massacres, even if it were my son, he needs to be punished. But if he is innocent, he should be free. Like this, it was barbarian. But when you see the innocent taken, the cycle will continue.

To which her son added, with a tone of resignation, "There is the commune's court, but they do nothing. If you're a youth, and the military decide to take you, you can do nothing."

Sekimonyo's hope was that the two parties—those in exile and those who returned or had never left—could meet and see what has happened: "Then they might reconcile. But we wait for those others to return one day. The two could meet, talk. Without it, we won't be tranquil." As teacher, mother, wife, and community member, Sekimonyo could visualize a better day. When Reinhild asked her what gave her joy and beauty, she had this to say:

> When one is among one's own, we're content. That is enough. No member of the family is falsely accused, I'm content. What is beauty in my life? I can't reply. Things, flowers, gardens, decorations for the house; the crops growing—beans, bananas—they're beautiful. We had cattle before the war, but all were killed and eaten. What is beautiful to me? To see my loved ones around me.

Uwintije, too, was able to speak of a better life despite the horrors beyond imagination. "Now after the war, death is no big thing. Before, family came and brought food, and so on." In answer to the question of why there was no crying among the Rwandans, she said, "Because of the enormity of the tragedy, because everybody has lost people." To the questions of what gives her joy, what is beautiful to her, Uwintije responded:

> That I have saved the young girls and that I see them before me; that my husband is gentle and that he loves people *[C'est que mon mari est doux, il aime des gens]*. Flowers. The grace of God gives me joy, I want to sing all the time that He has wrought miracles during the war.

Her hope for the future was "That the Interahamwe would not continue killing; that we can live, educate our children; that we can raise these girls."

Ndayambaje, whose harrowing experiences might have left him bitter, appeared to have learned the difference between good and bad people. He was particularly full of praise for his godfather, a Hutu who had saved his life, just as many Muslim Hutu saved Tutsi by hiding them in their homes. Of his godfather, he said "he has a joyful heart." Those who had killed were another matter for Ndayambaje. He recounted his experience of meeting up with one of his tormentors.

> Some who killed were taken to prison by the administration. I know who they are, they were from here. They have an evil heart. I saw one of these men who hit me while we were distributing seeds with Jacques [of the Salvation Army].
>
> I asked him, "Do you remember me?" He said yes.
>
> I pressed him, "Do you accept that you hurt me?"
>
> "Yes."

> But he asked me to pardon him. I said, "If you admit that you did it, I'll forgive you."

Ndayambaje thought it would be possible for there to be reconciliation like this between the two sides, especially if there was not another war. He spoke of his own personal reasons for being able to forgive his adversary: "If God forgives me, I should pardon others. I continue to praise God, who is stronger than all other powers."

Remembering the Dead

Ndayambaje took me (John) behind the cooperative warehouse to the communal pit for the disposal of diseased animals into which he had jumped and where he had been entombed among the corpses for 10 days before being rescued by his godfather. As we stood there and I photographed the pit (see Figure 30) with its human bones and debris visible about 20 feet down, he said that about 90 people had been thrown into it.

In late December 1994 Nkurikiyinka was preoccupied with the size of plastic sheeting he would request from the Salvation Army, Kayenzi's NGO partner in reconstruction. This plastic sheeting, of the kind that dotted all Rwanda and the refugee camps, would be used to line and cover the mass graves into which the victims in the open pits around Kayenzi were to be reburied. A memorial service and reburial was planned for January 3, 1995. Two mass graves would measure 2.5 m long by 1.5 m wide by 2.5 m deep. Into them would be put the remains of some of the mass graves hastily dug and filled in April and May 1994. For Nkurikiyinka, whose own flesh and blood were in those horrible sites, this would be the first step toward proper recognition of the victims of the war, including most of his lineage of the Gesera clan of Kayenzi.

Updates

In a letter to us in March 1996 Mujyambere wrote from the Muku camp in Zaire about developments in Kayenzi.

> Things are becoming more and more complicated in our commune. The news is not good, for many have been imprisoned, assassinated. In the communal prison there are now 400 detained. Our homes are occupied by refugees and others who have returned to the commune.

He pleaded with us to send them cash support and offered in his next writing to tell much news of the region. That would not be possible because Bukavu and the regions of the camps were overrun by the Zairian liberation forces led by the Banyamulenge and Laurent Kabila in November 1996. Although a few of the refugees in the camps near Bukavu trickled back to Rwanda, most fled westward ahead of Kabila and the Rwandan forces. Many apparently died from the ordeals of flight through the rainforest, from disease, and reprisals.

Sekimonyo wrote from Kayenzi in mid-1996 that Uwintije's husband and two of the girls had died from sickness. Their families were otherwise well, she said, but life was difficult. She asked whether we could help her son obtain a scholarship for studies in the United States. She wrote again in mid-1999 and related, among other news, that Nkurikiyinka continued to be the mayor.

A 1996 United Nations report would cite Kayenzi for human rights abuses of prisoners, but Sekimonyo noted in her 1999 letter that Kayenzi was more secure.

Ironies and Imponderable Questions

Many questions arise from this glimpse of Kayenzi, but there are few answers. As exceptional as the buildup of a killing machine and the transformation of individuals willing to go along with it was the seemingly common reaction of others to risk their lives to save those who were threatened. At the same time as mayor Mbarubukeye shot his own communal veterinarian and the agronomist, Uwintije and her husband took in and fled with the three Tutsi girls; Ndayambaje was so inspired by the bold acts of rescue of his Hutu godfather that he could forgive his unsuccessful would-be killers. The extreme divergence of members of one and the same community under the pressure of ideological mass hysteria challenges us to find an analysis that illuminates what drove people on the two sides.

Other questions and ironies call out for answers. What moved some of those who fled to return? Why did Uwintije and her family return from the French-occupied Zone Turquoise in southwest Rwanda? What compelled Sekimonyo and her family to return from Zaire? Was it knowing that their former neighbor Nkurikiyinka had become the new mayor? Then why did not Mujyambere and Makarakiza return, knowing that Nkurikiyinka so longed for it?

What can we learn from the healing of Nkurikiyinka by Sekimonyo's return that can be applied to the healing of Rwandan society at large? Does Nkurikiyinka's authorization to have citizens of Kayenzi arrested and turned over to the Gitarama authorities without prospect of a prompt trial represent the kind of justice that Sekimonyo, Mbaduko, and Uwintije long for? If their relatives are among these, is this simply too painful to accept? Can a community such as Kayenzi tame the particular beast that is Rwandan (and Burundian) ethnicity, the fracture between Hutu and Tutsi? Can this best be done by "negating the lie" as Nkurikiyinka argues, or by accepting the cleavage, naming the historical categories, and trying to live together as Rwandans?

2.2 Resistance to Genocide in Giti

A Report of Normal Grieving

John Ruaue, an Irish medical doctor with the Irish Refugee Trust, was assigned by the Ministry of Rehabilitation to work at Rwesero Hospital in Giti commune, an hour's drive north of Kigali. In the Ste. Famille parish guesthouse in Kigali he met Harold Otto and told him that he had heard there had been few massacres in this area. His interest had been piqued when he brought the body of a child who had died in the hospital back to its natal community; the family and neighbors met him with a visible outpouring of grief, the first time he had seen this in Rwanda. This mourning stood in sharp contrast to the apparently emotionless response to experienced atrocities that he had seen in his practice. He thought the two phenomena—grieving of death and no massacres—might be related. We decided to go to Giti to learn more. Later, we would come to understand the case of Giti as a remarkable lesson in the consequences of the courage by authority figures to stand up to the spreading recourse to violence.

One informant for this story was Nsengiyumva Patrice, Ruaue's interpreter and a young humanities student from the area; Muhawe Naason, a medical assistant at Rwesero Hospital; Gatete Immanuel, Giti commune secretary and sector inspector; and Rubagumya Innocent, communal agronomist, provided details in one visit to the commune. Most important, Sebushumbe Edouard, a Hutu, was mayor of Giti throughout the war. As a member of the MRND party, he could have been as involved in the planning of a genocide as other MRND mayors, but he also had the authority to thwart preparations for such an eventuality. His account details the preparations for genocide, which he did not follow, as his commune became a refuge for those fleeing surrounding communes.

The War in Giti

We took a taxi to Rwesero Hospital along Lake Muhazi in the Buganza region. Once one leaves the paved road northward from Kigali to Uganda, the road to Rwesero follows the long narrow lake that is the southern boundary of Giti commune. Homesteads and fields cover the hillsides just as elsewhere in Rwanda, and small commercial centers and schools are strung along the roads. What makes the region around Lake Muhazi special is the rich opportunity for fishing in its waters. Boats were out every time we drove along Lake Muhazi, reputed to be an abundant source of big fish. This region was the center of Buganza, the original core of the Rwandan kingdom and the Nyiginya dynasty (Vansina 1962, p. 61).

Ruaue was taking a patient to Kigali when we arrived, and he entrusted us to his interpreter, Nsengiyumva, and medical assistant, Muhawe. Nsengiyumva was available because secondary schools were closed; Muhawe had been with the hospital since July 1994. We sat down around a local map in an examination room of Rwesero Hospital next to crowds of patients and care seekers on the veranda to discuss the course of the recent war in Giti (the interview took place on December 9, 1994).

Nsengiyumva and Muhawe confirmed that there had been no massacres in Giti. However, the area had been extensively affected by other consequences of the war. The commune had taken in thousands of displaced persons from the north in February 1993; their shelters were scattered around the commune. Nsengiyumva related:

> The displaced persons pillaged beans from food depots to find something to eat. There were about 25,000 of them. The people here told them, Stop this, or you will be attacked because people are unhappy about this. People were afraid of the displaced because there were extremists among them and the displaced were also against the RPF. People of this area began to ask themselves where they would find refuge. At the moment when the attacks from the Interahamwe and extremists were beginning from all sides, people said if we don't participate in the killing we—meaning the Tutsi—will be killed, and they began to hide. The RPF arrived Wednesday, April 15, and moved through on its way to Kigali. Then the killing stopped, they went right on through. After the death of the president, [Radio] Mille Collines broadcast had announced that no one dare leave their place. This is why there were so many dead people, because they stayed in their houses [and thus fell easy prey to the murderers]. People with machetes were going out to kill, telling others that they would work in the fields. People fabricated stories why they were out with

> their machetes. Some of these people fled to Kigali, others to Tanzania.

Nsengiyumva continued:

> The Muhura mayor had a Tutsi wife. He put his Tutsi family and others in a pickup to Kisiguro, not knowing that the massacres were underway in his commune. They came through a place where all Tutsi were killed. He and his Tutsi wife and children and a policeman were killed at a roadblock.
>
> When there had been the organization of militia, in general, people of Giti did not participate. There were many Tutsi in the population, but everyone lived in symbiosis, together. When the president's plane was shot down and the massacres began, here the mayor was against the massacres and arrested those people. In Gikomero commune to the south the hotheads grabbed their machetes. They killed people and threw them into Lake Muhazi.

Nsengiyumva, a student of African history, had read Jan Vansina, Alexis Kagame, and Ferdinand Nahimana, whom he considered the best sources on Rwandan history. He was quick to find a background reason in local history for the relative absence of massacres in Giti.

> Around Lake Muhazi the people consider themselves Baganza. They do not differentiate themselves between Hutu and Tutsi. Among the Baganza, Tutsi and Hutu merged, intermarried, and many "Hutu became Tutsi." Tutsi lent their cattle to Hutu, and they prospered. "With cattle, they became Tutsi." "Hutu meant poor," "Tutsi meant rich."

Nsengiyumva's and Muhawe's accounts of how Giti commune held out in the face of the genocidal massacres suggested a new picture of the unleashing of the atrocities. Where the Interahamwe were not organized by the communal administration and the mayor was not a party activist, at least not in this respect, it was difficult to launch the killings. With a mayor who went around calming the people and dissuading them from violence, little or no violence occurred. The social fabric remained intact. The main fault line in Giti commune was that between the displaced and the residents. But even this appeared to have been held in check. We resolved to speak to others about this remarkable alternative experience during the Rwandan war and to identify the individuals and the motives of those who stood up to the forces of destruction and death in those fateful days in April.

Flight and Return

Nsengiyumva had not actually been in Giti during the war. He was in Kigali when the killing began and fled with so many others westward to the Bukavu area. At Cyangugu, he and 22 other Tutsi paid an Interahamwe captain 50,000 Rwandan francs (about $150) each to spare their lives and row them across the lake into Zaire, where there was a Tutsi camp. In Zaire he helped to organize supplies and facilities. Eventually, he returned to his home area to learn that his father had been killed, but his mother, a younger brother, and a sister had survived.

Many others of Giti fled into the bushes and hillsides when the massacres began, to avoid the bombings of the confronting armies. A more typical flight and return is sketched by Nsengiyumva's sister, who drew for us her escape from the family homestead to Giti, then across Lake Muhazi to Gikoro, then back to Buyoga, Rutare, and home again (see Figures 33 and 34).

When we were with Nsengiyumva in early December 1994, he lived in Kigali, commuting twice a week to Giti to work at the hospital as an interpreter. Later, he moved home to the countryside near Muhura mission to oversee the restoration of the family, in place of his father. Some 60 members of his lineage had been killed (presumably elsewhere in the country), leaving many orphans to be cared for. His own family's house had been destroyed and needed to be rebuilt.

In late December 1994 we again returned to Giti. The communal secretary, Gatete, with figures tracked carefully in a notebook, said that by 1992 there were 70,000 displaced in Giti and Rutare in addition to the local prewar population of 47,314 in Giti (October 1994) (about 9,000 households). In 1994 there were 1,500 victims, including 387 disappeared among all refugees and residents (from an interview with Gatete Immanuel in Giti on December 27, 1994). However, these figures for the dead and disappeared cannot be reconciled with the claim that there had been no massacres. Other sources suggest that these figures include people killed by the RPF.

The refugees from Rutare wanted revenge. Rubagumya credited the arrival of the RPF with keeping the killing from breaking out. The extremists had their machetes, but people fled to save themselves. He continued:

> In most communes there were organized Interahamwe, here too, and they waited for the command to begin killing; however, no order was given here. They did their singing and manifestations, but they weren't very active. Even in the neighboring sectors, there wasn't much "heat." But if the RPF had

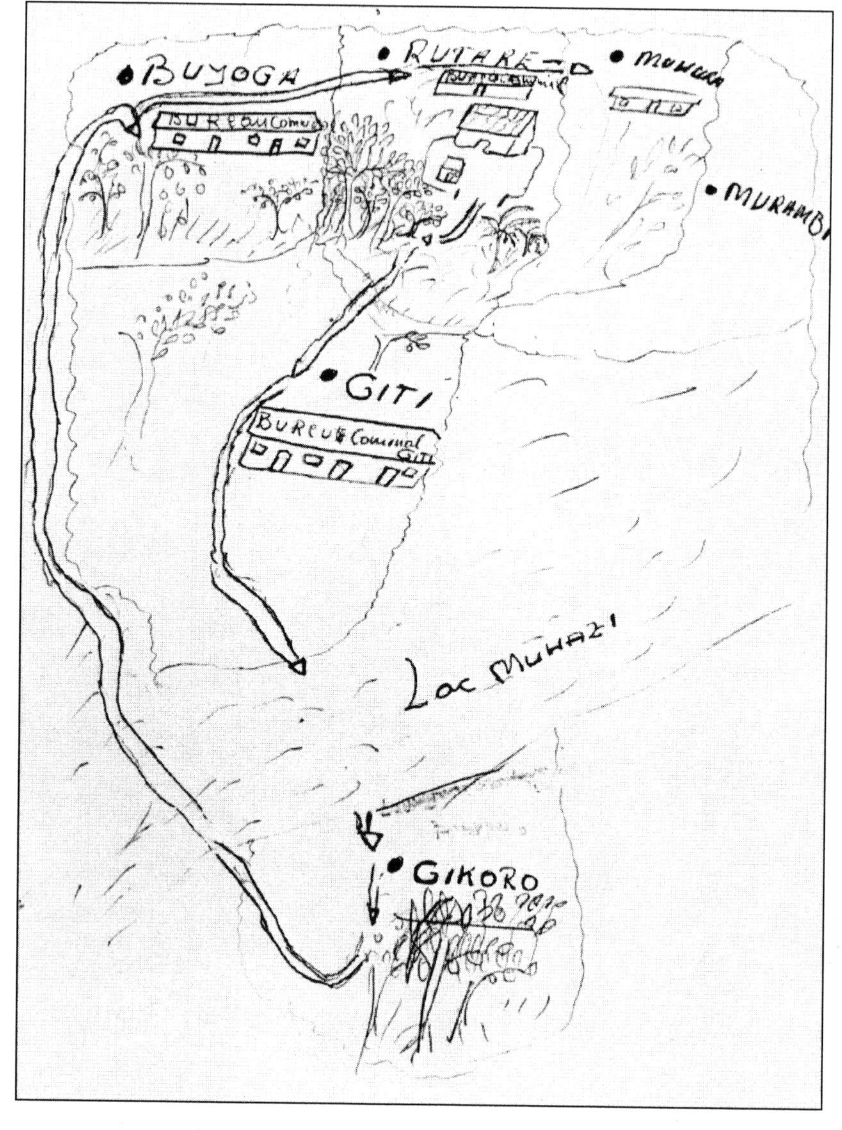

Figure 33. Route of flight and return home of the sister of Nsengiyumva Patrice from the family's compound in northern Giti commune across Lake Muhazi to Gikoro, back to Buyoga, onward to Rutare and then to Muhura. Drawn by Nsengiyumva's younger sister on December 27, 1994.

> not arrived, outsiders would have come to do it. Massacres began as soon as the president was killed, in neighboring communes. We saw houses burning to the south, and refugees were coming here. The mayor told the people to stay calm. Tutsi came from other communes. Some Tutsi were afraid and fled to Rutare, toward the RPF lines; they didn't return and may be among the 1,500 [who were killed]. After April 15, the panic switched sides. All Hutu were now afraid. People came through because Radio Mille Collines was broadcasting for them to leave. Some left for Kigali, Tanzania, others to Zaire, among the Interahamwe and with the other army. Some were killed too. Many people were afraid and fled their homes during the search for Interahamwe, but they returned home after a few days. The refugees who were here before, returned home to the north. Here there were no bombardments. But at Rutare, there was a battle with the old army.

Gatete, Rubagumya, and Nsengiyumva again sought to give reasons for this course of events in Giti that was different from almost everywhere else in Rwanda. One of them explained:

> The mayor risked his life and went around calming the people. People were ready with machetes, especially among the refugees. [But] the refugees noticed, "Everyone here is like Tutsi." The explanation, that there is intermarriage and neighborliness. The refugees were already extremists. But here even in 1959 there were no massacres. Hutu protected Tutsi. People remembered that now. Why? When the others began to kill Tutsis here, they were friends. Even before 1959, Hutu were treated better here. The same was true in 1963, in 1973, there was never killing of Tutsi in Giti.

Nsengiyumva strongly denied that the restraint in Giti was due to the church. In fact, at the

Catholic Seminary at Notre Dame de la Mercie, the Spanish and Rwandan priests were racists against the Baganza.

> The church is dead in Giti. In 1990, I was in the bush for weeks, and my family was displaced. The priests didn't help at all. The Rwandan priest even ordered machetes. When he heard the RPF was coming, he fled to Muhura and was killed by the RPF. The Spanish priest didn't support the Tutsi. He was in Burundi during the Bagaza era, coming here he was against the Tutsi. He's in Spain now. The majority of those who killed here were Christians. The bishops participated in politics, even after the Arusha Accords. They were divided among the parties, and those with the MRND supported the killing.
>
> One noteworthy exception was Father Mario [Falconi] at Muhura, an Italian priest, who protected refugees, got them to the parish. Others he took to Uganda. He also saved another group of people during a battle near Kigali. At Muhura and Rutare there are Pentecostals, Adventists, but a majority are Catholic.

Miracle at Muhura: Mario Falconi Tells His Story

In late December we hired a taxi to take us to Muhura parish to see the site and to talk with Father Mario Falconi, parish priest (interview on December 27, 1994). He served us coffee, bread, and biscuits in the refectory, which was decorated for the Christmas season. He described the events in the area from April 6 to April 27, 1994. There was intensive Interahamwe activity at Murambi commune to the east; the mayor there was active in this. Muhura was quiet at first, like Giti, although they had no refugees. On April 10 Father Falconi went to Muko for a mass and discovered that Tutsi had been slaughtered the night before. Attendance at mass was minimal that day, so afterward he suggested to his assistant that they pray for the dead. But his assistant was afraid, so Father Falconi went by himself. He found orphaned children in the houses of the dead. He gathered them and brought them to the church. On the way, he encountered people with machetes and asked them if they were really going to go kill; they sheepishly told him they also prayed to God. "What kind of prayers?" he asked mockingly. He quickly took the orphans in his vehicle and drove through the menacing crowd to Muhura. Within days, a thousand Tutsi were at the mission seeking refuge; they were put in a secured fenced-in area, an enclosed dormitory compound, while massacres raged in Murambi to the east and Gikomero to the south.

Some contingents of the RPF came through shortly afterward, driving on to Kigali. Father Fal-

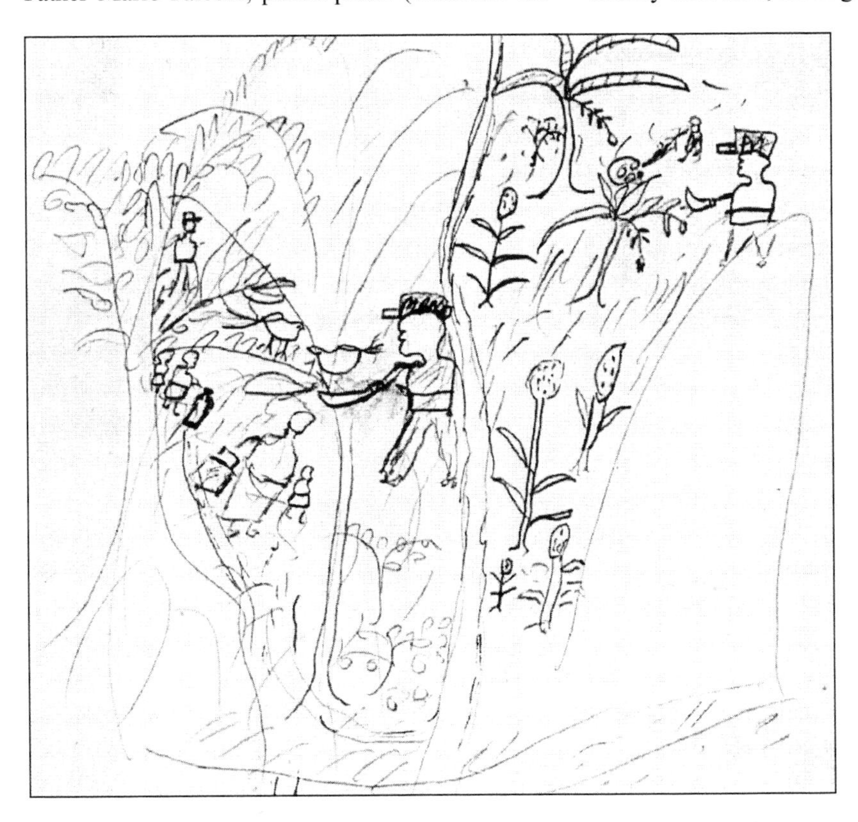

Figure 34. Detail from drawing by Nsengiyumva Patrice's younger sister of an Interahamwe soldier armed with machete hunting those who are hiding in fields and bush.

Figure 35. Mario Falconi with Reinhild Janzen, Nsengiyumva Patrice, and taxi driver in front of Muhura Catholic Mission church, where displaced Tutsi were harbored during the war.

coni had three communal police protecting the mission for a time, but they left or fled. The priests then purposefully spread the rumor that they had RPF protection to ward off Interahamwe. Meanwhile, the main body of RPF troops was advancing, creating panic among the Hutu, who also fled to the mission. Soon there were 100,000 displaced Hutu around the mission, surrounding the 1,000 Tutsi in the inner compound (Figure 35). Father Falconi and his colleagues fed these masses and kept them apart and peaceful, much to Father Falconi's and the two other priests' credit. "We were afraid on all sides," Father Falconi said.

UN helicopters stopped to evacuate the Italians, but the priests chose to stay on until April 27, 1994, when they organized a convoy of vehicles with orphans to Uganda, escorted by the RPF. Even the Rwandan priest from the seminary at Giti commune who had handed out machetes sought refuge at Muhura. After April 27 the RPF moved into the mission, set up house in the priests' and sisters' quarters, pillaged the place, and killed people in the area, including the Rwandan priest of Notre Dame de Mercie who had sought refuge there.

When Father Falconi returned to Muhura alone in early October 1994, the mission was empty, the buildings were in shambles, and the furniture was gone. But the church had been spared. Father Falconi's German shepherd dog was there, overjoyed to see his master.

On the day of our visit, December 27, 1994, Muhura mission was eerily calm and empty. Four long-horned cows grazed on the soccer field where 6 months earlier 100,000 Rwandans had huddled in fear of the invading army (Figure 36). The cooking hearths, hastily built of brick under Father Falconi's direction, still stood in the shed at the end of the playing field (Figure 37). On nearby hillsides hundreds of eucalyptus tree stumps bore mute witness to cutting of firewood to cook provisions of red beans. Smoke-stained walls in the dormitories of the mission school compound showed where terrorized Tutsi had done their cooking and kept warm.

Giti's Mayor Tells How He and His Council Averted Disaster

We tried to contact Sebushumbe Edouard through Nsengiyumva, but when we arrived at his house on December 27, 1994, he was in Kigali. So I (John) left a note with his wife explaining who we were and why we wished to see him. I invited him to come tell his unusual story of maintaining peace in the midst of war. I offered to pay the gas for his motorbike. His interest was clear by his note at the hotel the next day, saying he would be in Kigali on Friday (December 30), as invited.

Sebushumbe came early, sat down, took out a piece of paper when we began to talk, and went directly into his list of "facts to show that genocide was organized ahead of time."

1. Public demonstrations in January 1993 all over the country against the Arusha Accords, suggesting central organization and authorities' involvement of this effort. This was followed in February 1993 by a reactivation of hostilities against the RPF.

2. The distribution of arms to the peasants, rifles, etc., available at the prefectures where they were stocked.

3. Militia began to be organized and trained from the youth branches of the parties. These youth sections were active in a negative sort of way, but the communal governments were the ones to send them away for military training. Giti did not send any away [for such training]. What they learned was not appropriate for youth, things such as mounting and stopping a moving vehicle.

4. The refusal of the higher court, the *parquet,* to consider and judge penal cases which were sent up from the communes. The communes were supposed to send such cases, the persons with their dossiers, to the *parquet* court. After February 1993, many cases of stealing, burning houses, even killing were simply not handled; the *parquet* judges were intimidated by their superiors.[1] Giti sent up some cases of house burnings which weren't considered [in Byumba]; the perpetrators, having been arrested, were released a few weeks later. Thus criminals began to act with impunity, and this fueled the anarchy and killings, and all the miseries that followed.

5. In Giti, when people came to kill cows and commit other acts of anarchy, the communal police arrested them and put them in communal prison. Thereby others were dissuaded from pillaging and killing. As well, local people realized that local authorities were upholding the laws and keeping the peace; they were aware that justice was being done and refrained from developing a bad spirit.

6. Also, we made many patrols, day and night, throughout the commune, especially at the border with Murambi commune where the Interahamwe were very ferocious and would meet our gendarmes across the swamp and shout at them, "You are dogs, we'll come and get you![2]

Figure 36. Soccer playing field in front of Muhura Catholic Mission church where 100,000 Hutu were camped.

Figure 37. Remains of kitchen hearths of the Hutu refugees at far end of the soccer field, December 27, 1994.

> 7. We took in many refugees from Murambi [to the east], Gikoro [to the south], Gikomero [to the west]. Some were thrown into Lake Muhazi, so we told our people to go and rescue these who were still alive.

Sebushumbe mentioned these points to show that the authorities all around had encouraged the massacres. "A peasant does not take up arms against his neighbor on his own. It's natural that if authorities lead, the peasants will follow." He went on to elaborate these points and to raise others, sometimes in response to my questions.

> 8. We put the new refugees together in camps with the earlier ones from Mukarange commune in the north that had been with us since February '93 [driven from their homes by the RPF-FAR fighting]. There were some among these (old and new) who had arms, but we confiscated the arms, so they wouldn't incite the people of Giti.

Sebushumbe had also developed a strategy to contain the anarchic effects of multiparty political campaigns, even before February 1993, because, as he pointed out, political party speakers at that time wanted to gain adherents by any means, including "false promises, work for the unemployed, freedom for prisoners if elected."

> 9. We held meetings of information and reconnaissance to sensitize the people about the problems that could arise [from multipartisme]. We allowed meetings of all the parties, but they had to ask for permission so we could provide security. Then we forbade members of competing parties to be present. We thus forbade the youth from harassing each other. It was an education for everyone, and the meetings were not disturbed.

I asked Sebushumbe how he had found the wisdom for his actions. Without hesitation he said:

> One must be honest. I listened to my communal counselors. There were people who wanted to kill, but we kept the council united, and I consulted with [representatives of the 11 sectors]. I could have been replaced, but I stuck to my approach.

In answer to other questions, Sebushumbe elaborated on the role of the mayor in party politics as introduced in Rwanda.

> I was of course a member of the MRND, as were all mayors. They had been appointed by the president [Habyarimana]. Some changed parties and were replaced. Locally, a man named Habyarimana Evariste was head of the MRND, but he was a figurehead. The mayors were the leaders of the party locally. So, if there were massacres, the mayors would be the first to be implicated.

I asked Sebushumbe to respond to the reason given to me in the camps in Bukavu by the prefet and mayors for the massacres, namely, that the youth sections of the parties simply got out of hand and that the authorities had lost control. Was this true or plausible?

> Yes and no. If they were not punishing outlaws or pursuing justice, then things could easily have gotten out of hand. In Giti I would confront the culprit with the facts of the infraction. Some culprits would tell false stories about their imprisonment and the reasons for it. But if you would explain to them what they had done, they'd admit it. The mayor needed to know how to dare to impose law and justice. Otherwise, anarchy broke out.

I asked Sebushumbe whether he had had an awakening of conscience *(prise de conscience)* at any time regarding the course of events in his country.

> Yes, the demonstrations against the Arusha Accords in January 1993 when people were beaten set me to wondering. But mainly it was day-to-day issues needing to be dealt with that suggested what I must do. There were developments I didn't understand. For example, why give youth military training? Was it for civil defense? I didn't understand. When the president's plane fell, I understood that it had been planned. But no, one mustn't kill—I did my best to save people and the country. I never had the intention to kill. Rather, you do politics with ideas. Thus, each day after reflecting, I took account of the developments. But I don't need to explain why I don't kill or distribute arms, because these acts were illegal. Those who did it secretly, they must explain it.

I asked him whether there had been lists.

> I don't know. Perhaps among politicians but not among the peasants. Both Tutsi and Hutu were killed. More likely, [the reasons behind the pattern were that there were] reactions such as "X is wealthy, kill him for his riches, cars, house." In the countryside it was more like that. South of Giti, they first stole, then killed, but they fled doing theft to save themselves. Among politicians, I don't know.

I asked him what kinds of individuals had become Interahamwe.

> Some were educated, but many were petty bandits or uneducated boys who saw this as a way to advance themselves. Some like to kill, but others were horrified by it. These were forced or obligated to kill. Not all were assassins, just as not all MRND members were assassins.

I asked Sebushumbe whether there were any other mayors like him who actively intervened to halt the violence. He mentioned Gasamagera Evariste of Kicukiro commune in Kigali, who is a national deputy now. Otherwise he knew of none.

Sebushumbe's courageous actions in Giti commune were especially noteworthy between April 6, when the president's plane was downed, and April 16, when the RPF moved into Giti. He recalled that "during this time we kept things calm." I asked him how long he could have kept up the patrols, the meetings, and dealing with all the refugees had the RPF not arrived. He said, "There were Interahamwe all around and massacres. It is unlikely that we could have continued much longer."

On April 15, 1994, many fled into the bush in panic, but they stayed in the commune. The Interahamwe all fled, but Sebushumbe and his council returned from hiding after a week. A few of his people fled for Tanzania, but most stayed.

> They didn't have the spirit of war like those in the north. The RPF entered the commune looking for guns and documents. I don't know what they found. They installed themselves in the communal offices, forcing the commune to a new location. When I returned after a week, I continued in office until June 10—they said, "You did nothing wrong." Then they brought in another mayor, in a process somewhere between a nomination and an election, a university student from the commune, in a provisional appointment, someone who had not been of the old party.

In early 1995 Sebushumbe continued to live in his own house a few hundred yards between the RPF-occupied communal headquarters and the displaced new communal office located in the veterinary health center. Trained as a teacher at the Institut Pédagogique National (IPN) in Butare, he is now an independent merchant.

Sebushumbe had his own ideas about the region of Giti and why its people might have acted differently before and during the war. Although it is true that there were no massacres in Giti in 1959, he noted that there weren't any in most areas. Perhaps more important, Sebushumbe suggested, was the fact that there was simply less Hutu-Tutsi animosity. A Tutsi sous-chef stayed on in the region after 1959, becoming a communal judge (juge de canton) until 1970, but he stayed, whereas his brother left for Uganda. In Murambi commune things were more catastrophic in 1959.

> That the reason for Giti's calmness may lie in more ancient history is not convincing, although it is interesting. A number of the communes mentioned were all in the old Rwandan district Buganza. It was a region where there were many intermarriages between families and clans, enhancing solidarity. A marriage is a social pact that prohibits you from harming the family of your spouse. It's like a chain between different families, a man will not kill his wife or her brother or sister. . . . As a consequence of this type of marriage you feel yourself in a family . . . but there were also many such marriages in Murambi—they were also Baganza—and that did not deter the massacres. So I don't know what demon descended on that commune. I think it was largely the authorities, the politicians, who sought power any way possible. Some men even killed their wives. Unbelievable.

Finally, I asked Sebushumbe what had been the nature and use of Hutu and Tutsi labels or categories.

> We were aware of it, but we married and exchanged cows as signs of friendship in Buganza. Earlier Tutsi was defined as "Tutsi" [cattle keeping]. Now, no longer, for there are cattle-rich Hutu and Tutsi without cattle. Corveé labor used to define the relationship, but not now.

Yet Another Paradox of War

Because of its unique history and situation, Giti experienced a paradoxical need. At a time when relief agencies were ministering to communities in which savage massacres had raged, Giti needed food aid as badly as other communities and received none. For over a year—from February 1993 until after the war—Giti had harbored and fed thousands of displaced persons from the two communes to their north. Sebushumbe complained:

> Rutare to the north gets food, but Giti doesn't, although Giti fed a double population and experienced some drought, exhausting its stock. CARE distributed seeds, beans, and corn, but it didn't last long. Catholic Relief Service is at Rutare.
>
> Now, because there had not been massacres, we have no NGOs distributing food and seeds. We needed beans, potatoes, maize, soya, legumes; hoes, axes, saws, and pumps to spray plants against pests. Because we were spared the killing, we are now ignored. We need school materials and food until harvest. Beans and potatoes are the basic diet here; sweet potatoes were to be planted in April but weren't. So today there is nothing to eat. We were not helped with the refugees we harbored; they took our food. Diseases followed. Students skip school; they're hungry.

Despite the suffering of temporary hunger, Giti commune knew a far greater peace than communes elsewhere in Rwanda. Most of its residents had returned. There were far fewer victims of war to mourn. Most families and lineages were reorganizing, rebuilding, and getting on with their lives.

The case of Giti raises profound issues about the reasons and ways in which leaders can sway their people, for good or for ill. Sebushumbe Edouard was willing to obey the law for the sake of decency and civil society. His neighboring mayors were of a different mind and not only engaged in the massacres but also led them. Sebushumbe's argument for the rule of law is extraordinarily persuasive, for its own sake.

2.3 *The Fate of Institutions:* The Churches

Because our sponsoring organization, the MCC, usually works with national councils of churches in relief and development actions, we were encouraged to make contact with church leaders and local congregations, to listen to them, and to talk with them about their experiences, their hopes, and their plans for recovery. We met with a cross-section of leaders and laypersons of Catholic, Protestant, and Muslim faiths. We also discussed with numerous individuals the traditional Rwandan religion, Kubandwa. The religion of the Rwandans was of particular interest for many witnesses and observers after the 1994 tragedy because they found perplexing the juxtaposition of Rwanda being "the most Catholic country in Africa" and "genocide." The haunting specter of Christians killing Christians was part of the memory of this war, and it was deeply disturbing also to the Rwandan people.

The pervasiveness of religion in Rwanda, and of the churches in Rwandan national life meant that the churches revealed as well as any other institutions the contours of the political fractures of the early 1990s and the profound consequences of the war of 1994. Any attempt to describe these fractures needs to take into account the history of the churches in Rwanda, including the late colonial and early postcolonial history of Rwanda. Especially, the Catholic Church mirrored and channeled the power structure of the country (van Hoyweghen 1996 and Longman 1995a provide the most helpful overviews and general analyses of the fate of the Rwandan churches before and during the 1994 war). Until 1957 the Catholic Church had offered an avenue to power and influence for the Tutsi. Most of the priests and consecrated religious figures were therefore Tutsi. In 1958, however, with the swing of Belgian support to the Hutu and the emergence of a Hutu national party whose head was close to the Church, Gregoire Kayibanda, the power structure of the Catholic Church came to coalesce with Hutu influence. Although Kayibanda was killed a year after Habyarimana's coup of 1972, the Catholic Church continued to enjoy proximity to power in Rwanda. The earlier years of Tutsi church domination continued to be reflected in the numbers of Tutsi priests and clergy; the leadership from independence on reflected the Kayibanda-Habyarimana control of national and church politics. Especially during the Habyarimana years of the MRND's power monopoly, church leaders were often national political leaders as well. Thus the Rwandan archbishop Vincent Nsengiyumva was a member of the MRND national ruling council. Presbyterian Church president Twagirayesu Michel was a member of the MRND prefectural council in Kibuye.

With the attack of the Tutsi-dominated exile group, the RPF, in the 1990 October war and the introduction of multiparty politics in 1992, Rwandan church leadership was unable to address the deep social and political contradictions in national society with any degree of vision. Most Rwandan church leaders became so fully involved in single-party politics and the benefits of this power that they experienced a crisis of authority. With some exceptions and despite the best intentions of some, the Rwandan churches generally polarized along the lines of the national political divide. In the early 1990s "the Catholic clergy reflected the fissures within society: while 90 percent of the Christian population was Hutu, 70 percent of the lower clergy were Tutsi, and most bishops Hutu" (van Hoyweghen 1996, p. 382). As the war broke out, this contradictory tiered profile of members, lower clergy, and bishops produced a lethal internal struggle within the Catholic Church. Christians killed Christians. Most of the Tutsi clergy were killed. The church buildings that had afforded sanctuary in earlier attacks on Tutsi became sites of mass murder, a strategy that the officials of the genocide used willfully. Sometimes even the Hutu priests conducting mass were drawn into the killing. Many Rwandans and outside observers alike declared that "the Rwandese Church is dead," not just in a physical sense but also in moral terms.

The Protestant churches were also affected by the same forces of national division, with similar consequences during the war. As a general rule the more centralized the church organization, the more its leaders were involved in national politics of the MRND as a single party. Therefore the centralized national Protestant churches such as the Anglican, Presbyterian, Lutheran, and Baptist churches were torn up the most. Much less serious were the consequences of the political polarization and war on decentralized religious communities in which the local congregation was largely autonomous, features characteristic of the Pentecostals, the Church of the Brethren,[3] the Evangelical Friends, the Seventh Day Adventists, and the Muslims in Rwanda. Wartime stories abounded of how these groups maintained their solidarity during the war or refused to identify their ethnicity when confronted by Interahamwe militia. Particularly remarkable was the story of one Butare Pentecostal congregation that welcomed the Interahamwe while singing a hymn. When asked to produce their identity cards so Tutsi could be separated from Hutu, they said, "We will not single out individuals in our midst. . . . You can kill us all." On that day the Interahamwe left without doing their dirty work. There were also examples of this in Catholic churches as well, to be sure.

In this section we sketch a brief general background of the fate of several denominations in Rwanda during the 1994 war to profile those individuals with whom we held extensive conversations. We focus on the Catholic Church, to put into context our conversation with Cathedral Vicar Mungwarareba Modest and head of the bishop's commission of postwar pastoral renewal, Laurien Ntezimana. We also spoke with Presbyterian church leaders in the Muku camp in Zaire and in Kigali and with Baptist church leaders in Kigali.

The Catholic Church

The whiplash-like effects of the 1994 war on the Catholic Church of Rwanda destroyed not only the leadership but also the legitimacy of the church. Of the 400 prewar clergy, about half of these—almost all Tutsi—were massacred in the early phases of the genocide (Nzabahimana 1994; Van Hoyweghen 1996, p. 395). In the second phase of the war the Hutu top leadership, such as Archbishop Nsengiyumva of Kigali, Bishop Thadee Nsengiyumva of Kabgayi, and Bishop Ruzindana of Byumba, was also killed, with the effect of decapitating the Catholic Church (Van Hoyweghen 1996, p. 395). About 60 priests fled to the Goma area refugee camps, where Zairian bishop Monsignor Ngabu sought to maintain the prewar orientation of the church (Van Hoyweghen 1996, p. 395). What remained was thus a highly polarized clergy with less than half its original numbers inside the country.

Some of the actions of the clergy before and during the war had also de-legitimatized the church. The image of the priest of Ste. Famille parish in Kigali conducting mass and then pulling out a pistol to shoot Tutsi in attendance—witnessed by a passing journalist—had a chilling effect on any trust that may have remained in the church. When this priest fled to France and was further protected by the church, even less credibility remained. Only a handful of parishioners were in attendance for mass in the vast sanctuary of Ste. Famille, we noticed, when we stayed at the parish guesthouse in early December 1994.

Van Hoyweghen's (1996) analysis of the loss of legitimacy of the Rwandan Catholic Church includes its conservatism toward the reforms of the Vatican II Council, in which a less formal mass, the use of vernacular languages, and a greater attention to social injustices were emphasized. The Rwandan Catholic Church remained a highly liturgical church that kept its distance from political issues. According to van Hoyweghen (1996), it had lost most of its prophetic voice as its leaders became engulfed in the politics of protecting the national party of President Habyarimana and participating in the privilege of the political class.

The abuses of privilege by the top Rwandan clergy were related by some European Catholics whom we met. Rudolf Fischer and his wife, who headed the Rheinland-Pfalz Rwanda Partnerschaft, an organization that provided people-to-people programs in Rwanda for many years, were as Catholics particularly disgusted by the behavior of the archbishop at the opening of a children's project. He arrived late in his helicopter. At the meal, when he was served beer, he asked, "Where's my wine?" Later, having received the wine, he demanded, "Where's my cognac?" Mrs. Fischer said she did not even want to go to Goma to work with the Catholic clergy in exile there because she did not want to face the confrontation with church officials she knew were implicated in the massacres. The Catholic Church had forgotten the poor; it had become preoccupied with privilege and ceremony.

The complicity of the national Catholic Church in the genocidal regime put those clergy and those institutions who remained after the war under considerable suspicion with the new regime. The Vatican was well aware of this situation and sought outside clergy to work in the Rwandan Catholic Church. Where foreign clergy such as Father Falconi in Muhura had heroically mediated the war's conflict in his parish, the church maintained its credibility. Meanwhile, the Rwandan bishop of Byumba had been killed, as had the priest of a nearby seminary because they had been part of the genocidal plan, going so far as to order machetes for the massacres, according to our Rwandan guide Nsengiyumva Patrice. The dilemma of the Catholic Church in Rwanda was that there were too few Catholics like Father Falconi. Nsengiyumva could in one and the same sentence tell us that Father Falconi was his hero and that the Catholic Church was dead in Giti.

What we found in Butare was confirmed three years later by van Hoyweghen (1996), who singled out the diocese of Butare as an exception to the rule of the fate of the Rwandan Catholic Church. Only in Butare did the church seem to be "pulling itself together" through a program that was called Commission pour la Réprise des Activités Pastorales (CRAP) (Commission for the Renewal of Pastoral Activities) (van Hoyweghen 1996, p. 396). Because we spoke with the organizers of this activity several times and collected their pamphlets, we present the Butare initiative later in this chapter (section 2.5).

The Presbyterian Church

The modernist building of the Eglise Presbyterienne Kiyovu-Kigali sustained serious damage in the war, when a bomb or artillery shell scored a hit right through the roof, exploding in the sanctuary. We walked by this building several times during our stays in Kigali and wondered how the war had affected the Presbyterian Church. When we returned from Zaire just before Christmas, we knew we wanted to speak to the General Secretary Gakinda Gédéon about our visit with church president Twagirayesu Michel in the Muku camp. Christmas is celebrated in Rwanda; thus few offices were open in Kigali approaching this holiday. The emergencies of the postwar period taxed most officials we called on. Thus, on our first attempt to call on Gakinda he was in a meeting with a representative of a European agency. He came out to say hello briefly; I gave him the letter I had been carrying from Twagirayesu in Zaire, and we agreed on a meeting time several days after Christmas.

When we began our meeting on December 28, 1994, Gakinda was eager to hear about his boss in Zaire, Twagirayesu. Twagirayesu emphasized to us his eagerness to meet and work together with Gakinda, but he made reference to the need to speak the "same language" and for there to be "mutual pardon." Gakinda was satisfied with the tone of the report and went on to present a picture of two segments of his church that did not have a conflict (thus no reconciliation was needed) but were involved in a situation that was taking the two farther apart and could contribute to misunderstanding and the general drift toward another catastrophe if not resolved.

> The church is alive here [in Rwanda]: People are here, they are meeting, and we must reorganize now. There had been a large presence at the Christmas service in the bombed sanctuary at Kiyovu in Kigali. The pastors of the parishes had met to select representatives; they had to replace those who had been killed in the war. Now there was a need to look at the functioning of schools and health centers, including two hospitals. Directors needed to be found to get on with the work. NGOs had begun to help with the hospitals, and all this required legal work, thus legal representation. This, not some conflict, was the imperative pushing them toward replacing those who had fled.
>
> What to do? The boss, the head of the church [Twagirayesu] is in exile. Occasional letters hardly suffice to provide leadership. Yet, as long as security was not what it should be, it would be unwise for the others to return. After all, the Catholic Church has lost its bishops at Kibuye.[4]

In his comments to us Gakinda acknowledged the helpfulness of leadership mediation councils such as the Pan African Christian Leadership Conference at Nairobi; later, the Presbyterians would send one pastor to the Mwanza, Tanzania, meeting sponsored by the MCC and AEE. But he emphasized that what they faced was an "institutional crisis" resulting from the division of the leadership, even though they had not followed the quota system but had met as Christians to elect the best people. Coincidentally, the Presbyterians had thus come up with six regional presidents, half of whom were Tutsi and half of whom were Hutu. For the clergy their vocation and education were the sole criteria for nomination. Gakinda was against ever again using the quota approach.

Despite all this, a certain frustration had entered church ranks with all the shifting and moving of people, the dislocation. The refugees of 30 years ago had gained wealth and took up arms to come home.

> We're afraid that another catastrophe is in the making; the new refugees will be alienated from the nation if they stay away for long. We need to cultivate national unity at all cost.
>
> The church must avoid the ideologies of both sides, whether this be the MRND's position on negotiations or the RPF's position on war crimes trials. The synod asked the leaders to be there for all, not be partisan. Yes, the church must critique the powers, it must be prophetic; but justice and order are our allies.

When asked how they would resolve the institutional crisis of the legal representative position, Gakinda suggested that

> the Synod is the real leader of the church, and the position of the legal representative is renewed each year by it. So, the next Synod will have to decide; hopefully, Twagirayesu Michel will be there.

Gakinda spoke of the reason Twagirayesu was in Zaire and he in Kigali.

> We all left Kigali for the zone Turquoise in the southwest. I said, "Let's stay [in Rwanda]." Michel said, "Let's go, my wife is scared." After Kigali had been taken, I returned. They believed the false rumors from Radio Mille Collines that the RPF would kill the elites. I said, I want to verify it. When I got to Kigali, I heard the radio there announce that all people should gather to pray. That is what gave me strength.
>
> But my house is still occupied by the military [Gakinda lives in a church residence in Kiyovu]. We try to occupy all of the church residences to keep military from taking them. The representatives of Protestant churches met with the president recently regarding all the illegal occupancies of their houses. "Give me lists," he asked, offering to help. If this doesn't do it, I'll go to the parquet, after the commune, where he's already been.

We engaged Gakinda in discussion of some tough issues, such as church members' involvement in the genocide and other events. His response was that

> church people killed, but they were not Christians who killed. There have been no public confessions so far, although we have received confessions from, and have forgiven, those who killed spouses, or whose spouses killed. But when I tell the youth to confess, they just laugh at me. How to deal with youth and children who saw their parents kill? I fear most the sentiment of vengeance.

The Baptist Church

In late December 1994 we met in Kigali with Reverend Pastor Bashaka Faustin, the president (legal representative) of the Association of Baptist Churches in Rwanda (AEBR) and the assistant legal representative of the Protestant Council of Rwanda. He was joined by Patricia Mukabadege, Head of Sunday Schools of the AEBR.

Rev. Bashaka told us that he had first heard the word Mennonite at Goma, when a Mennonite pastor, Harold Miller, from the All Africa Council of Churches in Nairobi and a representative of the African Association of Evangelicals with him also identified himself as Mennonite. Rev. Bashaka described for us the postwar status of the Rwandan Baptist Church.

> Before the war there were 100,000 members in the Baptist Church, 114 parishes, 224 chapels or smaller groups, 100 primary schools, 2 health centers, 3 youth centers, and 70 literacy centers. But after the war, when we took stock, seven pastors had been killed. Seventy pastors and evangelists who had fled are now back in the country. Sixty thousand members are in the country, about 40,000 are still in the camps, but we don't have exact figures. The Baptist Church of Rwanda was founded from Zaire. Most members are in the west of the country near the Zairian borders. When I left for Goma many pastors followed me.

We asked him whether he had been afraid to return to Rwanda.

> It was a personal matter. It's not up to me to judge someone who is evil. I only must bring God's love. When they returned, people said that church members had killed. People did die in the churches, but it is important to take up the work of the churches again so that this terrible thing doesn't happen again. We've started up again, but things are very difficult. We must pray for the government because authority comes from God. These are all the reasons why I wanted to return. The church's job is healing.

How will the church do that?

> Talk to the president, because there are things the government knows regarding the return of refugees and the whole question of housing. And what can the church do in this process of bringing people back and bringing peace? So the church has to help the state. We did meet with the president who said healing and reconciliation is what you can do best. The president said that the state needs the church. We tried to counteract the accusation that the church was the setting of killing. Those who return from Uganda are integrating into existing

> churches; this is what the Justice Minister suggested, otherwise there would be division again. So now there are new church members from Uganda in these churches. A lot of widows in the churches in the south and the west.

We asked Rev. Bashaka and Mukabadege whether they had female catechists and pastors and whether female leadership was possible in this situation. Mukabadege responded that there are some women catechists. But Rev. Bashaka addressed the question of female clergy in the church.

> The Baptists don't have women preachers. But my wife was a national deputy from 1989 to 1993. In 1993 things started to go bad with politics, so she withdrew. Party politics became too mean-spirited. She got into politics because she was a church leader. There would be no problem for her now to participate in politics because she was a good person, was a member of the MDR party. My wife's brother is ambassador to Switzerland. All his siblings are here.

Rev. Bashaka said that his church was sheltering Tutsi. He was behind the lines of the RPF for three months. Soldiers were not pleased to see the mixture of people in the Baptist Church. The RPF put them all into the Hospital Faisal, a camp of 6,000; the UN military forces wanted refugee representation, so Rev. Bashaka was elected representative by the others.

> The old army was bombing this area, bombs fell right near the hospital. The UN evacuated us before June to Gisenyi in the west, so we fled west from there when the war got there a week and a half later. We were part of the World Relief and UNHCR relief actions. I became involved in the coordination of that work.

Rev. Bashaka decided after awhile that he needed to return home, however difficult it was.

> There are Christians in difficulty and they needed leadership. In August I made visits to World Relief, contacted the US ambassador, but not many people were here and everybody was afraid. You could count on one hand the people who came from Gisenyi to Kigali. I contacted a ministry before they had offices. The US ambassador helped us find them. So we returned to Goma to contact other pastors to return. Some stayed. I made contact with African Evangelistic Enterprises to have a seminar for pastors to overcome their fears and to bring the church back to life. With these seminars by AEE the church became active again. [AEE] helped us establish contact with other churches. I stayed in the Baptist Center in Goma, so the Interahamwe didn't bother me. I visited many of the camps in the Goma area but I wasn't interfered with. I went with other agencies into the camps, in their vehicles. The Interahamwe organized after people were there in the camps.

We asked why some of the pastors did not want to return to Rwanda.

> To return would be to support the new government and they needed to support the refugees in camps.
>
> My role is not to judge one government over another, rather to support the church. Some of the other Baptist pastors see me as an enemy because I returned. They formed an alliance of evangelical churches in exile. They don't want me to come there, so that is the real problem. But word is getting around that I have worked on both sides to keep the church going. I have had contact with the group in exile, and they asked to be forgiven and this gives us anticipation of possibilities.
>
> What can be done in the future? The refugees have lived a catastrophe, they have nothing in their houses, nothing to eat. Nobody is receiving a salary. The family needs to survive, that is the first need: to combat the famine. If they can be encouraged to return, the government would accept that. To cultivate their fields, they need seeds; then we can have reconciliation after that. People are afraid of the future because the Interahamwe say they will return and attack the country.

We returned to the condition of the churches torn between leaders now scattered in Rwanda, Zaire, Tanzania, and Nairobi. We asked Rev. Bashaka whether he thought a meeting in a neutral setting of the Baptist pastors, like that sponsored by the All Africa Council of Churches in Nairobi earlier in 1994, would be helpful for his church.

> Yes, it would. It would change [the pastors'] thinking. Also seminars with good outsiders to talk about reconciliation. About 25 pastors [of 70] remain outside the country, 12 in Tanzania, 12 in Goma. [Life continues dangerously for these pastors.] A pastor and his wife and children were killed in a recent skirmish between Zairian soldiers and Interahamwe at Goma.

Peace Conferences for the Churches

As the political climate in Rwanda polarized in the early 1990s, the churches sought to play the role of peacemaker between the Habyarimana government and the RPF. As Presbyterian Church president Twagirayesu recalled in our conversation in the Muku camp, the churches had created a *Comité de Contacts* intended to bring together the warring parties. He had played a role in this. This committee's efforts to bring about a peace accord before the war were reviewed in a document drawn up in Nairobi by exiled Rwandan church leaders in late 1994 (Dirigeants d' Eglises rwandaises 1994). This recital of peace-promoting initiatives by church leaders in exile echoes the Hutu perspective that the war was in large part precipitated by the RPF and that the new government in Kigali could not be fully trusted. On several occasions before the 1994 war the committee made contact with representatives of the RPF in Nairobi and Bujumbura. In particular, the meeting in Nairobi contributed to the peace negotiations of the Arusha Accords. In November 1993 the committee held a colloquium in Mombasa on the theme of seeking a durable peace. Even in February 1994 Catholic and Protestant authorities met to encourage the division of power as proposed by the Arusha Accords. Public meetings at diocesan and parish levels sought to reinforce the spirit of peace.

The exiled leaders in Nairobi also noted, in their review of church efforts at peace, that even after April 6, 1994, they continued to condemn the massacres and urged the belligerent sides to sit down to talk. They were rebuffed by the RPF. The document (Dirigeants d'Eglises rwandaises 1994) defensively raises the question, What then should the church have done? Even the president of the committee, a Catholic bishop, stayed with a large Tutsi mass of internal refugees at Kabgayi and had been killed by the RPF (for which the RPF blamed inexperienced junior soldiers, one of whom was executed for the killing of three bishops). The document in effect blamed the RPF for the flight of many Rwandans and church people and for internal persecution of church leaders. It also suggested that some of the church leaders who are in Rwanda appear to be playing the political games of the RPF by suggesting that those who refuse to return are guilty of complicity in the genocide and by calling into question the legitimacy of those leaders who remain abroad. The document concluded with a call for a church-wide program of reconciliation, rehabilitation, and reconstruction.

This document drawn up by the exiled Rwandan church leaders in Nairobi reflected the gulf that emerged between those clergy who fled for whatever reason and those who remained or who returned early after the war. This state of affairs affected all the national churches of Rwanda. If they were to play a significant role in the restoration of civil society, they would themselves need to be internally reconciled.

In this climate a number of international church agencies fostered reconciliation within the Rwandan church denominations, between those leaders who had left the country and for whatever reason hesitated to return and those who had stayed or who had returned and were trying to carry on as best they could. Nairobi was an important center of these initiatives, because of the presence there of the headquarters of the All Africa Council of Churches. It is obviously not possible here to detail the many agencies and meetings that were involved at various times to reconcile Rwandan church leaders after the war, an effort that continues to this day. Instead, we close this section with an account of one such reconciliation meeting held in Mwanza, Tanzania, in December 1994, in which the MCC had a part.

The Mwanza reconciliation meeting of some 30 Rwandan Protestant pastors from several denominations was organized by the Kigali office of the AEE, whose new president, Antoine Rutayisire, a trained linguist, had taken over from his predecessor, who was killed in the war. The AEE is an East African network of businessmen and public leaders who foster prayer breakfasts at which public figures can meet to socialize, meditate, and talk rather than to fight. Other figures and organizations in the background of the Mwanza meeting included MCC Peace Scholar Harold Miller, also a staff member of the All Africa Council of Churches in Nairobi; Hizkias Assefa, an Eritrean mediation expert who with a Ghanian colleague operates the Nairobi Peace Initiative, a network that works behind the scenes in African conflicts[5]; Zairian Mennonite pastor Mukambu ya'Namwisi from Kinshasa, who was working in the Kivu refugee camps as part of the MCC team; and finally, Dave Brubaker, of Conflict Management Services of Casa Grande, Arizona, whom the MCC asked to assess the dimensions and results of such reconciliation meetings (Brubaker 1994). The MCC sponsored the Mwanza meeting for $15,000, which was spent entirely on airfare and room and board for the participants.

The Mwanza reconciliation meeting occurred over a three-day period in December 1994. Our account is based on Mukambu's report when he returned to Bukavu. Assefa served as chair of the gathering. Mukambu was an observer and held some private counseling sessions with the Rwandan pastors. According to Mukambu, the Rwandans arrived from Nairobi, Zaire, Tanzania, and

Rwanda. They had not seen one another since the war; they did not even know who would be present. Therefore the first encounter was one of greeting, of embraces, of joy that each had survived the war, but also of taking stock of who had been killed. The first encounters were often tearful.

The more difficult part came on following days when, as a group and in smaller groups, they began to discern the lines of division among themselves, as church people and as Rwandans. Accusations, disappointments, and some confessions emerged—and again tears. In the end these men were able to talk to and about each other as fellow Christians and Rwandans rather than as RPF or MRND or as Hutu and Tutsi. All returned to their respective camps, places of refuge, or their home communities.

Mukambu's assessment was that the meeting had been an immense eye-opener for him. He thought it served the purpose of moving these church leaders from fear and suspicion to a point where they could talk to each other. The terror within the Rwandan community was made apparent to him when a Rwandan travel companion, a resident in a refugee camp in Zaire, realized mid-flight that the small plane in which they were traveling would land in Kigali on its way to Mwanza and not fly directly to Tanzania. The man became terrified, believing that he had been tricked into this return to Rwanda that would surely be his death. Mukambu's amazement at this man's fear was tempered only by a belated sense of humor over the incident. The man had begun to tremble and could not contain his bowels. On arriving in Kigali, he would not leave the plane and was calmed only once they were airborne and out of Rwandan air space.

Importance of the Laity in the Renewal of the Church

If any hope remained for the churches of Rwanda to be institutions of civil society and renewed morality, it was not to be found in the clergy and the top administrators who had allowed themselves to be drawn into the country's political elite. Hope and determination to rebuild the church were certainly embodied in those Hutu clergy such as Gakinda and Rev. Bashaka who stayed or returned from exile to be with their parishes inside Rwanda. But of special note were the lay people who were unsullied, who would try to restore integrity in the parishes by learning to speak the truth about what had occurred and not just lead liturgies while keeping silent about the injustices and the violence that had and continued to occur. Laurien Ntezimana of the Butare Catholic diocese and Antoine Rutayisire of the AEE were laymen committed to the restoration of the church in Rwanda. Their perspectives on this challenge are given in the following sections.

2.4 Throwing Water on the Flames

Will you not revive us again that your people may rejoice in you?—Psalm 85:6, the motto over Antoine Rutayisire's desk

Antoine Rutayisire was the newly appointed executive secretary of AEE, which helped to restore the Rwandan churches. AEE is a transnational eastern and southern Africa group that brings together intellectuals, politicians, and national elites from each country to "eat, talk, and pray in lieu of fighting," according to Don Jacobs, one of its founding members.

Rutayisire conducted graduate studies in modern literature at the University of Rwanda, where he had received his M.A. degree. He also had studied applied linguistics at the University of North Wales. As an academic and a teacher, he had been a board member of AEE, but the 1994 war thrust him into the position of executive secretary because most of the executive committee and staff had been killed. The victims of the genocide included his immediate predecessor, who was a Hutu and an outspoken critic of the Habyarimana regime and advocate of the Arusha discussions, another staff member who was a Tutsi, and a third member who was a "Hutu who looked like a Tutsi." Rutayisire was our first conversation partner in Rwanda for whom ethnicity was a tool politicians used to gain or retain control and power. Later, we would identify a number who shared this insight.

How Rutayisire regarded his own identity and what he thought of ethnicity in Rwanda soon emerged in our conversations with him one morning, December 8, 1994, in his office in Kigali. His account of the organization he headed was interspersed with his own life story and how he had escaped assassination in the opening days of the genocide. We began by asking what he and AEE were doing in response to the national situation.

> We've been trying to throw some water on the flames. We began reconciliation work from October 4, 1990 [after the RPF attack on Akagera]. The night of the 4th was a kind of drama, a make-believe, not real, war. On October 5 people were told to stay at home. From this time on there was a psychology of fear; feelings of suspicion grew. Arrests were made. False accusation of arms possessions had been made and were made. This went on for two years. Radio was used to say, "Watch out; your neighbor may be an accomplice of the RPF," and that all Tutsi supported the RPF.
>
> From 1991 on we tried to convince people that what was said over the radio and hearsay was *not* true, that reality was different. We also said, Don't get confused, because this is a fight for power, not ethnic conflict.
>
> In 1959 the king was overthrown; the elite Tutsi then left the country. In the kingdom the pyramid of power was in the hands of *very few people* in the country.
>
> Even the greatest chiefs served the king. The stronger one's army, the more powerful you were. Then after 1959 it was said that the Tutsi have been ruling you—which was not true. This was the first political mistake. My grandfather was very poor; he was a servant. My mother—a Tutsi—was a servant in the house of one of the kings. My father had been sick of the system and fled to Uganda, but he came back in 1955, when the feudal system was suppressed.
>
> Elections for local councils were held. So that's when the problem started. . . .
>
> In 1959 the kings, chiefs, and subchiefs fled. In 1961–63 the poor [Tutsi] got massacred during attacks by those outside of the country, from Burundi, from Uganda; in 1963 my father was killed in a wave of reprisals. Many Tutsi fled again. In 1966–67 there was another attack from the refugees outside the country, followed by massacres of Tutsi in the country. Every time they play this ethnic card in order to gain or keep power. There is an ethnic factor. There is a bad legacy from the parents of ethnic hatred; it has been transmitted from father to son. When there is no fight for power, there is no fight in the population.
>
> When multiparty democracy started in 1959, there were many parties until 1965. Then they were strangled and disappeared. In 1965 there was a one-party election. In 1973 the notion of party was supplanted by that of "movement," meaning the MRND. This continued until 1991, during which time all had to be members of the MRND. All Rwandans were members and paid contributions. They had to; everyone was obliged to be a member, otherwise people were put into jail. Those who aired frustration, also some preachers, were reprimanded "not to preach politics" but to "stick to the gospel."

In 1991, with the introduction of multiple parties, the ethnic card was played again. *Multipartisme* was imposed under pressure from other countries, with the leverage of economic aid. The RPF was the only party with an army. They organized themselves into a guerrilla army, and in October 1990 they attacked.

[In the next few years] some soldiers began to ask, "Why are we fighting, what are we fighting for?" Morale was low. They started to organize the militia across the country. We saw them training in small groups. By 1993 they had become a menace, and then they started Radio-Television Mille Collines because they were losing ground. They were thinking, "Whoever is not on the side of the MRND is not for the country."

When the Arusha document was signed to share power, we saw people from the opposition side with the MRND. Then both sides hardened their position. That is when the plane got shot down, at the time of confrontation. But who shot it down? I don't know. Some say the RPF, others say Hutu radicals, some say the Belgians. Each would have had their reasons. [In any case] that day the militia, who must have been trained for it, [began to attack]. Someone gave the signal.

If the massacres would not have happened, the MRND could have won out. Habyarimana had control of the process; he could have come out a stronger politician.

Massacres started already the very night the plane was shot down, there where the militia was strong. In the south they started only in May—it took a whole month to convince people to kill. In a poor country people are easily convinced to kill someone in order to get their things. People killed out of instigation and menace, not out of hate. They were forced to kill. But, by the end, it became a kind of pleasure to kill. I need proof from ordinary life to show me that there was hatred between people. My father was killed by a Hutu, but my studies were paid by a Hutu. My neighbor was a militiaman and told me to pray because I was in danger. This very militiaman passed by my house on his way to kill. It's a miracle of God that I survived. Many Tutsi were killed in my neighborhood near the stadium, near [United Nations Rwanda Emergency Operations] headquarters.

Then RPF soldiers arrived from the battalion of 600 soldiers stationed [at the stadium] and met the militia in front of my gate. The RPF shot militia at the checkpoints and they shot the militia near my gate. The fighting wasn't really equal.

I (John) asked how AEE looked at the events that transpired in Rwanda.

We look at this from the biblical point of view. First, this helps you to get an objective point of view. The Bible helps one see that this is a fight for interest: *James* 3:16, "For where you have envy and selfish ambition, there you find disorder and every evil practice." It is not a matter of ethnic strife. We get a broader and clearer view by looking at things from the biblical perspective.

The real question is, Who is interested in helping the population? This is a country of traumatized people, but because if you see your father being killed, that does not allow you to kill. And [we promote] a call to repentance to those who participated in the massacres—if we can get them to confess. We tell the people, "You are not allowed to kill and not have hatred in your heart. Don't transmit your hatred to your children." The Bible has something to say on everything, on political, economic, social issues. We use a holistic approach. We are working with widows, unaccompanied children, and orphans.

Our main objective is to strengthen the churches to give morale to discouraged pastors—to give a new vision to the pastors, to show them that they still have a role to play. Then to go and preach reconciliation—it is not easy to say you have to forgive.

I noted that some say justice must come first, then forgiveness. Rutayisire replied:

But what type of justice, because I cannot judge someone out of hatred. Hearts have to be changed. Who hasn't done wrong things? This is a very dangerous question—we are not out there to make ourselves a name.

I asked, "What can outside agencies do?"

Help with rebuilding the country physically, to rebuild churches, hospitals, schools, all of which are in ruins. There is a need for money. People can help with human resources. We have needs that are difficult to respond to. Doctors have been killed, judges too. We need trained teachers and nurses. If someone has a heart for that, there is room for good psychologists to do trauma counseling. And you can pray. Thirty minutes of prayer per day, that's a big contribution. (I lived in Europe and I've seen that people there are so busy. The average prayer time for American pastors is nine minutes per day!) The people you pray for, you are going to love. Because you think about them and try to understand them. Some people keep their distance from those whom they know have killed. But the challenge of the Christian message is to love the unlovable, even the criminals with blood on their hands. There is a lack of forgiveness for those who have killed. The person who killed my father, I know him and his children. It's a struggle to forgive; you can't do it by yourself. The problem is not the hatred but the bitterness. When you love someone he can feel it and see it.

I asked Rutayisire whether people can cease using their ethnic labels as instruments for getting power.

> How do you stop someone from using an easy means to get something? Yes, if we solved this question, we could solve the problems of our country. So we take the biblical point of view. If we could get a new heart for everyone in this country, we can solve it. You need transformed people to transform the system.

In answer to the question of whether the churches were involved in the massacres, Rutayisire answered:

> Not really. In all earlier massacres the people found refuge in churches. It was like an unspoken covenant, but this time the Interahamwe were *told* to kill people who sought refuge in the churches, to follow them into their sanctuary. But some Interahamwe hid and protected people in their own homes while they went off to kill people elsewhere.

I asked, "How did you acquire this 'instrumental' view of ethnicity?"

> I am a child of both worlds. I am Tutsi but a poor one with nothing to boast about. When you are born into a Tutsi family and your studies are paid by a Hutu, you find out your real friends and real enemies. My mother told us never to get involved with all these things. My mother is a very staunch Roman Catholic, but she is a disciplined person above all. Sometimes we went to the village diviner just to be sure. That was the kind of Christian she is. She was left with four children at 25 when my father was killed.

2.5 Renewal in the Catholic Diocese of Butare

War Losses in Butare Diocese

Not only did the desecration of the cathedrals by Interahamwe massacres take to the grave many thousands of good people, but it also shook the remaining community of believers to its core. In addition, the taint of political involvement in the politics of the genocide raised doubts that the Catholic Church could ever recover.

In Butare diocese alone, the effect of the devastation on the Catholic Church was severe. According to the records of the diocese, the Catholic population declined from 513,000 before the war to 260,000 after the war (in an overall population of 865,000 and 450,000, respectively); thus in both cases nearly 50% was lost to deaths and flight. A similar loss resulted in the decline of functioning parishes, from 18 before the war to only 9 after the war. Personnel was severely affected as well. The presence of foreign missionaries declined, through exodus, from 45 to 11. The number of Rwandan priests in Butare declined from 79 to 50 [nationally, 103 of 400 Rwandan priests were killed in the war, as were 3 of 9 bishops and many sisters, according to Kinyamateka (1994) and Nzabahimana (1994)]. Catholic schools in Butare Diocese were diminished from 12 to 4, and health centers dropped from 15 to 7 remaining with foreign staff. The estimated loss of material goods, including buildings (Figure 38), amounted to nearly $2 million according to a diocesan document (Diocese de Butare 1994a).

Launching the Initiative for Pastoral Renewal

Following the war, the bishop of Butare appointed a commission of pastoral initiative. So many priests had fled or been killed or been defamed in the war that an extraordinary effort was made to make the church credible. Laurien Ntezimana, a layman of Butare, was asked to head the Commission pour la Réprise des Activités Pastorales (CRAP), which later took on the name Service d'Animation Pastorale. The commission included five abbots; the vicar of the cathedral, Mungwarareba Modest; and other laymen.

In early January 1995, when we spoke with Ntezimana and Mungwarareba in their small office alongside the diocesan complex in the Economat, where the cars and supplies were kept, it was evident that this initiative was not business as usual. Both of these Tutsi men had survived the massacres in Butare by hiding in their homes. When they spoke about those fateful weeks, they seemed visibly shaken. But their concern was already in the present, in the restoration of the Catholic Church, at least in Butare. They were part of an experiment that would receive national and international recognition (van Hoyweghen 1996, p 396; de Heusch and de Bethune 1996). Neither man was wearing a habit. The walls were lined with current theological, historical, and sociological books, especially books about Central Africa, suggesting strongly that this initiative was in touch with current worldwide theological thinking. There was much human traffic through the office, with an air of urgency.

The core of this renewal initiative was a cadre of 24 lay people selected by the surviving members of the Butare parishes, two from each parish. The local clergy had been so decimated and defamed that it was no longer possible or desirable to work with them, suggested Ntezimana, putting this even stronger with the words, "Many of these pastors are morally wounded and broken, mortally. Let them go. We must help them to rest and to heal." I (John) raised with him the often heard phrase that "the church in Rwanda is dead" following the massacres and complicity in the genocide. He agreed:

> There are things that are dead that should stay dead. The big buildings, the ritual, the varnish—all that is superficial. The church can no longer just hand out sacraments. Worship is not just for feeling good. How can you go and receive the Eucharist at mass when you have thoughts of vengeance in your head? For us to be satisfied with the crowds of "believers" is dead. We can't be content with crowds anymore. We must deal with the spirit of vengeance first. People must excommunicate them-

Figure 38. Remains of the chapel of the Catholic secondary school, Butare, Rwanda, near the cathedral, facing diocesan offices and guesthouse. The building was destroyed in late April 1994 by Interahamwe militia, perhaps because it stood as a symbol of historical Tutsi privilege. Photo taken on January 4, 1995.

> selves and begin anew. We are not in a hurry. We must be vigilant, historically and through the spoken Word. Let the Word continue to live. We pray to be created anew by God. Our church is in diaspora; we must put the pieces of the puzzle together again.

The longer we spoke, the more it was clear that Ntezimana and Mungwarareba had a well-developed concept of what they were doing and that it would be more appropriate for us to read their writing in order to grasp their understanding of the nature of the destruction within the Rwandan church to understand how they thought they could rebuild it.

These two men, however, were like most with whom we spoke: eager to tell us how they had escaped the massacres in Butare. But they had already, apparently, told it to enough others that it was no longer oppressing for them, and they had been able to redirect their energies to their mission of rebuilding the diocese of Butare on a new footing.

A key document had been Ntezimana's (1994) essay on "rereading the Word and reading history, that is, current events." This was very much the foundation of the initiative in pastoral renewal through locally selected laity. Ntezimana's essay follows here in translation.

The Word of God As Principle of Human Maturation

> The tragic events that we have not yet concluded here in Rwanda oblige that remnant which remains of the church to reconsider its practice and its preaching of the Word of God, in view of creating new vessels for the ever new wine of the Good News.
>
> For the untruth and the murder that have ravaged this land and continue to suffocate it have proven such that Rwandans do not allow themselves to be penetrated by "the truth that sets free," because they have seriously misunderstood this truth. The "gospel of peace" has not found its way into the hearts of Rwandans, because it remains—90 years after the beginning of the teaching of this Good News in Rwanda—so irreconcilable [to the reality at hand], that it is enormously difficult to accept it [in the face of] so few scruples against the shedding of the blood of others.
>
> Whose responsibility is this failure of a certain teaching that is the Good News? More than just humans, to the "Christian system" no doubt ("truths to be believed, commandments to be observed, sacraments to be received"). The recent history of the country reveals that this system has not permitted the Word to penetrate personal and social reality so as to truly convert the mind so as to induce a society oriented toward increasing conviviality, as is expected from that which comes into play with the gospel message.
>
> History serves as a means of revealing the extent of good or bad inscription of the Good News into sociocultural realities. If a society is in large part Christian (as Rwanda) and it tends toward conviviality and its culture tends toward tolerance, then the inscription of the gospel is good. In the contrary case, [this inscription] is more or less false. And this is unhappily the case in Rwanda.
>
> To correct this inscription, it is necessary to attack the [faulty] processes, not humans as such (toward whom respect is essential).
>
> The failure of the teaching of the gospel in Rwanda is that it has been "congealed" *[figée]* into stereotypes, rather than renewed constantly in new syntheses elaborated in the face of history. It is thus the "process of rereading" the Word of God that has failed. This process, classic in the Bible, consists in this: that a theme is increasingly clarified thanks to the historical variations [in which it is manifested] and is increasingly better understood through generations of believers. When this process of rereading gets stuck, that of historicization is blocked accordingly.
>
> To "historicize," as written by F. Ebousi-Boulanga (1981, p. 190), is "to translate into the life of the city and in the public square that which [normally] is said and occurs only in the womb of the temple and liturgical gatherings; to produce outside that which one professes to achieve within, in the sanctuary of the soul and the heart." Thus, for example, to historicize the eucharistic mystery, in a world with totalitarian tendencies, would be among other emphases to recognize differences [among people].
>
> When this process of historicization fails, it leads to a counter-process of the ideologization of the Word, which is to say that this Word serves henceforth to camouflage practices which are the inverse of that which it proclaims. Thus, for example, the more one practices a policy of segregation, the more one preaches national unity; the more hate there is, the more there is talk of love, etc. This is what happened and continues to happen in Rwanda.
>
> To escape this condition, it is necessary to take up again the process of rereading, which then brings about historicization, which neutralizes the ideologization that has brought us such miseries. This [neutralization] is what we will undertake here, in trying to create—under the power of the Rwandan here and now—an operating synthesis of the diverse functions of the Word of God in the maturation of the human being, given that misfortunes and horrors as those which we have known in Rwanda are always due to human immaturity.

We cannot but put in perspective the work to be done and to indicate its steps, for, in truth, the work must be done in community.

The first thing to do is to try to see lucidly where we are: to make a "truthful affidavit," as Freud would say. Begin by taking stock of the abyss into which our lives have been thrown. It is from the center of this interpretation of our socio-historical situation that one must reread the Word of God in view of aiding people to mature in their tormented state.

The first purpose of the Word of God in human maturation found in a situation in which they have received serious wounds to their bodies, their emotions, their convictions, and their very humanity, is evidently to console them. This may cause some to smile; however, without consolation, the wounded human being can only pour out hate toward God and humanity. It is necessary, thus, before all else, to reread the Word (Writing and Tradition) in the sense of leading afflicted people to take stock of the tenderness of God to those who are broken and crushed, to allow them to accept the ointment of this tenderness on their wounds.

Surrounded by this consolation and putting roots into it opens the way to the therapeutic function of the Word. It is necessary here to reread the Word in such a manner as to put in process the forming of scar tissue of the wounds of humanity. These wounds will form this scar tissue when the "patient" accedes to the knowledge of that which has happened (not just knowing, but experiencing it). The light that the patient will receive will thus replace the ignorance of the causes of all the fear and greed which are at the basis of the lies and murder.

Contained in the therapeutic function as the active principle of healing is found the function of initiation to human life in God. It is necessary here to see that that which is in play in the Word and the Tradition, is nothing other than human maturity, the correct "information" (in the double sense of instruction and molding) of the human life.

At this stage the signs of human maturity begin to appear, which one must make well known so as to put aside the formidable and recurrent contempt that mistakes "spoiled children" for adults and merely violent persons for revolutionaries.

The first sign of human maturity is the capacity to ask forgiveness: to perceive one's limits, one's rancor and mistakes, to confess them at least to oneself, and to take oneself in charge to work out, with the grace of God, to better achieve a "self-in-God."

The second sign of human maturity is the capacity for expiation, to enter into the "play" of Christ by paying, following him and with him ("it is now my happiness to suffer for you," *Colossians* 1:24), the price of that which breaks the most immature brothers and sisters .

The sign of signs of full human maturity is the capacity for mercy *[misericord]*, to imitate God throughout the days in adopting his love with repentance toward other humans, this love that, says Paul, "excuses all, believes all, hopes all, endures all" (*I Corinthians* 13:7).

Here then, in a "strategic discourse," a manner to conceive of the Word of God and its teaching, induced to the situation that has traversed this land of a thousand hills, a thousand horrors, and a thousand mercies. To implicate the Christian communities, or what remains of them, in this strategy, such is the orientation that the Service of Theological Animation of the Catholic Diocese of Butare would like to take. Each and every criticism, in whatever fashion, will be welcome.

Discerning History and Reading the Word of God

The group of 24 lay pastoral leaders was visited regularly by Ntezimana and his team. These lay pastors were encouraged to listen to their parishioners and to document their stories—they needed cassette recorders, he thought—and to record the problems the people were expressing. This would offer a basis for a new beginning. Many of the 24 were volunteers, but they worked full-time. CRAP found some funding through a Canadian agency to support its work. However, two of the lay pastors were arrested on suspicion of collaboration with the former government.

Ntezimana shared with us some of the responses to this initiative. He also gave us pamphlets circulated from September 1994 on to guide the initiative. These pamphlets appear without authors' names and are intended to be semi-official guides to the work of the lay pastors and others, but they clearly continue to develop the work of church renewal from the perspective of Ntezimana's (1994) paper.

The September 21, 1994, pamphlet addressed the nature of the conflict in terms of the contradictory sentiments and feelings of several categories of people making up Rwandan society in the immediate postwar period. The church needed to listen to them all.

1. There were first of all those who "were supposed to die" (the Tutsi) and who had escaped or hidden or fled or those women who had allowed themselves to be violated by the Interahamwe to survive and who carried in their "body-soul" the consequences of those terrible months. Many of them harbored *thoughts of vengeance.*

> 2. Then there are those who "were not supposed to die" (the Hutu) who more or less did not or did not at all participate in the massacres and who fled and are returning. They are inspired by a *sentiment of fear of reprisal.*
>
> 3. There are the former refugees (of 1959, 1973, 1980) who are returning, above all from Burundi, Uganda, and elsewhere, and [who] are inspired by a *sentiment of victory,* finally at home in their Rwanda.
>
> 4. Then, [there are] those foreigners living in Rwanda, who stayed during the storm or who fled and are now returned, and those members of the NGOs working in Rwanda. They are inspired by a sentiment more difficult to define, but it may depend on their sympathy or antipathy toward one or another of the protagonists in the Rwandan conflict.
>
> 5. Finally, last but not least, [there are] the soldiers of the RPF who are now in power in this beautiful land of a thousand horrors and a thousand mercies. It is necessary to be very attentive to this group, some of whom keep their distance from all that is the Catholic Church and who pursue without pity the Interahamwe killers.
>
> All of these categories have in common a loss: materially (no food, clothing, often no housing) and morally (all are wounded in one or another manner, bodily, in their heart, convictions, and above all, in their humanity).

The pamphlet considered that the roots of this morass of fear and self-centeredness lie in a number of former troubles: depersonalizing education and the inadequate resolution *(guhagama)* of previous historical traumas, including the demands of the royalist and the colonial epoch. The roots of the crisis also lay in the dehumanization of the previous regime. The line of thinking stressed that each problem has a historical foundation that must be uncovered and understood before it can be adequately addressed in the work of the church. This perspective bears a close resemblance to a psychoanalytical understanding of what happens to an individual when trauma is not treated. Its damages linger on, continuing to obstruct the sufferer's unfolding humanity, which the initiative speaks of as maturation.

As for the church's role in all this, the pamphlet acknowledged that, except for a few individuals for whom the love of the other was stronger than death, the majority were not at their best. In other words, there were many in the church who participated in the killing in one form or another. How could this have happened? The pamphlet explained by admitting that the gospel was not well taught. But more than this, it was due to cultural compromise with power in the Rwandan church. This too has its historical roots that need to be examined and whose effects need to be counteracted by a more evangelical posture of the church. CRAP made several recommendations for immediate action: (1) The new pastoral teams should discreetly identify those believers who remained true to their faith and praise them at the appropriate occasions. (2) The pastoral teams should encourage and bring together the remnant parishes that refused to give up and reinforce them, in connection with item 1. (3) The pastoral teams should not simply stop the practice of the Eucharist but celebrate the deaths of the innocent and proclaim the Resurrection to strengthen the feeble hope of those who are on their knees. They should localize the sanctions to those parishes that were profaned but try to determine the degree of profanation and come up with measures to rehabilitate the site. (4) Above all, the pastoral teams should emphasize the curative aspect of the eucharistic celebration and combine it with weekly catechistic teachings in public and with everyone present. The diocese must give itself the task of grieving for a time, to give the Christians the opportunity to acknowledge and overcome their own betrayal. The clergy must share in this process and work with the congregants to break with old prejudices and bad habits.

The Work of Grieving

In late September another pamphlet (September 26, 1994), titled "The Work of Grieving," opened with a reexamination of the roots and the depths of the genocide. What is the explanation for the fragility of the Rwandan social fabric that permitted it to degenerate into genocide, even within the nuclear family and the marriage bond? How could a woman kill her own husband? a man his wife? a son his mother (to demonstrate that he had no pity)? and a mother her own children? Is this due, CRAP asked, to the weakness of the relationship? Or is it due to the fragility of the personality, that is, the weakness of Rwandan personhood? Few Rwandans, noted the pamphlet, demonstrated their capacity to "prefer dying to betrayal." As a consequence, it is necessary not only to encourage reconciliation but also to enhance personhood through leading grieving to make the mourners "weep bitterly" and to become "faithful to martyrdom" (following Peter after his betrayal).

CRAP took the position that the betrayal of the church was in large part due to the reluctance of church leaders to integrate the reforms of the Vatican II Council. The leadership was urged to engage in self-criticism and to publicly ask forgiveness of the faithful, and the Christians were asked to forgive the nation for not having averted the holocaust. After all, they pretended to be the most human part of the society.

CRAP suggested that each community announce its time of mourning, in connection with Advent, culminating in the Christmas celebration. In preparing for this season of grieving, the workers *(animators)* were to compile lists of those who died for the celebration of "communion of the saints." They were directed to research, rehabilitate, and bring back into use the symbolic language that Rwandans had used in mourning. They were to train priests to be good masters of ceremony, insofar as speaking, singing, gestures, and attitudes were concerned. Finally, the lay workers were encouraged to use the mass's liturgy as a vehicle for maturation and ripening. But at all cost, this could not be preached in a way that would rebuff the congregants. That would have been a sacrilege and would not have changed a thing. Realizing how difficult it would be to change priests' habits, the lay workers were told to be ready to take charge of the services.

Figure 39. Cathedral drums, Butare, Rwanda. These *ngoma* drums are used in mass and worship celebrations across Central Africa. They are symbols of power and expressions of spiritual energy. In the Butare post-war renewal initiative, drums were to be silent during the period of grieving in preparation for the communion of the saints, the recognition of the dead.

Sharing the Word

During this time of mourning, CRAP recommended that all drums be silenced and all dancing be suspended (Figure 39). Weekday masses were to be replaced with times of "sharing the Word" *(gusangira ijambo)*. Leaders were asked to avoid just reading the texts and encouraged to read and try to interpret the contents. Above all, the teachers were encouraged to "make the bridge between history in process in our country and that of which the text is speaking" (from the second CRAP pamphlet, September 26, 1994, p. 4).

The inclusion of preaching, sharing the Word, within the context of the mass was sufficiently disturbing to some congregants and members of the Catholic community that they spoke up about it. In response, CRAP addressed the special status of the modification of canonical liturgy. The modification was seen to be admissible under the principle of the unity of the three charges or functions of the priest, to teach, sanctify, and govern the parish. Under the banner of the priest's responsibility and the "prophetic freedom of the believer" these variations in the liturgy were defensible. In any case, the first principle of the liturgy, suggested the pamphlet, is that of *metanoia,* the participant's conversion to the conscious acceptance of the willingness to give one's body and blood for the reconciliation of humanity with God and with each other. The model for this stance of giving oneself for peace must be that of Christ in Gesthemane, sweating blood for the other. This was seen as such an important task in Rwanda that the liturgy must incorporate teaching to change from the status quo, when the liturgy masked all kinds of evil emotions.

The Creative Spirit in the Crisis

The CRAP pamphlet messages express the desire that the crisis become a time of learning, of growth. For that to come about, the creative spirit that emerges in great crises must be allowed to flourish (CRAP pamphlet 4, November 11, 1994). This is necessary because there are really no experts in the enormous work awaiting Rwandans in such a moment as this. Even the so-called experts must not dominate the process because one of the central needs is for Rwandans to learn to take their own affairs in hand again. This was true of the Rwandan evangelist, the new pastoral worker, just as it was true of the foreign helpers so prominent in Rwanda. All groups of believers still intact in their *collines* were to be allowed and were encouraged to participate and work together. The human community of the parish was encouraged to come back to life, although the costly buildings may not be rehabilitated. The parish was pushed to become a community on a human scale. It is doubtful that all the social services formerly administered by the church can ever be taken up again. The church had become too much of a social service administration, which may have inhibited its apostolic mission.

Justice

The CRAP pamphlets are bold enough to address the divided concerns of their parishes and all Rwandans regarding the impact of arrests, rumors of attacks, and imprisonment of those thought by some to be innocent. This is a highly delicate subject for CRAP to be addressing, because two of the 24 lay pastors had been arrested and imprisoned on such charges. The fifth CRAP pamphlet, issued on December 25, 1994, reviewed the various responses to these arrests. Some people said the arrests were unjust; others said that they merely appeared to be unjust; others were for protective custody. The pamphlet writer urged readers to let "justice be allowed to be just," adding that there are ways to assist in this. The pamphlet encouraged people to visit those in detention, encourage them, but also to visit the jailers, those making the arrests, and those in charge of the prisons to help them keep their humanity. The pamphlet writer warned of becoming too enthusiastic about mediation and of being overly eager about "settling scores once and for all" with those who committed the massacres. In other words, it is necessary to reserve judgment and to let justice take its course. In this, it is important for the pastoral worker to keep a spirit of softness and tenderness, for it is the comforting word that heals, not the harsh or cold or aloof word. This too is part of the work of grieving.

Genocide, Impunity, and Reconciliation

The writers of the CRAP pamphlets were concerned, in their Christmas issue, with the way in which the word *genocide* was being used in the international press, including the East African Catholic press. They argued that its use had obscured (rendered "occult") the human dimension of events. They wondered about the silence in these writings of the involvement of France, Egypt, and the United Nations in the armaments and the withdrawal of troops in the formative moments of the war. They were not trying to avoid the use of the term, as if to negate it. In fact, they were trying to deal with it head on. The true horrors of the genocide were sometimes masked by feature stories on the fantastic humanitarian work by international agencies. Also, there was considerable manipulation of information in the Rwandan national and regional press. A case mentioned in the fifth pamphlet was the handling by a now Belgium-based editorial group of the Rwandan Catholic magazine *Dialogue* and Ntezimana's publication of an article, "De Charybde en Scylla?" The editors added the question mark to the title and in a byline suggested that Ntezimana had been killed by the RPF for his remarks, something that has not worried him to this point. Blaming others is a common distortion in the media, in particular the Rwandan media, and is a block to healing.

Fearlessly, the pamphlet writer also mentioned the disorderly arrests in Rwanda, the disappearing persons, and accusations that impede the return of refugees. Finally, the writer suggested that the delay of the tribunals was perhaps the major stumbling block for peace in Rwanda. As long as justice was delayed, who could doubt the temptation to exercise reprisals? So long as there was no justice, it was hypocritical to preach forgiveness, the sine qua non of reconciliation, without appearing to reinforce impunity. These are all problems that also affect the work of the church in bringing about its renewal. In terms of Ntezimana's (1994) essay, they represent a reading of current history in the light of the Word of God.

New Year's Drums in Butare

Whatever constraints had been placed on the traditional high celebrations of the Rwandan Catholic Church by CRAP's work of grieving, there was no constraint on drums and the Eucharist for everyone on New Year's day in Butare Cathedral (Figure 40 and 41). The two services of that morning were filled to capacity. A cathedral choir with drum accompaniment led rhythmic singing that reverberated throughout the soaring spaces of the cathedral. The vicar's admonitions in Kinyarwanda mentioned the heavy themes of national guilt and the need for repentance and the recollection of the dead, but this only heightened the auspiciousness of the day. When the Eucharist was offered, everyone, including hundreds of children, came to the aisles to receive the wafer from attendants. Many of the participants that day were displaced persons (i.e., mostly Tutsi) from Gikongoro who had fled

Figure 40. Butare Cathedral, built in 1935 with funds from Queen Astrid of Belgium. Photo taken on January 1, 1995.

Figure 41. Drum-led mass and open communion on January 1, 1995. Many participants in the service were Tutsi displaced survivors of the Gikongoro massacres, living in temporary shelter in the dormitories of the Butare Secondary School near the cathedral under heavy military protection.

the Interahamwe and were living in the camp that had been erected in the fenced-in grounds of the Catholic secondary school near the cathedral, guarded by RPF soldiers. These were the "supposed to die" of the first item in CRAP's first pamphlet who had survived the attacks and probably "harbored thoughts of vengeance."

Ntezimana (1994) believed that the Eucharist should not be taken unless the thoughts of vengeance had been cleansed. It was apparent that the initiative of pastoral renewal as formulated by CRAP did not represent everyone's sentiment. For some, the church's liturgy continued to bless power, and everyone could take the Eucharist. This was the sentiment of the returned refugees of 1959, 1973, and 1980 and of the RPF soldiers (the third and the fifth group in CRAP's first pamphlet). What about the second group, those who "were not supposed to die" and who were inspired by a sentiment of fear of reprisal?

CRAP's concept for renewal of Rwandan society was focused on a new way of reading current history and reading the Word of God. Embedded sentiments long harbored as a result of former injustices, not properly dealt with, were supposed to be brought out into the open light of the gospel truth. There was supposed to be grieving, weeping, at the horrible crimes committed, at the betrayal of others. Only if earlier crimes and sentiments were expunged, as in the confessions of a psychoanalytical session, could full human maturity be realized. In this understanding the blockage of repressed or unsolved earlier injustices (formulated in the Kinyarwanda term *guhagama*) or congealed as stereotypes needed to be removed through full disclosure.

The Butare initiative for renewal was being adopted by many groups outside the Butare Diocese and by non-Catholics. It represented the most systematic rethinking of organized religion we encountered, the most thorough analysis of the impact of the war on the souls of a people, and the best thought-out approach to genuine, lasting peace.

2.6 *The Fate of Institutions:* The National Research Institute

Customs have been erased, tabula rasa; there is no morality.—Professor Karangwa, Butare, January 2, 1995

It was New Year's day, 1995, in Butare, Rwanda. We had walked with philosopher Abbot Lucien Rwabashi from the diocesan guesthouse to the Hotel Ibis to have a drink. At a table in the hotel courtyard we were joined by Innocent Mandali, a doctor who had studied medicine in Zaire and had worked in Kikwit, Zaire, on leprosy and respirology for an American NGO, and Kalinda Ezechiel, newly appointed research director at the Centre Universitaire de la Recherche Pharmaceutique et Médicine Traditionelle (University Center for Pharmaceutical and Medical Research) (CURPHARMETRA). From time to time we were also joined by a tipsy Burundian journalist who had been in California and elsewhere to study electronics. He had come to Rwanda for the first time in his life in August to find his roots; his parents were from Gitarama. He said it was great to be home. These men were all southern Tutsi and as such were out of favor with the Habyarimana regime. All except the abbot were living in exile because they would not have been able to receive university education in Rwanda in the time of the quotas. In late 1994 they, like many others, were back to fill central positions in the new Rwanda's research and educational institutions.

Soon the conversation turned to the events of the war, as it always did. Mandali said outright, "I'm Tutsi," and we were getting quite another perspective. He spoke of repression and blockage in education. Not in primary school, where they hardly knew of Hutu and Tutsi, but at the end of secondary school, when it came time for scholarships for study abroad. They were simply told to go teach in the north, and others—meaning Hutu—were given study abroad opportunities. Mandali had gone to Zaire to study medicine. Kalinda had gone to Burundi.

The others said they had suffered big losses in their families but suggested that the African families would come together again—"Where there's a will, there's a way." Mandali said that even all the orphans would be taken in by extended family members who probably had not found each other yet. They thought that it would be possible to rebuild the country.

They denied they were anti-Hutu, pointing out that their Hutu neighbors had helped their families bury their dead and that Mandali had even been greeted and helped by old neighbors he himself had been afraid to greet on first returning from Zaire. He planned to return to settle permanently in several months. He was confident that he could find work as a physician.

The abbot, the doctor, and the pharmacologist were unanimous in depicting the perpetrators of the genocide of April 1994 as a clique comparable to the Nazis, the KKK, and the Black Panthers—cynical killers who the abbot said were "sans foi, sans loi" (without faith, without law) and who the pharmacologist said believed in neither God nor the Devil. Many of the influential refugees who had fled to Zaire were using their alleged fear of returning as a justification for their involvement in the genocide. Granted, there were many innocents in Zaire, but they were hostages of the clique, held by fear of being killed by their old leaders should they try to return. Thus saying there is instability in Rwanda covers for them and they do not have to confront the clique that wants to keep them in Zaire. Hopefully, the international tribunal will bring out all the guilty. The three men rejected our suggestion that negotiations with those in exile might be necessary for there to be a lasting peace in Rwanda, saying it was impossible to negotiate with a government of assassins. They acknowledged that there were still many antagonists in Rwanda.

The three men suggested that the Hutu-Tutsi rhetoric of today had nothing to do with the traditional meanings of these terms; it was a rhetoric of division used by fascists of the worst kind to hang on to power by eliminating "the other."

The Institut de Recherche Scientifique et de Technologie

The next day Kalinda took us to the Institut de Recherche Scientifique et de Technologie (IRST). We saw the main buildings of the institute, which had been broken into and pillaged: fine sturdy structures built in the era of Belgian colonialism in a beautiful landscape setting. Windows had been smashed and computers stolen, but otherwise records and some furniture had been left intact. We were impressed by the atmosphere of this, a working research institution, open and conducting business so few months after such a devastating war. Eventually we would learn that most of the researchers were recent returnees, Tutsi, from neighboring countries. Of the prewar mostly Hutu staff, all had fled or been killed, except for the acting director of the National Museum, Bazatsinda Thomas (see section 2.7). We were not able to visit the university because we did not possess the special permit required to get through the military barricade on the road leading there.

The institute, including the central research center, the National Museum, the CURPHARMETRA, and sections of the main campus of the University of Rwanda, had all been created in the independent era. The research establishments were a re-creation of the colonial Institut de Recherche Scientifique Agriculturel et Culturelle (IRSAEC), founded in 1951. After independence, in 1964, the term *national* was added to the title to make it the Institut National de Recherche Scientifique (INRS). The present emphasis on technology was added during Habyarimana's rule to emphasize practical Rwandan concerns, in reaction to the Belgian colonial emphasis on basic research.

The most extreme destruction we saw was at the CURPHARMETRA, where offices had been ransacked and computers and equipment of any value had been taken. Kalinda showed us the laboratories where the medicinal plant specimens were still on the table as they had been when the place was destroyed. The large botanical gardens stood nearby, but they were unkempt. Six of eight workers and their families had been killed.

Kalinda told us more about his background, recent and more distant. As a Tutsi, he had been unable to get his advanced education and work in prewar Rwanda. He had been teaching biology in a secondary school in Burundi. He returned to Butare in August 1994 and was hired by the laboratory of CURPHARMETRA. Before he could continue with the tour of the institute, he wanted to tell us of his family's fate in the war.

> My family was nearly decimated in the massacres. Two uncles and most of their families were killed, a brother too. All that survive are some nieces and nephews and a sister-in-law and me. We used to be a large family of herders in Kibuye on Lake Kivu, traced back eight generations, but none remain there. I am now the family head and take my responsibilities seriously. My nieces and nephews aren't really orphans; the African family will handle this disaster.

Discussions with the Director on Science and Religion

Later in the afternoon Kalinda accompanied us to the home of the director of IRST, Professor Karangwa. He had not been at the institute that morning because he was sick with the flu or malaria, but he indicated he was willing to meet with us. We mentioned our visit with the Zairian educator Bishikwabo Chubaka in Bukavu, with whom he had stayed early in the war. We had discussed at length with Bishikwabo the continuing interest in the traditional Great Lakes region religion Kubandwa (also know as Imandwa, after Imaana, God), the rites of which explicitly included Hutu, Tutsi, and Twa. One of the topics of conversation we explored with scholars and others in Zaire, Rwanda, and Burundi was the possible role of this regional rite and set of beliefs as a basis for societal repair. A major colloquium had been held on Kubandwa in the heyday of the Vatican II's influence on the theology of African religions (CERUKI 1976). The scholars with whom we spoke, such as Bishikwabo, University of Bukavu rector Vincent Mulago, and the late Rwandan scholar Alexis Kagame, had explored the correspondences between Central African traditional religion and Christianity. Lyangombe, the martyr hero, clearly compared to Christ. The local Kubandwa rites featured a kind of inclusive communion that compared to Christian ideals. Now, several decades later, after a horrific war in which the Christian churches had not only engaged in divisive and murderous politics but also had been the place of violence, was it not time to look at these inclusive religious roots for moral renewal?

Karangwa came out of his sickroom to meet us. He had been in Zaire before the war, as a university research chemist. We told him about our mission and the question of Kubandwa's and Lyangombe's relevance to the postwar period. He seemed interested but suggested that we speak to Thomas Kamanzi, head of IRST's Rwandan Studies section, which we did later. Karangwa welcomed the suggestion of a colloquium on Lyangombe but said that the institute was certainly in no position to hold it now. He did offer his views on the Catholic Church in Rwanda.

> Rwanda has certainly been the most evangelized country in Africa, yet today the general sentiment is that the church has failed. The church has been demonstrated to have a superficial hold on people, yet the religious system that was there before has been largely destroyed. If Kubandwa is observed today, it is in secret. The church has succeeded in persuading the vast majority that it was sin to practice it. There is a need to look at, evaluate this, and begin from ground zero to determine how to evangelize. Kubandwa was more active in the north, although it extended throughout the [Great Lakes] area. A colloquium would be good.

Dinner Conversation with the Abbot

That evening, at dinner at the Butare diocesan guesthouse, Abbot Rwabashi told us of his experiences in the war after we reported of our day with Kalinda. He had taken the initiative earlier in our stay of sitting with us at the dining table. We had much in common as academics. The experiences he related were so horrendous that we wondered how he could have engaged in casual small talk about university life and authors. Once again we had been caught in the incongruity of this almost normal life around us and terrible memories of the genocide just beneath the surface.

> My family stems from a hill in Gikongoro, where three brothers and their families were all destroyed. The massacres were particularly systematic in Gikongoro. I had fled Butare [when the war broke out] to be with my family. [When the massacres broke out there,] my family sought shelter in the church. But this was one of the worst massacre scenes, with more than 5,000 dead. Hand grenades, rifles, and machetes were used. Homes were burned. Entire hills are burned-out ruins. I was one of only four or five who survived the massacre in Gikongoro cathedral, hidden under corpses.

We were deeply shocked by this dinner story and could barely continue with our meal. We immediately associated Abbot Rwabashi's account with the ambiguous justifications of the war we had heard from the lips of Gikongoro préfet Laurent Bucyibaruta in the Muku camp in Zaire. So we asked Abbot Rwabashi about Bucyibaruta and the role of the prefet in the massacres.

> By his failure to stop the killing he would be guilty. But the préfet was usually actively involved in the massacres. The orders came from the *chef d'état major* of the army, and the préfet would have to have been informed and involved.

But Abbot Rwabashi had clearly been at work coming to terms with his experience. Although all his books, clothes, diaries, and notes had been destroyed, he said he was in the process of writing about his experience, now that he had a new home in the guesthouse.

> I find consolation in history and scripture for my ordeal, which I will never forget. There is the biblical account of Herod's purge of all boys under two (*Matthew*, ch. 2) and Jesus' family's escape to Egypt. This is particularly appropriate. Note that Matthew refers back to Jeremiah, to another massacre: "We have heard the cries of Ramah, weeping and great lamentations; Rachel weeps for her children, she was not to be consoled, because they no longer exist" (*Jeremiah* 31:15; *Matthew* 2:18).

Colonial Anthropology, Mission Christianity, and the Origins of Division in Rwandan Society

We spoke with Thomas Kamanzi on two occasions during our days in Butare. Kamanzi, a trained structural linguist, lived in Burundi from 1973 until August 1994, thus during all of the Habyarimana era and the ensuing war. He taught at the university. The turn of events of the war had not been entirely bad for him. Amazingly, he said, when he returned to Butare, his old house, which he built before 1972, was empty. The colonel who had lived in it had fled. This was the colonel who become the préfet of Butare during the war, and when the tide turned, he fled. "Amazing good fortune," Kamanzi observed. Speaking of préfets, or governors, in the area, we mentioned Bucyibaruta. Kamanzi had known him well. In fact, they had been together at the INRS in 1972, on the eve of Habyarimana's coup. They had been colleagues at the National Museum. Yet from that time on their careers went in opposite directions; a better illustration could not be imagined of what national Rwandan society had experienced.

> After the 1972 coup, [Bucyibaruta] became a bourgmestre and a préfet, I went into exile. [Bucyibaruta] was a really bad instigator of massacres and repression. He would hardly escape capital punishment if arrested and tried.

Kamanzi had much to say about Rwandan religion, scholarship, and the conditions that led to the conflict in Rwanda. As did many of our contacts, he began with his personal story during the war. Because he had been in exile during the war, he had not been personally assaulted. But as a

Tutsi, he needed to relate the terrible things that happened in his home community in Kibayi commune near the Burundi border. This was told in connection with a general discussion of Rwandan religion.

> I was raised in a Catholic family where Imaana, Kiranga, Lyangombe, and Nyabingi were never mentioned. Rwandans were accused of being animists. All that—being pagan—was forbidden. The big substitution began. Today in Rwanda, it's deceptive. Tutsi were accused of being communists in the 1950s by the church and others. Ethnicity was used to polarize the people. Hutu were peasants, who were close to the voice of God. Pope John XXIII presented himself here in messages as a peasant's son. His predecessor, Pius XII, was an aristocrat, and the Tutsi were privileged. So the Catholic Church divided the people. Evangelization was always accompanied by division. Now, all has been destroyed—Mary and Joseph's statues were beheaded because they were held to be Tutsi. This kind of iconoclasm. The church in my home parish of Mugombwa was destroyed with Tutsi in it. There is now no mission left, no services; the church is destroyed. This is common throughout the country. Even more regrettable than all this is the profanation of the person and all that was sacred. This is a central characteristic of the massacres. I understand nothing of all this. The techniques that were used in the massacres were depersonalization and demonization, but this was preached a long time. The people of the Rwandan Patriotic Front were described as beasts, the Tutsi were said to have been abandoned by Imaana. All this continued for a long time. To be a true Rwandan, was to be of northwestern origin and Hutu. This is why the Hutu of the south were massacred as well.

Kamanzi went on to identify another source of divisive thinking, namely, the anthropological scholarship during the colonial era, and the division between scholars now.

> Such thinking was long in preparation. It has its roots in the identity card system, which is rooted in the work of the first anthropologists who came here to study differences between the people, scholars such as Jacques Maquet—who used such notions as "premises of inequality"—and Marcel d'Hertefelt.[6] The southern Tutsi were disfavored. I'm the only linguist in this Center. The northern scholars are now in exile. The evil that was done to intellectuals is terrible. Northwest intellectuals participated in the massacres; they are now in exile. Southern Tutsis were marginalized. The land is empty. The Akazu, the family of the ex-president who was from the northwest, was where the Hutu chiefs, or little kings, were from. So the big culprit was the anthropology of division applied to colonial ends. But the work of Luc de Heusch, who worked independently, and of Jan Vansina and Pierre de Maret is valid and good.

Finally, Kamanzi spoke of Kubandwa and the churches.

> Kubandwa was a national religion to God—Imaana. Kubandwa was a national religion, for everyone, although the services were held at the level of each ridge. Divination for misfortunes was private. So during the Catholic era [the rites of] Kubandwa became private as well, even secretive. Adherents met privately in caves, with Kubandwa services occurring in the midst of nocturnal wakes for the dead. This was a camouflaged form, however. My father-in-law died without Christian baptism; he explained to the priests he couldn't be baptized because he was already baptized.

Kamanzi related a consideration of the inclusion of Kubandwa in the pressing problems of the moment.

> The churches have a lot to learn. A discussion of Kubandwa should be totally open, to exclude no one. It is a propitious moment for this discussion. It's not for specialists, but for human beings. How to help Rwandese find a way to keep vengeance from being done. The young soldier whose whole family was killed, he can't behave like an angel.

2.7 Surviving Cultural "Scorched Earth" at the National Museum of Rwanda

I don't do politics, but the politics came to me.—
Bazatsinda Thomas, Acting Director and Curator of the National Museum of Rwanda, January 3, 1995

Hugging the western slope of a green-meadowed hill and alongside the road that leads from Butare north to Kigali and south to Burundi stands the National Museum of Rwanda. The building's horizontal expanse of brick and glass is given visual counterpoint by a series of steep gables that shape the roof. The cast-bronze dedication plaque, dated 1989, explains that this museum was a gift from Belgium to Rwanda. The exhibit concept was developed by the Rwandan Ministry of Education and the Institute of Rwandan Studies at the University of Butare in collaboration with Jean Baptist Cuypers and staff at the Musée Royal de l'Afrique Central, Tervuren, Belgium.

It was Friday, December 2, 1994, a cool rainy day, when we first stopped at the museum (see R.K. Janzen, 1995). The large glass panels of the entry doors were shattered, the only remaining outwardly visible sign that the 1994 war in Rwanda had also raged here. The next, less obvious sign of postwar improvisation was the director's desk set up temporarily in the spacious entry lobby, which doubles as gift shop, bar, and performance hall. And there were more not-so-subtle signs of a country under siege: after two young women received our admission of 300 Rwandan francs (then the equivalent of $1) each, we walked through the immaculately kept exhibition halls in the company of a few visiting Canadian UN soldiers in camouflage uniforms and were watched by Rwandan boy soldiers carrying automatic weapons.

The museum sequence acquaints the viewer first with the geography, geology, and ancient history, including the development of cattle raising and agriculture, and migrations of the Great Lakes region that contains today's Rwanda. Common subsistence tools pertaining to livestock tending, bee keeping, beer brewing, and agriculture and to metallurgy, pottery, and basketry are shown as well as a full-size reconstruction of a magnificent Rwandan round dwelling, complete with furnishings. Another hall displays artifacts and photographs related to traditional medicine, music, games and toys, the religious cult of Kubandwa, burial practices, and chiefship and kingship. Here the key exhibits are two drums, named Busarure and Rwagagaza. Busarure was used in the Umutege dynasty, and Rwagagaza was an 18th-century war trophy drum from Burundi. Also on exhibit was the late 18th-century burial of King Cyrima II Rujugira. The exhibits do not, however, present colonial or postcolonial history and culture of Rwanda.

On our return visits a month later, on January 2 and 3, 1995, acting director and curator Bazatsinda Thomas told us of the toll the war had taken on Rwanda's National Museum. Initiated under Belgian colonial guidance between 1951 and 1952 most of the collections were assembled in the first decade of the museum's operation. Until the museum was moved to its new site, it was housed at the INRS.

When he began to work in the new museum in the fall of 1989, Bazatsinda immediately started research in the field, to collect objects *with* circumstantial identification to eventually exchange these documented materials with the undocumented objects. This work was continued systematically by region until 1990, when the war broke out. At that time the government subventions and thus their research efforts were stopped. In fact, the outbreak of the war took Bazatsinda totally by surprise because he was doing research in the countryside just then.

After the civil war broke out again on April 6, 1994, and the front moved south from Kigali to Butare, Bazatsinda had to go into hiding. He tried to evacuate the collections, but the van driver he wanted to hire turned out to be planning to kill him, so he could not remove the collections after all. What he did do was leave the museum's keys behind and leave the windows and doors open so that they at least would not be broken by the invading and pillaging soldiers. Bazatsinda then tried to escape to Burundi but had to divert to the Zone Turquoise, that is, the region under French military protection, where he stayed in hiding and consequently got sick. He returned to Butare on July 25 and to the National Museum on August 2, after having sought and been granted authorization from the ruling military and the préfet of Kigali to open the museum again.

Chaos and disaster awaited him. He found that the museum shop had been pillaged, that some photos had been taken from the exhibits, and that President Habyarimana's photo had been destroyed. Some of the domestic utensils on display had been taken to be used by the recently dispossessed. The museum's atelier of sculpture had been pillaged, and the design laboratory and workshop had been plundered, as was all maintenance equipment. The conservation laboratory's equipment, including all the chemicals, had been taken. All office equipment, such as typewriters and photocopier, had been stolen. The museum's three vehicles had been stolen as well.

Worse than the material losses, however, was the destruction of all the museum's primary research, inventory, and catalogue records, losses that are irreplaceable. Administrative records were also destroyed, so that Bazatsinda did not even know how much money was left in the museum bank accounts when the war broke out in 1994. Before that moment the museum's annual budget had been about 25 million Rwandan francs per year.

The biggest loss was the field research the museum had done over the previous five years under Bazatsinda's direction. In addition, he lost the radio broadcast recordings that were part of his collecting efforts on contemporary culture. Bazatsinda, a historian trained in Moscow and Niger, had documented the war from October 1990 until July 1994 on 420 cassettes of radio broadcasts from many different international and national radio stations. Some of his own colleagues destroyed 200 of these tapes, which were stored at the museum, and 200 more tapes were taken away from him on his flight. He was left with eight cassettes of the radio broadcasts, which he is now in the process of transcribing. "It is extraordinary how systematic this destruction was," he remarked.

Bazatsinda explained that these losses occurred in two phases of destruction and pillaging. The first phase of destruction was committed by insiders. Many of the former staff, 40 in all and mostly Hutu, destroyed records and materials before fleeing the RPF soldiers as an act of sabotage, as an act of "scorched earth." Bazatsinda knows that three of his former colleagues participated in the massacres and that one of them wanted his job. He came to Bazatsinda's house, looking to kill him. Four of the former museum workers died in the war; most of the others fled the country. The second phase of destruction occurred when Butare was besieged by the people from the area who took things for themselves or for sale.

When asked about his future plans for the National Museum, Bazatsinda first replied with the words he received from the Ministry of Education: "There is no money. Culture is not a priority now." So he bought a case of Fanta to sell to thirsty visitors, at that time mostly NGO and UN personnel; beer and Coke were added a little later for variety. Artisans were asked to supply objects once again for sale in the emptied gift shop, and together with a guard and a cashier Bazatsinda is seeing to his most important immediate task: keeping the doors of the National Museum open and receiving visitors. Bazatsinda is working with students from secondary schools to assist with receiving the public and to help clean the collections. A basket maker and a sculptor were demonstrating their crafts in two of the exhibition halls.

In addition, the museum had already developed musical and dance performances that could be made available to visitors on 30-minute advance notice. For example, an ensemble of seven drums, the dance known as *intore,* a performance on wind instruments *(amakondera)*, song and dance performances accompanied by the sitar *(inanga)*, lamellophone *(ikembe)*, and the musical bow *(umuduri)* could be ordered for an audience of one or 50, ranging in price from 2,000 Rwandan francs to 15,000 Rwandan francs. That all this talent lived near the museum was demonstrated to us when we wanted to purchase an *ikembe* from the museum store. Bazatsinda called on one of the grounds workers, who selected an instrument for us with connoisseurship, tuning, playing, and singing to the sound of three of these instruments until he handed us what he considered to be the best.

Future plans for collections and exhibitions include the assemblage of a systematic Rwandan numismatics collection up to 1989, collections of clothing since the arrival of Europeans, and a variety of projects on the colonial history of Rwanda, utilizing photographic collections from the private archives of the bishoprics. For May 1994 an exhibition on Rwanda and German colonial rule was planned, but it was obviously aborted because of the war. "Now we must put in order that which we have and start a new collection program, as we have to start over again. Above all we must have a new team," Bazatsinda remarked. For that, he has already told the ministry what kinds of professionals he needs for this work, which is to be done in collaboration with the university and the Institute of Rwandan Studies in Butare, both of which reopened their doors under new leadership in January 1995.

There are two other museums in Rwanda. The Geology Museum in the Ministry of Commerce and Industry in Kigali is located in the Building of the Ministry of Planning. However, at this time there are no personnel to oversee the collections. The oldest museum in Rwanda is at Kabgaye. This museum was founded by the Catholic Mission in the 1940s. The collections were contributed by the king and the chiefs of the region.

2.8 Who Wants the Children of War?

"Unaccompanied Children," Not "Orphans"

The Rwandan tragedy of 1994 left many children without parents. The men who were killed, especially the Tutsi men in Rwanda, left widows with children. Often these orphaned children and widows with children were taken in by other families in their lineages or in their friendship circle, as did Uwintije Celestine in Kayenzi. These were the fortunate ones. Many more children reached the borders of Burundi, Zaire, or Tanzania with the floods of adult refugees. Many of those who fled with their parents lost them during the flight or in the epidemics in the Zairian border camps.

In late 1994 the UNHRC and the International Red Cross estimated that the war had left 300,000 Rwandan children without parents or separated from their parents. These children, who populated entire camps in Zaire, Burundi, and Rwanda, are identified in the language of the international organizations as "unaccompanied children," not "orphans." This designation promotes the assumption that they may well be reunited with their parents or with other extended family members. The designation "unaccompanied child" protects the child from the active international children's market.

Committed to the strengthening of families within national cultures, the Red Cross went to great lengths to reunite unaccompanied children with their parents or with another extended family member. To facilitate this process, the International Red Cross developed a computerized list of names or known identities of all unaccompanied children of the war. In most camps these lists were posted publicly in the hope that a parent or a relative would see them and notify the Red Cross so that the child could be joined with a responsible adult. We saw this happen a few times in the Bukavu camps, and great was the joy of those parents to see their child again, well clothed and healthy. By June 1995 the International Red Cross had reunited about 3,000 children with their parents (United Nations 1995).

The process of finding an appropriate home for the children of war takes many different forms and different outcomes. The African family, if it is there, is able to extend itself to take care of its own if one wage-earning adult is willing to take charge. But there is also the frightening specter of the international children's trade and the way it preys on the third world's war victims.

Reconstituting Families

Transferring Children to Another Family

In the Ste. Famille guesthouse dining room in Kigali we met Nyinawabibi Charlotte. A consecrated nurse from Butare who was in training in Bukavu when the war occurred, she told us of the fate of Butare. Since 1990 the préfet and assistant préfet of that region, priests, and others had tried to suppress the use of Tutsi and Hutu identity. There had been general peace in the area until early April 1994. The region's authorities held out for three weeks after the beginning of the massacres, until April 20. Then, the provisional MRND government replaced all the Butare government heads and brought in militias and the army and began killing Hutus who had opposed the MRND, then doctors, priests, university people, students, and Tutsi generally. Thus, Nyinawabibi lamented, in a region where Tutsi and Hutu had lived together, there was suddenly much killing and destruction. She passionately blamed the upper-level politicians of the MRND for inciting ethnic hatred and division, and she singled out the French army for protecting these people and their militias.

Nyinawabibi was in Kigali to deposit her papers at the Ministry of Health to begin working as a nurse-midwife. She was also there to retrieve three children of her mother's younger sister who were orphaned in April when their mother was killed. They were being kept by religious sisters in Kigali. Nyinawabibi asked a friend in her home community, Nyanza, near Butare, who had only one child of her own, to take care of these three, and she had agreed. When Nyinawabibi was finished with her errands in Kigali, she would return to Nyanza with the girls. She herself had lost two brothers, but several remained.

Assuming the Role of Lineage Head

Kalinda Ezechiel, introduced in section 2.6, returned to Rwanda in August 1994 to work at the INRS and to become family head. His family was nearly wiped out in the massacres. A brother, two uncles, and most of their families were killed. All that survive are several nieces and nephews, children of his sister-in-law. His lineage used to be a large group of herders in Kibuye on Lake Kivu. Their ancestral genealogy could be traced back eight generations. None remain in Kibuye now. Kalinda became the lineage head and takes his responsibilities seriously. This explained his remark during our first encounter, that "his nieces and nephews weren't really orphans and that the African family could handle this kind of disaster."

Busloads of Children Return Home

The 300 unaccompanied Rwandan children in the Terres des Hommes camp in Bujumbura, Burundi, were evacuated during the war from Butare in six buses. The children were sheltered by Terres des Hommes in a former toilet paper factory that had gone bankrupt. The children slept on foam mattress on the floor and ate in a bamboo and thatched-roof "dining room". Latrines were built for them. Meals of relief food were prepared in a makeshift kitchen with charcoal fires. Airy classrooms were also constructed of bamboo and thatch roof in a pleasant, shaded courtyard.

Debbie Baxton (a former Peace Corps math teacher in Bujumbura) and Rwandan refugee Pierre Damien Nzabakira were the main caretakers of the children. Other Rwandan, Burundian, and expatriate volunteer workers constituted the staff of cooks, teachers, and primary caretakers. A Belgian from Zaire, now living in Bujumbura, was working on many art projects with the children and was developing a puppet theater performance on cross-cultural understanding. To avoid racial stereotyping, he created featureless puppet heads from gourds.

By late November 1994, when Reinhild visited the camp, only 100 of the children remained. Two hundred had already been returned to Rwanda to their families or to surviving relatives and friends. The remaining 100 were returned in early December.

Adoption across Continents

Making Contact through Aid Agencies

Not all unaccompanied children were returned to their kin, as in the cases just recounted. In some cases international workers and foreign couples eager to adopt children figured out methods of taking Rwandan "orphans" for adoption. We encountered a number of these cases and "baby brokers" in our work and document them here to point out the sinister world of traffic in human beings following a war. While we were staying at the Isimbi Hotel in Kigali in late December 1994, we met a German couple who had come to Rwanda to "pick up their child."

A young Rwandan woman was expecting a baby in late December 1994. All of her family had been killed, and she had no way to take care of the child. Her aunt, a secretary of a German-Rwandan cooperation agency who might normally have looked after this niece and her child, learned through her supervisor of a German couple who was eager to adopt a Rwandan baby. The German staff member contacted his acquaintances in Germany, a couple who had been trying to adopt a child for some years but without success. A year earlier they had traveled to El Salvador to pick up a child, but red tape there had made that impossible. When the Rwandan child was born, just before Christmas day, the German couple came to Kigali. In the Isimbi Hotel coffee shop they told us their story the morning after their arrival. They had tried for close to eight years to have their own child but in vain. Then they had decided to adopt a child, but it was almost impossible to find a child in Germany. So they decided to look for a third world child. The wife was tense with anticipation, following the long flight. She said she had not slept at all this first night in Kigali, the night before she was to see "their" child, "her" child.

Later in the day we met the couple again. They had seen the child and had held it. But they needed to take several more steps in the paperwork to make the adoption complete. They were still quite anxious because they were determined to not repeat their devastating experience in El Salvador.

An Orphan Business?

We met Joseph Houdusse in Bukavu several times in December 1994. He had been director and professor of theology of an independent Baptist seminary in Butare, Rwanda, until the 1994 war. He remained in Butare during the war to stand by his students and to take care of a group of about 25 children from the island of Ijwi in Lake Kivu, children he had taken in some time earlier.

As he spoke to us, his mood was morose and distant, as if he were suffering from the same shock as the Rwandans who had seen killing and horror and had themselves been threatened but had survived. He was eager to talk about what he had seen and knew of the war. Butare was at first spared involvement in the war because the governor of this southern province, representing many of the people, did not wish to participate. On April 20, 1994, the interim government that had been reconstituted after Habyarimana's death sent military and militias to begin the attack on Butare. The governor was replaced by a military commissar, and the militia was brought in to begin the exterminations.

Houdusse described to us the way in which his own seminary students were drawn into the killing. It was so terrible he could hardly talk about it. He saw students who, weeks earlier, had been studying to be preachers and Bible teachers become polarized along ethnic lines and eventually even kill each other. This, more than anything else, shattered his sense of a life worth living. He had given many years to Rwanda but with what result?

As the war raged on, Houdusse and the children sought protection from the bullets and the assassins in their compound. They spent days and nights huddled in bathtubs to be safe. "It was the apocalypse," he said. Moderate Hutu as well as Tutsi were targeted for killing. Hutus who did not wish to be involved were forced at gunpoint to decapitate people with machetes, told to kill 10 or 15 or more.

Houdusse's children remained in Butare after the war. But their lot was troubled, their status was unclear, and there was no easy way to care for them in Butare. Thus Houdusse was in Bukavu trying to arrange the papers for these Zairian children to be sent to Germany, where his wife lived. Three were already there. He had received the necessary papers from the German consulate in Kinshasa but needed the signatures of the governor of Kivu, local authorities, in this case the king *(Mwami)* of Ijwi, and the German ambassador. The papers already carried the signature of the *Mwami* of Ijwi, but he lacked the other signatures. He hoped to use the connections of the Mennonite group to plead his case before the governor of Kivu. One Mennonite team member from Kinshasa knew the governor personally in school, and Houdusse thought that connection would help. Another member of the team, Daniel, was French and would surely be willing to help a fellow Frenchman.

However, other church and humanitarian workers warned about Houdusse. They cautioned that one should avoid becoming entangled in his projects, in particular, those having anything to do with the transnational movement of children. Upon hearing this and upon learning more about Houdusse's need for help in completing paperwork for transit of Zairian children to Germany, the Mennonite team's director and regional coordinator told Houdusse in no uncertain terms that the team could not help him, and he forbade Mennonite unit members from further involvement with Houdusse's children's project.

Several troubling questions begged for an answer in this case. What did the *Mwami's* signature on the forms suggest about his involvement in the transportation across international lines of these children without appropriate papers? Why were three of the children already in Germany when Houdusse was seeking signatures for their legal travel to Europe? He stated they would stay in Europe for recovery and then be brought back, which is what the papers were requesting. However, it was not clear under what circumstances they had been taken from Ijwi in the first place, where there had not been a war nor even a recent remembered famine. Nor was it clear how much money was being transferred for this children's traffic.

Ndjoko, one of the Zairian members of the Mennonite team, told of a similar "orphanage" in Kinshasa to which poor families had taken their children for temporary shelter and care. However, one day a family went to fetch its children and the orphanage was empty. The children were gone; they had all been transported to Europe, and the director had vanished with large sums of money paid by European couples who wished to have these children as their own.

It was not clear to us just what Houdusse's plan was for his Zairian children in Butare and Germany. He seemed to feel a powerful obligation to them, to care for them. Perhaps he believed in his own good motives and believed that he was truly saving these children of Ijwi from a further terrible fate.

First World Child Custody Ruling Denies Rwandan Family Reassembly

Exiled king Kigeli V, Jean-Baptiste Ndahindurwa, visited Kansas in March 1995 to attend a requiem mass for Rwanda in Kansas City and to promote the cause of the children of Rwanda. During his visit to the University of Kansas, where he gave a lecture, he met with fellow Rwandan Amos Sibose who had come to plead his case to his king. Sibose had tried, so far in vain, to regain custody of his 10-year-old nephew and his 8-year-old niece, who had been adopted by a Kansas City couple, attorney Tedrick Housh and his wife, Shelly Peterson; the couple has no other children. When the couple heard that Sibose was coming to Kansas to claim custody of the children, they filed for legal custody. In a court decision Commissioner Geoffrey Allen of the Family Court Division of the Circuit Court of Jackson County, Missouri, stated that although Sibose and his wife loved the children and would be able to care for them, he nevertheless awarded custody to the Kansas City couple.

The background story of how the children got to Kansas City from Rwanda in the first place and were separated from their uncle is an intricate tale of the consequences of the conflict in Rwanda. As Sibose told the story and as it was published in the newspaper (Bradley 1994), the children were born in Burundi in the mid-1980s to Rwandese parents living in Bujumbura. After the father was killed, Sibose took in his brother's family for four years, following African custom. When their mother died, the children were taken in by their aunt, Rose Kayetesi, Sibose's cousin, where they joined Kayetesi's only child by birth, a daughter. Sadly, Kayetesi was HIV-positive and sought, however possible, to go to America for treatment. In 1991 a Zairian man approached her about the possibility of an immigration file for a family to move to America. Kayetesi and her children assumed the Zairian name Mampuya; someone else took her physical examination to hide her HIV status. She arrived in Kansas City in March 1991 with her own daughter and the two young children, all of whom now carried the assumed name Mampuya. Kayetesi, upon learning about Tedrick Housh, who had spent time in the Peace Corps in Africa, called him and they became friends. In spring 1994 when Kayetesi went to Sweden to visit Sibose, she asked Housh and Peterson to watch the children. When she returned, she became ill and died. This is when the Kansas City couple filed for custody of the children.

Mary Reynolds, an advocate for Sibose, claims that Kayetesi, on her deathbed, pleaded that the children be returned to Rwanda, to the custody of their uncle Sibose, who is now married and lives in Sweden. Kayetesi's daughter wishes to stay in Kansas City and believes she can care for the children. Sibose, however, argues that she is not Tutsi but has grown up in Nairobi and speaks Swahili, not Kinyarwanda. Sibose has spent his life's savings to gain custody, so that his family can be reassembled. His lineage has lost over 40 of its members and needs every child alive. But the Kansas City Family Court denied a rehearing of the case.

Fate of the Children of War and Society's Future

Yet other fates await the Rwandan children of war. Being taken in by another family may not work out. Even kinsmen may neglect these adopted children. A Salvation Army nurse in Kayenzi related to us that their nutrition policy had been revised to include not only the adopted children of war taken in by kin and neighbors but also the caregiving family's children, because there were too many cases of mothers taking the orphans' food and giving it to their own children who were hungry. Unattached young boys were regularly taken into the RPA as a way of giving them a home and work, lest they become like the roaming gangs of unattached youth in Mini Leonard's drawing *Consequences of War* (see section 3.1).

The children are the future of a society. Unless they are taken care of, nurtured and loved, and given a home, the deep scars of war will live on to reproduce more horrors in the next generation.

Notes

1. Rudolf Fischer, German representative of the Rheinland-Pfalz Rwanda Partnerschaft in Kigali, told us that in some cases taken up in 1993–1994 by Amnesty International, the judges were threatened with having their families killed if they followed through on prosecutions.

2. Murambi mayor Jean-Baptiste Gatete is mentioned in a reporter's manuscript as having openly led the killings in his commune. He is also listed in the Rwanda government "List of Planners and Organizers of the Genocide."

3. British workers Jane and Peter Andrews, with the Church of the Brethren, told us that the Rwandan Church of the Brethren had maintained its solidarity during the war.

4. Gakinda refers here to the killing of bishops by RPF soldiers. See Reyntjens (1994).

5. Before becoming involved in Rwanda, the Nairobi Peace Initiative had been involved in peace making in Eritrea and Ethiopia and in Mozambique, Angola, and Burundi.

6. Kamanzi critiques here the scholarly introduction of "caste" to describe Rwandan society. This perspective was highlighted by Jacques Maquet's *Premise of Inequality in Ruanda* (1961). Marcel d'Hertefelt (1971) has both used and critiqued the notion of caste. Maquet's principal informants in *Premise* were the royal family, where in-marriage was pervasive and a caste-like attitude of separateness prevailed in relation to commoners and court servants. The extension of this view to all of Rwandan society has been discredited by scholars.

3. Visual Memories
of Peace and War

The Rwandan refugee children's drawings, the drawings by children in the Kayenzi and Giti communes discussed in chapter 2, and the Rwandan artists' images presented in this chapter are voices just like the spoken ones. By including visual memories of a prewar relatively peaceful Rwanda before April 1994 together with images of the war's effects on people's lives, the message of postwar images becomes even more poignant. In addition to the images' value as historical documentation, their drawing, just like the telling of stories, has a pronounced therapeutic effect. In the process of drawing, of telling a story visually, the child or the adult explains and integrates traumatic experience and thus gives meaning to what otherwise would remain chaotic and therefore meaningless.

The significance of visual records or visually expressed memories as opposed to spoken or written accounts lies in the power of immediacy that an image can communicate across language and culture barriers. Furthermore, when an experience is too difficult or too complex to put into words or when an experience is suppressed, it can sometimes be articulated more easily in images. This may be particularly true for children.

As hard as we tried to find out whether there were Rwandan artists who had translated their personal experiences of war into images, we saw only one such work. This was Mini Leonard's poster *The Consequences of War* (Figure 42), commissioned by the Bureau de Formation Medicale Agréé Rwanda (BUFMAR), a nonprofit public health organization funded by the World Council of Churches. The poster was printed on the national presses of Rwanda. Meant as a tool for public education and not as a work of art, the poster does not bear the artist's signature. He may have wanted to stay anonymous for reasons of personal safety. By visiting the BUFMAR offices, we were able to discover his identity and meet him. He told us of his only remaining prewar paintings for French cultural institutions in Kigali and Butare, which we were able to locate and photograph (Figure 43). Seen together, Mini Leonard's renderings of a rural, peacefully idealized, pregenocide Rwanda and his postgenocide Rwanda landscape of destruction, desolation, and horror constitute an instructive and tragic visual record of history. He was still in shock and barely able to work at his designer and illustrator jobs and not at all able—yet—to work creatively as an artist. His only wish was to forget, preferably by leaving the country and making a fresh start.

Mini told us of at least two other Rwandan artist friends of his, but we were not able to make contacts. The constraints of time and circumstances did not permit any systematic study of the effects of the genocide on visual artists. But by mere chance, again, we saw and were able to document paintings of the RPF's military leaders and of the Virgin Mary created for the open market (see Figure 76). These paintings attest to the making of icons of the new military government endorsed by the authority of religion.

Mini's prewar public artworks and his postwar poster parallel the before and after drawings by unaccompanied children in Bukavu and in the Mushweshwe refugee camp. The children's drawings of their home settings as they remembered them from before the war are idyllic and mostly rural; their drawings of their experiences of war are of acts of destruction, killing, and flight. Seen together, all images presented here manifest both Tutsi and Hutu perspectives. The girls from Kayenzi, Mini Leonard, and Philippe Baptiste (section 3.3) make it clear that Tutsi were among the victims but also among the victors of the war, whereas the unaccompanied refugee children in and near Bukavu showed Hutu as victims.

Figure 42. Mini Leonard's poster *Ingaruka Z'Intambara* ("the consequences of war"). BUFMAR-MEMISA, Kigali, Rwanda, 1994.

TAMBARA
Tiré sur les presses de l'Imprimerie Nationale du Rwanda.

Figure 43. A Rwandan landscape painted by Mini Leonard ca. 1993, for the Loiret-Butare French Cultural Center, which was transformed after the war into a United Nations military barracks for the French Canadian contingent. French Canadian soldier on right agreed to pose in the landscape, January 2, 1995.

3.1 *Consequences of War:* A Rwandan Artist's Memory

Since the war I am not calm.—Mini Leonard, artist and graphic designer

On Friday, December 2, 1994, pinned to the bulletin board of the United Nations Rwanda Emergency Operation (UNREO) headquarters in Kigali, we saw a poster that we could not forget (Figure 42). It depicts a desolate landscape watched over by a large vulture, saliva dripping from its beak in anticipation of all the ready carrion. Nearby, two vultures feed on a human cadaver, collapsed next to a demolished car. "Vultures are not normally seen in Rwanda," said the artist who created this work, "but after the killing there were many vultures around, as were dogs feeding on human corpses and dismembered body parts." A swollen corpse floats in the stagnant river water and skeletal remains lie stranded on the river's banks. All of nature is dead in this landscape; the tree is barren, and the well is dry and broken. The leafless tree, the cactus, and the dry well suggest famine.

All human institutions are destroyed and broken as well: the dispensary, the school, the church, the family farmsteads, the power lines, and the roads and bridges. In the operating room of a hospital doctors ask with frustration, "What can we do without any materials? Where can we transfer the patient?" And there are no answers. Fittingly, the poster is titled *Ingaruka Z'Intambara,* which means "the consequences of war."

"I gave prominence to the child in the foreground, because children suffered so much. They lost limbs because of mines and because the militias mutilated even children, hacking off both their arms and legs," explained Mini Leonard, the designer of the poster. We saw such a mutilated boy begging in the market of Butare, both arms cut off just below the elbow. On the poster, near the crippled child on crutches, we see an old man who has become a fool because he has seen unspeakable horrors. He pulls a toy like a child and wears mismatched shoes and socks. His mind has fled into laughter, and he roams aimlessly. A woman, all alone, mourns the death of her family while another woman, obviously pregnant, asks her neighbor, "What will I tell my fiancé about my pregnancy brought on by an Interahamwe rapist?" But her neighbor, a widow whose child is clutching her skirts, does not respond because she is too overwhelmed by her own problems and has no empathy left for the problems of others. Street children, that is, children whose families were killed in the war and who are thus left to their own devices, find shelter near or in gutters. They are shown as being on their way to becoming the asocial criminal element of tomorrow.

We first met Mini during our second visit to the BUFMAR offices, which had published the poster and where earlier we had been presented with two copies. The first time we tried to meet Mini we were told that he had worked late into the night to meet his deadline for a UN commissioned poster on human rights and therefore was not in. On our second try to meet him, Mini agreed to come to the Isimbi Hotel for more conversation after our initial introduction at the office.

"Since the war I am not calm. I could not work on my own art. This poster was a way to work out what I have seen. It is my expression of the hopelessness that I feel," said Mini. "Some people cry when they see this poster." He added that he had seen much worse than what he depicted in the poster. The poster barely scratched the surface. He wanted to forget the killing of his family, the loss of his five sisters and one younger brother. He wanted to study abroad and to start over again. Mini came to our hotel at the agreed-on time. He preferred the privacy of our room to the public lounge; he was soft-spoken and guarded about his family history. He spoke of the great tension between those who had been born and had grown up in Rwanda and those who had returned to Rwanda from elsewhere. As far as he was concerned, he simply called himself "Rwandais," otherwise "people's prejudices prevent one from getting ahead, or one might get killed."

Mini is a young man who attended the only secondary school in the country that offered fine arts programs in sculpture, graphic arts, cinema, photography and graphic design: the Ecole d'Arts de Nyundo at Gisenyi. The school is a private Catholic school that, like all schools and universities, was shut down during the war. After his graduation, Mini worked as a freelance designer for GTZ, a German development organization for technical assistance. In 1993 he began to work for the BUFMAR. It was this organization that commissioned and produced Mini's poster in addition to his regular design work of illustrative posters on public health issues, such as rudimentary hygiene.

When we asked Mini whether he could show us other examples of his art, he said that all his works, including photo documentation, and all his other documents were burned during the war; he lost everything that was in his house. Examples of some of his book illustrations can be found in publications of the Education Ministry and the Youth Ministry, financed by GTZ. The only pre-1994 paintings of his that remain are two murals, one in the Mission de Cooperation Français next to the French embassy in Kigali and the other in the Loiret-Butare French Cultural Center (Butare and Loiret, France, are sister cities) (Figure 43).

It was not exactly easy to gain access to either one of these buildings to find Mini's murals. The French embassy in Kigali was still closed, but a friendly gatekeeper got us access to the back stairs of the adjacent deserted Mission de Cooperation Français, where another friendly watchman showed us the sunny office where Mini had decorated an expanse of wall, 3 m by 5 m, with a bright painting: a bucolic Rwandan landscape scene. A young shepherd plays his wooden flute *(umwironge)* while standing in verdant pasture near the shore of a lake. He is surrounded by grazing sheep and long-horned cattle. In the background stands his small hut, or perhaps it is the traditional shepherd's umbrella woven of twigs and banana leaves. On the lake fishermen cast their nets from their canoe. In a nearby narrow hallway, one of Mini's schoolmates and fellow artists, Karangway Evariste, decorated a wall with a similarly bucolic landscape of a Rwandan *colline* complete with circular homestead and agricultural activity.

In Butare we found the Loiret-Butare French Cultural Center occupied by UN troops from Canada and Malawi. They were involved in resettling refugees from internal camps in their home communities and were glad for the diversion of English-speaking visitors. They gave us access through the barred and armed gates. In a large room turned into a soldiers' dormitory, one entire wall had been transformed by Mini into a pastoral scene of a peaceful countryside (Figure 43). A white-haired elder and a young man are seated across from each other at a game board *(igisoro)* in the palisaded yard of a traditional homestead with three thatched roundhouses. A narrow-necked gourd used to drink milk or sorghum beer is placed near the old man. Both men are dressed in traditional garments. Goats feed in the foreground, and a Central African long-horned cow stands gazing at the onlooker. A young woman enters the court of the homestead, carrying a load on her head. There is also a large spherical clay utility pot lying on the ground between the third house and the fence. This landscape, painted in the 1990s, contains—like Mini's wall painting in Kigali's Mission de Cooperation Français—a veritable inventory of Rwandan traditional material culture and blocks out any references to the Rwanda of the late 20th century. But on January 2, 1995, the bunk beds, mosquito nets, and personal belongings of UN soldiers literally invaded and occupied this idyllic Rwandan landscape painted on the wall.

A cataclysm is visible between Mini's prewar pastoral scenes of an idyllic, preindustrial Rwanda at peace and the postwar poster of desolation and hopelessness. In the aftermath of the war in Rwanda a pastoral image of preindustrial Rwanda, such as the ones Mini created for public art commissions before the genocide of 1994, was used as a didactic tool to hold up values in precolonial Rwanda and Burundi that should be emulated in rebuilding social bonds. For example, the French language paper *L'Arc en Ciel* (December 16, 1994, p. 10), published in Kigali, featured a drawing of a traditional scene of milking cows near a corral and distributing the fresh milk to a group of hungry children. The caption interpreted the image of sharing milk as a symbol of an ongoing pact between the people and communities of Rwanda and Burundi. Somewhere in town we had seen the same drawing used as a poster or flyer to advertise Kalisa Tharcisse's new peace play *Le lieu ou se sont assis les rois a Nyaruteja* ("the place of Nyaruteja where the kings sat down together"). But is the political use of such idealized imagery in the context of the genocide's aftermath in Rwanda not tantamount to denial? In contrast, Mini's poster remains the only artwork that we know of that speaks the truth and thus allows the necessary catharsis.

3.2 *"Ayiwewe"*: War-Traumatized Children Draw Their Memories[1]

Here also you see how we live. Life is complicated.—Mukayisenga Diane, age 15, Mushweshwe refugee camp, December 1994

Most Rwandan children and especially those who became refugees experienced events that are outside the range of usual human experience. Yet these children are the future of Rwanda, and it is therefore as critical to hear their voices as it is to hear those of the adults as first steps toward healing. As circumstances permitted, we invited children in four distinct settings to express their experiences in drawings: two communities in Rwanda, a center in Bukavu run by Zairians for unaccompanied children from Rwanda who had lost or become separated from their parents during the flight from the war, and a refugee camp outside of Bukavu, where the children lived with their parents. Of the 94 drawings that we were able to collect, a selection of those most illustrative of the children's trauma is discussed here.

We had two purposes for giving children an opportunity to express their emotions about what had happened in their lives. First, drawing a picture as a way of self-expression offers the child a way to cope and "helps children avoid destructive burial of feelings of insecurity, anxiety, fear, terror, mistrustfulness, and unhappiness produced by the impact of major disruption, violence, and despair" (Kilbourn 1994, pp. 59, 202, 205). "One of the worst traumas of children in war is separation from significant others" and "disruption of attachment relationships" (Garabino et. al. 1991, p. 17). In a study by UNICEF, over 50% of the unaccompanied children interviewed had witnessed the killing of a family member (Baker 1994, p. A16). Second, the children's drawings are powerful firsthand documentation that carries a level of authenticity that foreign journalists' cameras cannot capture.

Unaccompanied Children in Bukavu

The 2 million Rwandans who fled westward to Zaire in 1994 included many diverse groups of people. At first, the Tutsi fled the genocidal massacres, but later the refugees included the Interahamwe militia and the Rwandan army fleeing the advancing RPF. In addition, the refugees included government officials who had participated in the killing and their families and many innocent civilians who were afraid of retributions by the RPF. A fateful category that also formed was children who fled with everyone else and whose parents had been killed or children who became detached from their fleeing parents. Entire refugee camps of children were set up by the UNHCR and the International Red Cross. Based on prior experience in other disasters, these agencies intended to regroup families if at all possible and to discourage, if not outrightly forbid, the speculative international adoption of children. By late 1994 there were 200,000 to 300,000 unaccompanied Rwandan children (Lorch 1994; United Nations 1995).

At the Protestant guesthouse in Bukavu, a group of over 30 unaccompanied children were cared for by members of the local Protestant churches in one of the houses of the compound where the MCC team of volunteer workers was housed. We know the home communities of most of the unaccompanied children at the guesthouse because they wrote that information (or tried to) along with their names and their ages on their drawings: eight came from Cyangugu Prefecture and its different communes of Gisuma, "Nyenzi," "Nakabuye," Bunyenga, and Kimbogo (Cyimbogo); eight children said they were from Gikongoro Prefecture and its communes "Komini" and Rukondo; three were from Kigali Prefecture and the communes Rytongo, "Gashora," and "Nutenga"; and two children said they had fled the communes Ntyazo and Ngoma in Butare Prefecture.

Our MCC team frequently assisted with feeding these children, being concerned that they were not getting sufficient amounts of fruit and vegetables. Members of the team also played with them on occasion. According to their Zairian caretaker, Miruho Nyamulinduka, some children understood themselves as Tutsi, others as Hutu, and as a consequence animosity flared up between them; it became necessary for an adult to sleep with the children at night to prevent harassment and fighting. In this way the world of the children mirrored that of the adults in the refugee camps. As part of his effort to reconcile the children with each other, Miruho involved them in a play he developed that dealt with the theme of brotherly love. The children learned their parts in French, a new language for many of the younger ones, for the sake of the Zairian audience.

We invited Miruho to bring some of the children over to the guesthouse to do some drawing, dividing them into 2 groups of 14 and 12, respectively. In each group the children's age ranged from 6 to 15 years. Drawing, if not to say art activity, that emphasizes the individual's unique creative vision is not usually part of these children's experience, nor that of the children's caretaker. He asked whether we could show the children how to draw, whether we could give them a model or a prototype of what to draw, and whether the children could be given a ruler so their drawings would be "neat." But we emphasized that we wanted the drawings to reflect each child's own unique experience and that neatness was not the issue.

The children in the first group came twice, on two consecutive evenings (Figure 44). On the first evening we asked them to begin by drawing their memory of their home and their family in Rwanda. We wanted to see how these drawings would differ from those that would follow, about the traumatic experience of war, of fleeing, and of losing family. Also, we did not want to begin our first meeting with their most disturbing memory. The children's caregiver translated our instructions into Kinyarwanda, because most of the youngsters did not understand French.

The contrast of before and after drawings allows us a glimpse into the normal lives of these children and how they viewed their dislocation (Figure 45). Children of war have lost the structures that supported their lives before the war: Community, school, friends, peers, and their normal, healthy family life are no longer in place (Kilbourn 1994, p. 143). This vital structure that once was theirs is what the children drew in the before pictures. The drawings constitute a rich inventory of the children's world at home in Rwanda: comfortable houses, crops grown by hand in small fields (e.g., avocado trees, banana trees, cabbage, beans, sorghum, corn), and the animals (chicken, goats, sheep, cattle) that children are often responsible for as herders (Figures 46–49). Even the typical Rwandan beehive, a tubular basket placed horizontally in the fork of a tree, occurs in several drawings (e.g., Figure 50). The children drew many objects of daily use, such as baskets and pots, but most prominently featured next to the children's homes are members of their families. In several drawings the figures of father and mother, sometimes of brothers and sisters are identified by name (see Figures 46a, 47a, 48a, 51a, and 52a). The Rwandan home place is richly illustrated (see Figures 47 and 48).

On the following afternoon the same group came again, and this time they were asked to draw the experience of their flight from Rwanda to Zaire. This task was given to the second group of

Figure 44. Unaccompanied children draw their memories. Centre d'Acceuil Protestant, Bukavu, Zaire, December 1994. Looking at you is little Nshimiyimana, who drew his home and family as it was before the war and after the war (see Figure 45).

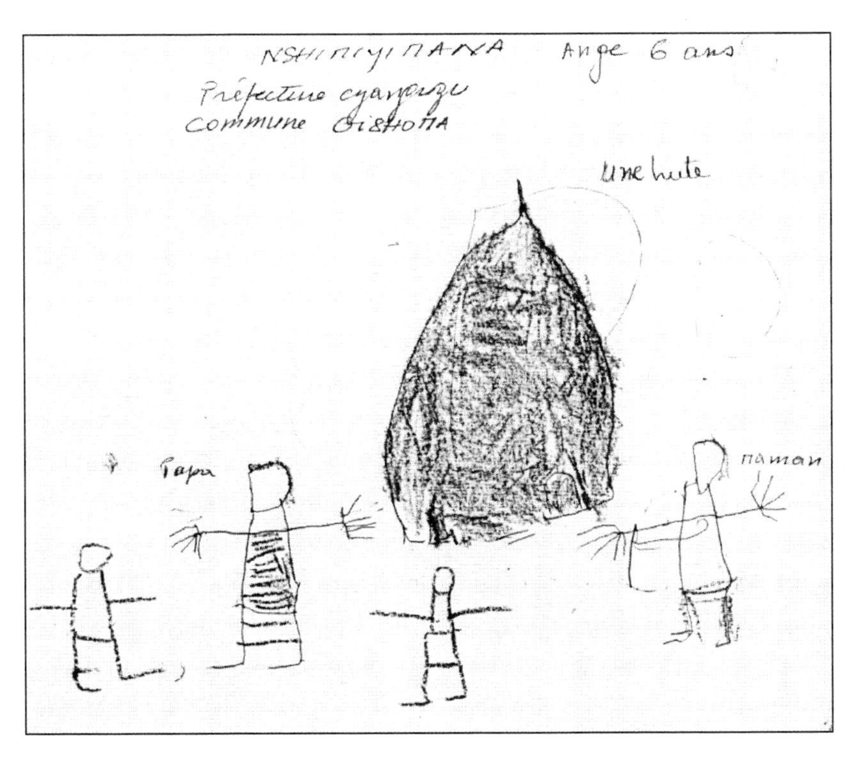

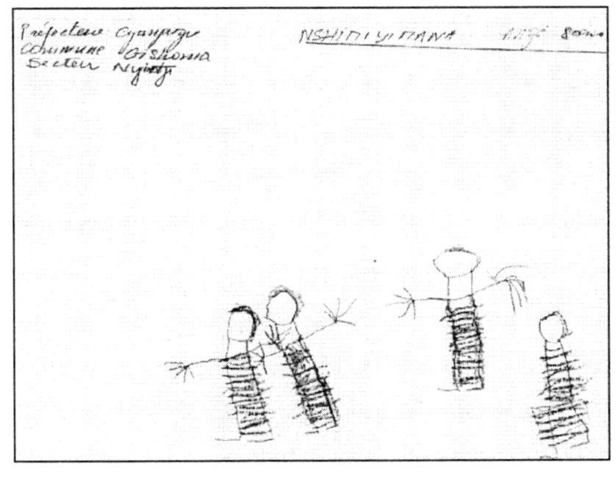

Figure 45 a + b. Nshimiyimana's drawing of his life (a) before and (b) after the war. After the war the house is missing, but his entire family is intact in his imagination, although he was unaccompanied and did not know what had happened to his parents.

children who came on a third afternoon. During each of these sessions the children worked seriously and intently on their drawings for an hour and a half, without interruption and without getting up from their chairs. We did have to emphasize that we wanted them not to copy from each other but to draw from their own personal memory. Some of the older children wanted to use their pencils as rulers and draw with straight lines.

Several pictures were executed as continuous narratives, with a linear sequencing of events. Such narrative in which the child essentially explains and integrates disruptive experience can give meaning to what otherwise would remain meaningless and chaotic. Many of these pictures feature scenes of travel, that is, flight (Figure 53), taking the child from the everyday lives of home, school, and play to their new lives as refugees. This transition is often symbolized by long lines of people on a road, people in trucks and cars, people crossing the Ruzizi River bridge on foot or crossing Lake Kivu in a boat to reach Zaire (Figures 46b, 47b, 48b, 52, and 54b), or other poignant scenes of flight.

That the children were aware of the explanations of the start of the war is evident in the many drawings that include the shooting down of President Habyarimana's plane; the depictions contra-

Text continues on page 138.

Figure 46 a + b. "Before and After," by Safari, age 13, from Cyangugu Prefecture, commune of Nyakabuye. Centre d'Acceuil Protestant, Bukavu, December 1994; pencil and crayon on paper. (a) Before the war Safari shows his home, his parents, himself, and perhaps a sibling or relative and his parents' garden with cabbage plants and avocado and banana trees. On the following

day he drew himself as he flees the gunfire of the opposing armies, with the shot-down presidential plane above (b). He carries his possessions on his head. He then crossed the bridge over the Ruzizi River into the safety of a refugee camp in Zaire where he is welcomed.

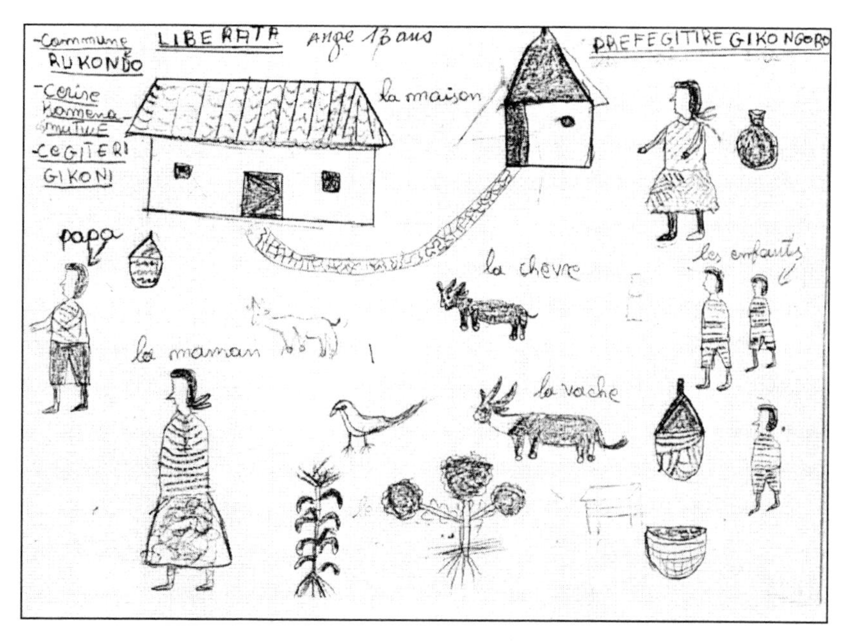

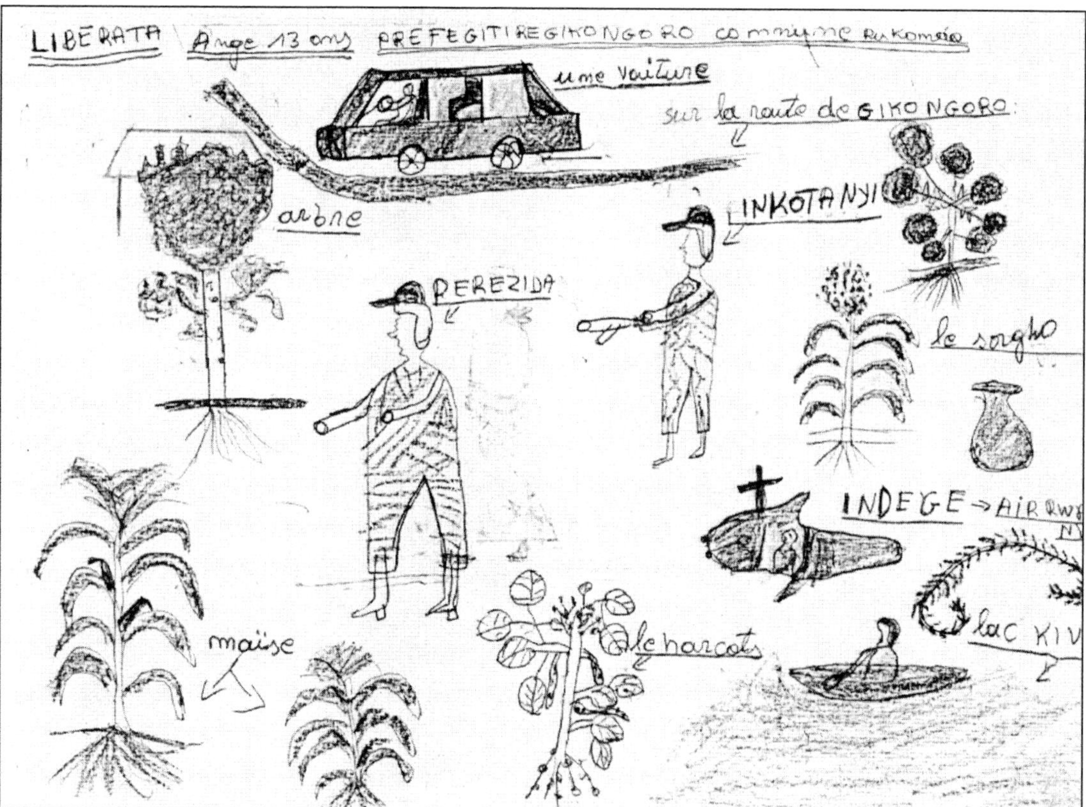

Figure 47 a + b. "Before and After," by Liberata, age 13, from the Prefecture Gikongoro. Centre d'Acceuil Protestant, Bukavu, December 1994; pencil and crayon on paper. (a) In her before picture Liberata identifies her parents, her siblings, her home, her family's livestock, plants and three woven utility baskets. (b) In her after picture she includes as cause of her flight a soldier of the RFP *(inkontanyi)* aiming his gun at the president and the president's fateful plane. The route of her flight may have been partially by car, partially by boat crossing Lake Kivu. But curiously, all of this is surrounded by the plants she had learned to cultivate in her home: corn, beans, sorghum, flowers, and trees.

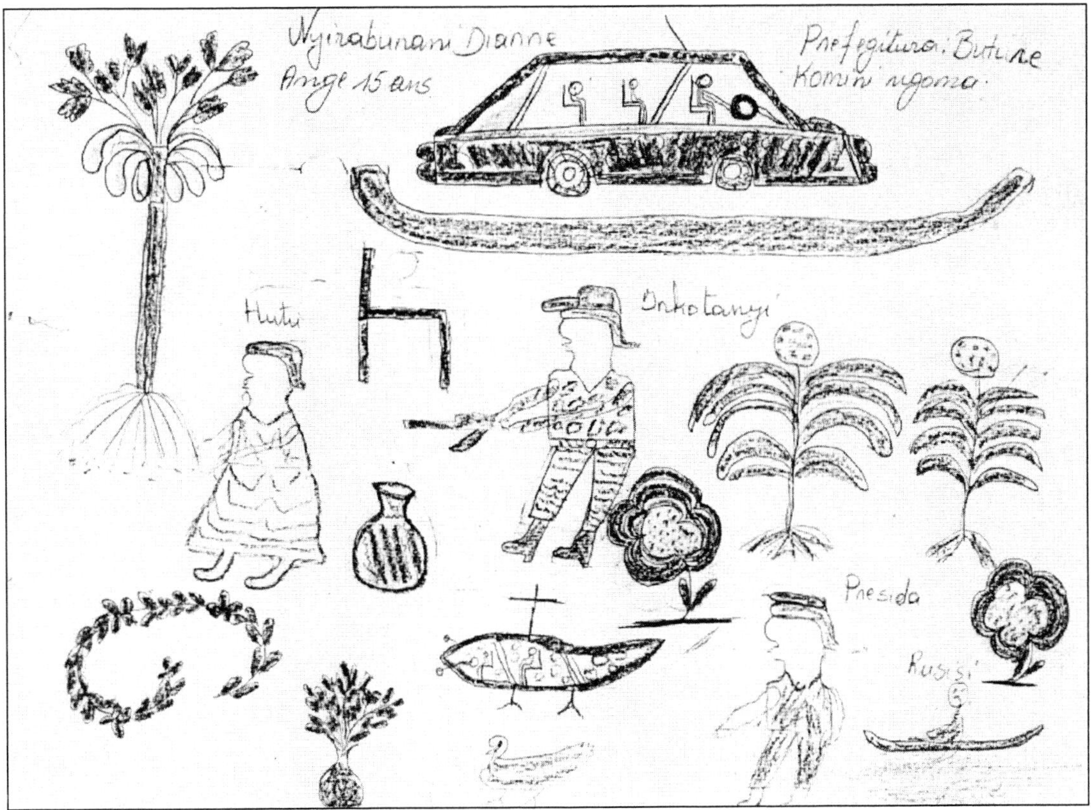

Figure 48 a + b. "Before and After," by Nyirabunani Dianne, age 15, from Butare Prefecture, commune of Ngoma. Centre d'Acceuil Protestant, Bukavu, December 1994; pencil and crayon on paper. (a) Home, parents, siblings, animals, plants, and household objects such as a lidded basket and a ceramic beer or water vessel figure prominently in the before picture, whereas the after picture (b) shows an RPF soldier *(inkotanyi)* aiming his gun at a woman identified as Hutu. The shooting of President Habyarimana's plane is alluded to as well.

Figure 49. "Herding Cattle," detail from the before picture drawn by Abayisenga, age 12. Centre d'Acceuil Protestant, Bukavu, December 1994; pencil on paper.

Figure 50. "Umuzinga" (beehive), detail from a remembrance of home in Rwanda by Lenzaho Alexi, age 12. Centre d'Acceuil Protestant, Bukavu, December 1994; pencil and crayon on paper.

Figure 51 a + b. "Before" and "After: War" by Ngabonziza Jean de Dieu, age 15, from Butare Prefecture, commune of Ntyazo. Centre d'Acceuil Protestant, Bukavu, December 1994; pencil and crayon on paper. (a) The before picture features the child's house, both parents, the child, and chickens. (b) On the after picture note that the child is alone on the road of flight, an armed ambush is nearby, and three more refugees flee on foot.

Figure 52. "Refugees," detail from the after picture by Donatira Mukandayisenga, age 12 (?), from Cyangugu Prefecture, commune of Nyenzi. Centre d'Acceuil Protestant, Bukavu, December 1994; pencil and crayon on paper.

Figure 53. "Fleeing," detail from the after picture by Shiminana Emmanuel, age 9, Cyangugu Prefecture. Centre d'Acceuil Protestant, Bukavu, December 1994.

Figure 54 a + b. "Ayiwewe," the before and after pictures by Gasana Diyonizi, age 14. Centre d'Acceuil Protestant, Bukavu, 1994; pencil and crayon on paper. (a) In his before picture Gasana shows himself crying "ayiwewe" in despair as an RPF soldier executes a family member, probably his father, in front of his home. The victim has fallen to the ground, bleeding from a fatal head wound. The outline of another armed soldier appears below. (b) In his after picture Gasana drew the cause and effect of the war that made him a refugee: a plane is shot down, people flee on bicycle and on foot, at the Ruzizi River or Lake Kivu a payment is made to be ferried to safety on the other side. The vehicle may allude to the presence of the UNHCR or other relief organization. Then again, boys like to draw cars, no matter what.

Figure 55. "Rwanda and Zaire," by Ngendahayo Providence, age 11, Mushweshwe refugee camp, Zaire, December. 1994; pencil, crayon, and ballpoint pen on paper. Ngendahayo's home has been destroyed by bullets; a huge RPF (FPR) soldier in camouflage points his gun at a group of people who have been canceled out, signifying their death. Refugees flee along the road toward the bridge over the Ruzizi River, carrying loads on their heads; others flee in cars or trucks. On the other side of the river in Zaire there is a camp of tents provided by the UNHCR.

dict those adults who think children are oblivious to the political aspects of the war and are shielded from the reality of the war (Stanton 1995, p. 8). Images of armed soldiers in camouflage uniforms, many aiming their guns at victims or destroying homes with gunfire and grenades, are prominent (Figures 46b, 48b, 51b, 54a, 55, and 56), and images of bombs or of machine guns can be identified in other drawings. Some of the soldiers are identified in writing as *Inkotanyi* meaning "the tough fighters," with the connotation of the old royal regiments (Prunier 1995, p. 367), the common designation given by the RPF to its soldiers (see Figures 47b, 48b, and 54a); other soldiers are identified with the letters FPR (French for RPF) (e.g., Figure 55). One 14-year-old identified a truck full of armed soldiers as MRND. At least two drawings show RPF soldiers having just killed a man and a woman, respectively; the victims lie prostrate on the ground, and red crayon shows the victim's blood flowing (Figures 54a and 55). Another drawing shows an RPF soldier, identified as *Inkotanyi,* pointing his gun at a woman identified as Hutu (Figure 48b). Such drawings thus underline the findings of a study conducted by UNICEF that revealed that over 50% of the children interviewed had witnessed the killing of a family member (Baker 1994).

Figure 56. "Rwanda and Zaire," by Myomugabo, age 5. Mushweshwe refugee camp, Zaire, December 1994; ballpoint pen and colored marker on paper. Near the child's home a soldier aims at a person (a child?) seeking refuge near a tree. Below, the child stands alone between two tents in the refugee camp.

Figure 57. "The Shooting of Habyarimana's plane," by Ntirenganya Myaka, age 14, from Kigali Prefecture, commune of Rutonga. Centre d'Acceuil Protestant, Bukavu, December 1994; pencil and crayon on paper.

Figure 58. Image by Bana, age 6. Centre d'Acceuil Protestant, Bukavu, December 1994; pencil on paper. In a series of three similar, deliberately executed drawings Bana expressed his experience of the inner and outer chaos in his life.

Another recurring motif is that of the shooting down of President Habyarimana's plane (which curiously appears as a helicopter in some of the children's drawings) (Figures 48b, 54b, and 57b). All drawings manifest that the pervasiveness of violence is vividly remembered by these children. The experience of a horrific explosion appears in a sequence of three drawings by a 6-year-old boy, Bana (Figure 58), and in the two drawings of 8-year-old Kamana (Figure 59), which shows two burning cars and a chaos of bodies and disconnected body parts thrown about. The incomplete images of people reflect the children's perception of the confusion and hysteria of the situation. These drawings express poignantly how the children's minds are filled with the "endless blur of terrifying scenes" (Elbedour et al. 1993, p. 806) that is war.

The flight for one's life is shown in the drawings. Some children drew streams of refugees fleeing on foot (Figures 45b and 52b), refugees crossing Lake Kivu in boats, or crossing the Ruzizi River (Figures 48b and 55). One of the many children who had to travel through the Nyungwe National Forest to reach a refugee camp commemorated that experience by putting a Nyungwe sign into the landscape of his flight. Particularly moving are motifs of the isolated, lonely child, the

Figure 59. "After," by Kamana, age 8, Centre d'Acceuil Protestant, Bukavu, December 1994; pencil and crayon on paper. Two cars are burning with bright orange flames. Incomplete silhouettes of people and animal body fragments are strewn around the burning cars.

child imploring the viewer to find his or her father (Figure 51), the child exclaiming despair with his hands held over his eyes crying out *"ayiwewe"* as a soldier of the RPF kills a family member in front of his home (Figure 54a), and an unaccompanied child fleeing the crossfire of the opposing armies (Figure 46b). In Figure 46b Safari, age 13, of Cyangugu Prefecture, shows himself as a refugee carrying a bag of possessions on his head, caught between the exchange of fire of a soldier from the RPF and a soldier of the former Rwandan army. In the lower scenes he crosses the bridge of the Ruzizi River and is welcomed at a refugee camp, indicated by the silhouette of a tent.

Many of the children wanted to know if they could come again for more drawing, an indication that they enjoyed the experience of expressing their emotions about the life-changing events that separated them from their homes and their families. The therapeutic effect of such self-expression has been observed and studied in other refugee settings. "One of the most crucial things adults can do is encourage the children to express their emotions. (Recovery for children and adults can only come through communication and expression (Dodge and Raundalen 1991, p. 116). In a study in Mozambique 75% of the children interviewed said they felt better after relating their experiences (Dodge and Raundalen 1991, p. 154). Kilbourn (1994) noted that children need encouragement and guidance from caregivers, especially in the absence of parents, to help them express their feelings in a protected and safe environment. "Children feel a sense of protection when they are with adults who allow the spontaneous expression of their understanding of their experiences. Children who are listened to and whose feelings are acknowledged by others begin to feel more secure, valued, loved and loving" (Kilbourn 1994, p. 202). Our MCC team thanked the children for their drawings by giving them a little party, with food and drink—only a bottle of Coke and a roll with honey for each child were available to us—and singing and dancing.

The drawings by the unaccompanied children at Bukavu revealed relatively stronger trauma and experiences of greater upheaval than do the drawings of refugee children who fled with family members. This is evident when the drawings of the unaccompanied children at Bukavu are compared with those of refugee children who lived with their families in the Mushweshwe camp. Research by Anna Freud on the effects of World War II on children showed that those who lived through the bombardment in the care of their own mothers or familiar mother substitutes were not psychologically devastated by their experiences (Garabino et al. 1991, p. 17). It is estimated that up to 85% of children who have the support of a parent or guardian can overcome their distress and live a "normal" life (Garabino et al. 1991, pp. 29–30). This is what we sensed in the children with family members in the camps, as opposed to the unaccompanied children in Bukavu.

Children in the Refugee Camps of South Kivu

In the small Mushweshwe camp of Rwandan refugees southwest of Bukavu, we met with the person responsible for the schooling of the refugee children, formerly a teacher in a commune of Rwanda. We sat in the teachers' office in the Zairian primary school that the Rwandan refugees were allowed to use to teach their children. Their class hours were in the afternoons, whereas the Zairian children attended school in the morning. We explained to the teacher that we would value drawings by a group of his students, age 6 to 15, that in this way they could share their experience with students and other people in North America, where we would show and explain their drawings. It is clear that many of the children understood their assignment as a form of visual letter to an unknown peer in the United States. This particular purpose of their drawing, this agenda to communicate to an imagined friend, was probably the impetus behind the linear progression of their picture stories, often enhanced with explanatory text, and the great amount of narrative detail found in these drawings. We gave the teacher paper, pencils, crayons, and color markers, and he promised to have the drawings done by the next afternoon. Many of these drawings convey the Hutu point of view, as do the drawings of the unaccompanied children at Bukavu, in that the refugees in Mushweshwe were Hutu fleeing the RPF army.

Most of the children divided their sheet of paper either horizontally or vertically, showing in one section peaceful scenes from their lives in Rwanda before the 1994 war: playing jump rope (Figures 60 and 61) or ball (Figure 62), going to school and to market (Figures 61–64), and enjoying vacation (Figures 61–65). They show their homes and furnishings, their father's car, their compounds with animals, the many different crops grown in their fields. The other section of the same paper is then filled with scenes of soldiers shooting at the plane of President Habyarimana (Figures 64, 66, and 67), hearing the news of the president's death on television (Figure 63), and hearing explosions and with scenes of war and destruction of houses and killing by the RPF (Figures 55, 56, 61, and 66–69). In one drawing a soldier identified as *Inkotanyi* (RPF) aims his gun at a fleeing woman, and in another drawing the soldier shooting at a home is also identified as *Inkotanyi* (Figure 70). Streams of refugees fleeing on foot under the threat of gunfire, crossing Lake Kivu by boat and the Ruzizi River by bridge, carrying loads on their heads, backs, or tied to their vehicles, are especially vivid in many drawings (Figures 61, 64, and 71–75). Particularly telling of the children's refugee experiences are their scenes of life in the camp. The crowdedness of the UNHCR-issued tents is made palpable through the lack of furnishings and the people shown sleeping on the tent's floors; also visible are the daily challenges of getting water for washing and cooking (Figures 62, 63, 68, and 71) and firewood for cooking (Figures 61 and 62) and trading for everyday commodities such as vegetables or canned goods (Figure 68).

Thus the set of drawings from this refugee camp documents the before and the after experiences of these children, as do the drawings done by the unaccompanied children in Bukavu. However, in the Mushweshwe camp the after drawings focus a great deal on life in the refugee camp as a totally other experience, opposite to the experience of home in Rwanda.

In both sets of drawings—by the unaccompanied refugee children and by refugee children who lived with their families in the Mushweshwe camp—some images look surprisingly controlled, in that the deliberate, careful organization of the images does not reveal the upheaval and trauma the child has experienced. Several explanations for some of these highly controlled drawings are possible. The orderliness that is imposed on the representation of a disorderly, disruptive, life-changing event may express the child's need to make the chaotic, disruptive, or disorderly experience and the present situation appear normal. That may make the acceptance of the traumatic change easier. The orderly or highly controlled drawings also may be a symptom of the child who shows no outward signs of trauma. Some children of war appear competent and self-sufficient and do not complain (Kilbourn 1994, p. 142). In these children the experience of war has created an inner chaos that has become "so dense that they have lost all ability to communicate their true feelings, thoughts, and emotions to the outside. The soul of the child is silent" (Kilbourn 1994, p. 142). From a psychological point of view, these children may suffer the greatest degree of trauma and usually need more long-term care than children who do display symptoms of trauma.

Text continues on page 150.

Figure 60. "Rwanda" and "Zaire," by Uwingabire Marie Liliane, age 15. Mushweshwe camp, Zaire, December 15, 1994; pencil on paper. Rwanda and Zaire are separated by a river, but more important for Uwingabire they are connected by a strong bridge, which she places prominently in the center of her picture. It is the emblem of her rescue, of her survival. The landscapes of the two countries are the same, hilly and wooded. But while her single home compound and playing children dominate the Rwanda side of her picture, the UNHCR sheeting of the tent city in Mushweshwe fills the Zaire side, where a mother with four children has just arrived. The infant is carried on the mother's back, and a sleeping mat and food and clothes are bundled on her head. A younger child minds a toddler, and one of the children carries the all-important plastic water container.

Figure 61. "Rwanda" and "Zaire," by Mukantwali Roseline, age 12. Mushweshwe camp, Zaire, December 1994; pencil and color marker on paper. At home in Rwanda Mukantwali enjoyed jumping rope and going to school (note the arithmetic lesson on the blackboard), and she depicts her tree-shaded home. After the death of President Habyarimana the news of which she has apparently followed on television, the war begins. She draws a grueling scene of a soldier shooting at a group of women carrying loads on their heads. One of the women lies prostrate, her blood flowing profusely in bright red color. Below we see Lake Kivu with boats carrying people. One of the two boats seems to have capsized. In front of one of the UNHCR blue tents we see someone tending a cookpot over a fire; in another tent two people sleep on the ground.

Figure 62. "Rwanda" and "Zaire," by Bigirimana Jean Pierre, age 14. Mushweshwe camp, Zaire, December 1994; pencil and color marker on paper. The boy's homestead in Rwanda is neatly fenced; he plays soccer and goes to school. The bridge crossing the Ruzizi River constitutes once again the critical transition point from home to exile. The center of the picture is occupied by two children carrying water in a gasoline pail and letting the faucet run into a pot. Someone is cooking in front of the UNHCR tent on the ground over an open fire, and finally, Bigirimana shows his audience how the refugees sleep: "on the ground simply, like this."

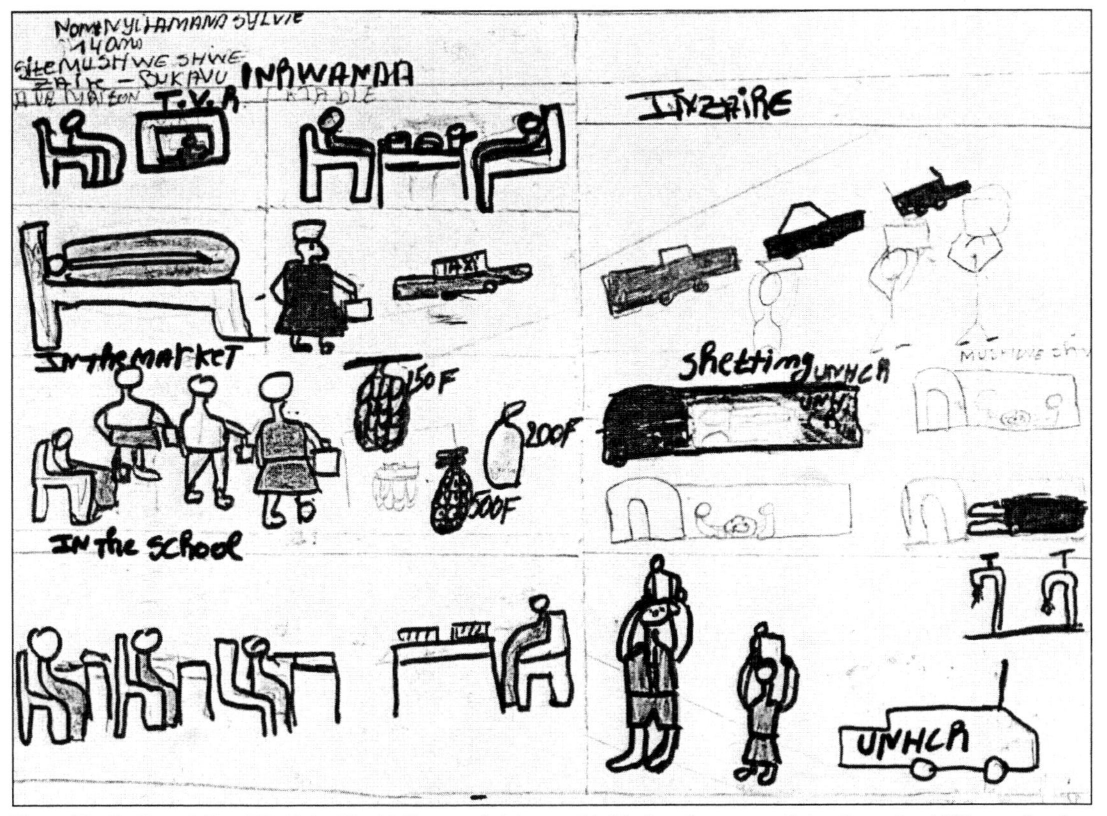

Figure 63. "In Rwanda" and "In Zaire," by Nyilamana Sylvie, age 14. Mushweshwe camp, Zaire, December 1994; pencil and color markers on paper. The Rwanda side of the drawing shows normal life at home (watching television, eating at a dining table, sleeping in a bed), going to market, and going to school. The story of Zaire begins with refugees carrying their belongings on their heads, others fleeing in cars, the plastic tent sheeting provided by UNHCR, people in their tents sitting on the floor, sleeping on the floor, and carrying water from the public open-air faucets in gasoline containers, and the UNHCR vehicle as much lifeline as is the water.

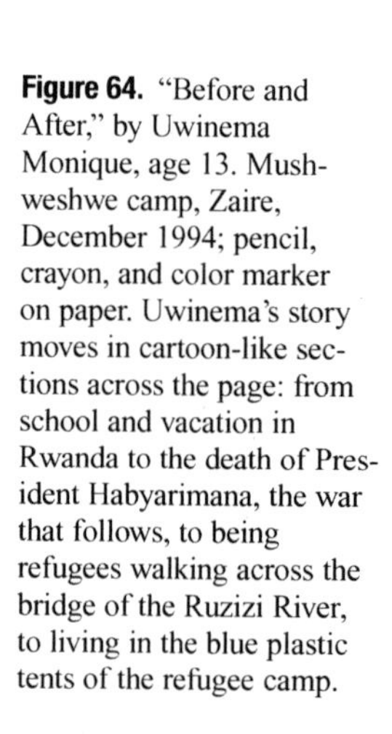

Figure 64. "Before and After," by Uwinema Monique, age 13. Mushweshwe camp, Zaire, December 1994; pencil, crayon, and color marker on paper. Uwinema's story moves in cartoon-like sections across the page: from school and vacation in Rwanda to the death of President Habyarimana, the war that follows, to being refugees walking across the bridge of the Ruzizi River, to living in the blue plastic tents of the refugee camp.

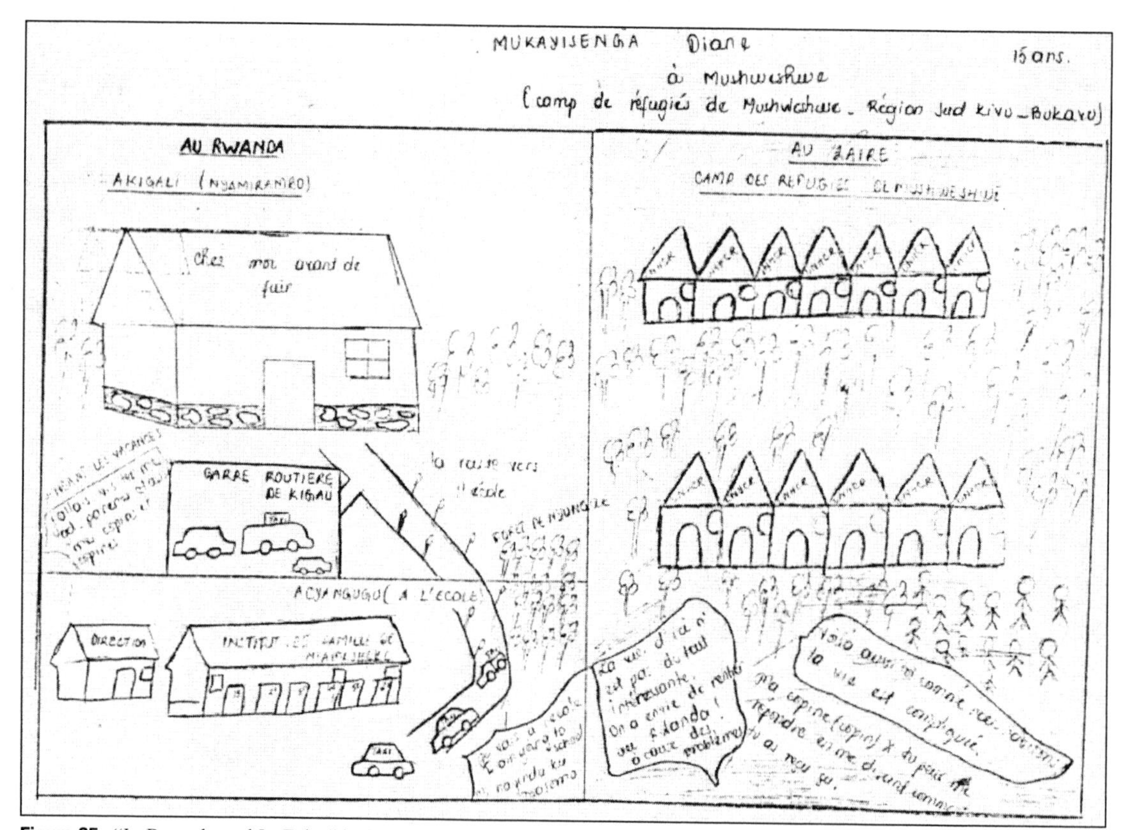

Figure 65. "In Rwanda and In Zaire," by Mukayisenga Diane, age 15. Mushweshwe camp, Zaire, December 1994; pencil on paper. On the left half of the page Mukayisenga shows her home before her flight, at Nyamirambo, Kigali Prefecture, with references to visiting her grandparents during vacations and her school at Nyamirambo. On the right side is the tent city of Mushweshwe, situated in a region with much forest. The UNHCR is accredited for each plastic sheeting that makes up the tents; door and window openings are neatly aligned, and lots of little stick-figure people inhabit the place. The thought bubble complains: ". . . Here life is not at all interesting. . . . We wish we could return to Rwanda. . . ."

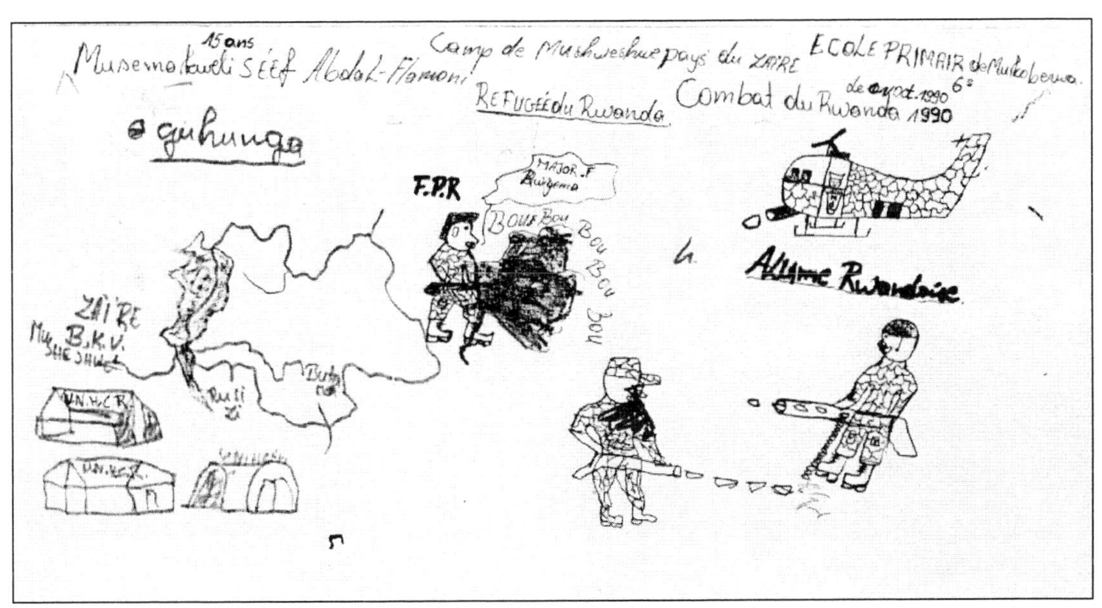

Figure 66. "The battle of Rwanda, October 1990," by Musemakweli Seef Abdah-Hamani, age 15. Mushweshwe camp, Zaire, December 1994; pen and color marker on paper. This student rendered a history lesson about the conflict of 1990 between the Rwandan army (FAR) and the RPF in which General Fred Rwigema lost his life in the battle with the then Rwandan government army and who has since become a hero and martyr of the RPF. The death of Rwigema is vividly shown here, as is the fatal wounding of another RPF soldier.

Figure 67. "Zaire and Rwanda," by Rutagengwa Yves, age 10. Mushweshwe camp, Zaire, December 1994; pencil and color marker on paper. The right side of the page shows the war in Kigali, the shooting of President Habyarimana's plane, and bombing of a house from which people are fleeing on foot. The bridge across the Ruzizi River leads to the tent city of Mushweshwe and its school.

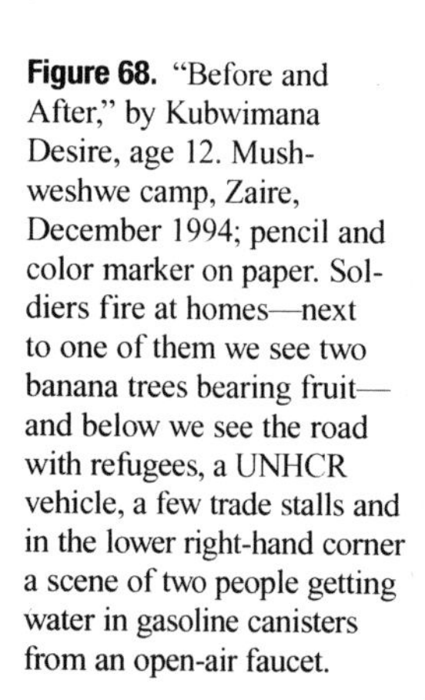
Figure 68. "Before and After," by Kubwimana Desire, age 12. Mushweshwe camp, Zaire, December 1994; pencil and color marker on paper. Soldiers fire at homes—next to one of them we see two banana trees bearing fruit—and below we see the road with refugees, a UNHCR vehicle, a few trade stalls and in the lower right-hand corner a scene of two people getting water in gasoline canisters from an open-air faucet.

Figure 69. "Before and Now," by Njemubeza Eric, age 15. Mushweshwe camp, Zaire, December 15, 1994; ballpoint pen and color marker on paper. Eric's narrative of his before and now experiences is explained in English for the imagined American audience. The sunlit peace of the family's compound in the hilly countryside is interrupted by the sound of explosions and artillery of war. Next we see the family in flight, on foot, carrying their belongings, including the plastic container for water; the baby is tied to the mother's back, and she is worrying about the house, the fields, and the cows that were left behind. They walk toward the crowded tent city in Mushweshwe, where CARE, CARITAS, and the Red Cross have mounted their logos, where the UNHCR is distributing plastic sheeting, and where water is fetched from a single outdoor faucet. Mennonites, who did not publicize their presence with flags, are nevertheless acknowledged and cheered by Njemubeza, who feels good enough about himself and his fate that he can wish others well.

Figure 70. "Bombe," detail of drawing by Nsanzimana Philbert, age 15. Mushweshwe camp, Zaire, December 1994; ballpoint pen and color marker on paper. A soldier of the RPF, here identified as *inkotanyi* shoots at the boy's home in Rwanda.

Figure 71. "Rwanda and Zaire," by Niwenshuti Jean Claude, age 15. Mushweshwe camp, Zaire, December 1994. Niwenshuti is conscious of the bridge across the Ruzizi River that will be the life saver for the refugees once the obstacles of customs and a militant Zairian border soldier are passed. Part of life in the tent city is the arrival of UNHCR vehicles with humanitarian aid and the chore of fetching water and carrying it back to the tents, here done by an adult and a child.

Figure 72. "Regardez les refugies," by Habimana Christophe, age 12, Mushweshwe camp, Zaire, December 1994; pencil and color marker on paper. Habimana's family's home, car, grove of trees, and fields are left behind. The thought bubbles that appear above the heads of a group of refugees carrying their belongings on their heads say "Where are my sheep?" "Your sheep are there," and "I don't see it." Vehicles of all sorts crowded with people move in a caravan along the road toward the Ruzizi River. The tents of the refugee camp are crowded with people.

Figure 73. "Rwanda and Zaire," by Mukeshimana Pelagie, age 13. Mushweshwe camp, Zaire, December 1994; color marker on paper. From a fancy home surrounded by flowers and trees the family flees by car, possessions piled on top. Refugees in cars and on foot find shelter in the UNHCR-supported camps; people crowd around a UNHCR truck that is delivering goods.

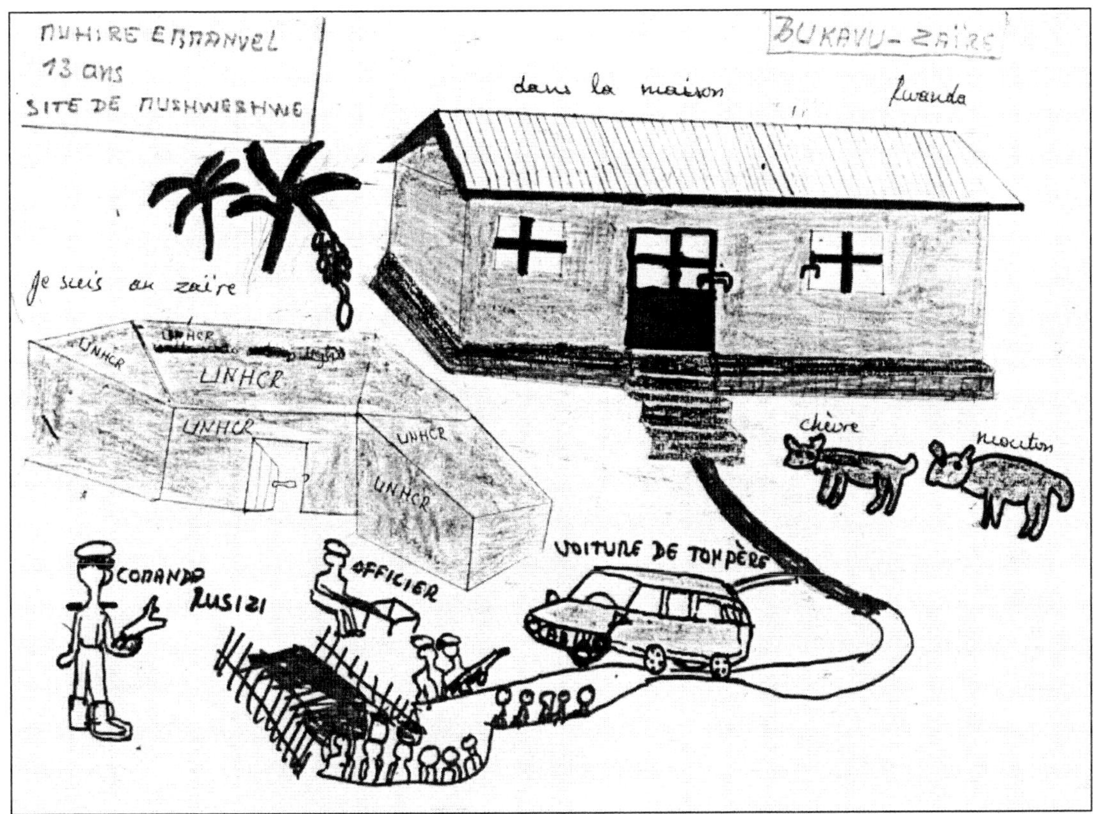

Figure 74. "Crossing the border," detail from "Zaire and Rwanda" by Muhire Emmanuel, age 13. Mushweshwe camp, Zaire, December 1994; crayon, color markers, and pencil on paper. A long line of refugees at the bridge that is also the border between Rwanda and Zaire are stopped by Zairian armed border guards.

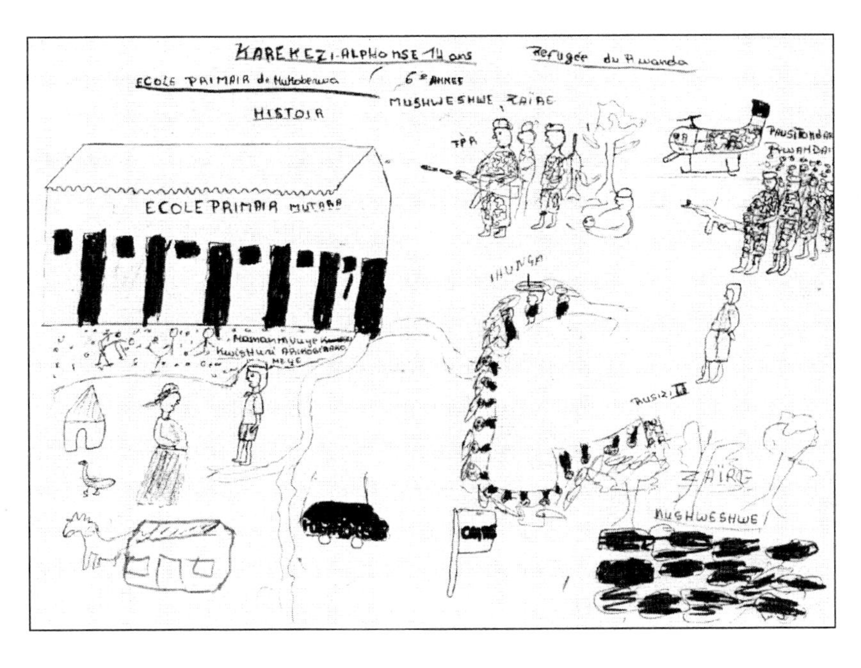

Figure 75. "Refugee of Rwanda," by Karekezi Alphonse, age 14. Mushweshwe camp, Zaire, December 1994; pen and color marker on paper. In the before picture Karekezi stands near the primary school of Mutara (the primary school of Mukobenwa is shown above) and is speaking to his mother near their home compound. Then he shows (himself?) as a lone figure between a long file of refugees headed toward the Ruzizi River toward refugee camps in Zaire with the two armies above him. Karekezi has a clear picture of the RPF and the Rwandan army facing off against each other.

A third explanation was offered by long-time MCC workers Terry Sawatsky and Cathy Hodder (personal communication, August 14, 1995) in Zaire, who were critically involved in first emergency assistance in the Bukavu area Rwandan refugee camps. They suggested that the controlled element in the drawings might be a result of the children being "very controlled by the prevailing authority in the camps." In their experience it was not easy to get children to speak for themselves. "Authorities gave a simple and clear message. 'We are victims; it is not our fault.'" Sawatsky added that in contrast to the children who lived in the camps with their families, the unaccompanied children were "more open about their experiences and less likely to think about what the adults wanted them to say."

One such controlled drawing is by 15-year-old Mukayisenga Diane (Figure 65). Using only pencil, opting against color, she drew neat rows of tents, conveying the crowdedness of the camp site by having the tents touch each other. Her drawing of her home near Kigali on the other half of the paper occupies a large space and stands prominently alone. This juxtaposition between the single-family dwelling in its compound and the crowdedness of the tents is a dominant motif in all the children's drawings. Mukayisenga included in her careful drawing short explanations and messages (in French) to an imagined friend in the United States, even including a little bit of the English she had learned in school:

> In Rwanda before fleeing I go to school. During vacations my friends and I visit our grandparents. Here [in the refugee camp] life is not at all interesting. We long to return to Rwanda! Because of the problems [incomplete] Here also you see how we live. Life is complicated.

In this last short sentence lies the expression of the whole weight of her frustration.

Other children expressed a surprising sense of hope, despite the upheaval of their war experience and their loss of the familiar and of security. Njemubeza Eric's drawing (Figure 69) includes his hope for peace—a sign that this child has a positive attitude toward the future, that as an adult he might be one of those ready for reconciliation, ready to break the cycle of violence. This kind of document, then, corroborates studies that have shown that children who experienced violence need not necessarily become perpetrators of violence as adults, that cycles of violence can be broken. For example, the many years of conflict in Uganda created many children who were tired of war and who wanted peace. Their goals for their future were based on positive role models, such as nurses, doctors, the Red Cross, or UNICEF employees (Stanton 1995, p. 14).

The children's drawings shown here and the larger group from which they are selected are a powerful and subjective documentation of the Rwandan War. No doubt our selection reflects our particular route of travel and work. Perhaps the results would have been more nuanced had we been able to speak and work with the children directly over a longer period of time and on an individual basis. In the five years since the children drew their experiences for us, a further lens of bias and control has become apparent: the adult ideological supervision of the children. All the drawings from Rwanda, Bukavu, and the Mushweshwe camp were directed by the children's adult supervisors (two of whom were teachers), except for two (Figures 33 and 34) and even those drawings were directed a little by the child's older brother. The Bukavu drawings directed by a Zairian were done with no or at least less political bias on the part of the adult who supervised the drawing, but there was some peer pressure among the children. It is noteworthy that Hutu refugee children who may well have seen or been party to the killing of Tutsi do not associate this with the reasons for their flight (the only reason they acknowledge visually is President Habyarimana's shot-down plane), and they do not show Interahamwe militia violence against Tutsi, nor do Tutsi children include in their drawings violence committed on the part of the RPF against Hutu. They both block out what most of the adults block out.

3.3 Emergence of New Icons

While walking along Kigali's Avenue de la Justice on December 22, 1994, we saw three brightly colored paintings displayed in front of a small shop. What caught our attention was the fact that the portraits of General Paul Kagame and General Fred Rwigema were shown flanking an image of the Sacred Heart of Mary (Figure 76). All three paintings were of the same format, done in acrylic on canvas in the style that was prevalent in the many painted shop signs across town and in the countryside. The shopkeeper told us that the paintings had been done by Philippe Baptiste, who was living in Burundi, but the works themselves bore no signature. When we asked for permission to photograph the images, we were asked to pay a fee of 3,000 Rwandan francs (approximately $15). We were not willing to pay, certainly not this much, for taking three photographs, so we left. But as was the case with Mini Leonard's poster *Consequences of War*, we could not forget this constellation of images.

We returned at our next opportunity, on Friday, December 30, 1994, to again ask permission to photograph these paintings, only to be told that the vendor had taken them to the big market and that we should come back after 2 p.m. the same day. When we came back again at the suggested time "our" paintings and three more were stacked with their faces against the wall of the little shop. After explaining our interest, we got permission to photograph without having to pay. Just as we photographed General Kagame's portrait on the veranda in front of the shop and in full sight of the street, a military personnel vehicle drove by, its passengers looking at what we were doing. This made the shopkeeper so nervous that we were not allowed to photograph the remaining paintings, which we had not yet seen and whose subjects remain unknown to us. "That's enough," he said, and we were sent on our way.

The constellation of the life-size portraits of General Rwigema, who led the RPF attack on northeast Rwanda in October 1990 and who lost his life in the battle with the then Rwandan government army (FAR), and of General Kagame, who led the 1994 war that unseated the govern-

Figure 76. Heroes of the RPF framing the Virgin of the Sacred Heart. Three paintings seen on display and for sale in Kigali, December 1994, arranged in this sequence: (left) General Fred Rwigema led the RPF attack on Rwanda in October 1990 and lost his life in the battle with the then Rwandan government army. (right) General Paul Kagame, right, led the 1994 war that unseated the government of President Habyarimana and the MRND party.

ment of President Habyarimana and the MRND party, on either side of the Virgin Mary not only lent the generals a sanctified legitimacy but also elevated them to near sainthood. The message of this particular grouping of three images, the way they had been displayed to rouse interest in a potential buyer, certainly implied that the actions and the persons of Generals Rwigema and Kagame were—and are—blessed by the Virgin Mary. The iconography of the Madonna, which was copied by the artist from widely popular, mass-produced holy cards, is significant in this context because of its association with Catholic piety surrounding the cult of Mary and because of its association with martyrdom. The flaming heart encircled by the crown of thorns that Mary displays (known as the Sacred Heart of Mary) is a symbol of Christ's martyrdom and love for humankind. Viewed by themselves, the idealized portraits of the generals—their features a combination of purposefulness and benevolence and their camouflage uniform and emblems of rank expressions of the power of the RPF—have a strong iconic presence.

Notes

1. Portions of this section have been published elsewhere. An abbreviated version of this essay and illustrations were published by Jewsiewicki (1999) and the Lutheran Immigration and Refugee Service (1998).

4. Burundi

In many ways Burundi is similar to Rwanda. The two countries are neighbors in the Great Lakes region, and the two national languages, Kirundi and Kinyarwanda, are mutually intelligible. Burundi, too, was once a kingdom, in a region where "Hutu" kingdoms were gradually penetrated by "Tutsi" pastoralists who had long intermarried with and lived among them. With the support of the German colonial government in the 1890s, the Tutsi became the overlords of the Hutu and the Twa. In Burundi the Hima and the Ganwa, often considered part of the Tutsi class, are additional ethnic identities. The Burundi kingdom was more internally segmented than the Rwanda kingdom. The capital shifted from region to region, and no formal history was kept by court historians, as in Rwanda. Traditional judicial systems were similar. In Burundi justice was mainly in the hands of local councils of judges, the *bashingantahe,* who compared to the Rwandan *gacaca.* Both were drawn from all groups of society on the basis of the individuals' skills and reputations for wisdom. In both societies appeals could be made to chiefs and the king.

Burundi shares the legacy of post–World War I Belgian colonial rule with Rwanda; both were administered from Usumbura (today Bujumbura) in the region known as Ruanda-Urundi. In the early 1960s, although there was popular unrest and emerging Hutu nationalism, as in Rwanda, factionalism and rivalry within the Tutsi-Hima community led to the destruction of the kingship. Instead of a Hutu republic emerging, as in Rwanda in 1959, the first three presidents of independent Burundi were Hima from the southern region of Rutovu, and they ruled the small country as a military regime. The third president, Pierre Buyoya, opened the way for democratic reforms and the popular election in June 1993. Melchior Ndadaye, the first Hutu president of Burundi, was chosen. However, after a mere 100 days in office, Ndadaye was assassinated by elements of the army in October 1993, in an attempted coup d'état. This brutal act drew a strong reaction from Hutu partisans and an equally bloody reaction by the mostly Tutsi military, who sought to regain control of the country. For several years after Ndadaye's death Burundi's government was based on a tense and unstable coalition of FRODEBU [Front pour la Démocratie au Burundi (Democratic Front of Burundi), predominantly Hutu] and UPRONA [Union pour le Progrès National (Provisional National Union), predominantly Tutsi] administrators and military and political figures. Ndadaye's successor, Cyprien Ntaryamira, died in April 1994 in the downing of the plane in which Rwandan president Habyarimana was killed. His successor, Sylvestre Ntibantunganya, a Hutu, who was ratified by a divided parliament, was overthrown in 1996 by Tutsi military figure Pierre Buyoya, who ruled until the 1993 elections. Since about 1994, a Hutu resistance has operated from within and beyond Burundi's borders, often in some kind of league with Rwandan Hutu militants.

Despite these warlike circumstances, Burundi has averted the abyss of total violence that Rwanda experienced. A series of national meetings to promote moderation and to explore mediation have kept the hope alive that Burundi can return to its early 1990s status as a promising democracy.

Our visit to Burundi was arranged by Harold Otto and the local Quaker office. The MCC was working with the Burundian Quakers to distribute Canadian food grains within the delicate standoff of community elements in the Quaker region west of Gitega. The MCC also supported medical staff for the re-opening of a hospital at Kibimba that had been closed after the fighting of October 1993.

Later, the MCC would support peace work in this same area and in the country. In Bujumbura we lodged at the White Fathers Mission in the St. Michel Parish and at the Italian Xavier Fathers Guesthouse. In the Gitega region we stayed with Susan Seitz, an American nurse at the Quaker center in Kibimba. We were taken around by David Niyonzima and his staff. We owe almost all this writing to the hospitality and generous time offered to us by Niyonzima.

This ethnographic sketch concentrates on two settings: (1) the Quaker mission and commercial center of Kibimba, west of Gitega, and (2) several surrounding localities and Bujumbura, the capital, with a focus on several urban communes, in particular, Bwiza. Both these areas have been subject to local conflict, but in each instance local peace initiatives were undertaken. In Kibimba the violence at the time of Ndadaye's assassination tore apart the community, leaving many dead and displaced. In Bujumbura's communes, ethnic cleansing and guerrilla attacks similarly left many dead and displaced. But in each instance local leaders and organizations tried to stop the killing or to negotiate a settlement. Recent efforts have built bridges amid continuing killings.

The reasons behind this compression of community destruction and community building in Burundi are not easy to understand beyond the immediacy of outbursts of violence followed by voices of caution. It has been said that in Burundi violence takes on a life of its own. People do not have ready answers for the onset of the waves of killing that have convulsed the country in the past. However, some evidence points to planned and targeted violence staged by small activist groups of extremists to achieve their political aims.

A number of Burundian voices are presented here, standing for both sides of the conflict, that is, the Hutu and the Tutsi sides, although it would be illegal in Burundi to voice these words openly. Even this policy of whether one should suppress ethnic particularism or acknowledge it is contested. Representing the side of the majority, that is, the Hutu, is a Burundian ambassador with whom we spoke and who wished to remain anonymous. We also interviewed other figures, each of whom represents a particular perspective. Author and former mayor Katihabwa Sebastian is cited in several places; professor and Burundian Catholic Bishop's Council Secretary Adrien Ntabona represents the view of the well-educated Catholic Church hierarchy, which has historically been primarily Tutsi. Quaker leader David Niyonzima describes his personal approach to dealing with violence. This section closes with Zairian Ilumbe Mwanasala's interpretation of the paradoxical behavior of Burundians, who he says possess a character that is superficially friendly and cooperative but in fact is secretive and deceptive, a stance Ilumbe believes is at the root of the violence. Ilumbe, a secondary school humanities teacher in Burundi until October 1993, tried to understand what he experienced as violence engulfed his school and its staff.

4.1 A Landscape of Low-Intensity War

Deus spes nostra es [God is our hope].—embossed motto on the upholstery buttons in a deserted mission house at Kibimba hospital and school

Kibimba, November 1994

As the morning fog lifted over Kibimba, the sounds were of men, women, and children starting their day and of roosters crowing. The sights corresponded to the sounds. Women and children walked down the path past the houses and the hospital on their way to their fields of corn, sorghum, or beans, carrying baskets on their heads and hoes in their hands. A few men and boys were slowly driving their cattle ahead of them to graze in some pasture or alongside their coffee tree plots or banana groves. A little girl fastened a bright pink flower in her black hair. Later, we walked on narrow paths between plantings on the steep hillside below the hospital to see and to photograph the farming families' small mud-brick houses, which were whitewashed and painted with designs and inscriptions to announce the groom's marriage.

This image of normalcy and peace is surreal, however. The women and children on their way to their fields, driving their cattle, were not coming from their homes and compounds; they were walking down from the ridge where the Secondary School and the Church of Kibimba, an old Quaker mission, are located (Figure 77). The school and church serve as a refuge for about 3,000 widows and their children and a few men. The women are protected by a camp of Burundian soldiers garrisoned at the end and highest point on Kibimba ridge, just beyond the school and church buildings. From the ridge these internally displaced people go out daily, past a guarded barrier, to spend a few relatively safe hours in their fields near where their homes used to stand before they were destroyed in the events of October 1993 and where their husbands were massacred by their neighbors. Hunger and a desire to save what they can drive the women to return everyday to cultivate their fields to augment the meager rations handed out by relief agencies.

Downhill from the Kibimba mission, hospital, and schools, along the national highway from Bujumbura to Gitega, there had stood a commercial center with many shops, a gas station, eating places, and numerous homes. Hutu partisans, furious over the killing of President Ndadaye in an attempted coup d'état on October 23, 1993, took more than 20 Tutsi students of Kibimba Secondary School to the station, doused them with gasoline, put them inside the building, and set it on fire (Figure 78). Burundian soldiers, avenging the students' deaths and those of many other Tutsi, razed the buildings of the commercial center. Now, only the jagged silhouette of the ruins of cement block and pressed adobe walls stand starkly as reminders of the fury of that moment of revenge and counter-revenge. Near the ruins of Kibimba center, along a road leading away and over the hills, a mass grave, freshly decorated with a wreath for every child that perished and a wooden cross inscribed with the words "Enfants Victimes de Génocide, 23 octobre 1993," commemorates the students who were burned to death in the gas station (Figure 79).

As anyone who follows the news from Central Africa will realize, this was not the first massacre of its kind in Burundi. The country has been racked by periodic clashes and killings ever since the end of Belgian colonialism in 1962 and the collapse of the kingdom (Lemarchand 1994). Successive governments by the Tutsi (Ganwa) strongmen Michel Micombiero, Jean Baptiste Bagaza, and Pierre Buyoya built up a set of national institutions controlled by a predominantly Tutsi elite. The mostly Tutsi army is the backbone of this order. Under Buyoya, however, political reforms and a broadening of the range of those included in the political process led the way for popular elections. These brought Melchior Ndadaye, a Hutu, to power as the first democratically elected president in June 1993. He installed a government reflecting the coalition between his FRODEBU majority party and the minority UPRONA party. But Ndadaye had hardly 100 days to govern before he and a number of his ministers and high officials

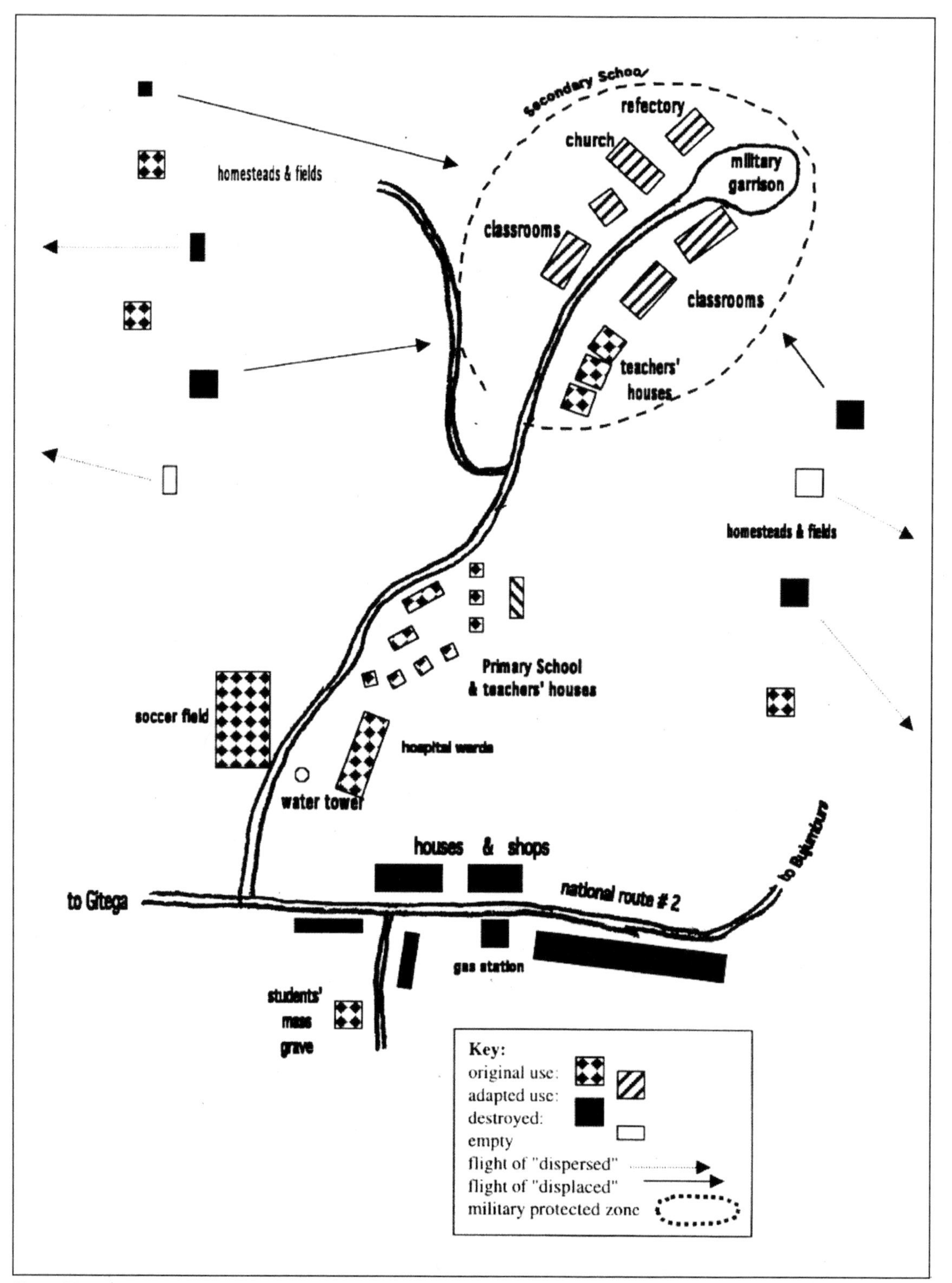

Figure 77. Kibimba, a local case study of Burundian ethnic separation. Note that most buildings are either destroyed, empty, or used for a purpose other than that for which it was originally intended. Only a few buildings are still in use for their original purpose, an indication of the extent of the internal displacement experienced in Burundian society. Arrows show the direction or location in which residents have fled. Map drawn by J. M. Janzen, November 1994, based on several local informants.

Figure 78. Ruins of Kibimba petrol station in which Tutsi students from Kibimba Secondary School were doused in gasoline and burned alive following the assassination of President Ndadaye in October 1993.

Figure 79. Mass grave and memorial to "Victims of genocide, October 21, 1993" for the Tutsi students of Kibimba, Burundi.

were assassinated by elements of the army. The UN Fact Finding Mission to Burundi, led by Ambassador Martin Huslid of Norway and Ambassador Simeon Ake of Cote d'Ivoire, established that a detachment of officers and soldiers had carried out the murder. Other members of the government were also killed. The perpetrators were not prosecuted, furthering the impression that this was an attempted military coup (United Nations 1994).

After the events of 1993 there followed popular uprisings against and attacks on the Tutsi and reprisals by the army on the people. Many Tutsi fled their homes to protected camps for the displaced. The army sought out and chased from their homes those it thought to be the perpetrators, who fled into the hills and bush; they and their kin became the dispersed. This war resulted in massive populational and social disarray. Homes were burned, fields destroyed, living conditions rendered difficult; disease outbreaks became common, especially water- and sewage-related diseases such as dysentery and cholera and respiratory infections among children. An estimated 50,000 to 100,000 persons were killed in this initial round of violence in October 1993; 280,000 were displaced internally, and 670,000 fled to neighboring Tanzania, Rwanda, and Zaire (US Agency for International Development 1994).

Kibimba took on national recognition in the tragedy of 1993, both for the shame and outrage over the brutal murder of the Tutsi students and for the resolve to let the immolation be a symbol of what must not happen again. The memorial to the students, at the site of their mass burial, was erected in late 1994. This occasion was attended by Burundian president Ntibantunganya and his military escort in an effort to show a united front between the mostly Hutu administration and the mostly Tutsi army. The president wished to make the point that the atrocities that occurred in Kibimba and throughout the country must never again be allowed to spoil the fragile fabric that is Burundian society.

At Kibimba mission itself the arrival of a courageous nurse, Susan Seitz, in the spring of 1994 was the beginning of hope for the people in the area. In the midst of the no-man's land between the two local camps of the opposing communities—mostly Tutsi displaced widows and children with their military protectors on the one hand and the dispersed Hutu peasants, shopkeepers, and craftsmen cowering in the wooded valleys and hillsides on the other hand—this American Quaker nurse came to reopen the hospital. She had been transferred from Somalia when her unit there was closed. In Kibimba—where all hospital staff had fled or been killed, where the storehouses with repair parts, goods, and medicines had been robbed empty, where the power generator had been stolen and there was therefore no electricity—Seitz moved into a long-abandoned house and with minimal provisions declared the hospital open. Supported by the Quakers of Burundi, themselves in hiding or fearful of meeting, Seitz, as an outsider, could reach both the Hutu and the Tutsi from the middle. Realizing that the displaced widows and the Tutsi soldiers were as afraid as the dispersed Hutu people in the countryside, Seitz made it a point to keep contact with both. Among her first patients in the hospital were many individuals critically ill with dysentery but also a man who had run full force into a tree while fleeing for his life at night. He died of internal injuries that Seitz was not equipped to deal with. Realizing that medical care was needed by both sides, she began to operate mobile clinics in the region, with special attention to infants and children. It became apparent that emergency food supplies were also needed. This is when the MCC offered assistance from the Canadian food bank and how the MCC began to work with the Burundian Quakers. In November 1994 there were relief food deliveries every two weeks from a relief distribution center in Miranda. Later, the MCC delivered Canadian food bank lentils to this camp of internally displaced widows at Kibimba and to the dispersed population.

War's Landscape: Tearing Apart the Threads of the Social Fabric

A map of Kibimba's hospital and schools complex (Figure 77), along a hilltop ridge, reveals the polarization affecting all of Burundi. This map, which reflects the situation of November 1994, is indicative of the less visible social and political polarization. The secondary school and church became a camp for displaced persons, mostly Tutsi women and children, although there were some Hutu there as well. Dozens of camps like this dotted the country. In the camp for displaced widows, stories abounded of husbands and families who had been attacked and massacred. The military garrison atop Kibimba ridge, manned by the Burundian army, which is mostly Tutsi, protected the camp and went out daily to set up roadblocks on the national highway and to attack suspected guerrillas "in the hills." Kibimba's commercial center was a burned-out shell from the October 1993 reprisal for the burning of Tutsi students in the gas station. Isolated by a roadblock and a strip of no-man's land on the lower end of the ridge was a complex of mission houses, the elementary school, and the hospital—the Hutu side of the same hill. The surrounding wooded hills and valleys were filled with the dispersed populace who had fled their homes. They ventured out only in daylight to work their fields or to go about their business but were afraid to be anywhere visible, such as at home, during the night. The army was convinced that armed bands were out to get them, and indeed there had been ambushes along the highway. The people complained, however, that the army planted weapons and created pretexts to drive fear into the hearts of the populace so that they could increase their control.

Many reporters and commentators simply called this conflict, as that in Rwanda, a tribal or ethnic one between the Tutsi, erstwhile pastoralists, and the Hutu, erstwhile peasants, while mentioning the Twa, erstwhile hunters. Tutsi, Hutu, and Twa served as class-based identities in a region where cattle were a traditional marker of wealth and status for millennia and working the land was something done by peasants for millennia; traditionally, the Twa were pottery makers. But the population of Burundi, as that of Rwanda, is unitary in many respects. All groups have lived locally together, all speak the same language, and they have intermarried extensively. Hutu, Tutsi, and Twa are social categories carried on by simple patrilineality, despite the fact that many families or households contain both identities. In other words, the conventional Central African societal building blocks of unilineal descent and exogamous marriage continue to operate here. "Embracing the other" in marriage provides a powerful integrating force to the overall social fabric. The usual forces of upward mobility have resulted in many peasant men marrying women of herders and the emergence of a folklore of the beautiful Tutsi woman. As a consequence, many households and families are interethnic in Burundi, as in Rwanda. However, this emphasis on lineal identity and cross-cutting marital integration is both a bane and a blessing.

In the common calculus of tension, the integrating forces of marriage fuel the tragedies, because one suspects not only the ethnic or class other, but even more the possible collaborator among one's own kin and neighbors. This is what makes the particular mixture of status differences and alleged blood line differences so volatile. It cuts through most neighborhoods and many families—in fact, the entire nation—providing a brittle breaking point for issues such as sibling rivalry, scarce land, limited positions in higher education, and competition for control of institutions inherited from the colonizers (Katihabwa 1991).

Thus, at a public level most Burundians emphasized the need for peace and harmony. Daily life seemed to be fairly normal most of the time. Even the Kibimba displaced widows, some of whom are Hutu with Tutsi children, went out to their fields during the daytime. But at night or when a national political crisis unfolded or when there was an incident in a local community, the rhetoric of ethnic extremism overwhelmed. The waves of violence that have been recently reported in Burundi have probably been instigated by a combination of the frustrations and contradictions of daily living and exacerbated by planned campaigns to take advantage of the opponent's weaknesses. However, no general statement of these matters can be as clear or as vivid as stories of individuals and families affected by or involved in the events. The following accounts were told by widows in the Kibimba camp, a hospital worker, a pastor, and a military garrison commander.

Stories of Massacre and Flight

Seven Widows

With the permission of Commander Adrien of the military garrison atop Kibimba ridge, we were able to speak with seven of the thousands of widows who, with their children and a few men, subsist in this camp of internally displaced persons (Figure 80). After we passed the military checkpoint at the entrance to the secondary school complex turned refugee camp, we were politely greeted and immediately surrounded by throngs of children, many plagued with eczema and snotty noses. Some were on their way to their class shift at the primary school, which had just opened again after a year of being closed. Others carried plastic water containers or bundles of firewood on their heads. Some girls played with a jump rope

Figure 80. Camp of the displaced in the meeting house and secondary school of Kibimba, Burundi.

Figure 81. Widows and children inside the meeting house where they have made their shelter, Kibimba, Burundi.

fashioned of vines or with balls made of tied-up plastic bags or rags. Boys constructed toy cars from bits of wood and toy weapons from scrap metal, with soldiers being the dominant role models in this setting. Everywhere cooking fires smoldered between hearthstones under the open sky. A mother was washing children at a water faucet along the road. A few heads of cattle were still corralled inside the mission cemetery, next to which a makeshift aviary safeguarded some chickens. Small boys were herding goats away from the camp toward more grassy areas.

We walked through the sanctuary of the cathedral-like brick meetinghouse and other school buildings that served as cramped, smoke-filled miserable shelter for thousands of women and children (Figure 81). People slept and spent many waking hours on layers of leaves or on grass mats on the ground. If they were lucky, they made a bed on a table, with their few belongings (e.g., cooking pots) piled within the narrow confines of each family group's bedding area. No privacy was possible, and the dismal, bestial circumstances were an enormous challenge to a person's dignity. Together with two interpreters who were assigned to us by the commander of the military garrison nearby, we gathered with seven women and some of their babies in a former science classroom. Charts on the growth cycle of the pineapple and chemistry formulas were still on the walls; otherwise there was a chaos of seed and furniture storage, a jumble of boxes of medicines, and piles of disposable needles. We sat in a circle and the women could hardly wait their turn to tell their stories.

Moabashisha Yolanda, with six children, spoke of her reason for being in the Kibimba camp.

> The Hutus chased us with their machetes on the 21st of October [1993]. In the morning, my husband was taken from our *colline* to the village of Kibimba 3 kilometers from here. My husband was killed. Then they went after the women to kill them with their children. We saw we were threatened, we fled here, but the killers pursued us. I arrived on the 24th, despite the barricades the Hutu had put up; the military came the 25th. The others came from 4 to 16 kilometers away, from four communes of Giheta, Bugendana, Rutegama, and Ndava.

Moabashisha told us that she had no bed and that she slept on the ground with her children. She wanted to go home or would do anything to build a new house and have school for her children. She wanted to go somewhere where she could settle and live in security.

Nsibimana Marie had come to the camp with her three children when her husband was killed in the events of October 21, 1993.

> I wish that you could intervene, to help give medical care to the displaced, who are sick. We need clothes. Those who have money can go to the hospital. We get 1 kilogram per household per week of grain. If I would go back, those who live around me would steal my goods and even kill me. The big problem is that all things were stolen; the officials who are in charge of justice, they killed my husband. The administration should be changed. There are [even] Hutu who could change things for the better. I would like to go back. We want to return, but there are all armed people there.

A young woman with one child, Nduwimana Mediatrice simply said that she had been a new bride when the massacres took her husband. She wanted to return, but her house had been burned.

The others added that they too wanted to return, but all around their houses were armed people who would do them harm.

Ndoruwigira Judith, with six children, said that life is difficult.

> There are orphans. If one is in here [in the displaced camp], you have no money for clothes or for school for your children. Help us to help the orphans and our own children.

She then revealed that the women in the circle had taken in orphans. She had taken in one child, and the new bride with one child had taken in three.

Inagatozi Degera, who had lost six of her eight children described, her ordeal.

> In the beginning, after the massacre, the youths said they would protect the widows and children. I had [eight] children, and passed many days hiding in the bush. Only two of my children survived. A Hutu hid us. But whenever I went to my field to get food, they attacked those who hid me. Hutu are not all bad—some protected us. But hostile words are still spoken to us. If you can help us, we don't know where to go. We still hear gunshots in the hills. I live too far away from my home for the military to protect me there [so I continue to live in the camp in Kibimba.]

Nizirazana Victoire had four children, of whom two survive. She told her story.

> That day they killed, it was a Sunday, the military told the people to stop. They were in the bush, hiding. Until today, the soldiers have protected us. We are very unhappy here. Food and clothing are scarce; the children have nothing to wear. We don't know how long this will go on. We have church here; a Giheta priest comes and we meet in the school assembly hall. The Protestants also meet there.

Ntacomaze Emmanuelle's husband was killed in the first round of attacks after the death of President Ndadaye; she fled with her eight children to the camp at Kibimba mission. She described her situation in the following terms.

> At 5:00 a.m. [on October 22, 1993] the *chef de colline* called people to put up barricades. And they began to bind up Tutsi and ran around to find others, beginning with the men, then the women. They were hunted even in the toilets where they were killed. Their houses were destroyed, and the contents stolen. Then they killed the women and children, even the pregnant women. Some *collines* now have no Tutsi left at all. Those widows who survive—most of us are widows here—and their children have nothing, no source of income. Some go to cultivate their fields, thanks to the military. They go to cultivate, but the Hutu who stayed harvest their fields. How do you get food here? The biggest evil is that those who killed are still in their positions. The administration should be changed. I am alive thanks to the military here. To go back would be impossible. Their objective is to eliminate the Tutsi. They look forward to the day when there are no more Tutsi. We have no hope for a better life.

Sitting in a circle of widows, we were surprised to hear Ntacomaze reveal her ethnic identity. "I am Hutu. I had a Tutsi husband. [So] I suffered like a Tutsi; and I continue to suffer like a Tutsi." By this logic, although she is Hutu, her children are Tutsi. Living amid a largely Tutsi camp, her life had been redefined into that of victim. She needed to protect her children.

A Novice Priest

Jovin, a novice for the priesthood, came to Kibimba to work with Susan Seitz in the hospital and to lend a hand with the emergency. His personal situation was tense but instructive. It was the inverse of Ntacomaze's. Because his father is Hutu, he is Hutu; however, his mother is Tutsi. In the cruel logic of Burundian ethnicity, he had been arrested twice by the Burundian soldiers, who are mostly Tutsi. But he had been able to buy his freedom each time because of his family's means. One afternoon Jovin came in to Seitz's house in Kibimba. He was agitated and told us that his parents' house and many others in a nearby settlement of nearly equal Hutu-Tutsi populace had been burned and that all his parents' provisions had been taken because soldiers had seen a Hutu armed with a pistol. As house owner, his father and he had been victimized in the reprisal. Jovin's younger brother escaped and was living with him at the mission.

A Pastor

David Niyonzima, legal representative of the Evangelical Quakers of Burundi, is a second-generation Burundian Quaker and a leader in his church and community. Of a quiet yet strong disposition, he has been a pillar for the Quakers in the recent turmoil and conflict. Normally, Niyonzima is the kind of person who would have no enemies. Although married to a Tutsi, as a Hutu he too was nearly a victim of the killings of October 1993.

When the army lashed out at the masses following the attack on Tutsi after the killing of President Ndadaye, a contingent of soldiers followed the road leading through the Quaker mission near Gitega. They came to the pastors' and teachers' training college at Kwibuka, rounded up several Hutu students, and shot them. Others were shot fleeing. Niyonzima found a hiding place and escaped.

The Quakers have always insisted that the church must be for everyone. Today, Burundian Quaker meetings are attended by members of all three identities—Hutu, Tutsi, and Twa—and in regions where there have been killings across ethnic lines, the Quakers have initiated house restoration and rebuilding projects within local parishes to demonstrate with their deeds that they affirm and proclaim the universality of the church, especially in Burundi. In Sunday morning services this openness to all persists, as the majority Hutu but also some Tutsi and Twa come to worship together, because they feel welcomed and safe.

Commander of Kibimba Garrison

Toward late afternoon we followed up on our early morning contact with Commander Adrien and walked to the end of the road, through the expansive secondary school compound, past the Kibimba church, now a camp of displaced widows and children, to the military camp. A big tent, a smaller metal shelter, and various small makeshift structures were scattered around. This barren and highest end of the Kibimba ridge commanded a vast open view of the surrounding hills. Far away we could see flames destroying a homestead. About 20–25 tall Tutsi soldiers in fatigues carrying bayonetted rifles and other weapons were standing around the camp; other soldiers were unloading large quantities of beer bottles from their trucks, stacking the orange plastic crates with military precision. (A big Amstel brewery is located in nearby Gitega.) There were women friends and young boys who cooked the evening meal over open fires. Commander Adrien greeted us, had wooden chairs brought out, and invited us to sit down in the drizzling cool dusk of the Central African highland. The commander was drinking a beer and offered us drinks, beer or, thoughtfully, soft drinks. After we introduced ourselves and shook hands, as a conversation starter, I (John) asked him, "What's going on in Burundi?" He gave us the pat answer of the three ethnic groups, suggesting that I should talk to Matthias, who was seated nearby, to get the local story. Matthias is the director of the primary school of Kibimba. He had experienced the horrible murder of his students in 1993 in the burning of the gas station. Commander Adrien went on: "Fear and defense keep us here in the garrison, protecting the Tutsi [women and children] and others." I asked him, then, directly, "Who's the enemy?" to which he replied, equally directly, "Armed bands of Hutu."

The commander's convoy had been ambushed several weeks earlier. We also knew that the soldiers of this garrison under this commander were responsible for some of the nearby roadblock hassles and killings. Matthias interjected at this point that those who had killed were still out there. He noted that it would take awhile to tell the whole story, but he reiterated the horror of the killing in the gas station and queried, "What kind of brutes could do that?" He was emotional on this point and emphasized that so long as that spirit was present in people, there was no hope. When asked what was needed, he emphasized the need to change the hearts of the people. Commander Adrien added, "Reading what's in the Bible and taking it to heart." The commander related to us his experience in the Soviet Union, where he had studied artillery and military theory from 1982 to 1986. He told us he had seen how inadequate the Soviets' atheism was, that it did not provide the goodness that people needed in their hearts to live together.

Both Commander Adrien and Matthias were certain there had been lists of Tutsi prepared and ready to guide the killings that started on October 21, 1993. The commander blamed the politicians for much of the trouble.

> They aren't serious; they seek self-aggrandizement. It's a poor third world country; politicians work on the side to make a living. They don't work for the good of the people. They try to get rich at it. If it wouldn't have been for the army, the country would have destroyed itself. The Belgians were also at fault. The Walloons and Flemish divided up the Burundian ethnic groups between them.

Commander Adrien projected the national army perspective, saying there were both Tutsi and Hutu in it, although not in the proportions of the population. When asked what outsiders like us could offer Burundi, he said, "Teach us peace. Help us with physical necessities. These are the two ways you can help in Burundi."

When night fell and the rain penetrated our wraps, we decided to end this macabre roundtable. Commander Adrien asked his adjutant to bring him his pistol and load it, and as he put it into its holster and accompanied us on foot to the farthest barricade beyond the secondary school, to the no-man's zone from where it was but a short distance to Seitz's house at the elementary school and hospital compound, he spoke of his desire for peace and of his overload of responsibility for the welfare of all the widows and children in the camp of the displaced.

Rebuilding at Kirambi Hill

"As Christians the idea was already in their hearts," said the elderly pastor of Nyabihanga's Quaker community when we visited the site where a war widow's house was being rebuilt by volunteers on Saturday, November 26, 1994. He estimated that at least 100 homes had been burned down on two hills in the commune since the war of 1993. Both sides in the conflict burned houses as acts of revenge.

Members of the local Quaker church were rebuilding the fourth house as part of their effort to restore a community torn apart by hatred—a tangible expression of help for those in need. As we walked through this widow's maize and banana grove toward the building site, we were passed by women and men carrying poles for the roof and bundles of grass for the thatch. We heard rhythmic singing and clapping, then saw a small group of church members who encouraged the building crew with their music. The mud-brick walls of the rectangular house had just been completed, and the pitch of the roof was being measured and the ridge pole was being put in place. The widow stood nearby, quietly watching the progress, telling us of her eight living children. There was a moment of tension when someone in our group asked her directly whether she was Hutu or Tutsi. She didn't know, she replied. The questioner was immediately reprimanded by another Burundian Quaker pastor, who pointed out that to ask this question was in fact illegal.

The morning's drive from Kibimba to Kirambi hill was through beautiful countryside. Along the way women, walking to market, balanced on their heads as many as seven spherical, black fired-clay pots, strapped together ingeniously with bamboo. Others carried big pots of home-brewed banana beer. We passed schoolchildren in their required khaki shirts, worn to mere rags, carrying their notebooks in dirt-red plastic sleeves. In one schoolyard at least seven large decorated drums were set up, ready for practice sessions for church services on Sunday. Here too, just as in Kibimba, many mud-brick houses were whitewashed and then decorated with painted profiles or whole figures of a man and a woman, marriage dates, and dedications (Figure 82). All the hillsides were blanketed with small terraced fields.

When this local Quaker community began their rebuilding effort regardless of the needy person's ethnic or religious identity (Figure 83), the non-Christians did not like it, said the pastor. But those who had been helped have since become members of the church. As Christians, this church community wanted to express by example that they do not support burning and killing. The pastor was convinced that the solution to the fighting would come

> when there [are] more people who love God. Many are just nominal Christians, but in their hearts nothing has changed. The message of God doesn't reach their hearts because their hearts are already

Figure 82. A peasant family on their farmstead in the Kibimba hills.

Figure 83. House rebuilding for a victim of the Burundian war by members of the Quaker parish of Kirambi Hill, Nyabihanga Commune, Saturday, November 26, 1994.

> occupied with search for power and money to get rich. When people are truly Christians, they won't fight for power and kill each other.

When asked what outsiders could do to help, the pastor suggested that

> they can give counsel, starting with government officials, so that those at the top don't discriminate against those at the lower level. The "whites" have money and can help in material ways, for example, with the material things needed in agricultural work, like hoes, seed, fertilizer. The one ton of bean seeds received from Mennonite Central Committee is not enough because there are so many people. We need more nails, doors, windows for the houses we are rebuilding. These things we cannot afford because they require money. For the house we are building here someone lent us money for the nails. Three kilograms of 8-cm nails cost 2,400 francs [$10].

The pastor also compared the political situation of Burundi with Rwanda's:

> Problems here are not the same as in Rwanda, where the problems were extreme. The meetings at Arusha were very good. The plans set there—that there was to be no more discrimination, that the parties were to be allowed to be represented in government, that RPF soldiers should join the Rwandan army—[were good]. But then the war destroyed everything. We have the same problem in Burundi, that is, when "others" don't want to join in leadership, that is, in the army and in the justice system. Outsiders could help in Rwanda by motivating refugees to return to Rwanda, into the country. Relief help is fine, but those who have fled must return to Rwanda.

Land, People, and Community in Central Burundi

On the drive through the countryside to Nyabihanga commune the local pastor and David Niyonzima explained to us how the countryside had changed in their lifetimes and that of their parents. In the words of the local pastor, whose family had been Hutu landowners:

> There used to be just one family on each hill. When I was a boy, I was a shepherd for my parents' cows. We had a roundhouse, a grass hut. It was easy to feed the cows. There was no cultivated land. Grazing places were larger than areas of cultivated fields now. There were two reasons for plentiful harvests: the many cows yielded a lot of manure, and there was enough grazing land for many cows. We did not cultivate on the same land every year. But now they cultivate the same place all the time and there is no place for cows. We never went hungry when I was a boy. Now there is no milk, children don't know what milk is. Now there are so many changes, so many houses. Now there is so much hunger.

Niyonzima described his Hutu family's background in relation to land tenure. His family had been in clientage to a Tutsi lord before his father went to the Quakers and became an early convert and prominent pastor. Niyonzima continued:

> The Tutsi had owned the land and the others had worked for them. There was no big thing made of Hutu and Tutsi. Today, by contrast, the landscape is divided into many small parcels, and cultivated very tightly in corn, millet, manioc, yams, eucalyp-

tus trees, tea, and coffee [Figure 84]. The Tutsi who live in the countryside are descendants of former landed lords. The Hutu have mostly bought land from the Tutsi. Most people live in separate homesteads on their plots of land. Burials used to be in these homesteads and provided strong sanctions against thieves and in the support of morality because family heads were there, in the place they had lived. Today Catholics and Protestants bury in separate cemeteries.

The Tutsi have in effect sold their land to Hutu for education and other ambitions and have thus used their land capital to move into the military, the clergy, business, and education. They run and control the country, although they are a minority.

Land ownership is not recorded anywhere. Under kingship, the king owned all the land and all the cattle. He would give cattle to people to reward them or take cattle away from people to punish them. With the end of kingship and the rampant buying and selling of land, without record, land security has greatly been reduced. There is nothing to prevent land from being taken away by force, which is what happens when houses are burned, people killed, and their inhabitants chased away. In the absence of a judiciary, what is their recourse?

Standing in the middle of a banana grove in central Burundi, this seminar on changes in land tenure seemed to illuminate the sources of the conflict. The breakdown of judicial recourse, the treatment of land as a commodity, and the threefold increase in population since independence seemed to account for the transformation of Burundi society into a class-divided society where hereditary land was used to acquire the techniques to control the upper class and the state.

The Peace Committee in Kibimba

The senseless killing of a hospital worker, shot in the back fleeing the military, in late October or early November 1994 inspired American Quaker nurse Susan Seitz and other Kibimba leaders to call a meeting of representatives of the various segments of the local community around Kibimba. She invited representatives of the community's varied groups, including several pastors of the dispersed Hutu of Kibimba, a representative of the commune, a representative of the camp of the displaced, a representative of the school, and the current commander of the military garrison. These individuals were asked to come to the football field near the hospital. Once assembled, Seitz, in her basic Kirundi (she knew no French) asked the committee to discuss and decide what such a peace committee should do. Then she left, because she judged this to be their task, not hers. Apparently they spent awhile talking about their fears and particular concerns but then eventually came around to the problems of the water system that supplied the hospital, the residences, the schools, the displaced camp, and the garrison. They closed their first meeting having decided to look into the water problem. They agreed to meet again in one week on the football field.

Figure 84. Freshly planted fields of maize and bananas on hillsides of Nyabihanga commune, central Burundi.

Figure 85. Kibimba/Gitongo Quaker church service in the open in a roofless church. The metal roof was in secret storage until the end of the war.

At a subsequent meeting they decided to have a football game between teams of both ethnic groups. This game, on Friday, November 25, 1994, was a peaceful encounter that prompted the committee to arrange another game on Sunday, November 27, this time between the garrison's soldiers and the villagers, that is, between the Tutsi protectors of the displaced refugee widows and children and the largely Hutu dispersed members of the community. The soldiers won this game, 3 to 2, in an event attended by a crowd of hundreds from both ethnic groups. Niyonzima arrived in Kibimba just as the game was completed and the crowd was dispersing; he was visibly relieved and happy over this first game on the Kibimba field in over a year, in fact since the killing of President Ndadaye.

Initially, through mid-July 1995 the peace held in Kibimba, despite some tense crises in Burundian national politics and local killings and reprisals in Bujumbura. The football games were events in a string of initiatives by the local community and members of both sides to create a common ground. One of the earliest such initiatives within the local Quaker congregations (Figure 85) included the staging of a Kirundian adaptation of Shakespeare's *Romeo and Juliet* by the congregational drama group. Dramas depicting conflict, the peace committee's discussion of the water system, and the football games provided suitable arenas for expression and interaction that were not confrontational in the sense that labeling and accusations and attacks are. These activities were a way back from the abstracted ideological negation of "the other" to a face-to-face sociability. They did not guarantee a lasting peace, but they were the beginnings of a conversation that can lead beyond catastrophe, to the hope for a just society. Unfortunately, an escalation of national political violence accompanied the formation of a Hutu opposition force in exile, which further destabilized the Kibimba area.

Ethnic Cleansing in Bujumbura

As horrible and tense as was the state of affairs in Kibimba and Kirambi Hill, an even more vicious face of this conflict during 1994–1995 was manifesting itself in the capital of Bujumbura. When we arrived in Bujumbura in late November 1994, workmen were reinforcing new high walls around the parish of St. Michel of the White Fathers with sharp metal spear points. When we returned at the beginning 1995, a 7:00 p.m. curfew placed an eerie calm over the city through which the sound of gunshots reverberated. We took no photographs of Bujumbura because of the pervasive presence of armed-to-the-teeth military and a nervous populace. While sitting at a pleasant little outdoor café, sipping a cool big glass of yogurt, we could read all eight and more of the country's newspapers in which the different parties launched vicious and vitriolic attacks on each other, intending to incite the readers.

During the first half of 1995 a series of assaults by Tutsi militia, sometimes backed by Burundian army units, on predominantly Hutu communes in greater Bujumbura—Bwiza, Buyenzi, Kamenge, Gasenyi, and Kinama (Figure 86)—resulted in scores of deaths and the flight of thousands into the hills or into neighboring Zaire. The military's and sometimes the government's rationale for this violence was that Hutu militias were operating within the predominantly Hutu communes and that these actions were necessary to rout the guerrillas. That there was a Hutu opposition armed movement is confirmed by announcements made in late 1994 by former parliamentarian Nyangoma Jean. From Zaire, he announced that he had taken up arms to fight the military, because governmental institutions had been sapped by the largely Tutsi military, and that there had effectively been a military takeover.

Other issues, including the interface with Rwanda, played into this militancy in Burundi. The war in Rwanda had brought many refugees, mostly Hutu, into northern Burundi. At the high point in the immediate aftermath of the 1994 Rwandan War, over 30 international agencies were feeding 800,000 people in northern Burundi (US Agency for International Development 1994). There were reports of Burundians attacking or holding up relief supply caravans because they were themselves hungry. But more than this, preemptive strikes against suspected Interahamwe militia in those camps by combined Burundian and Rwandan military and paramilitary units created upheaval among the refugees. On several occasions following such preemptive attacks on suspected perpetrators of genocide, thousands of Rwandan refugees sought to flee to Tanzania but were stopped by a closed border and agents of humanitarian organizations who tried to persuade them to return to their camps (Lorch 1995). Some Rwandan refugees, suspected of complicity in the Rwandan massacres, were even turned over to Rwandan authorities by Burundian military, in at least a technical breach of the human rights of refugees (Roberts 1995). (Of course, much depended on whether or not fleeing Interahamwe had rights as refugees.)

Because of the concentration of suspected Burundian Hutu militias in Bujumbura, the attacks in Bujumbura took their most severe form. In commune after commune the pattern was repeated. Initially, meetings between the extremist Tutsi groups Sans Echec ("Without Fail"), SOJEDEM (Société des Jeunesses Démocratiques), or AFOSANA (Association des Forces pour le Salut National) would resolve to clean out the Hutu gunmen with ruthlessness. Former president Bagaza was said to be present often at these meetings, and he was considered a leader of Tutsi extremists forces, the Tutsi-Burundian nationalist opposition outside the UPRONA mainstream party (Burundinet 1995). Some days or even hours later young militants would attack the commune in question. The public might or might not have been informed by official announcement that the army was conducting a campaign against guerrillas and that they should get out before the army began its "cleansing" work.

Bwiza, Kwijabe, and Buyenzi communes, which formed one of nine urban zones of greater Bujumbura (see Figure 86), remained relatively calm in October 1993, when President Ndadaye was assassinated, and subsequently Tutsi were killed by Hutu and the Tutsi militia or the army staged reprisals. Katihabwa Sebastian, who was mayor of this zone until 1992, gave us a possible reason for this relative calm, where ethnic cleansing and ethnic partition did not take the same toll as in other zones of Bujumbura.

What we learned about the Bwiza-Buyenzi zone, through Katihabwa, strongly suggests that this calm was not just a coincidence but a consequence of judicious political action. What was this action? In Katihabwa's telling, the zone had been troubled in prior years by the presence of Burundians and many settlers of other nationalities (Rwandans, Zairians, West Africans, Tanzanians, Ugandans) who tended to get into fights and misunderstandings. As mayor, he created a council of representatives elected by each of these communities that would meet periodically or whenever a crisis arose to discuss the issues and to search together for solutions. He also coordinated cultural activities, such as dramas and theater, to foster harmonious and peaceful coexistence between the groups.

In his earlier position of mayor in his home region of Kavumu near Gitega and from his own upbringing, Katihabwa had learned to hold in high esteem the historical council of notables. The *bashingantahe* were effective, he suggested, because they represented the local segments of society, namely, the cultivators (Hutu), the pastoralists (Tutsi), and the warriors. Such a council met as a judicial body to deal with conflicts and wrongdoing. The council that Katihabwa created in Bwiza-Buyenzi was thus an urban contemporary version of the *bashingantahe*.

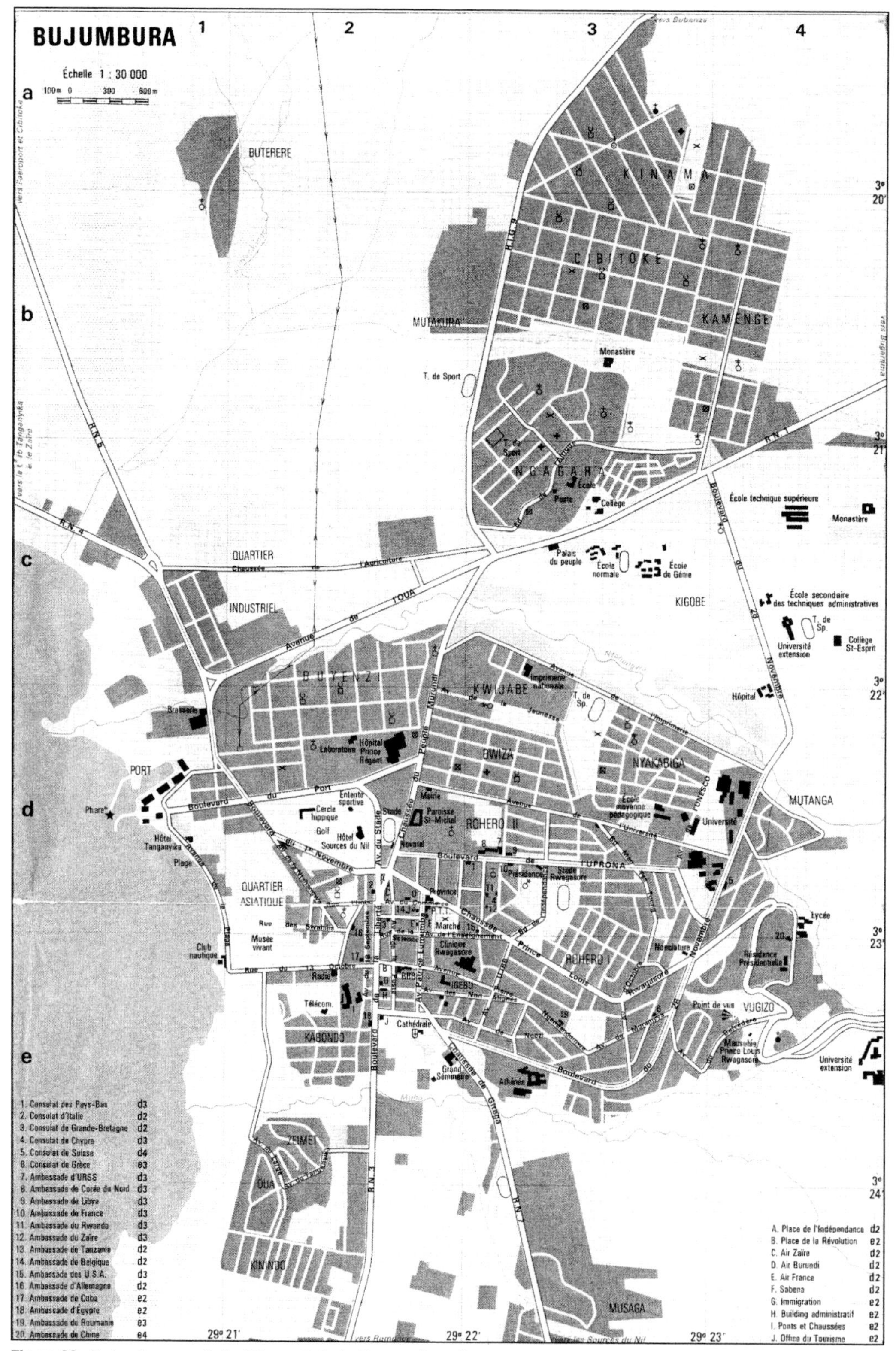

Figure 86. Bujumbura, capital of Burundi. Lake Tanganyika offers a major inland waterway, making Bujumbura an important trade hub of the entire Great Lakes region.

Although he was honored for this work in Bwiza-Buyenzi by urban authorities, Katihabwa's tenure as mayor ended in 1992. His successor did not understand his manner of working or the rationale for it; consequently, the councils were neglected and ceased to meet. When we spoke to Katihabwa in early January 1995, there had been ethnic cleansings of other communes (e.g., Kamenge), but Bwiza-Buyenzi remained relatively peaceful and pluralistic in its makeup. Then came the cycles of violence of March–June 1995 that brought major attacks by Tutsi extremist militias on the remaining communes of Bujumbura.

One weekend in March 1995 Bwiza and Buyenzi were "cleansed" of most Hutu residents in attacks by the militias, which were followed by mopping-up operations by the army. Scores, even hundreds, were killed (Associated Press, May 31, 1995). This was the sad ending of the story of a fragile community that had been created and cultivated with the help of a council, representing its diverse segments, that met to settle grievances and conflicts. The trust that had been built up over years was destroyed in one night of terror.

The "cleansing" of Bujumbura's communes continued in the first half of 1995. Kamenge commune was attacked in early June 1995. In this case the civilians were told to leave before the attack, and some 50,000 fled their homes. There was some confusion because the army commenced its operations at 6:00 a.m. when, in fact, the civilians had been given until 7:00 a.m. to leave. As a consequence, many civilians stayed and were the victims of the militia and the military attack. No casualties among the bodies seen strewn in the streets were members of the Hutu militia. They had fled days earlier, residents told reporters (Wallis 1995). To all appearances, the Burundian government was being held hostage by extremist Tutsi parties whom even the army does not control yet sometimes allows to do its dirty work.

In addition to the many innocent civilians who were killed in these attacks in the first half of 1995, the main victim was the idea of a multiethnic, multinational civil society. Former president Bagaza proclaimed that the houses of the uprooted Hutu would be given to displaced Tutsi, who would be installed with the protection of soldiers in armed troop carriers (Burundinet 1995).

The Hutu residents of those communes of Bujumbura that were cleansed fled either into exile in Zaire, into the hills around Bujumbura where they were often joined by Minani's guerilla fighters, or they were herded into detainment centers to the north of the city. The Burundian army hoped that the "citizens" could be kept from being infiltrated by the guerrilla fighters. By 1999 there were up to 60 of these detainment camps where conditions were miserable and unsanitary.

Threat to Moderates

In this situation those who seek to live in harmony or those who try to bridge the gap between Hutu and Tutsi are vulnerable, particularly if they are outspoken or have rubbed someone the wrong way. The fear of the ethnic other is clear, but even worse is the fear and mistrust of one's own associates. Techniques of attacking moderates range from infiltration to disinformation to vilification in party newspapers to outright assault in an attempt to frighten or kill.

This logic of extremism was apparent in the political reforms of the early 1990s and in the aftermath of the elections of 1993. Pierre Buyoya, a Tutsi moderate, achieved a remarkable broadening of the political center. He managed an unprecedented electoral campaign and fair elections. But he lost and was in fact seen by nationalists on both sides as a threat and a traitor. Many Tutsi opposed him for having opened up to the Hutu and permitting a Hutu to be elected president. Most of the Hutu were eager to elect one of their own.

In time, few moderate Tutsi voices spoke out because they were so vulnerable. A USAID report on Burundi suggested that fear among Burundian Tutsi elite of the collapse of the Rwandan government fuels their extremist element because of the general perception in some Tutsi circles that this is the only way to hold on to power, so as to keep from becoming themselves a minority driven out or worse, massacred (US Agency for International Development 1994). But the Hutu moderates, especially those who were adamant about the work of peace, were even more threatened: witness the assassinations in Burundi in February 1995 of the Minister of Mines and Energy and in Rwanda of the governor of Butare.

Adrien Ntabona, secretary of the Burundian bishop's conference, suggested that "the main problem in Burundi today is extremism, not ethnicity." But former president Buyoya himself was quoted to the effect that the real problem isn't the power of extremists but the weakness of the moderates who are afraid to denounce violence.

Katihabwa Sebastian began to devote his time to writing as a way of capturing the depth of the problems faced in Burundian society. Unresolved contradictions such as land disputes between brothers, uncared-for orphans, and politicians who became self-centered and alienated from their constituency can blow up into ethnic violence (Katihabwa 1991). The importance of the councils was thus to facilitate and frame the maintenance of a kind of local justice in day-to-day interpersonal, family, and community affairs. What happened in Burundi Katihabwa called the consequence of "deculturation".

4.2 An Ambassador Speaks

He had been Burundi's ambassador to countries in Europe and Asia and was currently an ambassador within Africa. We met him in downtown Bujumbura, in an office arranged by a third party. He came and left through a back door. As a member of the beleaguered Hutu in government service, he said he did not want us to use his name in publication. But he was eager to tell us his story and to tell us about Burundi from the perspective of a prominent Hutu.

> The situation here is a drama! The problem is that a democratically elected president was killed. The Tutsi continue to massacre the Hutu, as in 1973 when 300,000 were killed. The international community dare not let this continue. People continue to be killed by the army. It is the army that continues to kill and burn people's houses. My brother-in-law was killed four days ago. But it happens mainly at night now.

I (John) asked what the reasons were for the murder of President Ndadaye in 1993.

> [The assassination] was committed by several military to prevent democracy from happening. The three branches of the military are implicated, we know for sure. They danced when the putsch was announced. The Minister of Defense and the head of the gendarmerie were for the putsch, because they didn't want to accept that democracy would change the power of the army.

I asked the ambassador about the background of the resistance to democracy.

> During colonization and after independence, the Hutu were not given a chance at education; they were excluded from education. I myself was educated in the seminary. In the new government at independence, there were only two government ministers who were Hutu. It is simply common practice to exclude Hutu. The Tutsi do not want to share power. It is absolutely crazy. Tutsis are afraid of the loss of power. Twelve percent of the population controls the economy and the schools and diplomacy. It is all dominated by Tutsi.

The Burundian government of late 1994 was still the FRODEBU government that had been put together largely by the late President Ndadaye and his successor Cyprien Ntaryamira, who was killed in April 1994 with Rwanda's president. All of the predominately Hutu party FRODEBU ruled in a fragile coalition with the mostly Tutsi UPRONA party. Yet the ambassador spoke as if parties did not really matter much; it was the Tutsi repression of Hutu that clouded all efforts at peace in the land, despite the wisdom of those who ran the government.

> The current president knows that power needs to be shared, so he appointed Tutsi ministers from the opposition. The Hutu are richer than the Tutsi, because they work very hard. The Tutsi don't work. . . . The problem is ethnic. Tutsi don't allow the Hutu to achieve power.
>
> Yes, the Tutsi are afraid. But why did [the displaced Tutsi] go to the camps to the army for protection while the [dispersed] Hutu hid in the valleys without protection? The Hutu now, as a consequence of lack of protection, burn or murder for revenge. On the one hand, the Tutsi don't forgive, while the Hutu are looking for weapons to protect themselves from the army. In this situation, human life becomes cheapened; this is the revolt of the Hutu, the revolt against this violation of human rights. It has become clear that neither can live here having eliminated the other.

I asked, "What is a solution to this impasse?"

> Now the top officers of the army have understood the drama of Burundi. They understand that it is necessary to marginalize the extremists, but the problem is the army, which doesn't want democracy. It is necessary to respect fundamental human rights and freedoms!

"What about justice?" I probed further. The ambassador replied, "Justice does not function here, because it is 100% controlled by Tutsi."

Our conversation covered the attempt by the coalition government to bring Hutu recruits into the army to create a truly national army, instead of an army made up of all Tutsi. There were a few Hutu soldiers in the army at this time, several of whom acted as the ambassador's bodyguards. This line of our conversation led to a discussion of parliamentarian Nyangoma Jean (also a mathematician and physicist), who had promoted the recruitment of Hutu soldiers for the national army. The ambassador remarked, "One has to create a national army. The peasants are for and behind Nyangoma because they continue to die."

A few months after this conversation, Nyangoma announced that he had given up on the effort to bring Hutu soldiers into the national army and that he was moving outside Burundi to lead the resistance against the Tutsi-dominated army. The ambassador went on to describe the government's efforts to reform the army.

> The government requested military observers from the OAU [Organization of African Unity], but the army refused. The UN was also involved in studying reconciliation, and still people die. The UN authorized peace observers, but the army refused. The UN is preoccupied, however, with Rwanda, while Burundi slides toward disaster.

The ambassador had other complaints about the army's behavior toward the population, Hutu for the most part: "When the army 'disarms' the population, this doesn't mean that they may kill people in order to disarm them." He moved on to the role of the international community and the press in Burundi's fate.

> The international community should condemn atrocities, when they occur. The international press needs to be convinced of this first. The Burundian press incites people excessively. The army provokes too by firing guns to make people believe that the Hutu have armed bands. I lost two brothers-in-law this way, they were arrested and taken away at 2 o'clock in the morning.

I asked the ambassador, "What else shall we tell the world?" He importuned, "Tell the world that I am not an extremist. I just can't accept the violation of the sanctity of human life." He spoke then about spreading the truth about human rights violations.

> Burundians don't accept their own fault; they hardly ever tell the truth. Send people and get the international media involved. No arrests are being made. If justice would work, we wouldn't have this problem.

In a final comment, the ambassador tried to explain what was behind the Burundian impasse: "What the Tutsi can't tolerate is that the Hutu said no for the first time."

Less than a year later, Burundian Hutu president Sylvestre Ntibantunganya sought protection in the American embassy and former president and military leader Pierre Buyoya assumed the presidency. This was the effective end of the popular government ushered in by Ndadaye's election in 1993, and this change of hands amounted to a military coup in Burundi. We do not know what happened to the ambassador.

4.3 Preemptive Forgiveness and a Cup of Cold Water

On one of their several North American tours David Niyonzima and his wife, Felicity Ntikurako, spoke to a group of students at the University of Kansas about their experiences with coming to terms with the knowledge of who killed their close kin, in Niyonzima's case his brother and in Ntikurako's case her father. This was especially poignant because Niyonzima and Ntikurako's marriage, like many, bridges the national divide in Burundi: He is Hutu, she is Tutsi. But looking at them and listening to them, one would be at a loss to discern distinctions between the two identities. Indeed, when asked what the differences are, Niyonzima said, "There are none." Hutu and Tutsi speak the same language, live together, intermarry, and have a common history—unfortunately in recent decades of fear and suspicion and killing.

Of course, Niyonzima's answer was right in a physical and cultural sense in Burundi, because it is not possible to distinguish between Hutu and Tutsi by appearance, language, or demeanor, despite the well-known stereotypes. Also, for some years it has been a crime in Burundi to use the terms Hutu, Tutsi, and Twa in public discourse because the terms are so inflammatory. The colonial era identity cards were banned by postcolonial governments, and yet in a sociological and political sense the identities are real and provide the meta-language for conflict.

Because we had spent time in their circles in Burundi just a year earlier and knew their story somewhat, we asked Niyonzima whether he and Ntikurako would speak at a seminar of their own experience with conflict and conflict resolution or with coming to terms with living in the same local society as the people who had killed their family members. They agreed.

At the opening of the seminar (held at the Department of Psychology, University of Kansas, on February 14, 1996) Niyonzima and Ntikurako were asked whether they knew the people who killed his brother and her father in 1993. They answered, "Yes, we do." Niyonzima first spoke when asked what kind of relationship he has with these individuals today.

> One day in Bujumbura I recognized the two men who had killed my brother in the events of 1993. I approached them on the street and told them that I knew they had killed my brother. They were startled, but before they were able to do or say anything, I extended my hand to them and forgave them for what they had done.
>
> At first I had been terribly angry at my brother's murderers, ready to do a terrible thing to them, but that wouldn't have solved anything. Because they were afraid of me, they might have killed me just to remove me as a risk to them before I killed them. So I was in fact protecting myself by forgiving them.

Indeed, it seemed that this was the only way, under current Burundian circumstances, that one could break the potential cycle of vengeance between killer and victim's next of kin.

Ntikurako told of the man who sent the soldiers to kill her father.

> I don't blame the soldiers, because they are in uniform; soldiers act like that; but the man sent them. I knew him because my mother pointed him out to me one day. Then I recognized him one day when he appeared at our house and stood around as if he wanted something. Overcoming my fear, I went out to him and asked him what he wanted. He told me he was thirsty. So I brought him a cup of water. He drank it. We looked at each other for some time, but neither of us spoke. Then he left.

Niyonzima and Ntikurako were then asked if the relationship between them and the murderers of their family members had been cleared up by these acts. Niyonzima spoke first:

> The two men who killed my brother are now very humble toward me; they are morally "in my hands." They are open with me, because they are no longer afraid of me.

When asked whether they should be punished for their crime, he said that "their ongoing punishment is severe because society knows they did this deed."

Ntikurako was not as forthcoming in her comment on the relationship between herself and the man who had her father killed. "There is still something to make clean. The matter is not yet settled."

The context of these actions is a society in which there have been horrible killings and in which the killers walk around with impunity among the friends and family of the victims. The government courts are paralyzed. As the women in the Kibimba camp of displaced Tutsi refugees said, the local authorities are the ones who ordered the killings in 1993. As Katihabwa and Ntabona lamented, the local judges and councils have been destroyed. There is no justice.

Placating the Spirits of Vengeance

Niyonzima argues that "a change of heart" is the solution to Burundi's situation. This is what you would expect a Quaker pastor to say, but the comment recognizes an important dimension of peace making that is missing in a merely political settlement, whether local or national. If conflict is not truly resolved in the here and now, it lingers on as a legacy for the spirits of the dead. Central and southern Africa spirit hierarchies are filled with these unplacated spirits. The call of the unavenged dead is strong, especially where the victims died a violent death and were not properly buried; often there is the expectation of retribution upon the perpetrator or his descendants.

In Burundi the enemy one fears most is likely to be a neighbor with an old grudge against someone in one's own social category. And because the survivors and family of the victims of yesterday's killings walk the same paths, frequent the same markets, and go to the same schools as the perpetrators who enjoy complete impunity, the slightest incident can trigger renewed massacres. Local peace committees may offer a tenuous first step toward civility, but preemptive forgiveness (e.g., amnesty and truth commissions) is the only way to begin to diffuse the cycle of violence in a setting where the courts are paralyzed.

4.4 From the Heart of Africa

Adrien Ntabona is the secretary general of the Conference of Catholic Bishops of Burundi, a professor of the University of Burundi, and editor of the journal *Au Coeur de l'Afrique* ("at the heart of Africa"), a principal voice of the interdiocesan region of Burundi and Rwanda representing the White Fathers mission (Société des Missionnaires d'Afrique). As a university-trained philosopher, theologian, historian, and student of Burundian culture, Ntabona is an influential figure in Central African intellectual circles both within the Catholic Church and outside it. His dissertation was a 900-page study of Burundian proverbs and the way they embody knowledge and insight in Burundian culture.

In late November 1994, I (John) interviewed Ntabona in his office near the White Fathers guesthouse, where we were staying in Bujumbura. We conversed first as fellow anthropologists, then turned to issues of his research, and finally explored the current crisis in Burundi and the work of the bishops. We give here a summary of Ntabona's research on Central African culture and the Catholic Church and his interpretation of Burundian history and the emergence of the conflict.

Secrets of the Elders

Ntabona's best article, he suggested, is "*Ibaanga:* Faith in the immense potentiality of human insight—a study of Burundian proverbs" (Ntabona 1993). *Ibaanga* is one of those verbal nouns in a Bantu language that provides insight into the character of an entire people, in this case the people of Burundi, offers Ntabona. *Ibaanga* translates as "totalizing and irreversible obligation that establishes a relationship or a mutual commitment" (Ntabona 1993, p. 60). It can apply to relationships of husband to wife or to two households that exchange cattle or to Kubandwa cohorts belonging to a local congregation, to guerrilla warriors, or to any other set of relationships. The central defining attribute of the *ibaanga* relationship is the pact to share and protect a secret, even to death; thus it has a defense connotation. In the traditional sense this dimension of the *ibaanga* relationship gives "freshness of heart, of inner purpose."

Ntabona (1993, p. 10) wrote further that

> every adult in Burundi constantly uses the word *ibaanga* and willingly recognizes that it is at the basis of the framework of the sacred values of the land: in the role of conscience *(umutima)* in life, in the understanding of human dignity *(iteeka)*; in the mastery of suffering *(ukwiiyumaanganya)*; in the understanding of family, in neighborly relations; in the attention of everything ranging from having a sense of hospitality to recognizing one's social responsibility *(ubushingantahe)*, to knowing one's obligations in the political domain, and having respect for God and the authorities.

Reference to *ubushingantahe* in the foregoing semantic cluster[1] of referents of the basic verbal concept of *ibaanga* is also at the core of Ntabona's understanding of what is good in Burundian society and culture and of what should be used to improve the church's work. With many other Burundian leaders, including some already mentioned in other readings, the *bashingantahe,* the traditional councilmen or elders, who were previously drawn from all sectors of society, continue to be held up as a model to which Burundi should return. In Ntabona's explication of *ibaanga* among the elders, it is precisely the manipulation of secret knowledge that allows them to maintain their control of society and to mediate its conflicts. Therefore the role of the elders must be reasserted in the current crisis and its myriad local conflicts.

Ntabona believes that *ibaanga* can and must become a critical value for Christianity in Burundi. Under the missiological idea of inculturation, *ibaanga* is one of the indigenous values in Burundi that comes close to expressing the basic Christian doctrines of commitment to Christ and the church, of loyalty to Christ's ways, and obligation to one's fellow human being. Those aspects that do not fit the Christian way of life (such as the military defense of one's community or exacting retribution when someone with whom one has an *ibaanga* pact is attacked) must be changed to more loving and nonviolent understandings of the basic values (Ntabona 1993, p. 60). In this reinterpretation of Burundian culture, Ntabona represents the articulate, educated Catholic of Central Africa who is committed to the institution he serves and to its influence in his nation.

Burundi Society: Precolonial Origins

Ntabona, speaking of Burundi, used the terms *Hutu clans* and *Tutsi clans* that have long intermarried to speak of his society. Thus:

> At least since the Ntare dynasty, leading Tutsi clans had intermarried with leading Hutu clans who shared power, in the form of a pact—indeed, evidence suggested that the first of the Ntare kings was Hutu. It was the Hutu clans who kept the secrets of coronation and the blessing-of-the-sorghum rituals.
>
> In Burundi there were high status Tutsi and low-status Tutsi as well as high-status Hutu and low-status Hutu, both intermarried at their status levels. A third class emerged, made up of the princes of ruling families, the "children of kings." These were the Ganwa, who became major players in colonial and postcolonial politics in Burundi.

This view of Great Lakes regional society suggests that there was a division of labor between cattle keepers (Tutsi), cultivators (Hutu), and warriors. Each was represented by local and regional chiefs. They constituted the basis of a balance of power and justice. This view stresses the checks and balances on power in the precolonial state structure. Even more, the Queen Mother provided a constraining hand on the king and an equitable representation of all segments of the community in the council of notables, or judges, the *bashingantahe.* High office holders, even the kings, could be tried and judged as persons apart from their offices. Ntabona spoke of a society not only integrated but also imbued with a sense of justice and informed by a moral memory, although Burundi lacked the court historians that kept official memories in Rwanda.

Colonial Impact

Ntabona stressed that the balance of clanship and occupational groups was broken first by German and then by Belgian colonial powers. Not unlike colonialists elsewhere, the foreign governments sought to rule through the established elite.

> In Burundi the Belgians privileged the Ganwa and higher-class Tutsi over the Hutu and the Twa. They did this by supporting their rule as well as by creating in these groups an elite of modern rulers trained in French and European culture. Although mission schools were open to all Africans in principle, the Tutsi interests were promoted at the Queen Astrid College [in Butare], and the Hutu were encouraged to attend the "Little Seminary" at Gitega [in Burundi] and to seek training for manual trades and for cultivation.

In Rwanda things were similar, because the two regions were administered from Usumbura (later, Bujumbura) by the governor general of Ruanda-Urundi, using the same policies.

In addition, the Belgian colonial administration intervened in the structure of both kingdoms to streamline them, removing what they deemed unnecessary duplication of chiefs and creating in their stead a single hierarchical line of local, district, and national rulers, all under one king and the colonial governor. Structures of justice, which had previously been composed of an independent council of judges, were also subordinated to the new line of chiefs. Henceforth, the newly created chiefs, often created by decree of the king or the colony, wielded enormous power. Every semblance of checks and balances that had existed gave way to a leaner, more patrimonial, that is, personalistic, rule, with the colonial administrators becoming the ultimate arbiters of power.

Then, in the 1930s, the ethnic identity cards were instituted, requiring everyone in Rwanda and Burundi to select an identity. Ntabona pointed out that in Burundi many people were confused by this, because the high degree of intermarriage between occupational groups of cattle keepers and cultivators and hunters meant that people did not know what they were ethnically. As a result, the Belgians adopted a rule of thumb, the so-called ten cattle rule, to establish ethnicity of Rwandans and Burundians. Those men with ten or more cattle were declared Tutsi and those with less than ten were declared Hutu.[2]

As secretary of the bishop's conference, Ntabona was silent about the Catholic Church's role in extending privileges to those identified as Tutsi. By the 1950s a new generation of Rwandans and Burundians had grown up to learn that education was important in modern society, especially for access to public service jobs. Ntabona noted that the powerful in Burundian society got schooling and that the Tutsi in general grasped the opportunity to take advantage of education; schooling opened the way to modern occupations and government service. By contrast, the Hutu, who also may have desired an education, were blocked from the avenues of modern life that education provided. More than anything, status had come to be represented by ethnicity, and theirs was second-rate. This became the context in which colonization would end, party politics would begin, and the kingdoms would be discarded for republican nation-state government. The seeds of the current troubles certainly lie in the ranked ethnicity and authoritarian centrism of late colonial society.

Transition to Independence and Birth of the Republic

Independence in Ruanda-Urundi followed the logic of ethnic conflict that had been established, explained Ntabona.

> Many Tutsi pressed for independence, although those of Butare, that is, the southern Rwandan Tutsi, who were close to the Belgians, were against it. As Tutsi claims for independence grew, in the late 1950s, the Belgians both divided the Tutsi and advanced the cause of the Hutu as Hutu. Whereas previously the Catholic Church had fostered a Tutsi church, now priests who saw the oppression of the Hutu identified the gospel message as especially appropriate for the Hutu.

Frequently we heard this switch in Belgian Catholic support from the Tutsi to the Hutu explained in terms of Belgian ethnic divisions. Thus the early colonialists were often from the ranks of aristocratic Flemish who identified with the Tutsi overlords. Later, in the 1950s, the priests who came from the ranks of the Walloon worker class identified with the oppressed Hutu and against the Tutsi.

> For Belgium the Rwandan ethnic mix became the model for political development; thus the colony pressed for and obtained reforms in the way the chiefs were named, popular-based political parties, and in due course the abandonment of the kingdom. In 1959, with the first elections and the founding of a populist government led by Hutu priest Kayibanda, the first of many massacres of Tutsi occurred, leading other Tutsi to flee the country, thus creating the first wave of Rwandan Tutsi refugees.

Burundi Since Independence

Although the ethnic logic was at first the same in Burundi, the example of Rwanda and the establishment of a Hutu republic led to a different outcome in Burundi. Party politics in Burundi was such that the royalist party, UPRONA, was actually integrated ethnically, although led by a prince. Ntabona explained the origin of today's polarization.

> In the electioneering of 1965, Hutu extremists combined with the king against the Ganwa and the military, but the attempt by the king to be neutral and to hold together the center failed. Instead, the royal institution was itself destroyed after an attempted Hutu coup d'état and Tutsi military retaliation. Thereafter, the ethnic polarization of political parties was complete. After 1965 the military, mostly Tutsi, controlled the republic. The lines of the Congolese civil war threatened to engulf Burundi as well. Hutu attempts to strike back at Tutsi military domination were backed by Mulelist and Simba rebels from Congo, who often used drugs in fighting. Thus, in 1972, Hutu attacks, under the influence of drugs, led to many dead, followed by military reprisals against Hutu elite. This was a pattern that was to become typical of Burundi, where to this day the Tutsi minority, in control of the military, controlled the majority by striking at Hutu elites.

Ntabona traced Burundian political developments in the 1980s in greater detail than can be told here. But, as most political histories of the country tell, he described how military strongman Jean Baptiste Bagaza was succeeded by Pierre Buyoya who opened the way for reforms and multiparty elections in 1993. The FRODEBU party, an organization of numerous parties, including the secret extremist Hutu party Palipehutu, won the elections. FRODEBU candidate Melchior Ndadaye thus became the first popularly elected Hutu president in the history of Burundi, but he was to rule only a short 100 days. His death sparked the killing of as many as 100,000 mostly Tutsi and sympathetic Hutu and sent many more fleeing to internal camps of displaced people, protected by Tutsi military.

Surprisingly, Ntabona rejected the UN fact-finding mission's explanation that all the killing reflected an attempted military coup d'état (United Nations 1994). He stated:

> We simply do not know who killed Ndadaye. But the death of the president was the occasion, not the cause, to massacre Tutsi. With the assistance of Habyarimana of Rwanda, committees [of extremist Hutu] had been organized in local government and in the churches.

Despite his status as a ranking Burundian professor and churchman, Ntabona revealed his own ethnic slant. The implication was that Ndadaye was killed by extremist Hutu because he was not radical enough in the removal of Tutsi from power and in asserting Hutu dominance. Other partisans of the Tutsi cause would take this far beyond Ntabona's stance to suggest outright that the Hutu extremists cannot be trusted and must be rooted out and destroyed. Identifying the other as "Hutu extremists" justified the use of force for some; for others it meant that the other's extremists killed their own leader.

However, Ntabona's words on the current meaning of the terms Hutu and Tutsi or their euphemisms was accurately descriptive of the Burundian scene.

> Since the October 1993 killings the terms Hutu and Tutsi have no meaning in the ethnographic sense. They have become expressions of extremism, on both sides, of a kind of *violence identitaire* [identity violence], according to which if you don't kill "the other," you're a traitor.

Many refused to accept this new identity, Hutu as well as Tutsi. Ntabona argued that only a politics of power sharing between the minority military and the majority administration could solve the crisis. The center is fragile and needs to be reinforced, however possible. The moderates in both UPRONA and FRODEBU need to be supported; the extremists in both parties need to be condemned.

4.5 *The "Culture of Hypocrisy" in Hutu-Tutsi Societies:* An Attempt to Explain the Burundian Crisis

Ilumbe Mwanasala, like many Zairian teachers and educated workers, found his way to Burundi or Rwanda to work because the pay was better and because the working conditions were similar to what he would have known at home. From 1987 to 1993 Ilumbe taught humanities in a Burundian secondary school. It was a school in a rural area of Burundi, and he lived close to the Burundians. After several years of living and working there as a single man, Ilumbe married a Zairian woman, and she went to Burundi with him. Their first child was born there. Over the years Ilumbe discovered the many ways in which Zaire was different from Burundi and how different he was from Burundians.

In the secondary school in which Ilumbe taught, the events of October 1993 changed everything. The Zairians in the school were outside the conflict, in one sense. But late on the night after the killing of President Ndadaye, the Zairian teachers were called into the woods and surrounded by a group of Hutu colleagues demanding that they commit themselves in the conflict, to take sides, with them. Fearing the worst, the Zairians asked for time and withdrew to confer. Ilumbe was asked to speak because he was a Christian and of calm disposition. Back before his Burundian colleagues, Ilumbe argued that the Zairians were outside the conflict and begged to remain neutral. A professor from Kikwit, Zaire, calmed them. About a week later the Zairians along with other expatriates were evacuated by United Nations trucks.

Back home in Bukavu, Ilumbe and his wife were in shock. His wife vowed she would never return to Burundi. Although other colleagues had returned to their posts, Ilumbe had not and had no plans to do so. Instead, he tried to write about his Burundian experience. We met in the Pentecostal Church in Bukavu in mid-December 1994 and talked. He showed me a draft of his unfinished paper, "The Culture of Hypocrisy." The next day he came to the Protestant guesthouse to talk at length, and he gave me (John) an oral conclusion to his essay. Ilumbe said he could not complete the paper, but he wanted to give me the written portion and to tell me the rest. From notes he had with him, he told me the rest of the story, prefaced by his hypothesis of why the killing had occurred in Burundi. The following text is a translation of Ilumbe's written and then spoken essay, interspersed with our commentary. It is clear that Ilumbe continues to feel traumatized by the experience of late 1993 and grapples for ideas in which to frame his feelings. Not surprisingly, his conclusions contain their own stereotyped caricatures of Burundian people and society. The essay, however, offers an insight into the perception of Burundi among the neighbors to the west.

The Culture of Hypocrisy

The West knows Africa poorly! Africans also know their own continent poorly. No one can pretend to hold total mastery, the magic words that open forbidden doors to this immense darkness slashed and glossed by a complex evil. At the basis of multiple crises in our sad history there is this ignorance that deserves to be expunged as the shadows of the night are replaced by the light of day.

The case of Burundi— and that of Rwanda— confirms our project and compels the alpinists toward an ever higher climb. In effect, when, on October 21, 1993, Burundi plunged hands and feet into a grave crisis, it astonished more than one because, apparently, this crisis contrasted appreciably with the striking success of the entire electoral process. The Burundians themselves by the seriousness with which they undertook their work and by their actions seemed to have given proof of their capacity to achieve well-being.

The passing of power from Pierre Buyoya to Melchior Ndadaye (that is, from the minority Tutsi to the majority Hutu, or, to put it another way, from the army to civilian rule) elicited enthusiastic applause from all kinds of apologists. Burundi— alongside the contortions of the Zairians with an elastic and disfigured transition to the point of being a caricature of a caricature, alongside the dismal efforts of the Rwandans to establish a consensual government with the Rwandan Patriotic Front—seemed to have wisely traced its course along a very pleasing spectacle above all to the international community. Burundi for this reason had achieved a respectability it had missed for a long time.

However, as a beautiful and exalted dream that dawn drives away, Mr. Melchior Ndadaye was assassinated. Burundi exposed its full colors. It exploded and revealed its imperfections, its inconsistencies. Zaire, land of Luciferian miseries seemed like a haven of peace, a paradise for the thousands of refugees. During the months of collective madness, thousands of innocent people were piteously massacred. Spears and guns (the most rudimentary of the sophisticated arms) were widely distributed in the urban quarters and the villages. False prophets improvised ethnic discourses, in which such themes as the superiority of one's race or the legitimacy of vengeance were transparent. Why did this people, so good, so jovial, fall so low? Many explanations were voiced. Above all, these explanations leave us still thirsty. Here are some of the most common among them.

First Thesis. Colonization—especially Belgian colonialism—is at the basis of this crisis. Before the woeful arrival of the whites, relations between ethnic groups were harmonious to the extent that the entire people (that is to say, Tutsi, Hutu, and Twa) spoke as a single person and as a single person valiantly fought the enemies of the nation. But when the Westerners arrived, in order to reign, they created divisions, artificial antagonisms, that cynically destroyed the foundations of this paradise in Central Africa, the echoes of which are felt to this day.

Objection. This historicist explanation seems to us to be a straightforward refusal to take on the responsibilities, the heavy load, of one's mistakes. Is this not the same as to excavate the ideas of the 1930s and to say that they prevailed until the 1970s, when all those such as Senghor, Damas, and Césaire, dynamic prophets of Négritude, denounced slavery, colonialism, and an imported Christianity? Burundi has been independent for more than 30 years! To say that the colonialists are responsible is to declare that the Burundians have remained static, dumb, and guided by remote control.

It is true that colonization is the basis of many problems that we confront today, but we are not immature to the point of being incapable of seeing the reality in the face of how the African despots of the postindependence period have torn up their own countries by outrageous wars for the sole aim of presenting themselves as providential peacemakers and unifiers. They simulate coups d'état to eliminate elements irritating to them that arise each time there is a problem; they favor and encourage corruption for the sole purpose of enriching themselves. The West has exploited us and continues this destructive practice. But what are we doing with these concerns? It is a type of reasoning that Africans can no longer permit themselves.

Second thesis. Democracy is a poisonous gift, a trap set by the West to subject us anew. Because of it, the majority of our African countries are foundering in tribalism and killings of an unequaled savagery. The examples of Algeria, Togo, Gabon, Senegal, Zaire (above all Zaire!), Angola, and also Kenya prove that the democratic caravan ferociously burns those who are insufficiently prepared. In only the space of a few months (the case of Burundi) or several years, the experience [of democracy] has already left a bitter taste; Africa recoils back to the era before independence.

Objection. Democracy's detractors do not tell us if this trap is one of form or of substance. In any case, we know that most of those who brandish this thesis are nostalgic for dictatorship and single-party government. We do not agree with them. Furthermore, democracy appears first as a course with which to promote freedom and respect of the individual as well as of the society. We classify it as belonging to the rank of moral values, given that a democratic society remains in truth an ideal that is to be envisioned by the great thinkers of the human spirit. It is when man is free that he realizes great works. What of a value such as love? Would we call it a poisoned fruit? Note rather that it is the enemies of democracy that orchestrate cacophonous voices that nowadays sound in the ears of the African.

So, to affirm the [anti-democratic] thesis serves to devalue the African and to consider him as being inept and dumb. What is the intellectual or material level required to accede to democracy? When in the United States they put themselves to electing the presidents and when they wrote the Bill of Rights, was the number of university graduates comparable to that of the Algerian universities in 1990? Is it because of a high percentage of illiterates that a bloody tribal war rages in Yugoslavia? Or is it due to the low income level of the Serbs, the Muslims, the Croatians, and the Montenegrans? Is there one people capable of living in a democracy and another that is incapable of doing so? Is there a superior culture? These considerations are stumbling blocks for many, even the most shrewd.

Finally, democracy such as is preached in national conferences and popular demonstrations has been proposed as the solution to save a continent from the nightmarish quagmire into which the single-party systems plunged it. Dictatorship has failed because it is dedicated to the future of a single person, a single person made divine while crushing an entire people. Despite the emphatic discourses on total liberation and the definitive takeoff toward summits, underdeveloped countries have bound themselves by an absurd parasitism that pushes them today toward a beggar's existence before those whom they insulted only yesterday. Give democracy some time! You don't conclude that it can't walk when it is just learning to speak and crawls on all fours!

Third thesis. The Hutu are responsible for the massacres, say the Tutsi; the Tutsi are the true responsible ones, respond the Hutu. Each camp throws the ball back into the other's court. The other becomes a Machiavellian monster accused of fomenting anything in the aim of domination. The drama of Burundi resides in this duality: the two ethnic groups are faced off against each other with the virus of hegemony. Zaire with its 400 tribes is a dream [in comparison] because the hate between them is not carried to the top. According to this thesis, all the misery has its origin in the cohabitation of fraternal enemies.

Objection. Sociologically, the term ethnie is not correct as far as Burundi is concerned. A natural compound or calculus [concretion] unifies the Tutsi, Hutu, and Twa at every level: belief, language, subsistence activities (pastoralism and cultivation), even settlements. There are no villages of Hutu nor those of Tutsi. It is our opinion, rather, that it is most appropriate to speak of "race" because it is the size, the form of the nose, and even other subjective criteria to which the difference may be accredited.[3]

That the Hutu or the Tutsi are responsible somehow for the crisis, that is perhaps true. Follow them in their reflections, and the ethnic given invariably becomes a crystal ball. In schools, in administration, in the army, they take position immediately along the lines of this issue each time a little problem arises. However, because these "ethnic groups" have lived together for centuries and are condemned to cohabit, it seems useful to push the analysis much further so that in the future the kinds of slipups like those that followed the death of Melchior Ndadaye may be dampened or even avoided?

Our Position. When the spectacle is horrifying, international opinion consults journalists as well as the leaders of international organizations such as the Red Cross and the High Commission for Refugees [the UNHCR], individuals who for the most part [express their opinions from where they] lodge in hotels. We do not mean to say that their opinions are for this reason made aseptic or somehow sifted down; they are worth their weight in gold! But these people should also speak to the little blacks *[petits nègres]*, the economic and political refugees, who were close to the autochthonous as they fled from the interior of the banana groves and forests.

Two major advantages come from this approach. On the one hand, the peoples will know that their brothers and their neighbors watch and judge them sometimes mercilessly. On the other hand, the explanations they give will be diverse but will tend to clarify certain cultural aspects [of the setting]. If the culture is not impenetrable, it remains nevertheless a Gordian knot that tenaciously protects or hides its important secrets. This explanation can dig out the hidden truths and help master the miasma. In all of us there slumbers the childhood that mediates the edge of the days of life's journey. These are marks of childhood and/or marks of culture.

This is to say that for us this genre of explanation merits rigorous examination. Our people have cultivated certain errors that we must correct. We hold to be true the following definitions of culture:

Tylor: "Culture is this complex totality that includes knowledge, religious beliefs, art, morals, law, customs and all capabilities and habits that man has acquired as a member of society."

G. Rocher: "Culture is an ensemble of manners of thought, of feeling and of acting, more or less formalized, that, being learned and shared by a plurality of persons, serves at the same time in a subjective and symbolic manner, to constitute particular persons into a distinctive particular collectivity."

Ilumbe apologized for the abrupt ending of his incomplete essay. He said he had been unable to work on it further. Since Bukavu had been overwhelmed with Rwandan refugees, the Burundian disaster of the previous year had receded in importance for him. He wished me to incorporate this beginning with what he then told me directly.

Ilumbe set forth to construct his interpretation of Burundian culture, as he had experienced it in the seven years he taught there. The narrative continues here, interspersed with interpretive comments to clarify the reasoning where it seems elliptical.

Burundian society is divided between the sages (the *bashingantahe*) and the fools (the *basazi*). The former are examples, the others are marginal. The former are hypocrites. A true man does not say what he thinks. He may hate you, but he hides it and acts like your friend. He may think, "I will get you, or kill you; put poison in your beer as we're having a social visit." I encountered this in school meetings. In Burundi you aren't supposed to get excited openly about anything, but to stay calm, all the while they're thinking critically. They use many proverbs to hide the truth. All the while others think the speaker is a sage.

The fool, contrariwise, is he who says all he thinks. The Zairians are fools because they have no secrets. Burundi is therefore a society of silence. They don't cry. At the maternity for the first child, all the women who were crying out were Zairians. The Burundian women were all quiet. To cry would be to express your sentiments, to be a fool.

A people like this who don't cry, they don't sing either. In an African village, silence! At five years of age the Burundian children quit crying; at eight they are emotionally "grown up."

Ilumbe put his comments into the context of a novella he had written about a woman of his acquaintance in Burundi who had had an illegitimate child. She lived in the neighborhood of the school where he taught.

> The woman died, and the child was taken in by relatives, as is African custom. However, they more or less neglected the child. When it became sick, they let it remain sick. The child was obviously going to die. So I took the child myself for some days. Then the family took it back. But they lied to me about the child's well-being. I noticed that the city uncle of the child, the deceased mother's brother, came from Bujumbura to visit his very well placed brother. This "bourgeois" uncle told his family to "get this cadaver of a child out of here," referring to his very own nephew. One night he heard sounds of washing and moving around. The next morning everyone went about their work as normal. Later in the afternoon my domestic told me that the child had died. But the neighbor family never told me anything. They had washed the child and buried it without making a public event out of its death. A Zairian friend visited, who had known the child, and cried for it. An eight-year-old Burundian girl told this friend, "Why cry? That's how children without parents die here."

Ilumbe concluded this story by saying that Burundi "is a society in which people laugh and hug each other during the day, then at night they kill each other." He continued to spell out a principle that this observation revealed about Burundian society.

> Burundi is a tripartite society, ethnically, but it has a bipolar cosmogony; they think God created it this way: Hutu or Tutsi. As a Zairian, you are Hutu if you are short, Tutsi if you are tall. You learn first that "the other is bad." It is the same among the Hutu. I was appalled when my domestic told me, "I live with these people. But when the war breaks out, I know who I'll kill. And, just before the war breaks out, I must have killed my enemy first." Burundi is a society in which you deal with any contradiction by killing.

Ilumbe drew some consequences of this view.

> There is a failure of the Christian message, for one thing. Most Burundians are Catholic. They teach love for the other, while hating the other. They drink together but hate each other. The refugees from Burundi suffered a lot. The UN mission was told that everything was all right there [after the events]. But that was a lie. The Christian message and Western values aren't genuinely incorporated.
>
> Why is this so? Burundi's is a culture of hypocrisy. It is made up of two antagonistic complexes. First, the Tutsi complex is that they are convinced of the superiority of their race and their intelligence. To justify that, all kings and presidents were Tutsi. In the secondary school in Burundi where I taught, of 500 students, 450 were Tutsi. President Buyoya tried to change the system to national competition. Later, of 700 students, 300 were Hutu. A second part of the complex is that the Tutsi are convinced they are a minority. They must survive, and that requires staying in power. A Tutsi told me that President Buyoya was bad, because, although Tutsi, he opened the door to a Hutu president, Ndadaye; he sold out. I replied to him that illiteracy is the real enemy. In Zaire the Tutsi even try to become Zairians to rule.
>
> The Hutu's complex is this: First, the desire of vengeance, because they are convinced that they have been long-time victims; they are convinced of Tutsi evil, and they feel the need to right the wrongs. Furthermore, they are convinced that they are in the majority. Thus Buyoya was rejected. Many supported Buyoya, but they were opposed to him and voted for Ndadaye, an unknown, because he was Hutu, and so, finally, they were vindicated.
>
> In Burundian society, there is an ignorance of the message of love. It is evident in the way property is handled. The entire country is divided into little parcels, each his own house, a small parcel for each one and his field.[4] The consequences of this are that your land is yours, a victory of yours, you've won it. In Zaire the Burundians act the same way. They build fences around themselves. There is in this pattern of land tenure and building the absence of love, even between brothers. Inheritance is a serious problem. Traditionally, the oldest son got the largest part of the land. The others were left out. The oldest son therefore considered his junior brother to be an enemy, and vice versa. They find the chances to eliminate each other, and do it, but they laugh and drink together. What goes on between brothers, is the source of hate; they don't know love.[5]

Ilumbe further developed his point on the way this paradigm of relations between brothers became the way all of Burundian society operated.

> It is the same in institutions, in the government, and between ethnic groups in the entire country. At a higher level this hatred includes coalitions between Hutu and Tutsi, so that if a Hutu is opposed to a Tutsi, other Hutu will be in coalition with the enemy Tutsi against the Hutu. It is the same as in the family, between two brothers. In Burundian thinking the source of peace is the silence of the other, that is, his death. Silence equals the conquest of the other. Burundians are silent when there is killing.
>
> Ndadaye both empowered the Hutu and tried to give Tutsi security. He liberated political prisoners.

Ilumbe saw a polarization beginning in September 1993, and the killing began.

The Hutu fled to the hills, the Tutsi fled to the military camps. Buyoya and Ndadaye had succeeded in dividing the Tutsi and the Hutu. All who were with these two politicians, were killed. UPRONA was tainted with single party-ism; FRODEBU was the symbol of multi-party-ism. Ndadaye was thus killed by those who wanted to roll back the clock to single-party rule. He was accused of wanting to eliminate Tutsi; thus the ethnic card was played.

The president was killed by the culture. In initiation rites the Hutu "remove their skin" and become Tutsi. Among the refugees the Hutu in the government are probably considered Tutsi's Hutu.

Reconciliation is possible, accordingly, at the level of culture. Two conditions are necessary for both. The Tutsi must renounce their aspirations as people; the Hutu must guarantee protection to the Tutsi, including letting them become that of which they are capable. The trouble is that whenever anyone gets power, they hire only their own; they must renounce this. The Tutsi are losing out with their view of always going for the top power.

Above all, for reconciliation to occur, everyone must learn to tell the truth. They must unlearn the anti-value of lying, of not crying when you're sad. Cultural hypocrisy will only lead to more killing. Furthermore, they must become literate in loving—*alphabétisme de l'amour*.

Notes

1. Ntabona's analytical approach to Burundian proverbs is based on the semiotics of J. Greimas and J. Courtes, who emphasize semantic clusters or networks of meanings around particular lexical units, or words.

2. Thomas Kamanzi, long-time member and now director of the Institute for Rwandan Studies told us that research revealed that many sets of brothers and therefore their patrilineal descendants ended up on opposite sides of this ethnic divide because of the number of cattle owned at the time of the institution of the identity card.

3. For Ilumbe to reach for "race" here is a surprising turn in his argument, because he suggests that the real reason for the conflict is cultural. He appears to be using the race concept as a typological construct, almost as a stereotype of physical features, attitudes, and behavioral characteristics.

4. Ilumbe is here condemning a widespread settlement pattern that exists across much of East Africa and down to the Nguni region of southern Africa. From a Zairian (Congolese) perspective, where villages are the norm, isolated homesteads must seem highly abnormal and, here, a contributing factor to rivalry between close siblings.

5. Conflict between brothers is the theme of Burundian writer Katihabwa Sebastian's (1991) stories in his collection *Magume, ou Les Ombres du Sentier*. The story's title, "Les entrailles déchirées," refers to the mother's grief after her two sons fight over unequal number of cattle, land, and offspring, provoked by their wives' jealousy, leading one brother to try to kill the other.

PART II

Searching for Causes and Solutions

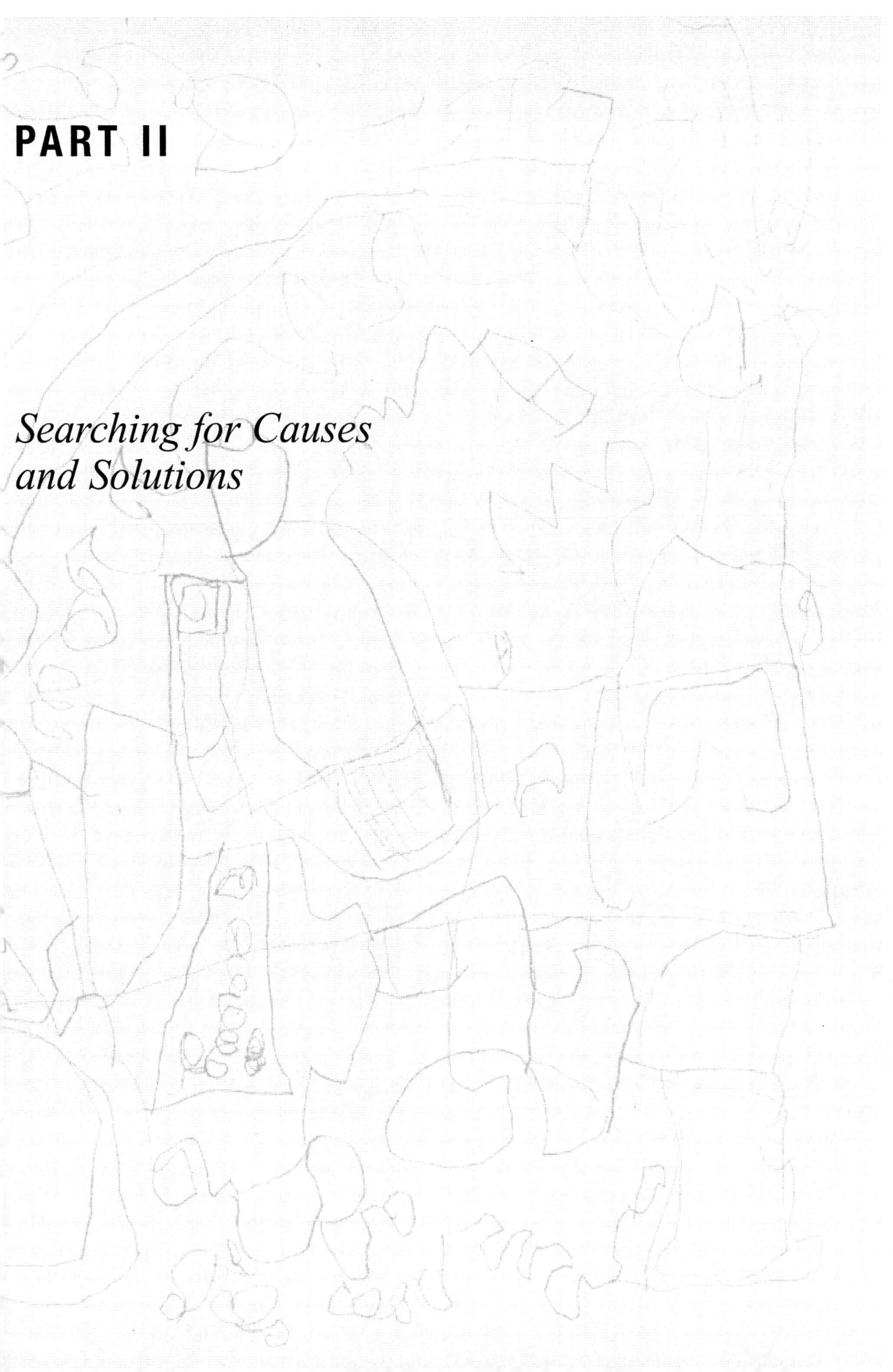

5. Understanding Conflict

in Rwanda and Burundi

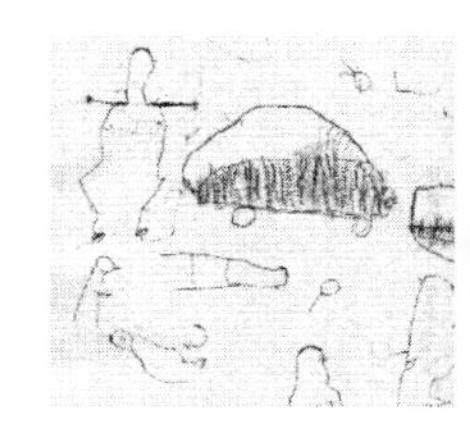

We begin this chapter with four frightening samples of the angry ethnic rhetoric heard in Rwanda and Burundi in the aftermath of the wars in those two countries. In their appeals to emotions and defensive debasement of "the other," they are extremely powerful and real because they are driven by a combination of fear and cynicism.

The Hutu love peace and physical work; they have a closer relationship with God. To kill is very difficult for them. If they have killed, they'll confess easily. The Hutu are naive and very fearful. The Tutsi are subtle; they never forget anything. If the chair is black, they can convince you that it is white. These are characteristics typical of a group that is a minority, necessary to protect themselves. In terms of accepting the Gospel, it is difficult and rare for Tutsi. Many are Catholic, but for a Tutsi to be Catholic is just like a custom. Tutsi are hypocritical.—spoken by a Burundian Hutu worker in an evangelistic Christian organization

Narrow nose like a European; tall; no recognizable heel tendons; black gums; a special kind of handshake that only they can tell.—consensus among a group of Zairians in Bukavu on the criteria for distinguishing a Tutsi from a Hutu

The statues of Joseph and Mary were mutilated in the massacres and pillages of April and May 1994. Joseph's nose was cut off, and Mary was decapitated, because they were considered Tutsi. Today cattle roam through the ruins of this Catholic parish church.—Thomas Kamanzi, linguist, newly appointed head of the Institute of Rwandan Studies, Butare, speaking of what happened to the church in his home community

Tutsi women who have known or who have married Hutu must know that they are first and foremost Tutsi. This is understood by our noble distinction. The mission of these women therefore is to spy on their husbands. Any children resulting from these Hutu are themselves Hutu. As these women have already committed treason, in any catastrophe, they have to save their own hide, but above all, they must not try to protect their children or their husbands.—from "The 17 Tutsi Commandments," *Ijambo,* no. 6, December 18, 1993

This rhetoric is famously effective because it appeals to people's fears and their visceral identities. However, the contradictions between the constructs expressed by this rhetoric and the understanding of current historical and linguistic research are apparent. Consistent objective markers to support the claims of the rhetoric are clearly absent. Thus, paradoxically, the rhetoric is as objectively false as it is emotionally real.

In this chapter we explore why the recourse to ethnic identification and vilification is so common. Section 5.1 presents yet another example of the range of understandings of the terms Hutu and Tutsi, this time among Rwandan intellectuals. Section 5.2 is our attempt to put together the current scholarship on the history of the Great Lakes region social categories and to understand why ethnic identity and conflict have emerged and why the ethnic card is played at particular moments and under particular circumstances.

5.1 *The Meaning of Hutu and Tutsi:* A Rwandanet Debate

On April 4–11, 1995, an international debate was held on Rwandanet concerning the meaning of the terms Hutu and Tutsi. This debate brought to computer screens around the world most of the positions on the meaning and nature of these categories and identities. The debate was launched by Pierre Ndilikilikesha, professor of Duke University, formerly of the University of Rwanda. For the sake of ready identification, the other participants are referred to by their given names only: Leonard, Venant, Merence, Theophile, Pierre-Claver, and David. Their additional identities become evident in their own voices and messages, insofar as they choose to present themselves. The debate is launched by Ndilikilikesha:

> It is my opinion that the tragic events in our country are not the result of a spontaneous explosion of centuries-old ethnic hatred, as some of my colleagues here have asserted. They are rather the consequence of a wicked but deliberate and masterfully executed policy by the Habyarimana clique of dividing us so as to perpetuate their control on power. . . . Some of us are convinced that Rwandan Hutus and Tutsis cannot live together peacefully because of major differences and disagreements between the two groups. If this is your position, would you please help us define the terms used. Specifically, could you define the terms "Hutu" and "Tutsi"? . . . In other words, who in your opinion is Hutu, and who is Tutsi? What does it take to be Hutu or Tutsi? How do you know personally who you are—Hutu or Tutsi?

Because Ndilikilikesha does not believe in the theory of inherent racial characteristics, he invites the respondents to compare Great Lakes region ethnic criteria with the ways in which the Nazis defined Jews and the apartheid government of South Africa defined Blacks and Coloreds.

Leonard is the first to respond to the opening question. He suggests in a contrived way that Ndilikilikesha is apparently confused about his own identity and that he knows full well who and what he is.

> While it is relatively easy to understand your apparent confusion about your ethnic appartenance *[sic]* in one of the groups that make up the Rwandan mix, it would be interesting to hear about what makes you think and "pretend" you are a Hutu despite your lack of sympathy for the millions of innocent Hutu in refugee camps inside or outside Rwanda.

Leonard equates Ndilikilikesha's questioning of the essence of Hutu identity as tantamount to lacking sympathy for the Hutu refugees and support for the RPF. He refuses to spell out the criteria by which one is or becomes Hutu.

Venant, in answer to the original request, makes a number of interesting comments about intermarriage, the uses of ethnicity by those in power, the lack of ethnicity among the weak, and the importance of representation in government so as to overcome ethnic divisions.

> I think that, given that there has been so much mixing between Hutu and Tutsi and that the marriage tie doesn't count in Rwandan society, it is very difficult to define who is Hutu or Tutsi. Often, it is a question of personal conviction! (e.g., the children of [former president Gregoire] Kayibanda, who for me were [no more Hutu than Tutsi]). Everyone knows that ethnicity and recently region have always played a role in our history, because those holding power have always used it to reinforce their own power. . . . All our chiefs did it, whether that be the Tutsi kings (key posts in the army were for Tutsi only), whether it be Kayibanda (the army had to be purely Hutu, which is why he recruited from the north, his region). Habyarimana above all demonstrated this. . . . His army was only there to protect him and his family.

"Personal conviction," that is, subjective identification, not race by birth, is the main principle enunciated by Venant for membership in an ethnic category. Such an identity can be used to build and keep a power base, that is, to control the state and exclude one's opponents. Venant uses this to explain why the Rwandan army turned on the population. He goes on to reinforce his point by noting that the weak have no ethnic differences.

> I believe that Tutsi and Hutu can live together, even the northerners and the southerners. Look at how Muslim Hutu and Tutsi don't even know this problem, because they have no power to dispute.

Venant draws from his illustrations the general conclusion that if Rwandan society is to live in harmony, it must define clearly the rules of power and, above all, respect the laws. First and foremost, the army must protect the people. The rulers have always used ethnicity to reinforce their power, whether in the kingdoms, the colonies, or the republics. He steers the argument back toward ethnicity and intrinsic polarization.

> Sadly, the result [of the conflict] is that today hundreds of thousands of innocent Hutu and Tutsi are dead because they were born Hutu and Tutsi. And I believe that the problem is no longer only one of power, it is an ethnic problem. Because of that I am more pessimistic concerning peaceful cohabitation. I think it is necessary to identify barriers to guarantee that ethnic manipulation is no longer translated into systematic massacres of an ethnic group.

Venant refers to the division of the Flemish and Walloons in Belgium into two districts, with the Flemish policed by Flemish police, and Walloons policed by Walloon police. It is a simpler problem. In Rwanda and Burundi things are not so simple. However, he concludes:

> It would be difficult to arrange our two countries in this wise, Tutsi governed by Tutsi, and Hutu by Hutu. But, personally, when I see the miseries and the population movements that have already been provoked by our civil wars, I believe that such a rearrangement would be the lesser evil.

Ndilikilikesha next responds to Leonard's accusatory message in which Leonard refused to give his criteria for ethnic labeling and rather suggested that Ndilikilikesha pretended to be confused. Ndilikilikesha repeats his invitation and lashes out at Leonard's "extremist agenda."

> Nice to meet you again on the net. I raised a very specific question; I challenged you to give me a definition of the terms Hutu and Tutsi, and what they mean in your own life and that of the people of Rwanda. I even gave you some hints as to how other racists in another era tried to define races. I was hoping that you would see immediately the absurdity of racial or ethnic politics. Instead, you still claim without any proof that one can "objectively recognize the ethnic group to which a given Rwandan belongs." That is exactly what my question was about: give us those "objective" criteria that you use to recognize people's ethnicity. I hope it is not a secret and proprietary method that only the Interahamwe (or RPF gunmen, if you want!) can use. I am sorry, but your response completely missed the point. I now address some of the cheap shots you directed at me. First, you accuse me of "lacking sympathy for the millions of innocent Hutu in refugee camps inside or outside Rwanda." I cannot see in any of my postings that lack of sympathy you accuse me of. Maybe you can provide a quote from my postings to illustrate your point. Believe me, I am as concerned as any of you about the well-being of the millions of Rwandans in the refugee camps. In fact, I have three sisters in Zaire and a brother in Uganda, not to mention the many members of my extended family, who are suffering in the various camps. Maybe you want to accuse me of insensitivity towards my own family! And you want us to believe that those who masterminded last year's massacres, those who desecrated our churches, polluted our rivers and lakes with the blood of our countrymen, those who destroyed our country's infrastructure . . . those monsters had "sympathy" for their countrymen? You want me to believe that those of you who persist in supporting or dismissing the excesses of the dreadful Interahamwe have the interests of the Rwandan people at heart? Stop hiding your extremist agenda behind the poor Rwandan masses! Their current tragic predicament is a direct result of the failed racist policies of people you admire and support, like Habyarimana, Bagosora, Leon Mugesera, etc. (By the way, I wish you a successful fundraising on Mugesera's behalf.)[2] The suffering of the Rwandan people will continue, and will probably intensify, as long as there are people like you who can only see Rwanda in the Hutu-Tutsi dichotomy.

Theophile writes Ndilikilikesha to say that the problems of ethnic division do not date from the reign of Habyarimana. To understand this, he says to begin with the monarchy and ask who was named chief or subchief in the north. Then:

> (1) From the monarchy to the first republic, did we gain or lose? (2) From the first republic to the second, did we gain or lose? (3) From the second republic to the current government, did we gain or lose? (4) Who leads the battle, who profits of the system put in place since the monarchy? . . . Everyone has the right to identify themselves as Hutu, Tutsi, Twa, animist, Muslim, Catholic, etc., but what is troubling and damaging is that such a label serves to exclude, to discriminate, and can lead to death, as has often been the case till now.

Theophile tells Ndilikilikesha that he is asking others to make an effort that he is incapable or unwilling to make, which he phrases in the form of this figure of speech:

> to recognize the weed in their own courtyard, and tear it out because it offends you. You consider that the weed in your yard does not offend anyone and that no one is able to notice it or identify it. That weed is egoism, the lack of a critical spirit. It is

> your right to adhere or fantasize such and such a political party; it is my right and that of the one who spews forth hateful writings to fight for a cause we judge to be noble. But where all this begins to hurt is when one loses control of oneself to the machinations or enslavements instigated by a fanatical political party for which one is struggling.

Theophile seems to suggest that the normal process of political struggle and self-identification can get lost in the swirls of egoism and manipulations. Sensing that Theophile is referring to him personally in the last paragraph, Ndilikilikesha responds within the hour.

> Theophile, I am completely in agreement with you. The history of Rwanda does not begin with Habyarimana's reign and the tragedy of last year. The problem is you accuse me of partisanship. I am not at all a member of the RPF, and even less, their fanatical wing. I am Hutu; my wife is Tutsi. My family has been brutalized by both actors of the Rwandan tragedy: the MRND/CDR/Interahamwe and the RPF and its commandos. My sister was assassinated by the Interahamwe in 1992; my beautiful (in-law) family was massacred by the same Interahamwe last year. As for the RPF, they assassinated my father. Was this because I affirmed on this net that I held Habyarimana responsible for the disintegration of our land, for this you accuse me of partisanship? Please explain.

Within two hours, Theophile replies to Ndilikilikesha, the essentials of his remarks being:

> The partisanship about which I speak applies to every person whose language consists in demonizing the ones and glorifying the others; every person who seeks to minimize the acts of such and such other party. I thought I sensed some of that in your writing, which otherwise had much of value. I do not mean to accuse anyone.

Pierre-Claver writes to Pierre and others on Rwandanet:

> I do not believe that one can find an "exact" definition of the terms Hutu and Tutsi. (In my natal region *umuhutu* also means "son.") But I believe that many Rwandans know how to differentiate most of the time the one from the other. This is why the error was never made of naming a Hutu to be king (just a joke!). Thus, in the region of Canada where I now live, Rwandan and Burundian Tutsis meet together for their social activities, and the Hutu for theirs alongside. Before the war (October 1990) they were all mixed together. Now, even the non-Rwandans know who is Hutu and who is Tutsi.
>
> As far as I'm concerned, I believe that Hutu are physically different from Tutsi, but this is not grounds for killing each other, nor to feel superior to the other. I am sure that the Rwandans of the two ethnic groups can live together, but I think that in both communities there are elements who would accept with difficulty to share power equitably and representatively. Unhappily, these are the "elements" which control and shape the events.

Ndilikilikesha returns five days later to raise the original question, singling out Leonard in particular.

> A week ago, I challenged Rwandanetters to define the terms "Hutu" and "Tutsi" that we so liberally use on this net. I got a number of responses, but most of the respondents, including yourself, did not really answer my question. Instead, they went on to repeat some of the old stereotypes about our ethnic groups. I would still like to see a definition of the concepts of Hutu and Tutsi. If you don't have a definition, you can always provide us with a "heuristic," an "algorithm," or a "rule of thumb" that you use to establish the ethnicity of a given Rwandan. I am still convinced that this would not be a trivial exercise. Actually, I am hoping that it would be therapeutic.

Addressing Leonard directly, Ndilikilikesha personalizes the issue, since both are Hutu men with Tutsi wives.

> Take for example your case. You claim that you can "objectively recognize the ethnic group to which a given Rwandan belongs." And you go on to say that [so-and-so] is "unquestionably a Hutu. . . ." Explain to us how you make these determinations. I mentioned earlier that I have known you for a number of years. So allow me to use examples from our own lives. Tell me, what is your own daughter's ethnic group? Is she Hutu? Tutsi? Explain! As I mentioned in my earlier note, it is definitely easier "to talk or write so passionately about some mythical enemy called Hutu or Tutsi," but what if the "enemy" is in your own family? Are you telling me that you can be a Tutsi when your dad or mom is a Hutu, or vice versa? What to make of the thousands, if not millions, of Rwandans who are the offspring of mixed ethnicity? What to make of this popular rule of thumb often heard in extremist northern circles that anybody who lives south of the River Base, anyone from Nduga, is Tutsi? And consequently, anyone north of Base is Hutu. Would this be the criterion you used to affirm that [so-and-so] is "unquestionably a Hutu"? Do you realize that, had you been in Rwanda with your family last April, the Interahamwe would have asked you to hack your own family to death? Why can't you face this horrible truth and help me and others on this net castigate the Interahamwe and their masters? I know that I

> will sound very annoying to some and too frank and personal to others, but I still don't understand how ethnic solidarity can blind us to such an extent as to not see or acknowledge the absurdity of this deadly ethnic game.

Finally Leonard responds, but not in such a way as to answer Ndilikilikesha's leading question.

> I think there is a short answer to your attempt to get me involved in the game you are playing since quite some time for an unknown reason. There is no interest to redefine the notion of Hutu or Tutsi on this net or anywhere else as an attempt to solve Rwandan problems. The first reason is I don't have time to commit to that agenda. The second reason is that as soon as the eventual redefinition of your terms is done, you will come up with new terms such as those you are suggesting in your posting, which you are pretending the Habyarimana regime used to divide Rwandans. The real reason you want people to commit their contributions to this dead-end issue is as an attempt to dilute the Rwanda ethnic cleavage as a major factor in the Rwanda crisis, as many supporters of the Tutsi minority group in power in Burundi have attempted since now many years with no success as we can see from the current genocide underway against the Hutu people in Burundi.
>
> How can you otherwise explain your attempt to deny the ethnic component of the Rwanda crisis while the RPF, the main victorious faction of the Rwanda war, defines itself by its ethnicity (Tutsi), and thousands of Tutsi were killed during the war because of their belonging to the Tutsi ethnic group and hence accused to be supporters of the RPF, and thousands of Hutu were killed during the war and up to now because of their belonging to the Hutu ethnic group and hence accused of supporting the Hutu militia.

The insinuation is that Ndilikilikesha, although a Hutu, is an RPF supporter and is merely dissimulating to provoke others who hold a more essentialist view of the conflict as, first and foremost, ethnic. Leonard continues:

> If there was to be a confusion about those two terms, it would be in your mind, not in the minds of RPF because they accurately know their next target, nor in the refugee camps where they accurately know who are their enemies. The problem is there is no confusion in your mind either because when you stated that you are a Hutu married to a Tutsi a couple of times ago, you knew exactly what you were talking about, and I doubt you are bringing up this wrong issue in good faith. Can you tell us what you really want?

The final Rwandanet participant on this issue was David from England, who summarized the debate and drew a few helpful conclusions. "This debate has been fascinating because it has struck at the paradox that ethnicity is both the form that conflict in Rwandese society takes and yet not the cause of that conflict." In other words, despite some suggestions of real differences between Hutu and Tutsi and Leonard's refusal to spell out the ways in which he reckons ethnicity, this ethnic identity was in fact socially constructed rather than biologically rooted. Therefore ethnic definition, if used at all, even if subjectively, must be considered real, but real as a kind of consciousness of belonging. For some this subjective belonging is defined by region, with the north and northwest identified as Hutu because it was the region of precolonial and early colonial Hutu kingdoms and chiefdoms and the south identified as Tutsi because it housed the capital of the Tutsi kingdom during the colonial era.

Others see this ethnicity as a symbol used to define a hold on power through the ethnicization of opponents. Several suggest that this has been standard practice throughout the history of the Great Lakes region, even up to the present. The reason ethnicity is used, some suggest, is that when all other forms of legitimacy erode, ethnicity is all that is left. Little basis, if any, for such ethnic identification remains, except to argue that everyone who is not for me or with me is against me, even if he carries the same formal identity. This explains why it is possible for Leonard to accuse fellow Hutu Ndilikilikesha, who would junk ethnicity, of not caring for the Hutu refugees and supporting the Tutsi RPF.

5.2 *Why Ethnicization?* The Scholarly Perspective

Ethnicization, although not found in most popular dictionaries, has become widespread in social science writing to describe the process by which all relationships in a society come to be subsumed in an ethnic rubric, as has occurred in the Balkans and other world regions, including the United States (Hobsbawm 1991; Young 1993; Williams 1989; Ignatieff 1994; Nash 1989), Rwanda and Burundi (Lemarchand 1994; Newbury 1988), and even some prehistoric societies (Wilmsen 1995).

Ethnicization in Great Lakes region African societies hinges, as we have seen, on the adoption of a tripartite view of society and its past, in which Hutu, Tutsi, and Twa are separate and have always constituted separate segments of society. The other side of this coin is the adoption of the unitary view of these societies and their past, according to which the region has been populated by a variety of peoples who have combined lifeways of hunting, cultivation, and herding and who have intermarried and spoken a single language and constituted a single culture. Which view is correct? What is the evidence? Here, we undertake a succinct review of the current understanding in scholarship.

Today's social rules governing membership in the categories and identities of Hutu, Tutsi, and Twa as well as membership in lineages and clans hold that one is a member of one's father's category or group, even in the many cases in which both parents of a family are of mixed identity. This rule of patrilineal membership is the basis of the premise for those who hold that the ethnic categories are races, that is, biologically transmitted populations with social and psychological characteristics, each with its own deep history and diverging origin. However, in speaking with Rwandans and Burundians, especially those who disbelieve the three-group ideology, mention is made of the olden days when it was possible for a Hutu to "become" Tutsi through the acquisition of wealth (cattle) and through the assumption of a status of prominence. For these individuals the iron-clad definition of Hutu, Tutsi, and Twa as patrilineally inherited quasi-racial identities is a lie, a false understanding of history.

Among the African scholars who sadly watch their region being torn apart by this false ideology, Congolese historian Bishikwabo Chubaka, longtime student of the Great Lakes region, founder of the Kivu Research Institute, and head of the Bukavu Teacher's Training College, points out what should be obvious. In Bashi society of the Kivu, which is historically an extension of the Rwandan cultural region, the Hutu-Tutsi cleavage does not exist; the terms are not used to categorize people at all. Therefore the ascendance of these terms as all-embracing social categories is more recent than the founding of these societies (Bishikwabo 1989). A review of some of the linguistic, archeological, biological, anthropological, and historical scholarship tends to support Bishikwabo. Unfortunately, the reality of the categories lies elsewhere, not in historical fact.

The Scholarly Record on History

The cultural historical record of the Great Lakes region, as found mainly in the linguistic historical and archeological record, establishes that the Bantu languages of the Great Lakes region (Kinyarwanda, Kirundi, and others) and cultivation, herding, and hunting—the economic functions around which Hutu, Tutsi, and Twa are defined—have been present in the region for at least 2,000 years (Schoenbrun 1995, who reflects the work of Pierre DeMaret, Christopher Ehret, and David W. Phillipson). Again, this suggests a common culture rather than three separate historical societies. The term Tutsi, which is most often identified with pastoralism, is demonstrated through historical linguistic analysis to have entered the Bantu languages of the Great Lakes region in the 8th century from South Nilotic languages without any suggestion of a racial connotation that is often implied in the use of today's category (Vansina 1993).

These disclaimers notwithstanding, what does research indicate concerning the claims of the racial identities of Hutu, Tutsi, and Twa? Bishikwabo (1989) approached this question from the perspective of colonial policy. He noted that many colonialists ruled through local elites but that not many did what happened in Ruanda-Urundi. Taking from the storehouse of antiquated racial ideas the example of the Hamites, the Catholic White Fathers proposed that the Tutsi were the African remnants of the Semitic offspring of Ham, one of the sons of Noah; by implication, the rest of Africans were "off the map" of biblical humans, therefore unworthy (MacGaffey 1970). The Tutsi, as a consequence, were privileged in schools and other colonial opportunities, whereas the majority (Hutu) were trained to be manual laborers. Especially, the Tutsi elite internalized this ideology of racial superiority. The ethnic references on the identity cards issued in the Belgian colony Ruanda-Urundi sealed these heretofore porous socioeconomic categories by giving them a patrilineal descent-based definition.

According to Bishikwabo (1989), a further reinforcement of the bipolar ideology of historical Hutu-Tutsi relations occurred with the 1961 publication of Jacques Maquet's *Premise of Inequality in Ruanda*. At the time Maquet's book was an authoritative work depicting the nature of the clientage exchange relationship between cattle keepers and planters as a type of African feudal serfdom, reinforced by endogamous (nonintermarrying) castes. Maquet's work was influential for a time, because it suggested that Rwanda was distinctive in Black Africa, where most people have stressed marrying one's neighbors (outside one's own unilineal descent group) and exchanging goods and services with them to cement ties for the long term good of society. It was later determined that Maquet's informants were all Tutsi aristocrats close to the king who supported such a top-down view of the society and exclusively married their own kind.

For Bishikwabo (1989) the most problematic legacy of late 19th- and early 20th-century constructs imposed on the interpretation of Great Lakes region history was the combination of race, culture, and migration accounts. For most colonial era writers Bantu and Hamite peoples are races who speak distinctive languages and possess distinctive behaviors. They were also seen as having migrated to their present location with these characteristics, unaltered since ancient times. This set of ideas combined with the unilineal descent theories of origin provides the elements of the current popular ethnicity terms in Rwanda and Burundi.

Race, defined as an exclusive breeding population, is no longer used in human studies, short of speaking of the human race. In any case, it could never be applied to patrilineal descent alone, which ignores the female contribution to progeny. Research on the distribution of genetic markers in Rwanda and other African areas demonstrates a degree of affinity between the Great Lakes region population and West Africa on the one hand and the Horn of Africa on the other hand. But these markers are scattered across so-called ethnic and clan lines (Hiernaux and Gauthier 1977). The inference is that there has been migration from elsewhere but also much crossbreeding, as is common in Africa, given the almost universal rules of descent group exogamy (meaning that one marries outside one's lineage and clan). There are, in any case, no separate races, let alone patrilineal races with distinctive physical, mental, and behavioral characteristics. The characteristics that are stereotyped in Rwandan society (e.g., height, facial features, nose shape) are to some extent based on varying alleles, and they are also determined by nutrition. Finally, they are only a few features among many thousands that the Rwandan population has in common. Unfortunately, such scientific refutation of separate races does not put to rest racist ideology, the reality of which lies in the rhetoric of what Malkki (1995) called mythohistories.

The case for a unitary and evolving society (in Rwanda, at least) is strongly supported by another set of data: the distribution of clans. Marcel d'Hertefelt (1971) established that most of the patrilineal clans of Rwanda have Hutu, Tutsi, and Twa members. He demonstrated from a sample of 20% of all Rwandan male registrants in the 1962 preelectoral census that 17 of the patrilineal clans include both Hutu and Tutsi and that ten include Twa (Table 1). On the surface of things this evidence is highly incongruous with the understanding of Rwandan society as made up of deep patrilineages and patrilineal clans. In short, how can the supposedly exogamous lineages and clans cross-cut the supposedly hereditary unilineal groupings of Hutu, Tutsi, and Twa? Such clan or regional groupings may represent distinctions between communities of what can be considered original inhabitants, the localized kingdoms that dotted the area since the 8th or 9th century, and communities associated with the pastoralists, or Tutsi identity, as embodied in the Nyiginya dynasty of the Rwandan kingdom. Rennie (1971) suggested that the periodic movement of herders,

Table 1.
Composition of Rwandan Patrilineal Clans[a]

Clan	% Hutu	% Tutsi	% Twa	% Total
Siinga	15.0	12.5	6.3	14.6
Siinda	14.9	5.6	8.8	13.3
Ziingaaba	12.9	4.4	9.3	11.5
Gesera	11.9	6.4	24.8	11.0
Nyiginya	7.5	29.0	6.3	10.9
Eega	7.5	10.7	11.8	8.0
Baanda	7.6	1.6	18.5	6.7
Cyaaba	6.6	5.7	2.5	6.5
Unngura (Hondogo)	6.8	0.8	3.4	5.8
Shaambo	3.0	9.0	3.4	3.9
Tsoobe	0.7	3.0	–	0.9
Kono	0.2	2.0	–	0.7
Ha	0.3	2.0	–	0.6
Nyakarama	0.1	2.0	–	0.4
Siita	0.1	0.5	–	0.3
Oongera	0.1	0.2	–	0.1
Eegengwe	0.003	0.01	–	0.004
Other	4.7	3.5	–	4.7

[a] Sample from 20% of all male registrants in the 1962 pre-electoral census.

pushed southward by drought in northern Uganda, Kenya, and the Sudan, brought about repeated contacts with the more sedentary cultivators. Given the dominance of African exogamy, these relationships would have fostered and brought about such a degree of mixing between local and incoming groups that, even though separate lineage and occupational identities may have been preserved, they were not thought of as distinct populations with identifiable cultures. Scholars have also pointed out that individuals migrate, not clans. Even if some of the Nilotic clan names are similar to Rwandan clan names, the fact that they are spread across Hutu, Tutsi, and Twa identities argues against their being submerged in these identities as unilineal descent groups. The missing ingredient of the analysis of Rwandan clans so far is power.

In an analysis that is finely reasoned and deeply rooted in research in the Great Lakes region, David Newbury (1980) offered a solution to the paradox of clans spanning the contemporary airtight categories of Hutu, Tutsi, and Twa. Newbury's hypothesis is important because it demonstrates the historical shifting of identities currently thought to be fixed and hereditary. First, Newbury (1980, p. 392) noted the distinction in Rwandan social concepts between clan *(ubwooko)* and lineage *(umuryaango)*. As is the case elsewhere in Central Africa, the term for clan is used to classify items in a category, such as a herd of cattle or a species, whereas the term for lineage is used to describe a corporate group with internal responsibilities. The clan is thus an identity rather than a group, although it is described as loosely patrilineal. By scrutinizing the regional distribution of clan names in d'Hertefelt's records as well as in his own work in western Rwanda and on the island of Ijwi, Newbury noted a pattern whereby clan identities apparently consolidated around dynasties that were dominant for a long period of time. Moreover, in regions with such dominant dynasties, there are fewer local terms than in regions where less widespread political consolidations have occurred. Newbury (1980, p. 394) demonstrated the process by which older local identities came to be associated with newer identities representing powerful descent groups with whom one might want to affiliate or to whom one might pay tribute and whose identity the local group would take over. For our purposes here, the enigmatic picture of clan identities that crisscrosses today's ethnic identities tells us that innumerable political groupings across the region of and around Rwanda and Burundi exerted an influence and consolidated cultural symbols in their reign. Newbury (1980, p. 396) also suggested that these clan concentrations had everything to do with perceptions and assimilation to a set of cultural norms affecting an entire local or regional population. In other words, explanation of today's circumstances by any single organizing principle—be it clan, ethnic group, or state—is too simplistic to be accurate. The stereotypes that are used to demonize a political opponent or a scapegoat are thus all the more grotesque and troublesome.

To return to the historical record, scholars seem to agree that a general process of political consolidations has been spawning chiefdoms or kingdoms in the Great Lakes region since the 10th century. These chiefdoms have included those of the western regions (the so-called Hutu dynasties), the Nyiginya dynasty that became dominant under German and Belgian rule, and the Gisaka and Bugesera dynasties, which were neither Hutu nor Tutsi (Pierre Ndilikilikesha, personal communication, June 10, 1999). The details of the rise and demise of these numerous dynasties is far too complex to consider in more than passing attention. Many of the western Rwandan dynasties evoked considerable interest and political attention as historical foundations of Hutu identity and for having been eclipsed or dismantled by Belgian colonialism (Nahimana 1993). Similarly of concern to scholars and state builders are the details of the rise of the Nyiginya dynasty that ruled in colonial Rwanda. The Nyiginya dynasty is held by most scholars to have emerged in the region of Lake Muhazi (today's Giti commune) in the 15th century, from where it expanded its control over all other contenders, especially with the help of German and Belgian colonialism in the 20th century (Vansina 1962). The historical basis of and the relationships between all these early kingdoms—the Hutu kingdoms in the western region and the Tutsi Nyiginya kingdom and the others—were hotly debated in Rwanda by academics in the notorious Ruhengeri conference titled "Ethnic Relations in Rwanda in the Light of the October 1990 Aggression" (Nyagahene 1991; Maniragaba-Balibutsa 1991). Intellectuals used historical scholarship to rescue the legitimacy of a beleaguered Hutu revolution and state by highlighting the Hutu kingdoms that predated the arrival of outside invading and usurping Tutsi. In this same vein, as the second Congolese civil war of 1998 was getting underway, allusions to the Tutsi-Hima conspiracy to recolonize Central Africa were again being mentioned in internet letters to justify attacking Tutsi or to counter the Tutsi-led invasion.

But alas, all scholarly evidence of a unitary Rwandan society with a deep history has not sufficed to dispel the creation and ascendancy of the image of three separate races or the image one group being an outside invader. This means that to understand the conflict in Rwanda and Burundi societies, one must look beyond the deep and rich social, biological, or linguistic history to the nature of ethnicity itself.

Scholarship on Ethnicity and Ethnicization

Scholars of the post–Cold War era now suggest that the ethnicization of society has its roots in the fragility of the nation-state and, ironically, in the introduction of the values of human rights and the hopes of democratic representation around the globe. Ethnicization comes about as elites in control of the state or a society's resources block others from access or as those disenfranchised from the society's and the state's goods voice that alienation and lay claim to their share. Caricaturing and demeaning "the other" are standard political playing cards in the process of ethnicization in Rwanda and Burundi and elsewhere in the world.

Through the voices of Burundians, Rwandans, and Zairians we have shown how in the old Belgian colonial region Ruanda-Urundi misrepresentation and marginalization planted the seeds of ethnic consciousness and ethnic polarization. The scholarship on ethnicity provides some helpful theoretical perspectives.

For some scholars modern ethnicity is all about the way elites have managed the nation-state (Hobsbawm 1991; Young 1993). For these scholars the recent rising tide of ethnicity, not just in the rubble of socialist empires but more widely across the world, is an indication of the declining stature and legitimacy of the state itself and of the continuing worldwide spread of the ideology of the right of all peoples to self-determination. Thus the beleaguered nation-state as an institution is increasingly unable to take care of citizens' rising expectations. The state steadily loses control and therefore sovereignty over juridical, economic, and communication arenas to international or transnational forces and institutions. In this view, ethnic polarization is a modern phenomenon rather than the continuation of ancient societal separations. The UNHCR recently identified the majority of worldwide refugees as the victims of ethnic civil wars.

Many studies of ethnicity are set in the late colonial era or early independence era in third world countries. A dominant theme is the origin of ethnic labels, categories, and identities being created by colonialists, or colonized elites, intent on dividing and ruling subject peoples. Many of the so-called tribes of these societies have their origin in this context, the result of labeling and classifying local society into convenient administrative units. Thus the ethnic terms that come to be used are often taken from some geographic, linguistic, or cultural vocabulary and are applied to a particular group that internalizes these labels.

According to many scholars, in the postcolonial setting these identities imposed by elites become the basis of actual subnational identities. The elite is rarely ethnic, because it wields power and controls the reins of the state. Those who are marginalized or blocked from access to the resources of society may appeal to their ethnic identity to rally support, just as those in power may come to defend their access to resources—jobs, education, wealth, status—from those so-identified as an ethnic "other." This is Catherine Newbury's (1988) analysis of the Rwandan situation. Newbury (1988, pp. 14–15 and 213–214) argued persuasively that the Hutu revolution in the late 1950s grew out of the frustration and poverty of the masses being deprived of the benefits of society, particularly education, which they saw the Tutsi enjoying while they themselves were stuck with deadend menial work and were barred from chiefship. Such a line of interpretation has often been called the instrumentalist analysis of ethnicity, in which ethnicity is seen as a language or code for elites to use to play on the insecurities and aspirations of their constituents in order to lay claim to material rewards and further their own political ambitions.

Yet to see ethnicity as a kind of card played by politicians with ulterior motives does not explain why ethnicization often can take on a frightening virulence that leads to violence toward the "other"; nor does it quite explain the mechanisms that operate in human relations and in rhetoric and sign manipulation to bring about the heightened emotionalism usually present in ethnicization.

In the 1960s some scholars used the phrase "primordial sentiments" or "primordial ties" (Shils and Geertz 1963) to speak about the symbolic potency of the appeal to blood ties, land, language, custom, and sometimes religion to forge alliances and gain popular support. Geertz (1963, p. 120) made the disturbing but prophetic point that "it is the very process of the formation of a sovereign civil state that, among other things, stimulates sentiments of parochialism, communalism, racialism, and so on, because it introduces into society a valuable new prize over which to fight and a frightening new force with which to contend."

The appeal to primordialism by scholars of ethnicity was received with mixed results. It opened up a respectable theoretical door for defenders of racist interpretations of behaviors they wished to see as inherent in the group they wished to malign or further repress. Primordialist explanations may have furthered racism in South Africa or in the United States. It is safe to say that in every society some individuals appear to act viscerally and irrationally and to do frightening things, but to call this behavior intrinsic or bound by human nature or to generalize it to group behavior is to say that it cannot be controlled and arises from intrinsic group character (e.g., the "Tutsi gene for lying," as used by a Hutu militant). This amounts to outright racism, an analysis no better than that which it seeks to explain and overcome (Williams 1989).

But rejecting racism does not explain the power of the appeals to blood, land, language, custom, and the sacred, nor does it explain why these types of symbols are invoked at particular junctures in the history of a society. The theory of signs has given scholars a more subtle and sophisticated analytical vocabulary with which to evaluate language, rhetoric, and nonverbal signs. Without minimizing the unequal power relations (i.e., class basis) in ethnicization, the process of forming group-specific symbols and identities may be closely scrutinized for the almost predictable semiotic sequence that is involved. Nash (1989) analyzed the ethnicization process by which a set of concrete index features emerges from the realm of blood (us versus them based on blood lines), bed (preferred and forbidden mating patterns), or cult (the truths and defense of revealed religion). The source of these features and the nature of the ethnic hardening follow the most readily available breaking points in the society, be they occupational, national, linguistic, or existing status markers. Because the index features emerge in association with bipolar break points, they become the basis for all sorts of elaborations, as associations are made from them to other aspects of life, groups, settings, and issues. For Nash, these index features (i.e., the idioms and images that concretize an identity in a material sign), once they are created, become recursive metaphors. They become recursive because they are rehearsed over and over to associate a group with a particular image or icon (e.g., the nose, the forehead, the stature). The calls for pure blood on one's own side or for the rape of the enemy's women or for the singling-out of facial or other physical features become almost clichés of choice in ethnic galvanization (Ignatieff 1994).

In the Rwandan civil war of 1994 the rhetoric of Radio Mille Collines is credited with creating and using such images with exceeding efficacy and with unprecedented tragic outcomes. The Tutsi and enemies of the regime became "cockroaches" that needed to be stamped out. In the rhetoric of the RPF the Rwandan government and its supporters became "vermin" or "rodents" "milling about in confusion," worthy of being displaced and chased out. Both sides used the language of "cleansing." In Burundi similar images became so powerful that in the remaining tenuous civil discourse they were taboo, as if obscene. In their place a series of euphemisms came into being. Thus the distinction between "displaced" and "dispersed" came to stand for Tutsi and Hutu, respectively. The displaced reside in safe havens protected by the army; the dispersed were forced to find refuge in the bush and sometimes were associated (by the army) with armed Hutu guerrillas.

Why the Ethnic Card Is Played

The understandings of ethnicity from scholarship may explain in a general way why the card of ethnicity is played and how it works. But something is still missing, namely, the timing of ethnicization, such as the occurrence of particular attacks in Burundi. We suggest that the explanation of the waves of violence is really as simple as a group of politicians scheming to use ethnicity to hang on to or grab power, mainly by frightening the general population or killing the other side's elites. The particular form this may take is to label a citizen with a weapon a Hutu militiaman, thereby justifying the attack on the community. Disinformation and planting incriminating evidence in the form of incendiary pamphlets or weapons is a common practice in Burundi. The appeal to ethnicity is a strategic choice used by both sides engaging in the conflict; that choice must be translated into particular speeches, newspaper essays, and actions. The constructivist school of ethnic studies, which may include much of the instrumentalist's subject matter, follows the postmodern inclination to look at social and cultural expression as discourse or text. Proponents of ethnicization evaluate the use of language, the manipulation of symbols, the timing of hard-line attacks, the messages through which political support is mobilized, and the particular myths and distortions that shape the reading of events and justifications of actions (Lemarchand 1994; Malkki 1995). Lemarchand (1994) suggested that historical memory in Burundi has often been couched in myths that are highly self-serving of factions. Such myths include the ideas (1) that ethnic conflict is a carryover of historical antagonisms (it's not; each episode is generated anew); (2) that ethnic conflict is a direct outcome of colonial rule; (3) that the 1972 killings were exclusively a Tutsi plot (there were mutual killings)[3]; and (4) that ethnic killing is the outcome of external subversion (it's not; it is usually local and always done by particular individuals against other particular individuals) (Lemarchand 1994).

Certainly, the ethnic cleansings of Bujumbura's suburbs in the spring of 1995 were planned. Usually the Sans Echec or other militant groups of Tutsi made the initial attacks; these were accompanied by army consent or by follow-up attacks. Similarly, there appear to have been plans to attack Rwandan (Hutu) refugee camps in Burundi to take out hard-core militia around the first anniversary of the beginning of the 1994 Rwandan war. National armies routing guerrillas or exasperated citizens defending their interests would not, as such, necessitate the appeal to ethnicity. In Burundi the appeal to ethnicity often seems to precede the violence. A hard-hitting newspaper editorial or propaganda article, an insulting cartoon (Figure 87), or an inflammatory speech is often followed by an armed attack. Does the first create the climate in which the second is condoned? Or are these merely phases of one and the same plan? In any case, the appeal to ethnic inflammation as a weapon or tool for political struggle is often followed by some people giving free reign to their emotions. The pattern is almost transparent, as if someone is using a page out of a manual titled "playing the ethnic card."

But in a broader sense, why would ethnicity be used? Burundian writer Katihabwa Sebastian, in an unpublished chronicle of a typical African refugee, shows how the fear of losing power drives leaders to play the ethnic card against their opponents, usually those alienated from power (Katihabwa, n.d.). This tactic is tempting because it is effective in the short term, but it is exceedingly volatile. According to Katihabwa, the tactic often arises from paranoia on the part of those in or

Figure 87. A Burundian political cartoon displays attributes of indexing and recursive metaphorization. The cartoon was on the front page of *Le temoin nyabusorongo* ("the diviner's oracle"), no. 10, December 1994. This cartoon caricatures four politicians whose heads, on the bodies of dogs, probably identifiable to most readers, are being chased or followed by figures wearing caps with the acronym UPRONA and carrying musical instruments or holding their hands high as if voting. UPRONA is the minority (mostly Tutsi) party that was the dominant and ethnically integrated party at the time of independence. Here, in a newspaper voicing the view of the majority party FRODEBU, UPRONA is parodied by the headline caption, which, translated, reads "recruitment of dogs to the core of the Union of Exploiters of the Nation." In a dialogue beneath the cartoon a stranger questions a certain Ciseau of UPRONA, who reveals that the party is indeed hiring dogs to do its dirty work, namely, eating the corpses of massacred Hutu in the campaigns to evict the enemy (Hutu) militia. The dogs, wearing sashes often worn by prominent public figures, are saying "Break Minani" (a reference to a struggle between the two parties over a parliamentary leader), "They must at all cost abide by our dictatorship," and "We have serious scores to settle with you dirty FRODEBU beasts." The cartoonist is thus casting the other party (and ethnic group) as running with killer dogs—extremists—and supporting the massacres of Hutu.

close to power, of those who are already caught up in the consciousness-raising process of struggling against their oppression. Their resistance and their struggle is, then, in the absence of fair elections or representative government or functioning courts, forced into an ethnic ideological framework. The end struggle of the Burundian version of ethnicization has been appropriately called, by Adrien Ntabona, *violence identitaire,* a deadend indeed. Katihabwa's response to this zero sum battle of identities and resources is the following poetic antidote to ethnicizing politics. The passage is from Katihabwa's novella (1991) profiling an independence-era politician who exploited everything and everyone to benefit himself; when he was pushed aside by younger opportunists and became a hermit, he offered these words to a young boy (p. 124):

When you no longer know thirst nor hunger
Keep them constantly in mind, my brother.
Many people suffer without end,
Even your own brothers, close to you.
When you no longer know desolation,
At each moment, keep it in mind, friend.
Not everyone has this true consolation
Especially where one is excluded.
When you no longer know injustice,
At each moment, keep it in mind, colleague.
For the majority of humans
It often recurs like a refrain.
In fact, all these people whose life is a burden,
Try to understand them to better help them.
You, my brother, will receive a divine gift,
A measure of enthusiasm and ardor in helping others.
Each time you adopt an attitude,
Know there will be a corresponding reaction
By those who will have made a study of you,
Even if subjective, to judge your own action.

Notes

1. Ndilikilikesha corrected this in another message, stating that Kayibanda was from the central region.

2. Bagosora Theoneste was a top general in Habyarimana's army who is said to have mentioned something about "returning to prepare the apocalypse" when Habyarimana agreed to the Arusha peace accords. He was indicted on August 9, 1996, of crimes against humanity by the International Criminal Tribunal for Rwanda in Arusha, Tanzania. Mugesera Léon, another top official in Habyarimana's government, was in prison in Canada, awaiting a court ruling on an extradition request by the government of Rwanda.

3. Recently, Lemarchand (1998, pp. 5–7) forcefully argued that the 1972 massacre in Burundi against Hutu elite and intellectuals was the first systematic use of genocide in the Great Lakes region coordinated by the Tutsi-controlled government and army. Therefore, for the region to find its way back to peace, this prolonged season of killing must be reconsidered carefully by all who wish to contribute to understanding and dealing with the recourse to mass killing as political process.

6. Healing and Justice

We suggested earlier that our realization of the depth of the trauma of war in the Great Lakes region of Africa came when we sensed that the flat, seemingly emotionless tone in many of the personal accounts of war experiences we heard were in fact evidence of shock. Again and again our interlocutors—church leaders, administrators, writers, artists, teachers—spoke of the tragedy in terms and tones conveying deep shock beyond the realm of normal discourse. When asked why there were so few tears in their horrible stories, we were told that the events were "beyond tears" or that the deeds were "bestial," that is, outside the realm of normal human and social action. Like many observers of this war situation, we came away convinced that just as these individuals had been emotionally destroyed, so their social conventions had been shattered and could no longer be used to right the wrongs that had been committed.

In these closing sections we offer our observations on how we saw the pieces of people's lives being put back together during our stay in the Great Lakes region eight to nine months after the massacre in Rwanda, and two years after the 1993 violence in Burundi. This is the most difficult part of our writing, to answer those who asked for our "profound analysis," "the truth—spiritual and scientific," and any thread of hope we may offer.

It seems that there are individual and collective levels to the consequences of war, and the ways in which the aftermath of war is entered. Individuals experienced the war differently, were differentially traumatized, and need different dimensions of healing. At the institutional or collective level the scars are more permanent and long term. Rebuilding may require totally new approaches to old problems.

One thing is certain, however, and that is that war leaves the tangled legacy of trauma, denial, thirst for revenge, and the danger of continuing cycles of violence. What is to be done? Without some kind of healing the violence is bound to continue. Tim Lind, a long-time worker with the MCC and observer of the Central African scene, said that unless the root issues of the Rwandan genocide are dealt with, the cycles of violence will continue (Lind 1996). The impulse for revenge that is driven by the open wound of unresolved war trauma is paralleled by the victim's cycles of fear and retaliation that come from the perpetrator's continuing impunity. How do we cut through this Gordian knot of fear, violence, and impunity? In the next two sections we explore the relationship between healing and the restoration of justice as the enabling steps toward peace. We review approaches to healing the wounds of war and the relationship of justice to peace. This area of concern has been the subject of much scholarship, which we summarize where relevant. We also highlight some of the distinctly African approaches to war trauma healing and justice that are effective in and integral to the wider region in coming to grips with the aftermath of war.

6.1 *Healing the Wounds of War:* Western and African Perspectives

If nothing is done to put a stop to the crisis, Burundi will know many social misfits and risks being transformed into a nation of savages and madmen.—Sylvestre Barancira, Burundian psychiatrist

Little of what we saw in war-torn Rwanda and Burundi resembled what we had read about the religion and healing of the region and what we ourselves had witnessed in research elsewhere in central and southern Africa, at least not at first. Divination, the hallmark of an African approach to the interpretation of misfortune, was nowhere to be seen. Rather, we heard numbed, shocked voices reciting atrocities and losses that seemed to defy meaningful interpretation or placement in any worldview of misfortune. We saw no healers ministering to the sick and wounded, except for the crowds of NGOs from abroad. We saw a traditional medicinal pharmaceutical center in Butare that had been the pride of the IRST; it was trashed by the Interahamwe, and its new director, who had returned from abroad, was trying to figure out where to begin. When we asked what had happened to the much researched Great Lakes region rite of Kubandwa (De Heusch 1966; CERUKI 1976), we were told repeatedly that it was a thing of the past no longer observed by modern individuals. Others said that Kubandwa is practiced by the uneducated or clandestinely by others because it was fought by the church. A recent work on changing concepts in Rwandan healing (Taylor 1992) identified the master metaphor of "flow and blockage" as central to how society and body are seen with "milk," "honey," and "money" providing the substance of exchanges to keep these "bodies" alive and healthy. We heard and witnessed nothing of all this. Rather, we saw Rwandan refugees in Zaire and internally displaced people in both Rwanda and Burundi speaking of their hunger, waiting for relief food handouts, fearing intestinal dysentery, and hoping to return home some day. We had the impression initially that all conventions and rubrics for the interpretation of misfortune had been shattered.

Perhaps the suggestion that there can be healing after a genocidal conflict is almost unforgivably obscene in the eyes and ears of some because their pain has been so total. Is this not comparable to suggesting that the survivors of the genocides of the 20th century—the Armenian massacre, the Stalinist gulag, the Holocaust, the Cambodian killing fields, the Balkan ethnic cleansing campaigns—can somehow be healed and made whole again? More likely, the appropriate phrase that we need to formulate is one of figuring out how to live with the images and the memories of what has happened and how to make sense of it, how to explain the gaping questions, Why? why me? why us? what does it mean?

And yet in the short time we were in Rwanda and Burundi, we were inspired when now and then we saw and heard healing and justice take form in surprising ways we had not anticipated. The Tutsi mayor of Kayenzi said he could begin his healing, despite the loss of most of his lineage, because his Hutu neighbor had returned from Zaire and was willing to take up life again as his neighbor. He could initiate the commune's reburial of the genocide victims' remains, thereby giving the community a human face with regard to these new ancestors. Another survivor, who had been in the pit of corpses for a week, could forgive the perpetrator who had tried to kill him once the would-be killer had been confronted and was willing to confess. This forgiveness was possible within the framework of the forgiver's Islamic faith. Similarly, a Burundian Quaker pastor could confront and forgive his brother's assassin. A church group rebuilt victims' houses. In Butare the Catholic diocese emphasized the truthful reading of history, to chip away at the formidable fortress of denial that plagued both camps after the war. As we were leaving Central Africa, communities were beginning to hold memorial services and to erect monuments, such as the one we witnessed earlier in Kibimba, Burundi.

In this section on approaches to healing we enumerate what we saw being undertaken to initiate healing in the aftermath of war from a variety of perspectives. We also review some of the perspectives on healing in the aftermath of war found in the literature and relate the Great Lakes region experience to what we saw in surrounding regions in central and southern Africa. We approach this subject from both a Western and an African perspective in the hope that out of the combination will come a better understanding of the ways that healing has occurred and can occur again. Even as we focus on healing and reconciliation efforts, we must emphasize that the bottom line of urgency is that unresolved conflict leads to more conflict, as indeed the Great Lakes region crisis has spread or joined with warfare that extends now to much of Central Africa.

War Trauma Healing and Reconciliation

Western Psychological Perspectives

War trauma, within the broader field of war's destructive effects, has been a Western concept since World War I. Since the Vietnam War, it has become the most serious affliction plaguing veterans. It has entered the mainstream as posttraumatic stress syndrome (Young 1993; Mays et al. 1998). The severe effects and long-term consequences of war trauma in this Western diagnostic sense were recognized by Burundi's only psychiatrist, Dr. Sylvestre Barancira, head of the Neuropsychiatric Center of Kamenge. He made the direct connection between low-grade warfare and the disastrous impact it was having on the psychological health of many Burundians. In an interview (Ndayizeye and Niyongere 1995) Barancira described the conditions leading to war trauma, and its consequences, in these terms:

> The sudden outbreak of collective violence, the noise of war, aggressive attacks and [fear of] imminent death, generalized insecurity without knowledge of its source, fatigue, sleep deprivation, and hunger lead to a considerable mental disorganization in the victim.
>
> . . . The experience of hostilities as victim, perpetrator, or spectator are accompanied by a massive destructuration of the psychic apparatus leading above all to the loss of moral values. The problem of ethnic conflict is so much the more dangerous because it creates a quasi-generalized paranoid suspicion between citizens of different ethnic groups. Simply seeing the other is accompanied by feelings of hostility, of persecution, of bitterness, or of vengeance.
>
> Regarding the seriousness of ethnic conflict, it is disquieting to see that the feelings of persecution persist even after the disappearance of the immediate danger. Not to know the whereabouts of one's loved ones, the dispersion of family, the impossibility of getting on with grieving as long as a body isn't identified are responsible for the crisis of anxiety, the feelings of guilt and of depression in survivors.
>
> It goes without saying that it is most urgent to bring about a quick end to these interethnic massacres, for Burundi already has enough orphans, enough displaced and broken families. If nothing is done to put a stop to the crisis, Burundi will know many social misfits and risks being transformed into a nation of savages and madmen.

Western therapists [e.g., Seppa (1996)] who have commented on the Rwandan postgenocide situation barely know where to begin. Just among the children there may be hundreds of thousands who are in need of some form of trauma therapy by Western psychotherapy standards. Estimates of children survivors who lost their parents are put at 80,000; many of these children saw their parents or a grown relative killed. The many child warriors who were trained to kill in the Interahamwe units have even more severe problems that make their moral maturation problematic (Seppa 1996, p. 14). Early in the postwar period a journalist interviewed a lone psychotherapist in Kigali who was able to see only several dozen cases per week. The editors of a recent special issue of *American Psychologist* devoted to ethnic conflict said that "the reality is that in the foreseeable future of many of the countries and nations most in need of ethnic conflict analysis and prevention, psychologists and other trained behavioral science professionals will be unavailable" (Mays et al. 1998, pp. 737–738). Even if such specialists were to become available, many conflicts in the world today are of such a nature that it is not altogether clear that the individualized Western approach would even be the most appropriate (Mays et al. 1998, p. 739). Furthermore, there is no unifying, agreed-on body of theory of conflict analysis and therapy. But May et al. emphasized the need for analysis of conflict in terms of its local cultural, political, and economic aspects and the importance of enhancing local skills and specialists in this area. Later, we present the work of Karl and Evelyn Bartsch, counseling psychologists who recently made an effort to train therapists and community leaders in trauma counseling in South Africa, but not before they had immersed themselves in the community setting where they listened to stories of trauma resulting from the apartheid years, the killing, the torture, and the transformation of their societies.

Within Religious Communities and the Truth and Reconciliation Commission

Although the churches were deeply compromised in the Rwandan genocide and war, with their leadership often involved in the politics of the single party that instigated the killing, some noteworthy initiatives emerged from those in the churches who tried to apply the spirit of Christ rather than pursue power politics. The most outstanding example of trauma healing and reconciliation within the framework of the Christian church in Rwanda is that of the Butare diocese. As presented in the writing of Laurien Ntezimana, the Butare initiative fuses a Christian perspective with a combined African and psychoanalytic understanding of individual trauma and trauma in community. The therapeutic model is built on the need, first, to deal with the denial that many Rwandans have of what they did or what happened to them and that the Catholic laymen thought was worsened or at best deferred by mindless repetition of liturgical rituals by assassins. Ntezimana suggested that this healing work must begin with "being there for" the parishioner as victim or perpetrator of the violence to affirm God's presence and then move toward a stronger reading of current history and a rereading of God's word (*New Testament* teaching) to confront the facts of evil. Acknowledgment of killing and of a spirit of vengeance must occur before reconciliation and forgiveness are possible. Ntezimana's perspective stresses the foundational character of each step in this process, much as therapists of abuse victims emphasize the need to tell the original story of pain to begin to rebuild. The Burundian bishops' conference was slowly moving toward dealing similarly with the issue of denial and the scars of war, "accepting error" after having looked at the facts.

Although many church members and their leaders participated in or at least facilitated the church's compromising position, others in individual and community settings acted out their convictions in amazing ways in defiance of the prevailing trends. We have told a few of these stories. There are surely more, although far too few. Confronting evil, saving life, and forgiving the perpetrator are the most common constellation of these initiatives, inspired by Christian, Islamic, and traditional Kubandwa belief. The positive consequences of these actions seem transparent, both from a mental health standpoint and from the viewpoint of restoring sociability. The power of forgiveness in resolving sentiments of revenge caught the attention not only of those involved in the conflicts but also of scholars. An exploratory research program, Scientific Studies on the Subject of Forgiveness, is examining the healing consequences of truth telling and forgiveness in 150 cases of perpetrators and victim-survivors who were involved in the South African Truth and Reconciliation Commission (Murray 1998). Others saw the similarity between these African approaches and initiatives rooted in the idea of forgiveness as a powerful tool for restorative justice and diplomacy (Lampman 1999a–c).

Mennonite Explorations

Although Mennonites, working within and beyond the MCC have promoted various peace and reconciliation efforts in North American, European, and other international contexts, little work of this nature had been done in Burundi and Rwanda before the 1993–1994 conflicts there. When the wars broke out, the MCC became involved in helping other agencies, primarily the Quakers and the Zairian Mennonites (from western Zaire). The MCC's actions were typically responses to specific requests received by field coordinators rather than directives from home offices. As already described, these measures included food distributions to both sides of the conflict in selected places in Burundi where local Quakers asked for assistance, seed grain distribution in Rwanda, and blanket and supplementary foods distribution in selected communities in Zaire, as determined by a Zairian-international team. Only after these material programs were in place in 1994 did longer term issues of trauma counseling and reconciliation work emerge as a part of the MCC's activity. These initiatives, like many others, were a combination of ideas and approaches imported from projects in other African settings, developed on the spot, or brought from the West. Here, a few of these initiatives suffice to sketch a picture of what emerged as the Mennonite approach to trauma healing and conflict resolution in the Great Lakes region.

In Bukavu trauma healing and reconciliation work took several directions. The Zairian and French pastors who were part of the Mennonite team in Bukavu were convinced that only repentance and forgiveness on the part of those who had committed atrocities would close the cycle of violence, because the killings were so common and the bitterness ran so deep. They thought that tribunals—without repentance and forgiveness—would only serve to drive the antagonism deeper and to rekindle cycle upon cycle of further vengeance. The ministers on our team included Mukambu ya'Namwisi and Ndjoko Mapombolo Jean of Kinshasa and Daniel Féver of France, who spent many hours speaking to Rwandan men about the need to confess. They were met for the most part with stony silence from men who nevertheless continued to attend the meetings and said they appreciated them.

Another focus of reconciliation and mediation work was in the public context of Bukavu and the South Kivu region—a combined Zairian and Rwandan society—with a great desire to avoid further conflict among Zairians, between Zairians and Rwandans, and among Rwandans. The UN operated as peacekeeper in the larger space of the region, to keep the various armies from engaging. On a smaller scale there were the tensions in the city and in the camps. The MCC was approached by Zairian mediation groups, which had organized several years earlier to respond to calls for help from citizens being harassed by the Zairian military. These groups became actively involved in the mediation of conflict between Zairians and Rwandans when the region was overrun by refugees. They asked for training in mediation skills and for support from international agencies. In early 1999 the MCC was still working with the groups, conducting training workshops and generally lending moral support. In Bukavu this work has gone hand in hand with selected material aid, in particular, a reforestation nursery to restore the hundreds of trees cut down by refugees from 1994 to 1996 and a distribution of blankets to Zairians immediately following the war of late 1996 when the alliance forces routed the Zairian army and drove out the refugees and the old Rwandan militias and military. An American-Zairian couple represents the MCC's interests in Bukavu on a continuing basis—when there is no war there.

A second area of trauma healing and reconciliation work by the MCC in the Great Lakes region of Africa has been in Burundi with the Quaker community—the Evangelical Friends, who have congregations in Rwanda and Burundi. Much of the MCC's involvement has been in the form of emergency food and blankets distributed through local Quaker institutions, with an emphasis on the equitable distribution to both sides in communities, such as Kibimba, that are being torn apart by low-grade warfare. The food being distributed is for the most part beans and lentils from the Canadian Food Bank. The MCC together with the Burundian Quakers endeavors to help where it can to maintain the middle in an otherwise polarized society. At one point this took the form of a "peace presence" of outsiders who worked in local schools or hospitals or who accompanied prominent leaders in their travels to facilitate their easier passage through military roadblocks. The MCC, through its representative in Bujumbura, also promoted dialogues and public forums for the open discussion of national issues. Being there for stressed Burundians to talk to has been a significant dimension of this work, offering hope and encouragement.

A third area of MCC work in the Great Lakes region has come in the form of initiatives among church and national leaders, with inspiration from the All Africa Council of Churches (AACC), headquartered in Nairobi. One of these initiatives was the Mwanza reconciliation meeting of Rwandan Protestant pastors in and outside the country and the background on a series of similar meetings of Rwandan clergy before, during, and following the war. These initiatives reflected the broad role that national councils of churches and ecumenical councils such as the AACC have played in bringing peace to African countries such as South Africa and Mozambique.

Mennonites are not the only players in this process, of course, but this is perhaps where their theology of peace and peacemaking has found direct expression in the ongoing struggle to overcome hostilities in the postcolonial African states. Harold Miller, MCC peace scholar and activist, represents Mennonite interests on the staff of the AACC in Nairobi. He has articulated a general perspective of this thinking in his *Peace and Reconciliation in Africa* (1993). Hizkias Assefa, Eritrean conciliator and mediation expert and head of the Nairobi Peace Initiative, chaired the Mwanza reconciliation meeting of Rwandan pastors and has worked with Mennonites in Somalia, Ethiopia, Mozambique, Sudan, and other African conflict settings. His experiences in these theaters of conflict have built up a background of understanding to the projects in which he becomes involved (see Assefa (1987) on the 1972 negotiations in Sudan). Within as well as beyond Mennonite circles, John Paul Lederach (1997) built up a common culture of knowledge about the potential of peacemaking in a range of conflicts in several dozen countries, including the United States.

A fourth area of Mennonite interest combines the peace perspective with professional experience in psychotherapeutic understanding of the impact of war and prolonged conflict on individuals. The arrival of this combination of interests in Mennonite work in Africa is no doubt due to a critical mass of professionalism in Mennonite institutions and circles as well as to accessibility to the front lines of rehabilitation work in the postwar scene in Africa. In North America a host of Mennonite psychologists, medical doctors, and clergy now routinely deal with the trauma of abuse, rape, victims of crime, and other types of mostly domestic situations. The application of this understanding to the African scene can be sketched in one project with implications for the Great Lakes region.

In 1995 Karl Bartsch, professor of counseling psychology at Pennsylvania State University, and his wife, Evelyn, who is a social worker, began a two-year project with the Diakonia Council of Churches and the Vuleka Trust of Durban, Natal, South Africa, to lead stress and trauma healing workshops for caregivers in South Africa and the Truth and Reconciliation Commission led by Desmond Tutu (Bartsch 1997, p. 5). They were particularly interested in looking at the process of transition to the new postapartheid South Africa and in determining how people who experienced a variety of traumas (bombings, killings, torture, and other kinds of violence) could be helped to find healing and to adjust to the new realities. The violence of Natal, South Africa, made this project timely. At the close of their time in South Africa, after workshops and encounters with many therapists and other resource contacts, the Bartsches prepared a manual (Bartsch 1998) for therapists, pastors, and healers that was quickly translated into Zulu and French. The Bartsches have since returned to private practice in Pennsylvania.

The Bartsches' project is noteworthy for both its highly cosmopolitan inspiration and its local application. The Bartsches' experience in Korea in the 1960s gave them a degree of global awareness as they entered their professional careers. By the time they came to South Africa, the global awareness of war trauma and its effects had become professional wisdom in psychology and affiliated fields of behavioral and social science. The Bartsches were able to participate in the Survivors of Torture Conference in Cape Town (November 1995), in which 80 countries participated, an MCC conference in Chicago in 1996 with therapists from three continents, and the International Conference on Children, War, and Persecution in Maputo in December 1996, with 30 countries represented (Bartsch 1997, p. 9). But their setting for developing caregivers' training was in a local parish in Durban and the Natal countryside and in regional seminars. Thus from the start the Bartsches were being instructed in the cultural context in which their training was to be applied. Perhaps a third feature that accounted for the success of this venture was that the Bartsches are humble senior professionals who realize their need to learn as much as to teach. Therefore they speak of their role as "consultant/trainers to midwives and gardeners" rather than as "professors" (Bartsch 1997, p. 10). In their training sessions they realized early on that they needed to work through what they called cultural gatekeepers, South African personnel who were eager to learn what they had to share but needed to stay in charge of the process (Bartsch 1997, p. 11). The Bartsches' sensitivity to the cultural embeddedness of the nature of trauma and trauma therapy is evident in their discussions of South African cultural diversity and their references to anthropological writings.

The diversity of South African culture led Karl Bartsch to claim that there are a few universal aspects of trauma but that the context and particular meaning of much else is variable. Bartsch described the varied experiences of trauma in the greater Durban area and KwaZulu-Natal Province and the common effects they produced.

> The transition stress was made worse by the ongoing violence. Those people who directly or indirectly experienced killings, house bombings, or other acts of terror knew the effects of trauma in their person, family, and community. For others, the persistent stress of adjusting to new realities weakened the fibers that made up the fabric of their lives. For some, the traumatic violence cut the fibers that held their lives together.
>
> Whether people wear out through accumulating stress or through sudden traumatic events, the effects are the same. Normal patterns of living are disrupted. People feel disconnected from others, feel helpless to manage the events, and often lose faith and hope. (Bartsch 1997, p. 5)

Here, it is possible to sketch only the main lines of Bartsch's approach to culture, trauma, and trauma healing. While holding fast to the core dimension of trauma's effects, much else is culturally variable; indeed, this was so in the cases Bartsch encountered in multicultural Durban and the KwaZulu-Natal Province. One of the core features of Bartsch's orientation is that all persons hold some type of spiritual sensitivity, whether that is formulated as Christian, Muslim, or traditional African belief. He conceptualized this spiritual being as having an inner soul or heart and an outer person or self-image. Through this prism of the person Bartsch delineated a number of dimensions or ranges that constitute the actual person as experienced in his cases. Some South Africans presented a fully Western individualized self-image, whereas others were more attuned to a communal or group identity. Time orientations also varied between future and past, which tended to reflect culture and education; the locus of control of the self ranged from internal to external; finally, the extent to which individuals were shaped psychologically by their social context varied as well, some being "high context" and others being "low context." This grid of contrasting types of persons-in-culture—Bartsch also spoke of them as tensions—permits the therapist to recognize the common and the culturally varying consequences of trauma and the ways in which therapy must bend to suit the individual.[1]

Bartsch also addressed the role of ancestors in identity formation of some of the patients he met in his workshops with trauma victims and other therapists. He saw the ancestors as an extension of the self, a dimension that must be kept in view while coming to terms with a traumatic experience. Bartsch incorporated Desmond Tutu's notion of *Ubuntu* to account for the importance of social relationships and the mutual influence of persons on one another in African society. This sense of human connectedness and of a past orientation is what compels traumatized Africans to want to know what happened to their kinsmen in the Truth and Reconciliation Commission hearings. However, Afrikaaners and other white South Africans, who are supposed to be future oriented, also want to know the truth (Bartsch 1997, p. 18), suggesting that there is more going on here than psychological character orientation. Bartsch's attempt to bridge Western academic psychology and religious worldview with Zulu and African culture in trauma and transition moves us forward in formulating an appropriate and adequate perspective on trauma healing and reconciliation. Especially, it provides important bridges back to the world of the Great Lakes region's trauma expressions, which still largely await attention, and to the paradigms in which they are couched.

Powerful Words and Poisons

For us one of the earliest points of connection to recognizable African perspectives on trauma accounting was Bugingo's observation on the pattern of misfortune in his life. As recounted in section 1.1, Bugingo suspected that his string of misfortunes—his trouble getting into schools despite his good scores, his difficulty with his marriage despite his own, his mother-in-law's, and the chaplain's efforts at mediation, his troubles with his military commanders, his near death in the war of 1990, his near death three times in 1994, his repeated trouble clearing his record of false charges, his situation as a refugee—were the result of sorcery, of others wishing and willing him harm. Although we tried to help him think of a new beginning, Bugingo's self-diagnosis was in keeping with a common line of explanation of misfortune in Central Africa. Although we spoke French with Bugingo, even some English, it was clear that the concept to which he referred was that which in Kinyarwanda is called *kuroga,* to "ensorcell."

A digression is required here to elaborate on this concept and to situate it within Central African beliefs about illness and approaches to healing. *Kuroga* is the Rwandan version of a widespread verbal concept that combines the motive of hostility with the means to carry it out. In other words, this concept encompasses both the anger or ill will toward another and the instrument expressing it (e.g., an injurious word, a blow to the head, or a bit of poison in the drink). This notion is so ancient in Africa that its ultimate root, reconstructed as **-dog* or **-dok,* is in Proto-Bantu lexica of at least 3,000 years ago, and modern derivations of it are found from Cameroon and the Congo coast in the west to the Swahili coast in the east to the Nguni speakers in South Africa and everywhere in between. The notion is not always associated with ill will; sometimes it is used simply to refer to the power of words or the use of powerful words used in curses, but also in blessings and oaths, which may well be its original and central semantic core.

When Bugingo lined up his misfortunes and recalled the exact words that had been spoken by others before those events about what would befall him, he was drawing the logical conclusion that these utterances had caused or could have led to his misfortunes. Had not his father warned him about letting others take his marital troubles to diviners? Had not his commanding officer told him "you will die" before the Battle of Akagera in 1990?

Although Bugingo was greatly relieved to hear us encourage him to forget the past and to try to live every day as if it counted anew, he still dwelled on the power of his own words and the power of our words to him. In his second letter to us in March 1995 he recalled the encounter of mid-December and conducted a mini-ritual to set straight his own world of words. He wrote:

> I want to go back [in thoughts] to our conversation. . . . Several sentences in [John's] counsel came to mind. Concerning the judgment of others, certainly leaders, I apologize and regret having often made judgments, rightly or wrongly, in this place being mostly revolted both internally and externally. This was totally groundless given that the work of leading is not easy, errors are always possible, such as the wrong appreciation of situations and individuals. May God forgive me in the name of our savior Jesus Christ.

Bugingo realized that his own words of criticism of those in power, whom he feared, and those in charge of the refugee camps, about whom he had complained, might actually affect his relationship with them. Before me, his new friend-diviner-confessor, he was retracting these possibly powerful words. He then sealed this retraction with more powerful words by invoking the name of Jesus Christ.

If misfortunes can be caused by the utterance of hurtful or condemning words as well as by other acts of aggression, then the injuries between humans might be healed through the intervention of blessed powerful words and medicines and the purging of poisons by other means. Communities can be healed by confessing and purifying and sacrificing before the spiritual authorities.

Although we connected with Rwandan ideas of misfortune and healing through the concept of *kuroga* (also spelled *kuloga*), there was more to learn about the Rwandan-African approach to healing in the aftermath of war, as suggested in late prewar writing by Pierre-Claver Rwangabo (1993). Rwangabo was a pharmacist who was instrumental in the development of the Butare-based INRS section on African medicine. After surviving the 1994 war as a moderate southern Hutu, he was appointed governor of Butare district. When we met him briefly in January 1995, he was busy with monetary changes that had been instituted by the new government. We congratulated him on his just-published book and promised to read it as soon as possible. Accompanied by a single soldier bodyguard, he appeared tired and vulnerable. Tragically, within a month he was assassinated in an ambush as he was returning from a meeting in Kigali. The government said it was Hutu guerrillas from Zaire; other sources suggested that he had criticized the government in which he served once too often and was thus eliminated. Did Rwangabo realize the extent of the truth of his own statement "It is not the poison itself which kills, but the malevolent words" (Rwangabo 1993). This is a perspective that proves helpful in understanding the likely course that healing the wounds of war may take.

Rwangabo presents Rwandan medicine as if it is a part of the modern reality in his country rather than a fossilized system at odds with modern medicine. Thus the causal domains of Rwandan medicine are divided at a general level between the "physical and mystical causes." Diseases range across a variety of types and can be attributed to either causal category. Rwangabo's medical training is evident in his listing of disease types, as follows: parasitic diseases, microbial diseases, systemic diseases and bodily accidents, gynecological and obstetric diseases, and psychomental and behavioral diseases. Under the last group he identified current psychopathological conditions that entail abnormal behavior as understood even in traditional thought and diseases believed to be caused by broken prohibitions and beliefs about ancestral *(abazimu)* and other spirits *(ibitega, amahembe, nyabingi, amasheitani, amaji)*, which often are identified in relation to mental illnesses.

Rwangabo (1993) noted that because most pathological conditions have a physical dimension and a mystical or nonphysical dimension, in African thinking the etiology affects the way a condition's therapy is arranged. The decision to seek physical therapy has to do with the context in which it occurs, its severity, the response to treatment, and other related matters. To show how this added dimension operates, Rwangabo discussed at greater length precisely those dimensions that postwar healing covers: poisoning *(uburozi)* and the ancestors *(abazimu)*.

The use of chemical poisons is a serious problem, with a variety of powerful concoctions known to kill with a small dosage. The extent and nature of the problem is highlighted by Taylor's (1992) research findings, which identified the most common type of poisoning as being that between brothers (22%) and various other lineage relationships (a total of 51%), as well as between neighbors (12%), between occupational and business associates or rivals (10%), and between spouses (16%) and other in-laws (Taylor 1992, p. 76). As already suggested, poisoning is seen as an extension of the power of words, in particular, harmful words. Rwandan therapy for poisoning consists of antidotes, prophylaxis, and purgatives taken to cleanse the stomach. It is also a kind of inverse purging of the system of undesirable elements, and in that sense it may be seen as an expression of the central paradigm of "flow and blockage" as Taylor understands Rwandan medicine. It is perhaps, then, not so surprising that in a society in which poisoning is so common, heightened political tension might escalate to genocide.[2]

The ancestors are accorded power to both inflict disease and to overcome, indeed prevent, disease and misfortune. *Abazimu,* the most common term in Rwanda and Burundi for ancestors, is also a widespread Proto-Bantu term found across central and southern Africa. The ancestors are considered to safeguard the health of their descendants and to sanction those who forget to remember them. In the well-known African view of ancestors, there are those who are near and those who are distant, those who are beneficent and those who are prone to be malevolent. Ancestors are considered the mediators to *Imaana* (God), and it is to them that prayers are given. With the war there was an entire host of new ancestors—the newly dead—who were there as part of the equation and with whom one needed to come to terms for life to go on. Would the next step be to avenge their deaths? Or would it be to somehow break the cycle of violence? From where would that inspiration originate?

Mizimu and Ngozi in the Aftermath of the Zimbabwean Civil War

Other wars approaching the Rwandan War in horror have been studied in the longer term. Years and decades rather than months are required to see the progress from mass dislocation and deep shock to emotional acknowledgment of the events, grieving, and the eventual reconstruction of a memory, including the recognition of the morally restorative ancestors. Werbner's *Tears of the Dead* (1991, p. 152), on the aftermath of war in Zimbabwe, showed that part of the response to war is to reestablish memory of the prewar ancestors—the *midzimu*—and to bring them back into closer range while putting in place those who died a violent death and were not properly buried—the *ngozi.*

In the Kalanga lineage of southern Zimbabwe that Werbner studied before the war and revisited in the late 1980s, these ancestors were reconnected to the community of the living within the Ndebele-inspired *ngoma* rituals. The dead were sorted out into good or useful mediums and threatening or harmful mediums, that is, the spirits of those who had died a violent death or had not been properly buried or those who had killed others wantonly. This 10-year sorting-out of ancestral spirits following a war calls to mind the spirit categories in Swaziland. There, *ngoma* spirits were regularly differentiated into those who were "victims of Swazi wars," "those who died by drowning and received no proper burial," nature spirits, and the lineal ancestors. The presence of a class of victims of Swazi meant that they remember the spirits of the early 19th-century wars. At least, the memories have been built, the stories are strong, and divination and healing rituals incorporate them almost as a paradigm in dealing with lesser traumas of today (Janzen 1992, pp. 95–96, 99).

The focused ritual operation of reconnecting to the prewar ancestors and marginalizing—or contextualizing—the *ngozi,* thus creating a nuanced worldview of healing (and of exorcism or mediumship), is a powerful trauma treatment. The ancestors are an extension of living humans who have suffered all the horrors of war; the ancestors themselves are the icons of those terrible moments, some having been killed and others having done the killing. What we saw in Rwanda was all about fear, shock, denial, blaming the other—all the emotions that Western therapists associate with long-term psychological damage that takes years if not lifetimes to heal. Because the collective trauma is so great, the spirit paradigms in the healing process may continue, as in Swaziland, for decades or even centuries.

The Dead Remembered

Not surprisingly, in light of the postwar rituals for the dead in Zimbabwe, in Rwanda tentative first steps were being taken to acknowledge what had happened and to begin building a memory of the dead. As was described in section 2.1, in late December 1994 bourgmestre Nkurikiyinka Damien requested plastic sheeting from the Salvation Army to line and cover the new burial pits into which would be reburied the remains of some of Kayenzi's 8,000 victims, to the extent that they could be found and disintered from the awful, hastily dug mass graves in the killing days of May and June 1994. We met a number of individuals who, as surviving adults, were seeking out widows and orphans of their lineages and reestablishing bonds. An uncle or aunt here, a niece or nephew there, would become the new unit within which memory of the dead parents, siblings, uncles and aunts, grandparents would be kept alive, that is, honored.

On April 6, 1995, at the one-year anniversary of the outbreak of the Rwandan catastrophe, the memorial services and commemorations increased in number; newspapers remembered the occasion and took stock of the state of affairs in Rwanda and Burundi. The following poem was among the most poignant written on this occasion (N'kuba 1995).

Our Dead Are Not Dead

It was twelve months ago
[Only] one hundred days sufficed
to cause a million of our people
to disappear.

Today, more than ever
Our dead call to us.

Dead children
Dead adults
Dead women
Dead elders?

They are here amongst us
They live in our souls
They animate our hearts.

They remain everywhere
They are in the wind
Which, alone, carried their last cry.

They are in the seas
Which swallowed their final breaths.
They are in the earth
Which devoured them alive.

Our dead are not dead!

The poem speaks eloquently and reverently of the living dead who are in their repose yet among the living. They continue to speak to the living.

In many places physical monuments were erected to remember the dead. In some communities the skulls of the mass murdered were piled up in a public shrinelike location and the rest of the remains were put in a mass burial. In other communities the sites of mass killings in churches and schools were left untouched to memorialize the victims and to remind all who passed by these places what had happened.

The school in Gikongoro in southern Rwanda is an example of this. The authorities who succeeded Laurent Bucyibaruta decided to leave the dead where they had been killed, in classrooms of a large school building. Tutsi were said to have been advised to gather "for their own protection" on April 7, 1994, the day after President Habyarimana's plane was shot down. From April 20 to April 23 about 25,000 Gikongoro Tutsi were killed by Hutu militias, according to local authorities. Few Tutsi survive in Gikongoro (Santoro 1997). Elsewhere, the dead who were killed under similar circumstances in churches were also left as a memorial of the Rwandan holocaust or were memorialized in a mass tomb, as in Kibimba.

Midwife Nyinawabibi Charlotte from Butare told us that new babies (i.e., those born after the genocide) are named after murdered family members, that people plant trees surrounding sites of mass graves, and that special belongings of the deceased (such as a chair or a spear) are guarded and not used by surviving family members, to thus honor the deceased's memory.

These are but a few examples of how the survivors were beginning to hold memorial services, conduct reburials where possible, and reestablish social ties to remnants of their families. Others were trying to deal with guilt in addition to grief, wondering why they killed or how to find cleansing and release from the nightmares that haunt them.

In Burundi many people hope that they will be able to get through each crisis without sliding into a Rwanda-style conflagration. There is little time or political certainty for memory building. Even the recognition of victims of the massacres of 1993 as "victims of genocide" is seen by some as divisive partisanship.

The Dead and the Drums

Invoking ancestors to come to terms with the recently dead of course raised the question of whose ancestors and images were to be invoked. Drums, drumming, rhythm, song, and dance have been used in many Central African settings to couch the active memory of ancestors in the lives of living humans. The voices of the ancestors are widely held to speak through song and dance and drum rhythms and the dreams, visions, and trances experienced in connection with their performances. Yet even in this regard, Katihabwa's deculturation hypothesis for explaining the crisis in Rwanda and Burundi seems to apply. In our experience and in the experience of those we spoke with, the absence of a legitimate format in which to lament, to call for help, was painfully evident. Ilumbe Mwanasala (section 4.5) observed that the Burundians do not sing, do not cry, do not dance. Although we may call into question his assertion, there may be some truth in his perception that the Burundians were not able readily to express their strongest feelings in the midst of crisis and violence.

Drum idioms were extremely highly centralized in Rwanda and Burundi and were co-opted by the structures of the kingdoms, which were destroyed in the early 1960s. What happened to official drum culture in Rwanda is evident in the National Museum, as explained by acting director Bazatsinda Thomas (see section 2.7). The exhibits retained some of their most potent symbols of Rwandan nationhood in prominently displayed drums, specifically, two drums named Busarure and Rwagagaza, which Bazatsinda said represented aspects of the composite power and authority of the traditional Rwandan state. Before the collapse of the kingdom, the full array of state power represented in drums included (1) the national drum, representing the sovereignty of the kingdom; (2) the war drum, which was sounded whenever the need arose to call the army together (when it was beaten once, all the local *colline* drums would repeat the call); and (3) the Queen Mother drum, which represented the principle of alternative power to that of the national or royal drum, in the sense of a check on abuses of royal power. Then there were Busarure and Rwagagaza, representing the powers and procedures of transition, or succession, of enthronement. Busarure, covered with blood, its two drumsticks resting on a traditional drum stand, evidenced the animal sacrifices that had commemorated the shifts in state power during the dangerous moment of interregnum and succession.

The first three drums were presumably destroyed, thought Bazatsinda, in connection with the populist Palipehutu revolution in 1959.[3] But why had the two drums of enthronement survived? One answer, reflecting the Hutu Republic under whose rule the National Museum was built, might be that these two drums, as functions of statecraft, were associated with earlier kingdoms in western Rwanda from which the historical institutions of state had originated centuries earlier.[4]

In Bazatsinda's telling, the final chapter of the Rwandan royal drums came with the kings' conversion to Catholicism. Somewhat ruefully, he told us that "King Kigeri V gave his drums to Jesus," as if he had really abdicated power, thus ending the dynasty. Rwandan drum rhythms are now carried on by musical groups and in churches and schools, he said. These museum drums reminded us of other ghosts of former empires, such as the Hapsburgs in Vienna and the Romanovs in St. Petersburg. Although the dynasties were closed, the trappings of empire lingered on, and the haunting echoes of former power continued to sound. But we may well ask whether anything has replaced the condensed symbolic power of these dynasties—the drums of state in Rwanda and Burundi—as the nuanced tools of social processes, especially for weeping, expressing illness, pain, and grief.

In many societies surrounding Rwanda and Burundi drum and song and dance culture—regularly translated as "drum of affliction" from *ngoma*[5] (drum), with song and dance being an association of the commonly afflicted around a particular adversity—is integrally used in coming to terms with the spirits of the dead and with misfortune. Drums of affliction have often been identified with a selected range of issues having to do with either internal societal experience or perceived external threat. Internal societal experiences can be such dilemmas as infertility or fetal wastage; chronic headaches, hernias, or other physical afflictions; occupational difficulties such as chronic failure in hunting and difficulties with particular types of game; family organizational problems such as segmentation and leadership or getting reconnected with the lineal ancestors; environmental dilemmas such as poisonous vipers and handling them, rainmaking and rain stopping; and social factors of long-term changes that adversely affect the domestic community, such as those having to do with long-distance trade, labor migration, and perceived diseases and social breakdown conditions accompanying these issues. In Zimbabwe the restless spirits of those killed in war live on in the memories of the drums, rhythms, songs, and performances. In Swaziland *sangoma* diviner-healers (those who "do *ngoma*") come to terms with a category of spirit—the victims of Swazi warriors, thus "our former enemies"—that died a violent death and are still there, visiting, reminding, the living 200 years later. They are invoked to account for illness and are either exorcised or incorporated by the afflicted individual as a spiritual companion.

Ngoma orders have emerged in response to these types of issues at various times and places throughout the region where the notion and the term *ngoma* are in the cultural repertoire and where no other source of a solution exists, such as an excellent court structure to deal with injustices or inequities, a dynamic chiefship or state that handles solutions "from above," or a modern welfare society that can support the persons struck by misfortunes. In the *ngoma* response to such adversities, it is the sufferers themselves who unite to listen to and support one another and to possibly shape the environment in which they live.

As a social institution or movement, a given *ngoma* order is usually characterized by a fairly fluid networklike organization, in which local nodes or cells meet occasionally to perform listening, singing, voicing, and drumming rituals—the core of doing *ngoma*. Individual novices, under the tutelage of their sponsoring healers, themselves former novice-patients, are brought together and encouraged to "bring out" their distress, to formulate their own stories in confessions, dream presentations, and outpourings of experiences, and thus to achieve mastery in the presentation of their own selves in every sense.

Articulating Metaphors of Difficult Experience

The songs and images of the self-presentation in the *ngoma* rituals, especially in the more advanced stages of the novitiate's therapy, feature the deft use of central metaphors of the affliction, trauma, or chronic distress. I (John) am using here the commonsensical definition of the metaphor as a figure of speech in which a word or phrase literally denoting one kind of object or idea is used in place of another to suggest a likeness or analogy between them. These articulations in visible images drawn from the stock of myths, proverbs, society, and common rhetoric give the inchoate and troublesome difficult experience a tangible expression that is less threatening and more amenable to some kind of treatment or accommodation. These images sometimes come from the dreams and fears of the sufferer-novice and may include ancestral and spirit figures, which must then be reformulated by the diviner or *ngoma* leader into the new self-presentation. Sometimes these self-expressions emerge from the call-and-response song-and-dance format in which the close co-singers and co-dancers help the sufferer to bring out the ill. Thus in one Cape Town session (Janzen 1992, p. 114), the *ngoma* participants repeated to a participant the phrase "come out of your pot . . . I have news of your household. Hey, . . . come out, I have news of your household."

The subject here was seen as confined, locked, choked off, in need of emerging to get in touch with his family. Other images are from the world of natural expressions often used in rituals of mediation with the mystical and the hidden. The crab, *nkala,* is a favorite image, because it scuttles from the sandy shores into the water or because it goes in and out of its holes that go beneath the water, the ambience of the spiritual and ancestral world, and reemerge into the visible world of human experience. The following song from the coastal Congo *ngoma* named Lemba exhibits a powerful three-part metaphor of the successful novice couple having overcome their ill and risen to priestly prominence just like the sun moves on its course across the sky (Janzen 1982, p. 118).

> That which was a "stitch" of pain
> Has become the path to the priesthood.
> It has caused to rise
> the sun of Lemba.
> My death occurred
> in the Lemba father.
> Now there is life in Lemba.

Widely, then, there is evidence in central and southern African healing traditions surrounding Rwanda and Burundi of the process by which chronic and crisis pain are transformed into sources of healing and strength. Although this takes on a culturally particular form in drum and song-and-dance ritual, it is clearly a more widespread human practice.

Imagination of Fresh Metaphors and the Search for New Beginnings

Where would new metaphors come from that would allow these war-torn societies to move toward overcoming the crisis that had festered and finally engulfed them? Following the massacres in

Burundi in 1993 and in Rwanda in 1994, many people were in denial, refusing to or not knowing how to grieve. Others were plotting revenge. The search for metaphors and new beginnings had just begun. But where could Rwandans and Burundians go to find new metaphors to replace the lost dynasties: the deculturation of which Katihabwa speaks, the mutual poisonings of siblings, the terrible hatred and bitterness between the two sides that have warred against each other for several decades and caused millions to die? Only the Rwandans and Burundians can create these metaphors. However, we can identify those initiatives we noticed that may be the beginning of collective rebuilding. Comparison with other societies that have gone through deep genocidal trauma suggests that fresh starts take decades, generations, and centuries, if they come at all.

At a conference on catastrophes in the 18th century (held at the University of California, Berkeley, in 1995) Nigerian scholar Olupona Jacob, on hearing our account of the impasses of Great Lakes society, recognized a situation similar to what his West African forebears faced during the interminable 19th-century slave wars between the city-states of Ile Ife, Oyo, and others. Many descendants of war victims and displaced exiles live today scattered throughout West Africa and the New World. The cult of Oduduwa, one of the many Orisha gods, moved into ascendance as a primary deity in parallel with the rise of a common Yoruba language and identity. A common identity transcended the particular city-state and regional identities.

Olupona also compared the challenge facing the Great Lakes region's people with that faced by the South Africans in putting apartheid behind them and moving on. One of the most commonly mentioned images for "the new South Africa" is the creation of a nonracial society in which the racial terms *black, colored,* and *white* are no longer used and the barriers are dissolved. The parallels to the Great Lakes region are easy enough to draw, and some individuals do indeed see the only hope for the future in rejecting the categorization spelled out by Hutu, Tutsi, and Twa. But attempts in Burundi to outlaw the use of these terms and their elimination from identity cards in Rwanda and Burundi have not brought to an end the violence committed on a categorical basis. As a consequence, these identity categories continue to be rallying points for those who see themselves as oppressed and excluded. However, it is hard to imagine a return to a peaceful society in the region without some attempt to create a culture of inclusion in which not only are these identity categories minimized but also an effort is made to create and use a collective image around which leaders and people can rally in the creation of a new legitimacy and moral grounding.

In these pages we have reported on those local and often private initiatives that create a local situation of neighborliness, which may be based on or certainly creates an image of a different and better society than that of civil war. For example, we heard of a Hutu neighbor who returned from Zaire to live next to his Tutsi neighbor, a Tutsi victim who confronted and forgave a Hutu perpetrator of violence, a Hutu victim who confronted and forgave the Tutsi killer of his close kin, and a Hutu woman who saved the lives of and adopted children of a Tutsi neighbor who was killed. These individual actions are clearly based on an image of a different society from that based on ethnic difference. They constitute many building blocks for an inclusive society.

Could the new metaphors arise from a rereading of the past? This was what the joint Rwandan-Burundian theater troupe Renaissance (Mutabaruka) suggested in their postwar play *Nyaruteja, the Place Where the Kings Sat Down.* Kalisa Tharcisse (a Rwandan Tutsi exile in Bujumbura) and Sibazuri Marie-Louise (a Burundian Hutu), president and vice-president of the Renaissance theater troupe, respectively, led their group to intentionally fashion itself as interethnic and international. By late 1994 *Nyaruteja* had been performed in Kigali and Butare. The drama recalls an 18th-century peace treaty made between the kingdoms of Rwanda and Burundi following a particularly horrific war at Kirundo, near today's border between the two countries, a place that even today has the connotation of "many dead Rwandans." The purpose of the play, said its producers, was to encourage the people to think of peace and to overcome the cycle of violence. The kings were remembered as heroes of peacemaking.

Perhaps new metaphors could be drawn from the widespread religion known as Kubandwa, which existed and continues to exist everywhere across the Great Lakes region as a popular ritual among commoners and the prominent alike in the centralized kingdoms that emerged from the 12th to the 15th century, societies such as Rwanda and

Burundi, Buganda, Ntoro, Soga, the Haya of Tanzania, and elsewhere (De Heusch 1966; CERUKI 1976; Pennacini 1998). Kubandwa is a common religion that worships the High God Imaana through the prophet Lyangombe (or Kiranga in Burundi). Kubandwa offers salvation to everyone, as an oft-repeated song of Lyangombe makes unambiguously clear: "that the Hutu worship me, that the Twa worship me, and that the Tutsi worship me" (CERUKI 1976, p. 120).

The identity of Lyangombe or Kiranga has been much debated. Some sources have him coming south from Ntoro, the 12th-century ancestor of Bunyoro in Uganda, as refugee of the BuCwezi dynasty there. The BuCwezi or Chwezi continue to be recognized as healing spirits over a wide region of eastern and central Africa. All sources, however, feature the martyr death of Lyangombe and his followers, although the circumstances and the import of their deaths seem unusual alongside the reverence offered them. The legends state that on his trek southward Lyangombe was gored by a buffalo during a hunt near present-day Butare and died, whereupon his followers followed him in death to honor him (CERUKI 1976, p. 23).

The possibility of Kubandwa and the cult of Lyangombe/Kiranga as a postgenocide object of restoration was on the minds of some Rwandans and Burundians with whom we spoke; they said that it could be studied and that this might bring Rwandans together around their common history. The scholars were interested in telling us how Kubandwa had been combated by the Catholic Church and how it had been transformed from open public ritual to secretive family practice in the homestead. Each household and family once had its priests, and many are said to still practice Kubandwa in secret or in conjunction with Christian festivities. Some puzzled as to why the missionaries had so strongly fought against Kubandwa, since the same God, Imaana, was supported by the churches. Thomas Kamanzi, newly appointed head of the Institute of Rwandan Studies in Butare, recalled the song to Lyangombe in the Kubandwa rites that had stressed that "all Tutsi, Hutu, and Twa must worship Lyangombe," and indeed memories of precolonial Kubandwa observations were that all worshipped together in a local community. The Renaissance theater group was in active contact with Kubandwa followers in some of the refugee camps, as a way of encouraging spiritual healing.

However, the reactions of others with whom we spoke about Kubandwa as a focus for grieving and for memory building was more ambiguous. Some said that Kubandwa had been discredited and was a matter of history. It was no longer a living tradition. Others were concerned about the recognition of ancestors, because those ancestors would encourage retribution on the descendants of their killers. Bugingo, the Rwandan refugee in Zaire (section 1.1) whose parents had followed Kubandwa and were not Christian, defended Christ as mediator for the following reasons:

> Lyangombe and Christ were different. Under Lyangombe it was acceptable to take vengeance; Christ did not offer this. In Kubandwa adherents would dream of their ancestors or receive visions from them, with instructions to seek vengeance on the descendants of their own killers. Thus this sentiment is at the source of killing and may account for the seemingly random pattern of killing. Christ does not condone it, even though Christians might kill. Many Christians practice other rites in secret, such as Kubandwa, and their duplicitous character weakens their morals, so that when there is tension, they explode.

It remains unclear from our vantage point which confession or cultural ideology such a process of imagining the metaphors of social wholeness might take in Rwanda and Burundi. Even the restoration of a powerful state will need to establish the authority of balance of power and methods of succession, not to mention democratic representation. But in Rwanda all prior norms were shattered and central symbols were desecrated. Katihabwa's deculturation hypothesis rings profoundly true.

As in other horrendous catastrophes in other societies in the past, newly invented practices may emerge to provide understanding of the Rwandan holocaust. Perhaps the pastoral renewal movement of Butare will offer an adequate explanatory system within Christianity. Perhaps there will be a revival of Kubandwa around the martyr figure of Lyangombe. Or perhaps there will be a flourishing of independent Christian prophets and healers.

This work of creating new metaphors on the ash heaps of the crises and catastrophes of the past will need to engage poets, healers, priests and pastors, teachers, politicians, judges, and everyone else as an exercise in imagining community (Anderson 1983).

6.2 *Justice:* The Precondition to Peace

In the domain of Mbuye, in precolonial Burundi, according to memory, a peasant sought justice following the king's attempt to take his land. The peasant, named Murima, was accused by the king's people of having encroached on the king's lands near the court. Murima, fearing for his life, took refuge with the Queen Mother. Mwenzi, the king, pursued Murima, but he was protected by the Queen Mother, who told the king that "all contacts with Murima will take place through the abashingantahe.*" When the hearing convened, Murima claimed long-time occupancy of the land. There were witnesses: each side's [witnesses] planted the lance and brought beer before the Queen Mother. When the* bashingantahe *ruled, they said that "Murima had spoken well," for no one could openly say that the king was wrong. But because of the ruling the king returned the land. Murima concluded, "The cause of my joy is the refuge given me by the wife of Lyangombe."*—Nsanze (1980, pp. 17–18)

In Ruhango, near Gitarama, there is a rock called the Rock of Kamegeli. It is named after Kamegeli, a councilor of the Mwami of Rwanda, who falsely accused another man. He was found out, and received the punishment he had requested for the other man. Kamagori's village was destroyed, he was taken captive. The Mwami said, "You're an evil man; you deserve to be roasted alive as you were going to do to the innocent man." The rock was heated, and he was grilled alive on it. This was the Mwami's justice and wisdom.—Laurent Bucyibaruta, former governor of the Rwandan prefecture of Gikongoro, in Mushweshwe refugee camp, eastern Zaire

The victims of genocide, in their eternal rest, are watching us all. They are dead, victims of a tyrannical regime. They dream, for those who escaped and other groups making up Rwandan society, of a Rwanda in which justice wins over brute force.—the Rwandan "attorney general" (Procureur de la République près le Tribunal de Première Instance de Kigali) Nsanzuwera François-Xavier, at a press conference in Brussels, Belgium, May 11, 1995, to explain why he took a leave of absence from his post in Kigali to plead before the international community for help in restoring the courts

These pithy accounts of judicial institutions live on in memory in Rwanda and Burundi in which modern justice has so terribly failed the people. The first story, from Burundi, exalts the principle of justice not corrupted by power. It shows the judicial force of the council of judges that represents all of society's segments and classes and of the Queen Mother who offsets the power of the king. In the second story, from Rwanda, the king defends the falsely accused innocent and punishes the corrupt court councilor, a punishment so severe that it makes us cringe. Ironically, this story was told to us by a man who allegedly was instrumental in the genocide in the region where he governed (see section 1.5). These stories are remembered because people long for the principles that are illustrated in them and the peace that comes from the integrity they embody.

The third quotation is about the struggle to reestablish the machinery of justice in postwar Rwanda. Attorney General Nsanzuwera François-Xavier, exhausted and overwhelmed, took leave from his post in April 1995 and appeared in Europe, where he gave a press conference to voice his frustrations (Nsanzuwera 1995). Apparently, he was one of the few judges to survive the genocide and the war and could speak from a historical perspective. In 1993 Nsanzuwera wrote a book warning that the Rwandan judiciary had fallen into the grip of executive power and, "more than ever, fear reigned and few dared to denounce arbitrary actions. They took refuge behind silence" (Nsanzuwera 1993) In 1995 his fears and disappointments were of a different order. He expressed his disappointment in the international community for not helping reconstitute the Rwandan judiciary after the genocide. Meanwhile, the underfunded UNHCR was slowly preparing the International Tribunal of the Genocide in Arusha. Not only had judicial institutions failed to avert the conflicts that led to war, but they were also still in a weak or paralyzed condition. Many judges had been killed in Rwanda before or during the war; others fled and were in exile. Several who had stayed were killed or quit their posts. The Supreme Court had yet to be named by early 1995.

In this section we seek to identify the link between justice and peace in the current setting of Rwanda and Burundi to discern the nature of the link between the quest for "just peace" (Lederach 1999) and the winding down of the continuing cycle of violence. We explore a kind of hypothesis that rests on an analogy between the victim's continuing war trauma and the perpetrator's abuse of justice or the continuation of impunity. The impulse for revenge that is driven by the open wound of unresolved war trauma is paralleled by the cycles of fear and retaliation that come from the absence of retributive justice.

To be sure, the principles of justice and the rule of law were violated repeatedly and massively not only during the recent troubles of 1993 and 1994 in Rwanda and Burundi but also in the months and years leading up to them. More seriously, these principles continue to be violated. In Burundi the widows of Kibimba complained that their husbands' assassins were still at large, that they were in fact still in office in the local communes. Others complained that President Ndadaye's assassins were free and circulating with total impunity. The Supreme Court in Gitega was closed indefinitely and had been since the president's slaying in October 1993. In Rwanda judges were afraid for their lives during the latter days of the MRND regime, fearing to prosecute cases sent up to them by lower courts. The survivors of the genocide complained that justice was slow in coming. The few judicial officials who remained were barely making a dent in the dossiers piled on their desks. The refugees in Zaire complained that many people were being falsely accused of involvement in the massacres and arbitrarily arrested, causing them to fear returning home. The Rwandan prisons were overflowing with those accused of human rights violations, although there were many complaints of arrests on trumped-up charges against the innocent.

Two Courts Come To Life To Try the Perpetrators of Genocide

In Rwanda, despite the complete destruction of the courts and the abuse of justice leading up to the war, judicial institutions were restored to come to terms with the genocide. The International Criminal Tribunal for Rwanda (ICTR) was established by UN Security Council Resolution 955 in November 1994 as part of a response to the ethnic cleansing wars in the former Yugoslavia (United Nations 1997). The Rwandan part of the court was set up in Arusha, Tanzania, whereas the court for Yugoslavian war crimes sat in The Hague. South African judge Richard Goldstone, who had presided over some of the court cases of the crimes of apartheid, was selected to create the working infrastructure of the court and the basis of its investigations. When we were in Rwanda in late 1994 and early 1995, we met the first international investigators and their Rwandan counterparts in Kigali preparing to comb the countryside for evidence and witnesses. Despite delays caused by diplomatic and bureaucratic wrangling, shortages of funds for equipped chambers in Arusha, and criticism of corruption and the slow pace of action, six judges had been elected by the UN Security Council by 1995. By 1996 they had indicted 21 of the major perpetrators, 13 of whom were actually in detention. Cases began to be heard in 1997. The UN Security Council had laid out the basic terms of judgment and procedures. However, many Rwandans were disappointed that the ICTR could deliver only a judgment of life imprisonment, especially since it went after major offenders.

Meanwhile, the Rwandan government set about to reconstruct its national court, with far fewer resources, a decimated judiciary, and circumstances that were totally overwhelming for those who survived (as seen in the case of Attorney General Nsanzuwera), with Rwanda's dismal prisons crammed with up to 130,000 suspects. Nevertheless, under the direction of Gerald Gahima, *Chef de Cabinet* of the Ministry of Justice, offices for investigations were set up, the judicial staff was given crash training courses, and a functioning court began to take form. Rwanda benefited from some financial support for these initiatives from several Western countries that realized the importance of the restoration of a judiciary to the ultimate hope of restoring peace. The Parliament argued and approved unique legislation (called the Organic Law of August 30, 1996) for crimes against humanity perpetrated from October 1990 to December 1994. This included the War of 1990 about which Bugingo told (see section 1.1), the massacres of 1992, the genocide and war of 1994, and the killings of the RPF as they took control of the country. Criminal charges were identified as belonging in four categories:

> Category 1 included (a) the planners, organizers, instigators, supervisors, and leaders of genocide or a crime against humanity; (b) people in positions of authority at national, prefectoral, communal, sector, or cell level, or in a political party, the army, religious organizations, or in a militia who perpetrated or fostered such crimes; (c) notorious murderers who by virtue of the zeal or excessive malice with which they committed atrocities, distinguished themselves in their areas of residence or wherever they passed; (d) persons who committed acts of sexual torture. Category 2 included persons whose criminal acts or whose acts of criminal participation place them among perpetrators, conspirators, or accomplices of intentional homicide or serious assault against a person, causing his or her death; Category 3 was defined as people whose criminal acts made them guilty of other serious assaults against the person; Category 4 was reserved for people who committed offenses against property. (Rwanda Embassy Web site).

The Organic Law stipulated the obligatory death penalty for Category 1 offenders, if convicted. Of the more than 100,000 accused prisoners, only about 2,000 were considered in a preliminary listing to be in this category; they were identified on the Rwandan Embassy Internet List of "Planners, Organizers, Instigators, Supervisors, and Leaders of Genocide" (see Figure 21). Moving at a much more rapid pace than the Arusha court, the Rwandan court tried its first cases by late December 1996, and by February 16, 1997, the Rwandan court had sentenced 11 of 12 Category 1 suspects to death (the other suspect was defined as a Category 2 and was given life imprisonment). In April 1998, 22 of those convicted of Category 1 crimes were executed by firing squad at several well-publicized venues in Rwanda (Pan African News Agency 1998; Brittain 1998).

The strategy of the Arusha and Rwandan courts and the consequences of their actions on the waiting and watching world—the people of Rwanda, those in prison, and those in one of the four categories but still at large—began to become apparent in the days and weeks that followed these first executions. The Rwandan court had closely followed the proceedings of the South African Truth and Reconciliation Commission as a prospective model for some of the masses of prisoners in categories 2–4. These suspects were offered reductions in sentence if they entered guilty pleas, detailed their criminal actions, and identified those who had been with them in crime. Only after the executions did prisoners begin to enter guilty pleas. In May 1997 one of the "top fish" in custody in Arusha, former Prime Minister Kambanda Jean, pleaded guilty to having helped direct the genocide (Brittain 1998). It remains to be seen whether this strategy will turn the minds of those thousands who are still awaiting trial.

Although the Rwandan court was at first criticized for its slow pace, later it came under heavy criticism for its rapid jury-less trials that basically gave the defendants no rights to counsel. Changes have been made to permit defense attorneys access to the convicted, although in effect Rwanda has said that this is a luxury it cannot afford. Under pressure from international civil rights and human rights agencies, Rwanda has instituted various measures to assist defendants in their preparations. A screening commission called the Commission de Triage has been formed; with the help of foreign legal groups, the Commission provides a semblance of counsel for defendants. There is a keen realization that unless the government of Rwanda wins the hearts and minds of its people, it is fighting an uphill battle. It must be seen as dispensing justice evenhandedly. This is difficult because almost all prisoners are Hutu, and the government is perceived as Tutsi dominated. But, as one writer observed, it is to the Rwandan government's credit that the thousands of prisoners who languish in jails have not been summarily killed. A move was afoot at the time of this writing to release the 2,000 children in Rwanda's prisons.

A serious problem for both the Arusha and Rwandan courts has been the vulnerability of witnesses. In 1996 over 200 genocide survivors were killed by former military, militia, or others who had returned to Rwanda from Zaire or who made raids back into Rwanda for this purpose (United Nations 1997). In one such raid in 1997 in the northwest region, 600 prisoners were released. Such actions scare those who know something or someone and who fear that someone knows that they know it. This fear leads directly to the hardening of the sentiment of impunity of the perpetrators of crimes and the prospect of further conflict as those perpetrators eliminate witnesses against them. The ICTR, following the killings of a number of witnesses in its celebrity cases, instituted measures to protect the witnesses from being identified, such as shielding their voices from being directly heard in the courtroom and using aliases to identify them.

Judicial Situation in Burundi

Unfortunately, the picture of the judiciary in Burundi evidences little progress toward "just peace." Indeed, President Sylvestre Ntibantunganya of the FRODEBU party sought refuge in the US Embassy in late 1996 when rumors circulated of imminent attacks on him and his government by the army and militia. The creeping military coup that had begun with Ndadaye's assassination in 1993 was effectively accomplished when strongman Pierre Buyoya, who had governed before the 1993 elections, again became de facto president of Burundi.

However, the international community and the community of neighboring rulers did not just sit by and permit Burundi to descend into turmoil again. By mid-1996 Tanzanian president Benjamin Mkapa and former president Julius Nyerere took the initiative to set up a summit on Burundi at Arusha. They called together presidents of the region, the chair of the Organization of African Unity, and representatives of Western governments. Following Buyoya's coup by year's end, this group initiated a trade embargo on Burundi as a sanction against what they saw as illegal military usurpation of the democratic process in Burundi. By the time of this writing, Buyoya's military rule has somewhat calmed the country, but the low-grade war continues with periodic reports of massacres of civilians by raids attributed to Hutu guerrillas and reprisals by the Tutsi army, a pattern that has become sickeningly familiar to observers of Burundi. Meanwhile, the Burundi summit in Arusha continues, and many Burundians continue to hope against odds that eventually peace and justice will come to this troubled land.

As sketched at the outset of this section, the paralysis of judicial institutions was worse in Burundi than it had been in Rwanda. In fact, there was virtually no justice at all in Burundi. Courts at every level were closed, with no prospect of their opening and with none of the energy of national or international agencies coming to their rescue as they had in Rwanda. The recital of the state of affairs of the Burundian courts by a Burundian student in 1995 still describes the situation at the time of this writing (Nkubanyi 1995). Total impunity in major crimes, such as the assassination of national leaders, retaliation murders, attacks on Hutu by Tutsi militia, and counterattacks on Tutsi by Hutu militia, beginning in 1964 and continuing in waves to the present, suggested nothing less than a nearly complete breakdown of orderly society. Nkubanyi (1995) noted, second, that the paralysis of the judiciary also featured what he called an absence of ethnic equilibrium among magistrates. Almost all judges are Tutsi, and the majority Hutu have no representation. Nkubanyi noted that in the past the ethnic adherence of judges was not an issue, but it had become that. Third, Nkubanyi noted that those magistrates who make unpopular rulings are threatened and sometimes killed. Thus the security of the magistrates is a problem in Burundi on a level with what was seen in Rwanda (or in Colombian regions controlled by drug czars). Nkubanyi also noted the interference by the executive in the judicial branch of government. Faced with judicial action against their political peers, leading party representatives intervene against the judiciary. Thus, although there are magistrates in Burundi, their work is completely paralyzed by circumstances. The only solution, Nkubanyi suggested, is the creation of an international commission that is neutral and that can focus on these incidents of interference and situations of blockage to reintroduce a sense of respect for law. Indeed, these are some of the measures that have been taken up by the peace summit in Arusha.

Coming to terms with all the political crimes that have been committed in the past 40 years in Burundi would be a "titanesque effort," suggested Nkubanyi (1995). But it is work that is essential if Burundi is to have a sane future. As much as anywhere else, the dictum that "there can be no peace without justice" would seem to apply to Burundi. And yet Burundians are willing, perhaps even eager, to sit down and talk to each other in the Arusha summit that has been at work since 1995.

Perceptions of Justice and the Legal Grounding of Genocide Charges

"The elimination of impunity is essential to ensure that the cycle of genocide is broken in Rwanda. National reconciliation will only be brought about when justice is seen to be done." These are the words of the authors of the United Nations report of 1997. They emphasize the thread that connects long-lasting peace and justice. But they also highlight that no technical definition of justice is sufficient in bringing about such peace. Rather, it is the sense of impunity that must be overcome. This means, quite simply, that the idea of the legitimacy of justice must become a reality that people believe in and that they believe will serve them when they need it. Lasting peace thus includes the appearance that justice is capable of being done.

Two examples illustrate this work of persuading the populace of the Great Lakes region and more widely of Africa that justice is possible and worthwhile. During the first trials of the ICTR of Arusha, Belgian legal scholar Filip Reyntjens prepared a case study of the first three days of the April 1994 massacres to reinforce the clarity of the charges of genocide (Reyntjens 1995, 1997). One would think that there would be no need to conduct legal-historical research to argue the case for genocide, but as it turns out there were many detractors. One has only to recall our conversations with the refugee Rwandan administrators in Zaire to lift out phrases such as "The killings were regrettable, but it was a war" or "There were killings on both sides." Others argued that the Tutsi were the greater aggressors over the long course of history, guilty themselves of genocide. Reyntjens cautioned that the case of genocide was not easy to make against those that the ICTR had indicted.

In his 1997 article Reyntjens focused on the case of Bagosora Theoneste, the "biggest fish" in the hands of the court, who, although he was not the sole mastermind, was one of the core group of one or two dozen who planned the massacres. As a member of the *akazu,* the "little house" around Habyarimana, he had a record of involvement with death squads in 1992 and of sabotaging the peace talks from mid-1992 to mid-1993. He is reported to have said that if the peace accords were implemented, he was returning to Kigali "to prepare for the apocalypse" (Reyntjens 1997). When the president's plane was shot down and the army chief of staff and other military leaders were killed, Bagosora was the remaining military leader. He was in charge when the army met during the evening and night of April 6–7, 1994, to plan the next steps. Reyntjens identified a dual track that was pursued by the military high command, on the one hand appearing to work with the UN peacekeeping mission but on the other hand setting in motion the killing machine whose first victims would be opposition politicians, the leaders of civil society, and Tutsi in general. The first victims were Prime Minister Uwiligiyimana Agathe and the ten Belgian paratroopers guarding her (Reyntjens 1997). In his trial Bagosora denied charges of genocide, stating instead that he was not able to control the military under his command.

Reyntjens (1997) argued that it is imperative to establish the link between the conception and engineering of genocide and its implementation. The demonstration of intent is crucial in making the distinction between atavistic massacres and calculated genocide. Some of the defendants may need to be offered immunity from prosecution in exchange for their testimony; they will need to be protected as well.

The wider ramifications of the ICTR, both for the conviction of the charges of genocide and for quelling the attitude of impunity at large, are also discussed by Peter (1997), associate professor of law at the University of Dar es Salaam, and defense counsel for indigent suspects and accused persons at the ICTR. The ICTR's importance and its challenge, suggested Peter, lie not in the number of cases it will be able to try but in the wider influence it has in Africa. Peter quoted Theodor Meron: "No matter how many atrocities cases these international tribunals may eventually try, their very existence sends a powerful message. Their statutes, rules of procedure and evidence, and practice stimulate the development of the law. The possible fear by States that the activities of such tribunals might preempt national prosecutions could also have the beneficial effect of spurring prosecutions before the national courts for serious violations of humanitarian law" (Meron 1995, p. 555). Furthermore, by creating such tribunals, the international community delivers a warning to those dictators and others who do not value human life. Finally, argued Peter (1997), the ICTR deals a blow to those African leaders who hide their crimes against humanity behind Article 3 of the Charter of the Organization of African Unity that provides for the noninterference in the internal affairs of member states. The court argues that human rights are everyone's concern. Although the ICTR has a four-year mandate, it is likely that the United Nations will seek to continue indefinitely the mandate of the courts that are now seated to try crimes against humanity. In such a world, killing with impunity is not as readily tolerated.

Lessons from Hindsight on the Legitimization of Judicial Practices

The efforts examined here to restore damaged or paralyzed institutions of justice or to recreate such institutions where they had been destroyed can be clarified further with a historical rearview-mirror-like regard to how such procedures and institutions were undone in the first place. The voices in this book relate stories that in hindsight portray a trail of judicial destruction leading to the apocalypse. There are the blatant examples from the time before the war in Rwanda, mentioned by the mayor of Giti. He noted that capital cases sent for trial to the district court were usually dismissed, possibly because of the intimidation of magistrates by political leaders or others. He also mentioned the inability or unwillingness of mayors to intervene in cases of brigandage that resulted from the introduction of multiple parties, leading to a failure to prosecute criminal acts. In Burundi the courts at all levels have been paralyzed since 1993, and many earlier cases of murder and violence have never been tried.

Reading through the voices in this book, we see other patterns that offer a backdrop of impunity. What is one to make of Bugingo's many examples of corruption: grade fixing by school directors, manipulation of ethnic categories in favor of officials' kin or region in the scholastic competitions for scarce university positions, rigged military tribunals, border patrols engaging in smuggling, and so on. Acts such as these are no doubt found in all societies of the world, but not everywhere do they lead as cumulatively to the destruction of "the other" as in Rwanda and Burundi.

The full story of the destruction of the judiciary in Rwanda and Burundi and the rise of violence and impunity no doubt go back to far earlier eras, including the colonial removal of structures of checks and balances in two hierarchical kingdoms and in the ways the courts operated. In both Rwanda and Burundi precolonial judicial institutions were formally retained by the colonial regime. Although a popular palaver court (the *gacaca*), is described for Rwanda (Reyntjens 1990), it was mainly used for local civil crimes of property and fights between kin within community. The chiefs held courts of appeal on more serious matters, and the king held the ultimate authority and could order executions, as the tale of the Rock of Kamegeli suggests. Leaving the prior set of tribunals intact as run by the chiefs and councils, the colonial government took over all capital cases and opened its own high court. The councils in effect lost their independent judicial authority, just as the chiefs merged their administrative roles for the colonial government with their judicial work. This merging of the various functions of government and the ensuing leaner single chain of command leading ultimately to the Governor General of Ruanda-Urundi had the effect of destroying the checks and balances that had existed previously among the several types of chiefs, the crown, and the Queen Mother and between the Queen Mother and the council. The Rwandan populace rejected this oppressive hierarchy and its Tutsi chiefs in 1959.

In place of this colonial system an effort was made in Rwanda to establish a judiciary independent of the new administrative structure, which no longer included the chiefs. The hierarchy of courts began with the canton or community level, followed by the court of first instance, the appeal court, and the Supreme Court. Most civil cases were handled by the *gacaca*, at the canton level, or at the court of first instance. Capital crimes were directed to the court of first instance. The magistrates, many of whom by 1980 held their law degrees, were appointed by the president. These new-style magistrates were supposed to be independent and make independent judgments. The national council of magistrates held the authority to sanction, even dismiss, judges. Although this judiciary system was in theory a modern independent judiciary, it was in fact taken hostage by the executive branch of the single ruling party, the MRND, and after multipartisme was introduced, it was drawn into the conflicts and turmoil of the day.

A striking feature of the decline in Rwandan and Burundian judicial institutions since independence is the absence of any semblance or trace of the well-known African customary tribunal. In many other settings this institution is either incorporated into national judicial affairs (e.g., as in Botswana) or convened by the people outside the rubric of the nation state's judiciary (e.g., as in Zaire). In Burundi there are calls for the resurrection of the *bashingantahe* councils (Ntabona 1992c), and periodic meetings of national reconciliation have the character of the customary tribunal with the exception that no one is actually judged, because that would be too explosive. In

Rwanda there is again talk of the importance of the popular civil tribunal, the *gacaca,* and that it be used to try the more than 100,000 imprisoned Rwandans who were charged with category 2, 3, and 4 offenses in 1994 (Fisher 1999).

Scholars of African jurisprudence emphasize the dynamic interaction of process over rules (Fallers 1969; Comaroff and Roberts 1981) to assess the way conflicts were presented to courts and adjudicated. African courts outside the modern nation-state context are not limited to the governments of chiefs or kings, where they have been described. In fact, the most elaborate judicial procedures are in segmented societies where the council of judges or speakers debates on behalf of their contesting clients. In the absence of a central authority, the onus falls on the speakers or judges to maneuver through the mine fields of tension to reach settlement. Some of the most elaborate juridical rituals, including proverbs, call-and-response persuasion songs, and a variety of truth-eliciting techniques, arise from these decentralized settings. In Kongo society of western Congo (formerly Zaire) these rituals have persisted into the present, providing the stock-in-trade of justice in the absence of an effective national judiciary (Mertens 1944–1952; Janzen 1998b; Wamba-dia-Wamba 1992). In such settings justice is more of a process that culminates in reconciliation (including payment of fines but also exchange of gifts and drinks, which leave the contestants on speaking terms) rather than a formal imposition of rules. Such courts recreate sociability. This is why the popular expectations of justice in many African societies are often quite exacting and the disappointment so great when justice falters.

In Burundi, whether or not there is an active memory of an effective elders council like the *bashingantahe,* the expectations of justice include reconciliation. In a general characterization of African justice, Fallers (1969) wrote, "Like many other African peoples, [the BaSoga] go to court readily and frequently; they admire and cultivate the arts of litigation and adjudication and they take great pleasure in discussing legal affairs" (p. 2). In the Burundian version of this tradition, law was institutionalized in the council of notables or judges, who came from all groups (Hutu, Tutsi, Twa)—the *bashingantahe.* The salient verb in this word is *tahe,* "to balance or reconcile" (Bigirumwami 1992, p. 488). This is the same verb as that used to speak of shaking or balancing the *ngombo* divination basket on the southern savanna *(tahiye ngombo)* so as to ferret out truth and understanding. *Bashingantahe* are thus "those who balance out an understanding," or justice, that is, those who bring form and substance to ideals of fairness and morality in society.

The calls for tribunals that are fair for all concerned echo this deep expectation founded in a memory of past renderings of justice. Although the colonial and postcolonial courts were well developed in the idiom of Western national jurisprudence, they became largely paralyzed by political conflicts. One has the impression that with the collapse of the kingdoms all aspects of former public sanctioning were abandoned for a course into the brave new world of the African single-party state. Where the procedures of the traditional judicial councils were maintained or incorporated into new institutions or ad hoc arrangements or where the centralized state's courts were truly kept operating, peace held longer.

Yet the conviction looms that for there to be not only a return to peace in Rwanda and Burundi—and other states of the region—but also a lasting peace, the very nature of the control of the state will need to be transformed to incorporate the rule of law in which every individual and every institution is equal before the law (Johnson 1998). The political base needed for such a legitimate modern state to flourish must necessarily be some kind of democracy with individual representation accompanied by access to economic opportunity for the masses. Johnson (1983, 1998), who has written on the slow emergence of the rule of law, offers five conditions that must obtain for a political system to maintain itself with just peace to avoid the descent into autocratic totalitarianism that ended Roman rule. In the West such rule of law resurfaced in the application of the church's canon law and in secular reforms in England with the *Magna Carta.* In such a society the constitution (whether written or oral) must be in the language of the common people; it should be subject to lawful change (possible but not easy); it must be open to interpretation in a conservative but enlightened manner; and the economy as well as all other institutions must remain subject to the courts. Equality before the law goes hand in hand with the right of individuals to vote. The rule of law so defined is for Johnson one of the greatest human achievements of the second millennium. Johnson (1998) emphasized that maintaining the independence of the courts is more important than exercising formal democracy. In fact, the substance of the rule of law is upholding the courts; formal democracy is its shadow.

In this spirit our parting words to our Rwandan and Burundian friends who asked us to give them our honest opinion about their countries and their futures would be this: We encourage you to build a society based on justice and equality, and there will be peace. Allow God to change your hearts and practice the *alphabetisme de l'amour.*

Notes

1. The main drawback in Bartsch's scheme is his tendency to create group stereotypes around psychological types that seem to evolve from one polar extreme to the other. Thus one reading of his text suggests that black Africans are moving from traditional to modern character types, from collective, past-oriented, high-social-context, other-shaped people to individualistic, future-oriented, low-context individualists characteristic of Westerners and urban South Africans. This kind of a model echoes the worst of colonial anthropology, if taken literally and to its full conclusion. At the same time Bartsch speaks of South African society as being highly multicultural, with many permutations and combinations of personality types. Fortunately, he tends to focus on real individuals and real problems, emphasizing that the main feature of overcoming the displacement of trauma is to have a stable loving environment in which the individual can sort through experience. Bartsch embraces both African healing and academic therapies, so long as they are suited to the expectations of the individual.

2. Pierre Ndilikilikesha doubts that poisonings are as common in Rwanda as suggested by Taylor (1992).

3. Of course, even these had been "reconstructed" at various times in the history of the kingdom, according to museum texts.

4. According to museum interpretive text, Busarure and Rwagagaza were symbols of the Umutege dynasty, whose ritual kings were second in importance only to the king among the *umwiru* ritualists in the Rwandan court. According to traditions, the ancestor of the Umutege was the ritualist of the Umurenge dynasty, in one of the so-called Hutu kingdoms, and governed a part of western Rwanda before the advent of the Nyiginya "Tutsi" dynasty. The Umutege ritualist transferred the royal ritual of the Umurenge to Gihaga, founder of the Nyiginya dynasty.

5. *Ngoma* in many central and southern African languages refers to "drum" (the instrument), to song and dance performance, and to the group that is involved in such a performance around public events or more limited groupings of the commonly afflicted for which specialized use of the phrase "drum of affliction" has been coined (Turner 1968). However, *ngoma* is by no means restricted to healing. Two works that sketch the issues of a fuller understanding of this aspect of African culture are Janzen (1992) and Van Dijk et al. (1999).

Bibliography

African Rights. 1995. *Rwanda: Death, Despair, Defiance,* rev. ed. London: African Rights.

African Rights.1997. *Bisesero: Resisting Genocide.* London: African Rights.

Anderson, Benedict. 1983. *Imagined Communities: Reflections on the Origin and Spread of Nationalism.* London: Verso.

Aron, Raymond. 1956. *Dimensions de la conscience historique.* Paris: Plon.

Assefa, Hizkias. 1987. *Mediation of Civil Wars: Approaches and Strategies—The Sudan Conflict.* Boulder, CO: Westview Press.

Baker, Gwendolyn. 1994. *We must do more to heal Rwanda's children.* New York Times 114:A16.

Bangamwabo, Francois-Xavier, Maniragaba-Baributsa, Eustache Munyantwali et al. 1991. *Rélations interethniques au Rwanda à la lumière de l'agresssion d'Octobre 1990.* Ruhengeri, Rwanda: Editions Universitaires du Rwanda.

Bartsch, Karl. 1997. *Reflections on Training Caregivers in a Cross-Cultural Setting.* Occasional Paper 23. Akron, PA: Mennonite Central Committee.

Bartsch, Karl. 1998. *Stress and Trauma Healing: A Manual for Caregivers.* Akron, PA: Mennonite Central Committee.

Bigirumwami, J. 1992. Le mot intahe: Terme du vocabulaire juridique kirundi. *Au Coeur de l'Afrique* 60(4):432–524.

Bishikwabo Chubaka. 1989. Rélecture de l'histoire des royaumes et empires africaines: Les peuples des grands lacs. *Cahiers du CERUKI,* n.s., 23:37–61

Bohannan, Paul. 1957. *Justice and Judgment among the Tiv.* London: Oxford University Press.

Bradley, Donald. 1994. Dreams, hopes of two families, cultures, collide. *Kansas City Star,* January 11.

Brittain, Victoria. 1998. Former Rwanda PM admits role in genocide. *Mail & Guardian* (Johannesburg), May 11 (electronic version).

Brubaker, David. 1994. *Report on Healing/Reconciliation Assignment.* Akron, PA: Mennonite Central Committee.

Burundinet. 1995. Anonymous letter, 8 June, to the Administrateur Général du Bureau Central des Renseignements à Bujumbura.

CERUKI (Centre de Recherche Universitaire du Kivu). 1976. *Lyangombe: Mythe et Rites.* Actes du Deuxième Colloque. Bukavu, Congo: CERUKI.

Comaroff, John L., and Simon Roberts. 1981. *Rules as Processes: The Cultural Logic of Dispute in an African Context.* Chicago: University of Chicago Press.

De Heusch, Luc. 1966. *Le Rwanda et la civilisation interlacustrine.* Brussels: Université Libre de Bruxelles.

De Heusch, Luc, and Kathleen de Bethune. 1996. *A Republic Gone Mad: Rwanda 1894–1994.* New York: First Run/Icarus Films. Film.

De Lame, Danielle. 1995. Refugees in South Kivu. *Relief and Rehabilitation Network Newsletter* 5:9–12.

De Lame, Danielle. 1996. *Une colline entre mille ou le calme avant la tempête: Transformations et blocages du Rwanda rural.* Tervuren, Belgium: Musée Royal de l'Afrique Centrale.

d'Hertefelt, Marcel. 1971. *Les clans du Rwanda ancien.* Series Sciences Humaines 70. Tervuren, Belgium: Musée Royal d'Afrique Central.

Diocèse de Butare. 1994a. Evaluation des dégâts après la guerre 1994 et plan de relance des activitiés. Mimeograph.

Diocèse de Butare. 1994b (Sept. 21). *Tentative de "Constat loyal."* Butare, Rwanda: Commission pour la Reprise des Activités Pastoral.

Diocèse de Butare. 1994c (Sept. 26). *Propositions concrètes pour le "travail de deuil."* Butare, Rwanda: Commission pour la Reprise des Activités Pastoral.

Diocèse de Butare. 1994d (Oct. 12). *L'esprit du "travail de deuil."* Butare, Rwanda: Commission pour la Reprise des Activités Pastoral.

Diocèse de Butare. 1994e (Nov. 11). *Pour que notre crise soit féconde.* Butare, Rwanda: Commission pour la Reprise des Activités Pastoral.

Diocèse de Butare. 1994f (Dec. 25). *De quelques obstacles à la relance des activités pastorales.* Butare, Rwanda: Commission pour la Reprise des Activités Pastoral.

Dirigeants d'Eglises rwandaises. 1994. Réunion entre les dirigeants d'Eglises protestantes du Rwanda et les organisations ecclésiastiques et para-ecclésiastiques basées à Nairobi. Aide-memoire, November 4 (unpublished).

Dodge, Cole P., and Magne Raundalen. 1991. *Reaching Children in War: Sudan, Uganda, and Mozambique.* Bergen, Norway: Scandinavian Institute for African Studies.

Ebousi-Boulanga, F. 1981. *Christianisme sans fétiche.* Paris: Présence Africaine.

Elbedour, Salman, Robert Bensel, and David T. Bastien. 1993. Ecological integrated model of children of war: Individual and social psychology. *Child Abuse and Neglect* 17:809–819.

Elias, T. Olawale. 1962. *The Nature of African Customary Law.* Manchester, England: Manchester University Press.

Fallers, Lloyd. 1969. *Law without Precedent: Legal Ideas in Action in the Courts of Colonial Busoga.* Chicago: University of Chicago Press.

Faulkingham, Ralph, and Mitzi Goheen. 1998a. The ongoing crisis in Central Africa. *African Studies Review* 41(1):vii.

Faulkingham, Ralph, and Mitzi Goheen, eds. 1998b. The ongoing crisis in Central Africa. Special issue of *African Studies Review,* 41(1).

Fisher, Ian. 1999. Massacres of '94: Rwanda seeks justice in villages. *New York Times,* April 21.

Garabino, James, Kathleen Kostelny, and Nancy Dubrow. 1991. *No Place To Be a Child: Growing Up in a War Zone.* Lexington, MA: Lexington Books.

Geertz, Clifford. 1963. The integrative revolution: Primordial sentiments and civil politics in the new states. In *Old Societies and New States,* E. Shils and C. Geertz, eds. New York: Free Press, 105–157.

Gluckman, Max. 1965. *The Ideas in Barotse Jurisprudence.* New Haven, CT: Yale University Press.

Goldhagen, Daniel Jonah. 1996. *Hitler's Willing Executioners: Ordinary Germans and the Holocaust.* New York: Alfred A. Knopf.

Gourevitch, Philip. 1997. *We Wish to Inform You That Tomorrow We Will Be Killed with Our Families: Stories from Rwanda.* New York: Farrar, Strauss & Giroux.

Hiernaux, Jean, and A.M. Gauthier. 1977. Comparison des affinités linguistiques et biologiques de douze populations de langue bantu. *Cahiers d'Etudes Africaines* 66/67:241–253.

Hinton, Alex. 1998. Why did the Nazis kill? Anthropology, genocide, and the Goldhagen controversy. *Anthropology Today* 14(5):9–15.

Hobsbawm, Eric. 1991. *Nations and Nationalisms since 1780.* Cambridge, England: Cambridge University Press.

Human Rights Watch. 1999. *Leave None to Tell the Story: Genocide in Rwanda.* London: Human Rights Watch.

Ignatieff, Michael. 1994. *Blood and Belonging: Journey into the New Nationalism.* New York: Farrar, Straus & Giroux.

Ijambo. 1993. The 17 Tutsi commandments. No. 6, December 18, 11–14.

Janzen, John M. 1982. *Lemba 1650–1930: A Drum of Affliction in Africa and the New World.* New York: Garland Publishing.

Janzen, John M. 1992. *Ngoma: Discourses of Healing in Central and Southern Africa.* Berkeley, CA: University of California Press.

Janzen, John M. 1995. The aftermath of war: Inside Rwanda and Burundi, 1994–5. *KU Anthropologist,* May 1, 13–15.

Janzen, John M. 1998a. *Kongo Reader.* Kansas City: Sharp Publications.

Janzen, John M. 1998b. A tale of two communes: Consciousness, genocide, and justice in Rwanda. Paper presented at the conference "The Future of the African Past." Oxford, England: St. Antony's College.

Janzen, John M .1999. Afterword. In *The Quest for Fruition through Ngoma: The Political Aspects of Healing in Southern Africa,* Rijk van Dijk, Ria Reis, and Marja Spierenburg, eds. Oxford: James Currey Publishers.

Janzen, Reinhild Kauenhoven. 1995. The Musée National de Rwanda, surviving the war. *African Arts* 28(3):62–63, 92.

Jewsiewicki, Bogumil, ed. 1999. Central Africa: Political dynamics of identities and representation. Special issue of *Canadian Journal of African Studies,* 32(2).

Johnson, Paul. 1983. *A History of the Modern World: From 1917 to the 1980s.* London: Weidenfeld, Nicolson.

Johnson, Paul. 1998. Laying down the law. *Wall Street Journal,* March 10.

Katihabwa Sabastien. 1991. *Magume, ou Les Ombres du Sentier.* Bujumbura, Burundi: Régie de Publication Pédagogique, Ministère de l'Education.

Katihabwa Sabastien. n.d. L'autre rive: chronique d'un refugie ordinaire d'Afrique. Unpublished.

Kilbourn, Phyllis, ed. 1994. *Healing the Children of War: A Handbook for Ministry to Children Who Have Suffered Deep Trauma.* Monrovia, CA: MARC (a division of World Vision International).

Kinyamateka. 1994. Liste des martyres. December.

Kotch, Nicholas. 1998. Former Rwandan P.M. pleads guilty to genocide. Yahoo News/Reuters News Service, May 1.

Lampman, Jane. 1999a. A diplomacy that disarms past conflicts. *Christian Science Monitor,* February 18.

Lampman, Jane. 1999b. A new model to deal with crime and its victims. *Christian Science Monitor,* February 4.

Lampman, Jane. 1999c. The power of forgiveness. *Christian Science Monitor,* January 28.

Lederach, John Paul. 1995. *Preparing for Peace: Conflict Transformation across Cultures.* Syracuse, NY: Syracuse University Press.
Lederach, John Paul. 1997. *Building Peace: Sustainable Reconciliation in Divided Societies.* Washington, DC: United States Institute of Peace Press
Lederach, John Paul. 1999. *Building Peace: The Promise and Challenge of the Millennium.* Bethel College Peace Lecture Series. North Newton, KS: Bethel College, January 9.
Lemarchand, René. 1994. *Burundi: Ethnocide as Discourse and Practice.* Cambridge: Cambridge University Press.
Lemarchand, René. 1995. Rwanda: The rationality of genocide. *Issue: A Journal of Opinion* 23(2):8–11.
Lemarchand. René. 1998. Genocide in the Great Lakes: Which genocide? Whose genocide? *African Studies Review* 41(1):3–17.
Le Temoin Nyabusorongo. 1994. Recrutement des chiens au sein de l'Union des profiteurs de la nation [cartoon]. *Le Temoin Nyabusorongo,* no. 10, December.
Lind, Tim. 1996. Chronology of disaster in central Africa. *MCC News Service,* November 8.
Longman, Timothy. 1995a. Christianity and democratisation in Rwanda: Assessing church responses to political crisis in the 1990s. In *Christianity and Democratisation in Africa,* Paul Gifford, ed. Leiden, the Netherlands: E.J. Brill, 188–204.
Longman, Timothy. 1995b. Genocide and sociopolitical change: Massacres in two Rwandan villages. *Issue: A Journal of Opinion* 23(2):18–21.
Longman, Timothy. 1998. Empowering the weak and protecting the powerful: The contradictory nature of churches in Central Africa. *African Studies Review* 41(1):49–72.
Lorch, Donatella. 1994. Children's drawings tell horror of Rwanda in colors of crayons. *New York Times* 143:A1.
Lorch, Donatella. 1995. Pledge of protection halts Hutu flight from Burundi. *New York Times,* April 3.
Lutheran Immigration and Refugee Service.1998. *Working with Refugee and Immigrant Children: Issues of Culture, Law, and Development.* New York: Lutheran Immigration and Refugee Service.
MacGaffey, Wyatt. 1970. Concepts of Race in the Historiography of Northeast Africa. In *Papers in African Prehistory,* J.D. Fage & R.A. Oliver, eds. Cambridge: Cambridge University Press., 99–115.
Magnarella, Paul J. 1995. Trying for peace through law: The UN Tribunal for the former Yugoslavia. *Human Peace* 10:3–8.
Magnarella, Paul J. 1996. Trying for peace through law: International Criminal Tribunal for Rwanda. *Human Peace* 11:3–9.
Malkki, Liisa H. 1995. *Purity and Exile: Violence, Memory, and National Cosmology among Hutu Refugees in Tanzania.* Chicago: University of Chicago Press.
Maniragaba-Balibutsa. 1991. Le myth des fils de Gihanga ou l'histoire d'une fraternité toujours manquée. In *Relations interethniques au Rwanda à la lumière de l'agresssion d'Octobre 1990,* François-Xavier Bangamwabo, Maniragaba-Baributsa, Eustache Munyantwali et al., eds. Ruhengeri, Rwanda: Editions Universitaires du Rwanda, 61–129.
Maquet, Jacques. 1961. *The Premise of Inequality in Ruanda.* London: Oxford University Press.
Maren, Michael. 1997. *The Road to Hell: The Ravaging Effects of Foreign Aid and International Charity.* New York: Free Press.
Masamba ma Mpolo, [Jean]. 1981. Kindoki as diagnosis and therapy. *Social Science and Medicine* 15B(3):405–414.
Mays, Vickie M., Merry Bullock, Mark Rosenzweig et al. 1998. Ethnic conflict: Global challenges and psychological perspectives. *American Psychologist* 53(7):737–742.
Meron, Theodor. 1995. The international criminalization of internal atrocities. *American Journal of International Law* 89:554.
Mertens, Joseph. 1944–1952, passim. La juridiction indigène chez les Bakongo orientaux. *Kongo-Overzee,* v. 10–18.
Miller, Harold F. 1993. *Peace and Reconciliation in Africa: A Preliminary Survey of Ecumenical Perspectives and Initiatives.* Occasional Paper 19. Akron, PA: Mennonite Central Committee.
Munyantwali, Eustache. 1991. La politique d'équilibre dans l'enseignement. In *Rélations interethniques au Rwanda à la lumière de l'agresssion d'Octobre 1990,* François-Xavier Bangamwabo, Maniragaba-Baributsa, Eustache Munyantwali et al., eds. Ruhengeri, Rwanda: Editions Universitaires du Rwanda, 300–307.
Murray, A. 1998. Researchers probe forgiveness in South Africa. *Monitor* (American Psychological Association), November.
Nahimana, Ferdinand. 1993. *Le Rwanda: Emergence d'un Etat.* Paris: L'Harmattan.
Nash, Manning. 1989. *The Cauldron of Ethnicity in the Modern World.* Chicago: University of Chicago Press.
Ndayizeye, Onesime, and Richard Niyongere. 1995. Entretien avec M. Sylvestre Barancira: La crise socio-politique au Burundi et ses répercussions sur l'appareil psychique du Murundi. *Le Rénouveau Quotidien Burundais d'Informations,* January 3.
Newbury, Catherine. 1988. *The Cohesion of Oppression: Clientship and Ethnicity in Rwanda, 1860–1960.* New York: Columbia University Press.
Newbury, Catherine. 1998. Ethnicity and the politics of history in Rwanda. *Africa Today* 45(1):7–24.
Newbury, David S. 1980. The clans of Rwanda: An historical hypothesis. *Africa* 50:389–404.

Newbury, David S., ed. 1995. Rwanda. Special issue of *Issue: A Journal of Opinion,* 23(2).
Newbury, David S. 1998. Understanding genocide. *African Studies Review* 41(1):73–98.
N'kuba Joseph-Marie. 1995. Nos morts ne sont pas morts. *Rwandanet,* April 7.
Nkubanyi, Melence. 1995. Comment sortir de l'impunité des crimes à caractere politico-ethnique au Burundi? Excerpt from "La victime dans le système juridique burundais." *Burundinet,* June 2.
Nsanze, Augustin. 1980. *Un domaine royal au Burundi, Mbuye, env. 1850–1945.* Paris: Société française d'histoire d'Outre-Mer; Bujumbura, Burundi: Université de Burundi.
Nsanzuwera, François Xavier. 1993. *La magistrature rwandaise dans l'étau du pouvoir exécutif: la peur et le silence, complices de l'arbitraire.* Kigali, Rwanda: Collectif des ligues et associa-tions de défense de droits de l'homme au Rwanda.
Nsanzuwera, François-Xavier. 1995. Rwanda: Et si demain il y avait un autre génocide? Press Conference, IPC, May 11, Brussels, Belgium; *Rwandanet,* June 23.
Ntabona, Adrien. 1992a. Famille et inculturation au Burundi. *Au Coeur de l'Afrique* 60(2–3):4–45.
Ntabona, Adrien. 1992b. L'institution des bashingantahe et la moralisation de la vie sociale et politique. *Au Coeur de l'Afrique* 60(4):432–481.
Ntabona, Adrien, ed. 1992c. Moralisation de la vie publique. Special issue of *Au Coeur de l'Afrique,* 60(4).
Ntabona, Adrien. 1993. *Ibaanga:* Une foi dans les immenses potentialités de l'intériorité humaine—une étude à partir des proverbes du Burundi. *Au Coeur de l'Afrique* 61(1):10–60.
Ntezimana, Laurien. 1994. *La parole de Dieu comme principe de maturation de l'homme.* Butare, Rwanda: Service d'Animation Theologique, Diocese de Butare.
Nyagahene, Antoine. 1991. Le cas de l'histoire du peuplement du Rwanda ancien. In *Rélations interethniques au Rwanda à la lumière de l'agresssion d'Octobre 1990,* François-Xavier Bangamwabo, Maniragaba-Baributsa, Eustache Munyantwali et al., eds. Ruhengeri, Rwanda: Editions Universitaires du Rwanda, 19–60.
Nzabahimana, François, ed. 1994. Les événements d'Avril-Juillet 1994. Special issue of *Dialogue,* 177(August–September).
Pan African News Agency. 1998. 15 Rwandan prisoners enter guilty plea. Web site article, May 7.
Pennacini, Cecilia. 1998. *Kubandwa: La possessione spiritica nell'Africa dei Grandi Laghi.* Torino, Italy: Il Segnalibro Editore.
Peter, Chris Maina. 1997. The International Criminal Tribunal for Rwanda: Bringing the killers to book. *International Review of the Red Cross* 321(1):695–704.
Pottier, Johan. 1996. Relief and repatriation: Views by Rwandan refugees—lessons for humanitarian aid workers. *African Affairs* 95:403–429.
Prendergast, John. 1997. Applying concepts to cases: Four African case studies. In *Building Peace: Sustainable Reconciliation in Divided Societies,* J.P. Lederach, ed. Washington, DC: United States Institute of Peace Press, 153–180.
Prunier, Gérard. 1995. *The Rwanda Crisis: History of a Genocide.* New York: Columbia University Press.
Rennie, T.J. 1971. The precolonial kingdom of Rwanda: A reinterpretation. *Transafrican Journal of History* (2)2:11–64.
Reyntjens, Filip. 1990. Le gacaca ou la justice du gazon au Rwanda. *Politique Africaine* 40:31–41.
Reyntjens, Filip. 1994. *Sujets d'inquiétude au Rwanda en Octobre 1994.* Working Paper, November 3. Antwerp, Belgium: University of Antwerp. [Reprinted in English as "Subjects of concern: October 1994," *Issues* 23(2):39–43 (1995).]
Reyntjens, Filip. 1994. *L'Afrique des Grands Lacs en crise: Rwanda, Burundi—1988–1994.* Paris: Karthala.
Reyntjens, Filip. 1995. *Burundi: Breaking the cycle of violence.* London: Minority Rights Group.
Reyntjens, Filip. 1996. *Rwanda: Trois jours qui ont fait basculer l'histoire.* Brussels and Paris: Institut Africain and l'Harmattan.
Reyntjens, Filip. 1997. "The Planner of Apocalypse": The case against Bagosora. InterPress Third World News Agency, May 7.
Roberts, Douglas. 1995. *UN Burundi/Rwanda* [correspondent's report]. Geneva: United Nations, May 9.
Rwanda Embassy. Rwanda: The embassy of the Republic of Rwanda. Available at www.rwandemb.org.
Rwangabo, Pierre-Claver. 1993. *La médecine traditionnelle au Rwanda.* Paris: Karthala.
Santoro, Lara. 1997. Rwanda massacre sites now grim memorials. *Christian Science Monitor,* August 4.
Schoenbrun, David Lee. 1995. *A Narrative History of People and Forests between the Great Lakes: ca. 1000 B.C. to ca. 1500 A.D.* Working Paper 194. Boston: Boston University African Studies Center.
Seppa, Nathan. 1996. Rwanda starts its long healing process. *Monitor* (American Psychological Association), August, 14–15.
Shils, Edward, and Clifford Geertz, eds. 1963. *Old Societies and New States: The Quest for Modernity in Asia and Africa.* New York: Free Press.
Smith, David Norman. 1998. The psychocultural roots of genocide: Legitimacy and crisis in Rwanda. *American Psychologist* 53(7):743–753.
Stanton, Carla. 1995. Children in the aftermath of war. Unpublished.
Taylor, Christopher. 1992. *Milk, Honey, and Money: Changing Concepts in Rwandan Healing.* Washington, DC: Smithsonian Institution Press.

Turner, Victor W.1968. *Drums of Affliction.* Oxford: Clarenden Press.
United Nations. 1951. Convention on the Prevention and Punishment of the Crime of Genocide. U.N.T.S. No. 1021, vol. 78, p. 277 [adopted by Resolution 260 (III) A of the United Nations General Assembly on 9 December 1948].
United Nations. 1994. *Report of the Preparatory Fact-Finding Mission to Burundi to the Secretary-General* [led by Ambassador Martin Huslid of Norway and Ambassador Simeon Ake of Cote d'Ivoire]. New York: United Nations, May 20.
United Nations. 1995. *Progress Report of the Secretary General on the United Nations Assistance Mission for Rwanda.* Report S/1995/297. New York: United Nations.
United Nations. 1996. Situation of human rights in Rwanda. UN Commission on Human Rights, 52d Session, Item 10 of Provisional Agenda, January.
United Nations. 1997. *The Rwandan Genocide Trials: Building Peace through Justice.* New York: UN Department of Humanitarian Affairs, March 7.
US Agency for International Development. 1994. *Report, US AID Office of Foreign Disaster Assistance for Burundi.* Bujumbura, Burundi: US Agency for International Development, March 16.
Uwizeyimana, Laurien. 1991a. La politique d'équilibre ethnique et regional dans l'emploi. In *Rélations interethniques au Rwanda à la lumière de l'agresssion d'Octobre 1990,* François-Xavier Bangamwabo, Maniragaba-Baributsa, Eustache Munyantwali et al., eds. Ruhengeri, Rwanda: Editions Universitaires du Rwanda, 308–322.
Uwizeyimana, Laurien. 1991b. Population, éspace et développement au Rwanda. In *Rélations interethniques au Rwanda à la lumière de l'agresssion d'Octobre 1990,* François-Xavier Bangamwabo, Maniragaba-Baributsa, Eustache Munyantwali et al., eds. Ruhengeri, Rwanda: Editions Universitaires du Rwanda, 271–299.
Van Dijk, Rijk, Ria Reis, and Marja Spierenburg, eds. 1999. *The Quest for Fruition through Ngoma: The Political Aspects of Healing in Southern Africa.* Oxford: James Currey Publishers.
Van Hoyweghen, Saskia. 1996. The disintegration of the Catholic Church of Rwanda. *African Affairs* 95:379–401.
Vansina, Jan. 1962. *L'évolution du royaume Rwanda des origines à 1900.* Classe des sciences morales et politiques, Memoir 8, n.s., no. 26(2). Brussels: Académie Royale des Sciences d'Outremer.
Vansina, Jan. 1993. Nieuws over de "Oorsprong" der Tuutsi. In *Liber amicorum Marcel d'Hertefelt: antropologische opstellen,* Patrick Wymeersch, ed. Brussels: Institut Africain, 315–321.
Wallis, William. 1995. Reuters News Service, Bujumbura, Burundi, June 8.
Wamba-dia-Wamba, Ernest. 1992. Beyond elite politics of democracy in Africa. *Quest (Lusaka)* 6(1):29–42.
Werbner, Richard. 1991. *Tears of the Dead.* Washington, DC: Smithsonian Institution Press.
Wilmsen, Edwin N. 1995. Who were the Bushmen? Historical process in the creation of an ethnic construct. In *Articulating Hidden Histories,* Jane Schneider and Rayna Rapp, eds. Los Angeles: University of California Press, 308–321.
Williams, Breackette F. 1989. A CLASS ACT: Anthropology and the race to nation across ethnic terrain. *Annual Reviews in Anthropology* 18:401–444.
Wymeersch, Patrick, ed. 1993. *Liber amicorum Marcel d'Hertefelt: antropologische opstellen.* Brussels: Institut africain.
Young, Crawford. 1993. *The Rising Tide of Cultural Pluralism: The Nation-State at Bay.* Madison, WI: University of Wisconsin Press.

Index